# *The Bristol Gunners*

The History of
The Gloucestershire Volunteer Artillery
1859 to 2014

Tim Anderson
In Collaboration with Derek Driscoll

The Bristol Gunners

© Tim Anderson 2013
First published in Great Britain 2013
Second Edition 2014

Published by Tim Anderson
Royce Close, Dunstable, UK LU6 2NT

*All rights reserved.*
*No part of this publication may be reproduced or transmitted in any form or by any means, electronic or mechanical, including photocopy, recording, or any information storage and retrieval system, without permission in writing from the copyright holder.*

## This book is dedicated to all who have served, who are serving, and who will serve with the Gloucestershire Volunteer Artillery.

*Photographs in this book are from archives of the Gloucestershire Volunteer Artillery. Exceptions are with kind permission as noted in relevant captions.*

*Cover illustration*
*Bristol gunners at rest in Italy, 1918. Photo with kind permission of Peter Shakespeare. This picture also appears on page 213.*

The Bristol Gunners

# Contents

List of Illustrations .................................................................. 4

Introduction ............................................................................ 5

Chapter 1  Genesis ................................................................. 8

Chapter 2  Marching to the sound of gunfire! ...................... 21

Chapter 3  The Roses Are Blooming In Picardy ................... 57

Chapter 4  The Battle of the Somme ..................................... 81

Chapter 5  1917, A Year of Changes ................................... 137

Chapter 6  Andiamo in Italia! .............................................. 188

Chapter 7  The Interwar Years ............................................. 250

Chapter 8  The Second World War ..................................... 274

Chapter 9  From Then Until Now ....................................... 328

Glossary ............................................................................... 348

Bibliography ........................................................................ 365

## The Bristol Gunners

# List of Illustrations

| | |
|---|---|
| Cover | Bristol Gunners at rest in Italy 1918. |
| Page 7 | BSM Derek Driscoll and L118 Light Gun. |
| Page 8 | Felice Orsini, whose actions prompted the formation of the GVA. |
| Page 9 | Major Henry Bouchier Osborne Savile, first Commanding Officer of the GVA. |
| Page 12 | 1881 GVA Group Photograph outside the HQ building. |
| Page 13 | 18 Pounder muzzle loader and crew. |
| Page 14 | Heavy gun drill at the Artillery Grounds. |
| Page 15 | 1901 Annual Inspection of the GVA at the Artillery Grounds. |
| Page 18 | Results of a premature shell explosion, Plymouth 1906. |
| Page 20 | Silver model of the 12 Pounder Whitworth Gun. |
| Page 36 | GVA march out of the Artillery Grounds, August 1914. |
| Page 56 | Lt. Fullerton & gun crew, Neuve Eglise, early April 1915. |
| Page 95 | Major Chester Todd DSO. |
| Page 96 | Lieutenant E L Gedye. |
| Page 137 | Signallers at work, Somme, late 1916. |
| Page 173 | Balloon photo Hill Top Farm, 1917. |
| Page 186 | Sergeants' mess group photo, autumn 1917. |
| Page 213 | Bristol gunners outside an accommodation hut in Italy, 1918. |
| Page 230 | Major R A Corsan MC DSO. |
| Page 232 | Major General Robert Fanshawe. |
| Page 256 | The original Beatles, 1919. |
| Page 259 | Gun team on the move, post war, 1919. |
| Page 260 | Lt. FS Gedye on his horse, Canada, 1919. |
| Page 264 | Morris gun tractors and 18 Pounders, 1933. |
| Page 267 | 1923 GVA officer group photo. |
| Page 294 | 3.7 Inch HAA gun in fixed position. |
| Page 295 | 3.7 Inch HAA gun in mobile form. |
| Page 312 | GVA Sergeants group photo, Italy 1944. |
| Page 327 | Captain Murley and visiting foreign generals. |
| Page 332 | Green Archer radar system. |
| Page 333 | GVA Matchless motorcycle in a stream. |
| Page 338 | Queen Elizabeth II inspects men of the GVA in 1956. |
| Page 344 | GVA Officers' Mess silver and trophy display. |
| Page 345 | OP team training in an FV432 APC. |
| Page 346 | GVA OP party giving a demonstration at RSA mid 1980s. |

The Bristol Gunners

# Introduction

This book tells the story of men who were ordinary citizens, and at the same time were extraordinary people. From 1859 to the present day they have volunteered their services to protect this country, and all that it stands for. They have come from every background, from the most humble sections of Bristol society, through to those families that were prominent in the local and national community. They have shared the challenges, the discomforts, the dangers, and the rewards of doing their duty. They have created a fellowship, which endures across the years to the present day, for the Gloucestershire Volunteer Artillery (GVA) serves our country still.

This story in detail is of Bristol men, but a similar story has been lived a thousand fold throughout our great country, in every city and town. Military Volunteer organisations have existed throughout the UK, and I hope that this story will, in a small way, represent all of them, for they are cut from the same cloth.

There are important features in being British. One of these traits is that of being a gifted amateur. Professionalism, especially in warfare, is something that we acquire only when are pressed by circumstances. We feel uncomfortable at being too proficient in the skills of war, yet repeatedly we have proved that we make excellent soldiers when we have needed to do so. We can be proud of our professional amateur soldiers who have made up our Territorial and Volunteer forces over the last century and a half, and who will form our Reserve Forces into the future.

I hope that the story of the GVA will engage your interest, will inform you, will entertain you, and moreover help you to better understand and appreciate our 'weekend warriors.'

Military men (and women) have the habit of using words and abbreviations that are not generally understood by those without military experience. Many people are confused by the habit of the military to use some words that have arcane, ambiguous or contradictory meanings. This text is necessarily full of these words of jargon. At the end of this book I have included a glossary which I hope you will be able to consult in order to improve your understanding of what is being said in the main body of

## The Bristol Gunners

the book. If, despite using the glossary, some terms still confuse you, I apologise to you, for that is not my intention.

The military also hold great store in naming units, and renaming them from time to time. Again I appreciate that the frequent change of unit title may confuse the casual reader. I have included these changes in military title as they occur, but have used the abbreviation 'GVA' consistently as I feel this may provide some continuity and clarity for you. This book is the story of the GVA, and other changes of titles have all proved to be transient, though important in their time.

I have included a bibliography of the sources of much of the information on which this book is based. If there is anything in this book that fires your imagination, or stimulates you to learn more of the subject, I would encourage you to start by reading some of these books in the hope that you will be able to satisfy your curiosity and interest.

The GVA were, and are, soldiers specialising in artillery. Their everyday life, when in uniform, was to serve their country by serving their guns. With the guns, they also had a range of vehicles, equipment, and other hardware to master and operate. In past times they also formed close bonds with their horses. They worked within systems and procedures that are mysterious to laymen. It is not my intention to explain how the GVA and artillerymen in general carried out these detailed tasks, others will be better placed than I am to do this. If you do, however, develop an interest in learning more of the artilleryman's craft then a little research into what other publications are available will, I am sure, be able to satisfy the enquiring mind.

I have had access to a range of information sources in compiling this history. Foremost among these is the mass of records and documents assembled after much hard work and dedication by Derek Driscoll, formerly Battery Sergeant Major of the GVA. He has worked tirelessly to assemble and transcribe large numbers of documents and information. Many of these records have come from former GVA men who wrote diaries, letters, and other accounts. Without these crucial, mostly contemporaneous, written records it would not have been possible to fully and justly recount this story. I am indebted to these men, for their help in understanding the GVA and its history. I am proud to have been their comrade, and feel myself highly privileged to have served in the

### The Bristol Gunners

same regiment as them, and to be able to share their tale with you. I hope that they will feel that I have done justice to them.

And, finally, I would like to thank my wife, my family, and my comrades in the GVA, especially BSM Derek Driscoll, for his help and encouragement in persevering with writing this account, and Eric Mellor for patiently proof reading and suggesting improvements to the text. This has been a real team effort, and, I hope, a rewarding result.

***Tim Anderson, Captain R.A.(V) TD (Retired)***

**Retired GVA Battery Sergeant Major Derek Driscoll in front of an L118 Light Gun on the Castle Mount in Bristol. BSM Driscoll is responsible for drawing together most of the information on which this book is based, and for continuing enthusiasm in recording the history of the GVA.**

The Bristol Gunners

# Chapter 1  Genesis

On the evening of 14th January 1858, an Italian revolutionary attempted to assassinate Napoleon III and his wife. The events following this resulted in the birth of the Gloucestershire Volunteer Artillery, which, in due course, would play a full part in achieving some of the aims of this revolutionary long after his own death.

Napoleon and his wife had been travelling to the opera in Paris. The Prince-Emperor survived, but eight bystanders died and some one hundred and forty two people were injured.

The revolutionary was one Felice Orsini, a dedicated and active campaigner for Italian unification (*Risorgimento*). The First War of Italian Independence, in 1848, had not achieved the hoped for unification of Italy. It had, however pointed out that Italians could not, on their own, eject the Austrians (Hapsburgs) from that part of 'Natural Italy' that Nationalists believed was an irredeemable part of their country and which they aspired to bring into the Italian State.

One major potential ally in achieving Italian unification had been Napoleon III. In his youth, and before coming to power, he had stated his support for Italian independence. He had subsequently done nothing practical to further his commitment. This lack of action prompted Orsini to attempt his assassination.

The bombs that Orsini threw were British. They were made in Sheffield, and were tested in the English West Country. These facts created a degree of tension between France and Britain. The British Government considered it possible that this might lead to war between the two countries. In addition, the recently fought Crimean War had highlighted the fact that Britain's small Regular Army could

**Felice Orsini, 19th Century campaigner for Italian Unification, whose actions in Paris prompted the creation of the GVA.** (Photo Wikimedia Commons)

## The Bristol Gunners

not prosecute an expeditionary war abroad as well as maintain sufficient forces at home to ensure secure defence of the homeland. Something would need to be done to put this right.

The French captured Orsini and they sentenced him to death. However, before this sentence was carried out, just two months after the assassination attempt, he wrote a letter to Napoleon III. In this letter, he urged the Prince-Emperor to take up once again the cause of Italian Independence. Orsini went to his death not knowing that he would achieve at least one of his aims. Napoleon III supported Sardinia in its war with the Austrians the next year, sending French forces into Italy. Significant parts of the country were liberated, and in subsequent years, yet more territory was unified into the Italian State. However, the northeastern provinces, including Trentino and Istria remained with Austria. These territories were termed the 'Irridenta', the unredeemed part of 'Natural Italy.' It remained an aim of Italian Nationalists to bring these areas into the Italian State. This would not be achieved until 1919. As part of the final acts of the First World War, the GVA and the British Army helped to liberate much of the Irridenta from the Austrians.

We will examine in more detail later the GVA's part in Italian Unification. By a strange coincidence the GVA were in northern Italy at the end of the Second World War, once again helping return control of the country to its people. For the time being, we will return to the events of 1858 and 1859.

Wars in Europe and The Crimea had highlighted to the British Government that the British Regular Army was too small to garrison the Empire, defend the UK mainland, as well as forming an expeditionary force. An expeditionary force may well be needed again; as the tensions rising and falling on the Continent could easily drag the UK into another war such as had been fought against Napoleon Bonaparte fifty years earlier.

Major Henry Bouchier Osborne Savile, the first Commander of the GVA on its formation in 1859.

## The Bristol Gunners

The British position was that any hostile power occupying the North Sea coast of the Continent would be able to threaten Britain by invasion, and it was therefore in our interests to maintain friendly or neutral regimes in Belgium and The Netherlands. Any threat to these countries, by, for example, the French or Germans, would, by default, carry a threat to Britain. An appropriate response from the British would be needed in the form of an expeditionary force able to secure our vital interests across the North Sea..

On 12th May 1859, in the midst of the rising alarm in Britain, the British Secretary of State for War issued a letter to the Lord Lieutenants of counties in England, Wales, and Scotland. This required them to raise Volunteer Rifle Corps in each county. The Volunteer Rifle Corps were formed specifically for defence in times of actual or threatened invasion, and were the responsibility of the Lord Lieutenants, that is, were not part of the War Office establishment. In September the Secretary of State for War (Lord Palmerston) issued an amended requirement to the effect that it was now preferred that in maritime counties Volunteer Corps should be of artillery in addition to Rifle Corps. Captain Henry Bouchier Osborne Savile, a local businessman and formerly an officer in the Royal Regiment of Artillery, was asked to form and command a Volunteer Artillery Corps based in Bristol. In December 1859, he was gazetted as major and appointed as commanding officer of the Gloucestershire Volunteer Artillery.

Major Savile did as he was bid. In a very short time, the Gloucestershire Volunteer Artillery Corps became a physical fact, ready to stand duty for the Crown. One can only imagine the urgency for action that there must have been throughout the country at this time, for so great a change and organisation to be created so quickly.

The motto *'Fidus et Audax'*, meaning Faithful and Audacious, was chosen for the Gloucestershire Volunteer Artillery on its formation in 1859. No records exist that explain why this particular motto was chosen, or what message, other than the obvious one, was intended. Fidelity, to the Crown, is a given in the British Military, and audacity obviously accords with martial prowess. At formation, as with other Volunteer Artillery Corps, the GVA was not part of the Royal Regiment of Artillery, but was the responsibility of the County, and therefore was not eligible to

## The Bristol Gunners

use the mottos of that regiment – *'Ubique'* (Everywhere) and *'Quo Fas et Gloria Ducunt'* (Where duty and glory lead).

It can be said that the GVA *Fidus et Audax* motto accords well with that of the Royal Regiment of Artillery and has been proudly preserved by the GVA through all the changes of the last century and a half, and is still the motto under which Bristol Gunners serve.

However, the Gloucestershire Volunteer Artillery was not the first artillery to be based in Bristol. In the 15th century Bristol was the second most important port in the country, with trading links with Ireland, Iceland, and Gascony. It therefore needed protection from foreign raiders or invaders. Artillery was based in Bristol soon after the Wars of the Roses (1485) to secure this important asset, through to the late 18th century, and then again briefly during the Napoleonic wars. This was due to the importance of the port and city in increasingly important trade routes across the Atlantic and to the New World. From 1814, though, artillery presence in the city ceased, until the 1859 crisis, when, once again, security for Bristol (and the port of Gloucester) became a concern for the government.

It is appropriate at this point to explain why an organisation based in Bristol, a city with county status, should be named after another county, Gloucestershire.

Bristol sits mostly on the north bank of the River Avon, forming an enclave within the county of Gloucestershire, and the Lord Lieutenant of Gloucestershire has historically also been the Lord Lieutenant of Bristol. Prior to the award of its Royal Charter in 1155 Bristol was part of Gloucestershire, and still maintains important links with that county. The War Office instructed the Lord Lieutenant to raise the Volunteer Corps in 1859, and it seems natural that he would chose to name these Corps after Gloucestershire rather than Bristol. Infantry units raised in Bristol under the Volunteer Rifle Corps scheme were also later assigned to the Gloucestershire Regiment.

The crisis of 1859, the threatened invasion from France, passed, and no invasion took place. The Volunteer Rifle Corps and the Volunteer Artillery Corps, though, continued in existence. The need for a permanent

The Bristol Gunners

home defence force had been recognised, and these Volunteer Corps fulfilled that need.

Throughout its life, the Gloucestershire Volunteer Artillery has been based in Bristol, at the Artillery Grounds in Whiteladies Road, Clifton.

A group photograph of 1881, in front of the entrance to the then headquarters building. The Fidus et Audax inscription is above the door.

In the first years from its establishment it comprised four batteries all based in Clifton. A battery is the basic unit of the artillery. It is made up of a number of guns (usually between four and eight) along with the men (between 75 and 125 depending on role and equipment), vehicles, equipment and horses needed to make it operational. A fifth battery was raised there in 1860, and in 1863 it was brigaded with the Gloucester, Clevedon (Somerset), and Newham Volunteer Artillery Corps to become titled as '1st Administrative Brigade and Gloucestershire Artillery Volunteers,' commanding a total of nine batteries.

## The Bristol Gunners

**GVA Crew with one of the original 18 Pounder Muzzle Loading guns, a relic of the Crimean War.**

By 1907, the Gloucestershire Brigade had grown to a total of thirteen batteries.

The first role of the GVA was coastal defence, and as such, it was modelled on the methods, equipment, and uniforms of the Royal Garrison Artillery (RGA). The first guns issued in 1860 were 18 pounder smooth bore guns (cannons, that is, muzzle loaders) originally destined for use in the earlier Crimean War. The Royal Navy brought these to the port of Bristol in April 1860. The inhabitants of the city celebrated the arrival of the guns with a parade through the streets.

As the Corps expanded, more guns and equipment were required and supplied from the Artillery Headquarters in Woolwich, London, or, by private subscription, as was the case for two Whitworth guns in 1863. A number of fund raising events were held in the Bristol area in order to pay for these guns and their upkeep.

## The Bristol Gunners

Most training was carried out locally, troops and guns being taken from the Artillery Grounds in Clifton and marching up to the Clifton Downs about one mile or so up the hill. There, the drills of coming into and out of action were practised.

Guns changed from time to time. Coastal gunners needed to be able to operate and fire a range of gun types, and practice with larger guns was usually carried out at the annual firing camps at Avonmouth and later Portishead. On occasion, the GVA were assessed in a variety of competitive events, and always found to be of a very high standard.

**Men of the GVA going through drill with a heavy gun in the late 19th century at the Artillery Grounds in Bristol.**

The GVA were on parade at a number of official events through the years, including the arrival of Princess Alexandra in London and her marriage to the Prince of Wales (later to become King Edward VII) in 1863. In 1864, on the opening of the Clifton Suspension Bridge, the GVA fired a salute on Clifton Downs. A Royal Guard was supplied when the Prince of Wales visited Bristol in July 1872. Queen Victoria reviewed the Volunteer Corps in Hyde Park in 1881, and the GVA were present and on parade on that occasion. In 1897 the GVA were at the Jubilee parade in Bristol where they provided a guard of honour to Queen Victoria as she processed through the city.

## The Bristol Gunners

Initially tasked with the defence of the Bristol Channel, in 1892 the GVA were re-tasked with the defence of Plymouth, and changed the location of annual firing camps to that area.

**Annual Inspection of the GVA at their headquarters in the Artillery Grounds, in 1901.**

During the South African War (Second Boer War) from 1899 to 1902, the GVA, as a home defence unit, was not mobilised. Volunteers were not required to serve overseas. However, in line with most other Militia and Volunteer units in Britain, a call was made for individuals to volunteer for Imperial Service (IS) and many members of the GVA answered the call and served, either in South Africa on active service, or in Britain to replace regular troops so that they in their turn could serve in South Africa.

In 1902 the GVA changed their title to 1st (Gloucestershire) Royal Garrison Artillery (Volunteers).

A little later, in 1908, the role of the GVA changed from coastal defence (Royal Garrison Artillery) to field (Royal Field Artillery, RFA). This change was the result of a review of the defence needs of the country, known as the Haldane reforms. These reforms made significant changes

The Bristol Gunners

to the future of the GVA and all other Volunteer Corps, Yeomanry and Militia throughout the UK.

The reforms were carried through by a government facing a range of new circumstances, largely resulting from the Indian Mutiny and the Boer War, and rising tensions with, and within, Europe.

The RFA provided mobile artillery for direct support of infantry formations. This process started for the GVA in 1872 with one battery using the Corps owned, (that is, not Ministry of War owned) Whitworth guns in range practice of Field Artillery methods.

Changing role to be part of the RFA required a change of uniforms, from the blue of RGA, to the khaki of RFA, and a complete change of guns and other equipment.

The British Government was concerned that after unification (in 1871), the Germans were intent on establishing an important role for themselves in the world. To counter this, and the Triple Alliance that the Germans had created with Austro-Hungary and Italy (1882), the British entered the Entente Cordiale (Triple Entente) with France and Russia (1904). The Entente Cordiale was an informal arrangement between these nations intent on mutual support in the event of war (with Germany or Austro-Hungary) and was initiated by King Edward VII. One result of the drawing together of Britain and France for mutual defence was that General Sir Henry Hughes Wilson took it on his own initiative to establish comprehensive contingency plans for the mobilisation of the BEF and its transport to the Continent. Wilson did this without formal approval by the War Office, and on his own initiative. Wilson had a strong relationship with General Dubail, French Chief of Staff, and shared his enthusiasm for Franco - British co-operation in military matters. In the event, Wilson's efforts had a significant effect on the outcome of the early part of the First World War by enabling the BEF to mobilise and deploy to France quickly and efficiently.

British defence policy of the time was based largely on the strength of the Royal Navy, and its ability to protect maritime trade and prevent any enemy from considering invasion of the UK. The Regular Army was organised largely as a colonial police force, with small units carrying out limited operations in support of the local administration or defence in

### The Bristol Gunners

small scale operations. Overseas wars (specifically the Boer Wars) had found the Regular Army to be inadequate for large scale operations, and certainly totally unprepared for a Continental war. Once again, the need for an expeditionary force had found the British military short of manpower and capability. With political tensions rising again over Europe in 1908, the need for maintaining home defence while permitting an effective expeditionary force to be constituted came to the fore once again. A major threat to the UK was invasion by the Germans in the event of war, and keeping them away from the North Sea coast of Belgium and The Netherlands was still seen as a vital interest. This preoccupation with that coast, and a focus on invasion (however unrealistic this threat) was to drive much of British strategy throughout the coming war.

The Haldane reforms created the requirement for the Regular Army to be able to form a six division expeditionary force (totalling around 125,000 men) in the event of war between France and Germany, to support the French and fulfil our commitments to protect Belgian neutrality. Defence of the UK would be the responsibility of the newly created Territorial Force, formed out of the Volunteer, Yeomanry and Militia forces. Their commitment would be to home service only, with volunteers forming a Special Reserve for 'Imperial Service' with the Regular Army.

These Territorial Forces were organised into fourteen divisions based on geographical groupings.

An army division at that time had an establishment of around twenty thousand men, mostly infantry, but with a balance of supporting arms, such as artillery, engineers, cavalry, veterinary, medical, and supply troops.

Thus, the GVA became the 1st (South Midland) Brigade Royal Field Artillery (Territorial Force), part of the 48th (South Midland) Division (Territorial Force). This is normally shortened to 1st (SM) Bde., RFA (TF) of 48th (SM) Div. (TF). This also marked the GVA changing permanently from coastal artillery to field artillery. That is, they were now to be equipped and trained to support infantry formations in mobile warfare. Their time spent in coastal defence would be useful to them in utilising modern gunnery techniques as they were introduced during the First World War in response to the conditions found on the battlefields.

The Bristol Gunners

**Training could be dangerous. A premature shell explosion damaged these guns and injured their crews at Plymouth camp in 1906.**

Another effect of the Haldane reforms was to address the issue of officer training. Under the 1859 establishment of the Volunteer Corps, officers were not appointed by the War Office, but by the Counties. Though many officers had previous military experience (the GVA's first commander was Major HBO Savile, a former regular artilleryman), some were appointed without a formal army training. These had honorary positions, having no formal military role, other than to maintain links between the military and the community, and raising and contributing the necessary funds. In addition, the officers and the County shared responsibility for financing, clothing and equipping their troops, so that standards and practices varied between units. Other reforms during the 19th century (Cardwell 1870, Childers 1881) had corrected some of these deficiencies and gradually brought the Volunteer Corps up to date and under control of the War Office, but the issue of standardised training and methods, especially in the officer element, needed further improvement.

The Haldane reforms established a formal Officer Training Corps (OTC). The Junior Division of this operated in public schools, and the Senior Division in universities. The intention was to ensure a steady supply of

The Bristol Gunners

well trained and suitable officers to command the Territorial Force. This particular element has been notably successful and most British universities still retain their OTC or share an OTC with other educational establishments.

These changes were to be put to their most severe test in 1914 and the outbreak of the First World War.

Local business and community leaders have always had an interest in security and stability in order to protect their commercial and trade interests, as well as from their natural loyalty to the crown.

The government had relied on the counties to form the volunteer corps in 1859, and this meant that the organisational and financial responsibility lay with the civil authorities, not the War Office. In 1881, under the Childers reforms, the Volunteer Corps came under the financial control of the War Office, but for the first twelve years, they were paid for by the local community, and were an integral part of that local community.

A number of family names recur in the ranks of the GVA, many of these being of prominent local families. The first commander, Henry Bouchier Osborne Savile, was in business locally, and was a member of the Bristol Society of Merchant Venturers. His father had been the MP for Taunton. One of his sons also served in the GVA, and was killed in the First World War, and another while serving with the Gloucestershire Regiment (TF). A cousin of Savile's died while a Captain in the Royal Navy. Major Chester William Todd, DSO, commanded 'A' Battery of the GVA until his death at the battle of Passchendaele in 1917. He was also a member of the Society of Merchant Venturers, and a brother and two cousins also served with the GVA in the First World War.

A list of officers of the GVA published in 1890 lists many men with notable histories and positions. There were local businessmen. For example, Joseph Weston-Stevens, director of two local manufacturing companies and president of the Anchor Society. There were baronets, there were aldermen, JPs, solicitors, doctors, engineers, landowners, even a circus performer (though he was also landed gentry). This points up the fact that the GVA was fully a part of, and was supported by, the Bristol civil community.

## The Bristol Gunners

**A Silver model of the 12 Pounder Whitworth gun bought through public subscription and donated to the GVA in 1863.**

The headquarters of the GVA has always been the Artillery Grounds in Whiteladies Road, Clifton, Bristol. The land which this occupies is owned by the Bristol Society of Merchant Venturers, and was supplied by them to the Lord Lieutenant in 1859 to enable the establishment and continued existence of the GVA. This land is still owned by the Society of Merchant Venturers, and is leased at a 'peppercorn' rent, on the proviso that it is to remain so as long as a formed body of Volunteers remain in occupation of the site.

The GVA would not, and could not, have been created and sustained throughout the last one hundred and fifty plus years without the full and continuing support of the local community, prominent organisations, and mostly with the active participation of local people to volunteer and serve. The GVA (as with most other military volunteer organisations) has been, and continues to be, intimately linked with its community.

Along with other military and civil organisations, the GVA has been fully engaged with Bristol City, and community life throughout its history.

The Bristol Gunners

## Chapter 2  Marching to the sound of gunfire!

Whether we like it or not, whether we take an interest or not, world politics and the ambitions of politicians do affect our everyday lives. So it was in the early part of the 20$^{th}$ century that the clash of ideas and objectives among the European nations led to a world war. This war did not fully resolve the tensions, and we will hear more of this later, however, for the time being we will address the events following the Haldane Reforms of 1908, and how these came to envelop the Bristol gunners.

The causes of the First World War are covered in many other places much better than I can do here. With your indulgence, I will ask you to accept that there were causes, and that in due course the British and their army became wrapped up in the war, and its outcomes.

As far as the GVA were concerned, the Haldane Reforms brought immediate and dramatic changes to their chosen professional amateur way of life. The change from coastal artillery to field artillery meant that all previous drills, equipment, practices, and organisation needed to be transformed. Even as coastal artillery, the GVA had not had the most up to date equipment and a full complement thereof. The thirteen battery structure was more administrative than operational, being a repository of trained manpower rather than an effective fighting organisation.

The new field structure meant a move to three field batteries, two in Bristol (Clifton) and one in Gloucester, and an ammunition column (wagons and men to carry artillery ammunition and gun supplies) organised as 1$^{st}$ (South Midland) Brigade RFA (TF).

Training for Territorial Force batteries was made up of morning or evening sessions, weekend practices, and an annual camp of two weeks. This annual camp was normally at an army camp and included live artillery and small arms firing on military ranges.

The War Office could not afford to issue all 151 Territorial Force batteries with the modern QF 18 Pounder gun. It decided instead to issue converted 15 pounder guns left over from the Boer War (BLC 15 Pounder). These guns had originally come into service in 1885. The conversion amounted to fitting a gun shield to protect the crew from

small arms and shrapnel fire, a recuperator mechanism to return the barrel to its position after each firing, and modifications to the trail to enable some improvement to traverse and stability. It was QF (Quick Fire) in that the ammunition came as a single piece, shell and cartridge case combined, which enabled the crew to load and fire the gun more quickly. Larger guns, which were not QF, had their shells and cartridge cases (propellant) loaded separately, this taking more time to complete, but giving the option of varying the amount of propellant loaded.

This gun also came equipped with an ammunition limber and was pulled (drawn) by a team of six horses with three drivers. A limber is a small cart which has specialised storage for artillery ammunition and seats for some of the gun crew. Combining a limber and gun allowed each gun crew to have its own supply of ammunition ready for immediate use. Further supplies of ammunition were carried on larger horse drawn wagons held in the battery. These were normally at the Brigade Ammunition Column (BAC) in rear of the actual firing position, also sometimes referred to as the 'wagon lines.' Each battery initially had four guns, organised as two sections of two guns each, with a gun crew (sub-section) of ten men to each gun. Each member of the crew had a defined set of tasks to perform, and these with roles were numbered from 1 to 10. Each soldier in a gun crew was trained and able to perform several of these numbered roles, so that the loss of one or more individual would not prevent the gun from staying in action.

This BLC 15 Pounder gun was entirely suitable for training. However, it became clear when it was deployed into active service in 1915 that it had severe shortcomings and would have to be replaced.

Each gun needed six horses to draw it, and ammunition wagons needed a team of horses as well. Officers needed 'chargers', and there were many other horses needed to draw wagons carrying food, kitchen equipment and spare stores. In total, a battery in the field would need to have around seventy horses to enable it to move around and operate effectively, a brigade of three batteries some three times that number.

The accommodation in Bristol and Gloucester was not big enough to stable a full complement of horses, and there were not enough full time staff, in any case, to properly feed, clean, and minister to them. The solution was a typical British compromise. Each battery had six horses

issued to it. These were just enough to draw one gun, and to enable the necessary practice drills to be carried out, such as getting the gun into action, and out of action again. The six horses were contracted out to local businesses and brought back when needed, for evening drills and annual camp for instance. The local business was paid to look after the horses and used them as they wished except when the army needed them. This system enabled the batteries to go to camp with enough horses to carry out single gun practises, but still a long way short of a full war establishment.

In the event of war, it was planned to requisition and purchase horses centrally from a number of sources in UK and overseas. The general standard of horses brought in this way when war did break out would lead to a number of problems.

This was a pragmatic solution but not a complete one. In the words of Captain C E Boyce, Adjutant in 1912:

*"Each battery had six horses, which were farmed out to business firms on the conditions, which included their being available for the riding drill in the school on certain evenings, for Saturday afternoon parades, for week end camps and the annual fortnight camp.*

*So there were 12 horses at Bristol and 6 at Gloucester and this gave each battery one 6-horse team most valuable for training the young soldier to take his place as a team driver. The Brigade Ammunition Column had no horses. And incidentally here was one of the difficulties of those days, to keep up the esprit de corps, the enthusiasm, the efficiency, and the numbers of a unit with no guns and no horses; only some ammunition wagons.*

*The only possible solution was the one carried into effect was to train them as a battery. With the co-operation of Major Walter Swayne [1st Battery] and Lieut-Col Wise [2nd Battery], the B.A.C. borrowed guns and horses from the two Bristol batteries, and at practice camp, trained as a battery."*

This innovative decision to train the brigade ammunition column as a battery and to practise firing guns was to have major benefits to the brigade when it went into action later. The drivers and others in the Brigade Ammunition Column (BAC) shared in the allocation of live

rounds available to the brigade and fired 'live' on the ranges. Multi tasking is a central part of an artilleryman's craft. Every man who wears the Artillery cap badge must be able to carry out efficiently any duty in serving the guns.

Field Artillery's role is immediate support to infantry in whatever phase of war they are engaged. Much of the operational doctrine of the time was based on a concept of manoeuvre warfare. In this, formations of troops use movement to attack and disrupt their enemies, and literally outmanoeuvre them to the point where they are defeated. The artillery would support the main arm, the infantry. They would do this in attack by reducing the enemy's manpower and ability to resist. In defence, when the infantry need to retain possession of ground, the artillery would disrupt and destroy enemy attacking forces (infantry and cavalry) before they could close with our forces. This required forces to emphasise mobility and speed. Thus artillery needed to able to match their supported arm (infantry or cavalry) in movement capability. The Royal Horse Artillery (RHA), supporting cavalry formations, was equipped with horses and lighter guns and equipment to enable the same cross country movement speed, and fast time into action, as the cavalry. The Royal Field Artillery had to match the manoeuvre speed of the infantry, which is essentially marching speed.

This manoeuvre warfare concept had been long established both in the Continental armies, as well as in British colonial policing actions. However, the Boer War had identified that some situations in war required a different approach. In addition, some military thinkers had identified the possibility that with modern industrial technology a stalemate may occur on the battlefield and that this could lead to static trench warfare in which the current organisation, equipment, and methods would not be effective. Before the First World War had started solutions were being thought up, but the key to unlocking a static trench front had not been resolved, and would not be so until after three years of hard won experience on all sides.

The method of controlling fire from the guns in battle was not standardised across the army. Even gun drills, that is, the methods and commands used by a crew when operating a gun, could vary between units and even within a unit. This situation clearly needed improvement.

We will see that as the conditions in France were experienced methods were standardised and improved beyond all measure.

As a supporting arm the artillery were judged by their 'masters', the infantry or cavalry, more on speed of response than accuracy, more on 'dash' than method. This would also change in the light of hard won experience during the Great War.

The GVA had a background in coastal artillery, and the methods used in this context were very different from Field. They were more technical and rational. In due course many of the techniques that had been used by coastal artillery for many decades would be brought into use by field artillery as the war progressed, to the point that British artillery became the most effective and feared (by its enemies) weapon in any army anywhere.

In both 'Horse' and 'Field' guns, the main shell was shrapnel, named after its inventor, Major Henry Shrapnel. This is a projectile filled with hundreds of lead balls which are ejected forward from the shell by an explosive charge into the face of the enemy troops, ejection being controlled by a timed fuse in the nose of the shell. This type of weapon was designed to kill or neutralise enemy troops in the open. This shell was of limited use in the conditions in which most of them came to be used, in trench warfare. Troops in trenches were largely protected from shrapnel balls which mostly flew past above them. Other types of shell and fuse were in use, but in relatively small quantities. As the Great War developed, it became necessary to introduce a wider range of more effective shells and fuses.

Following its conversion to field artillery, the GVA entered into an intensive programme of learning its new skills. There was a permanent staff of Regular Army personnel, a captain as adjutant, and seven senior NCOs (sergeant and above), spread between the batteries and BAC, including one as combined Brigade Regimental Sergeant Major (RSM) and Chief Clerk.

We have heard earlier that circumstances required officers and soldiers to make do with less than adequate equipment and methods. They made the best of what they did have, though. Again, in the words of the adjutant, Captain Boyce:

## The Bristol Gunners

*"The Brigade always went to camp each year at Whitsun for a fortnight – In 1912, to Pembray in Wales, in 1913 to Okehampton and in 1914 to Salisbury Plain.*

*Training was usually confined before Christmas to gun-drill, laying, rides and harness fitting with recruits. After Christmas, lectures and miniature range for officers, gun drill, laying, signalling and rides for N.C.O.s and men-were carried out in the evening. The serious work, though, began after Easter, and from then till camp, "Spring Drills" were held.*

*During this period, officers attended the miniature range under the adjutant on Mondays, Wednesdays, Thursdays, and Fridays from 7.15am to 8.0 am, and N.C.O.s and men could be seen daily out on the parade ground signalling and laying.*

*One could not fail to admire the spirit which imbued the men who voluntarily came down to learn to be gunners before going off to their daily work. And then every evening they were there again doing section or battery gun drill, laying drill, etc. all forms of training to make themselves and their unit efficient.*

*Saturday afternoon parades were, in 1912, mostly carried out on Durdham Downs. But this proved unsatisfactory, both on account of the public wandering about, getting in our way and distracting men's attention from the task in hand, and also in the nature of the ground which did not lend itself to the training in the occupation of positions.*

*Permission was therefore obtained to use Ashton park - this gave us all we wanted and we went there again in 1913 and 1914.*

*The two batteries and the B.A.C. at Bristol and the battery at Gloucester each and all gave of their very best. "Teacher" does indeed take off his hat to them.*

*Practice camp at Pembray in 1912 was of an elementary nature as far as actual practice was concerned, simple targets, simple schemes, to give us all confidence and to make certain we had the elementary part 'cold' before taking on more difficult tasks.*

## The Bristol Gunners

*Brigade H.Q. made all arrangements for travel and very little, if any, of the Q work was passed to batteries. Guns and transport went by one train, the personnel by another, and the horses arrived from all over the place by a third.*

*Luckily it was perfectly flat road from the station to the camp and we all eventually arrived without mishap. From the military point of view, and noted how all those who had been able to put in that ¾ hour before breakfast during the six weeks of spring drills were quicker and more 'au fait' with gun drill and orders. It was most marked. It was therefore essential before next camp to improve the miniature range which up to then had been merely a small sand table and a rod to indicate the fall of the shell.*

*By the end of the year the new miniature range was well on the road to completion, thanks to R.S.M. Le Gallé. It was a large sand model and was at the Whiteladies Road end of the Drill Hall. We then ran a gun in at the opposite end, and to this, with the aid of the 2$^{nd}$ Battery fitter who was untiring in his efforts, we fixed an air gun. A wire connected the trigger with the firing lever of the gun. The Subaltern officers carried out the whole operation of laying the gun etc, exactly as was done in the field, and the gun No1 gave all orders.*

*The officers who were not conducting the shoot were thus being taught their gun drill and the results showed itself in the improvement in the drill of the detachment at the next camp.*

*The air gun was on a screw and was by this means given an angle of depression equal to the angle of elevation plus the angle of sight, and so the slug when fired, went into the sand. The only variation from normal drill on the gun was that the No5 had to be round in front of the shield to load the air gun.*

*The next problem was how with one gun to represent four guns firing and so get distribution over the target. This was achieved by having 4 aiming posts numbered 1 to 4, and the layer laid on the number required; thus – if the order was 'Right Ranging 3600-3300' he laid at 3600 on to the No1 block through the dial sight and fired. Then he traversed his gun until the dial sight with the same setting was laid on No2 block, and with 3300 on the range drum, fired again. The blocks being set at the*

## The Bristol Gunners

*equivalent of 20 yards apart produced the affect of firing with two guns at 20 yards apart.*

*Every known [and unknown] type of target was practised with wonderful results when camp came along at Okehampton. 'Okey', as usual lived up to its reputation, though it might have been much worse. We got out most days without a wet skin.*

*As in 1912, guns went by one train, horses by another and personnel by a third. And this time there was no level road from station to camp, which had to be traversed with horses, which had never seen before and quite unaccustomed to the requirements as a member of a 6-horsed team. How the guns and wagons ever got up that hill - a hill that no one who was present will ever forget, history does not relate - but they did, and without any casualties, of any sort.*

*We all benefited from the help we had from the members of the regular army and the all-round improvement was most marked. But it was hard work the whole fortnight it was no joy ride, and the batteries were given more Q work to do than in 1912.*

*On return to Bristol, one thing stood out and above all else - we cannot go on in this old way of going to Camp in three batches - men, horses, vehicles, we are batteries and must work as such.*

*Colonel Balfour had a long and arduous battle over it with the County Association, but after 9 months, he won, and authority was given to go to camp as complete units.*

*In the meantime, the usual winter programme of battery dinners was duly carried through with their prizes giving, speeches and music. Oh! Happy days. None then foresaw being mobilised and on the east coast 12 months later. The training continued on similar but more advanced lines in 1914, and when we went to camp, it was as units.*

*We collected our horses at the Artillery Grounds - marched to the station as units entrained, detrained at Amesbury, and marched like the Regular Army to our camp. The value of this cannot be over - estimated and it proved some eight weeks later. It was a good camp and all batteries did well, on targets similar to those given to regular batteries. We had advanced a long way since Pembray days, the 1$^{st}$ battery*

28

*especially did well at the actual practice, and they were full of confidence that they would give a good account of themselves in the competition for the King's Cup."*

Thus, the last annual camp before war broke out was a dress rehearsal for many aspects of mobilisation that would be needed in August, a few weeks later.

As well as bringing the brigade up to full competence with his innovations, Captain Boyce also seemed to be something of a clairvoyant. On his appointment to the Brigade in 1912, and while giving an early address to the officers, he stated:

*"Before three years have passed, there will be war with Germany."*

In fact, as Boyce freely admitted, he did not have any foreknowledge; he was using every means at his disposal, including rhetoric, to enthuse his audience for the task in hand. As he states:

*"It was a prelude to a call for further efforts to increase the strength of the brigade, and not really a prophecy at all. It was produced in an attempt to imbue all ranks then serving with a desire to redouble their efforts to make the brigade an efficient fighting unit and the standard the speaker had in mind was that of a first class regular unit.*

*That standard was reached by the end of September 1914 and the Brigade was then definitely fit to take its place in the front line. More efficient than when, after some five months in Essex, it eventually sailed it could not be otherwise in the conditions under which it carried on during those five months...."*

Through the efforts of all ranks, when the call came, they were ready, willing, and able.

The First World War came to Britain on 4$^{th}$ August 1914. The spark that initiated the fuse to the powder keg of European tensions is generally accepted as being the assassination of the Austrian Archduke Franz Ferdinand in Sarajevo on 28$^{th}$ June 1914. The succeeding responses and events cascaded one on another until the Austro-Hungarians invaded Serbia on July 28$^{th}$ and the Germans launched their armies into France and Belgium on August 4$^{th}$. Later that same day Britain declared war on

The Bristol Gunners

Germany as we had guaranteed Belgium's neutrality, and the order went out to all military units to 'Mobilise!'

One invaluable skill in war is anticipation. Some did not wait for the order to take action. The permanent staff and volunteers of the GVA were on duty preparing for mobilisation some hours before the order came.

Britain had a comprehensive mobilisation plan thanks to General Henry Hughes Wilson, and all military units had made good preparations so that the act of mobilising went smoothly. British Regular Army troops started arriving in France on 7th August, and the famous Kitchener appeal for volunteers 'Your Country Needs You' started on August 11th. Within two weeks 100,000 men had signed up. However, it would take some months before these recruits could be equipped, trained, and fully prepared for front line service.

The British Expeditionary Force (BEF) would have to keep the Germans at bay until the Territorial Force had been fully organised and prepared for service. The BEF first met the Germans at Mons in Belgium on 23rd August.

The German attacks in the west were based on the Schlieffen Plan. The concept of this was to advance rapidly through Belgium and down the west of France encircling Paris, cutting the BEF off from its logistic bases on the coast, and forcing the French to surrender. At the same time, the Germans had to deal with the Russians to their east. Speed was paramount in removing the threat to them in the west before turning to the east.

The German strategy failed, in part to their own errors of executing the Schlieffen plan, and in part due to the extraordinary efforts of the French Army ably assisted by the BEF, but mostly by the delays imposed by the unexpectedly determined, skilful, and heroic resistance of the Belgians.

The Germans pushed the BEF back at Mons, all the way to Le Cateau in France where the BEF turned and stopped the Germans in a rearguard action. This bought time to complete an orderly withdrawal from contact with the Germans.

The German Army was finally halted north of Paris, on the Marne River, in early September. Here they mistakenly swung eastwards north of Paris

rather than south of the city. They were met by the Paris garrison driving to meet them in taxicabs requisitioned by French General Joseph Gallieni. After this high point in their advance, the Germans withdrew north again and consolidated their positions to shorten their supply lines. They had by now realised that the Schlieffen plan had to be abandoned.

The next phase in the war was the 'race to the sea.' In reality, this was an attempt by both sides to outflank the other, and lasted until the end of November when the open flanks of both sides ended at the North Sea coast at Nieuwpoort in Belgium, just over the border from France. Germans, French, Belgians, and the British then had little choice but to settle down for the winter where they stood, the Western Front trench line was to move little from that time until 1918.

While the BEF were crossing to France, meeting the Germans, helping to stop them, and then racing to the sea, the GVA were also busy.

Captain Boyce describes the activity well:

*"And so to the fourth of August 1914, when we find the Adjutant in his office studying mobilisation orders which he had gone through in detail during the spring with all officers and senior N.C.O.s and had explained their duties.*

*A growing crescendo of voices and rumbling wheels disturbs his thoughts.*

*"La Gallé, La Gallé, what is all that noise about outside?"*

*"Come and look out of your window, Sir," The R.S.M.'s reply brought him quickly to the window. And what a sight to see one so typical of the spirit that permeated the whole Brigade with its Esprit de Corps and keenness. There they were, some thirty to forty of them, at least eight hours before the order to mobilize was received, helping the permanent staff to run out and clean up the wagons and to tackle anything else that called for a bit of work.*

*As far as they were concerned, it would be a case of "Ready, Aye, Ready" when the call came to the 1st South Midland Brigade.*

## The Bristol Gunners

*War was in the air, but not until about 7pm was the telegram received that sent a real thrill through the Adjutant "MOBLIZE." The order was repeated to Gloucester and all officers warned.*

*Things were early astir on the 5$^{th}$, the permanent staff had slept on the premises and soon men were arriving in their hundreds.*

*First and most important was the Bounty. But the banks were shut; this had not been foreseen and it was not for an hour or so that the Adjutant was able to extract the money from the bank manager, and then not until the latter had phoned London for instructions and the Adjutant had worried the military authorities. In due course, we were all paid out, medically examined, and so on.*

*Mobilization vehicles and harness were got ready, etc etc. The second day of mobilization saw ammunition arrive from the magazine at Portishead by lorry. Horses, too, began to arrive. They were purchased for us, and we collected them, from Temple Meads station and brought them up and piqueted them on the grass in the grounds.*

*The third day continued on the same lines and by the evening of that day we were complete except for a few horses. The next day, Saturday, saw us leave by train for Plymouth; mobilization had been carried through without a single item going wrong, absolutely in accordance with the Brigade mobilization scheme.*

*And now we really did feel the benefit of our entraining for practice camp earlier in the year. One trembles to think what might have occurred without that experience. As it was, each battery and the B.A.C. [less the S.A.A. Section which was not to accompany us] marched to Temple Meads [or was it Pylle Hill?], and entrained as units with out a hitch. It really was a wonderful effort to mobilize complete in 3 ½ days and march out and entrain for the war station without a single hitch.*

*Every train left exactly to the minute according to schedule.*

*A word here about the S.A.A. Section of the B.A.C. They did not begin their real mobilization - the collection of horses etc, till after the rest of the Brigade had marched out.*

## The Bristol Gunners

*In addition to horses, they had to collect vehicles and harness, which were bought from civilian sources. In due course they left Bristol by route march to join the 1st South Midland Division, and then their troubles began in earnest. One might almost say harness of some vehicle broke every half-mile or a vehicle itself gave out under its unaccustomed load of S.A.A. They had a truly terrible time, and it speaks volumes for its commander, Lt A. Hopkins, that they ever reached their destination. The bills he incurred followed on for ages and caused reams of correspondence and explanations. The Army was not accustomed to finding bills run up by a subaltern without having obtained the "necessary authority" in triplicate, beforehand.*

*At this point mention must also be made of the sack of harness, which was lost on rail between Bristol and Plymouth. Here again the correspondence was colossal and some weeks elapsed before authority was received to indent for the contents of the missing sack. Naturally, all Brigade deficiencies during the intervening period had to be assumed to have been lost in it. The indent was truly wonderful in its demands.*

*Ordnance with a charm that became rather tarnished in later months wrote a reply of Chesterfieldian delicacy and said that, while under the exceptional circumstances, the indent was passed, the sack appeared to be of abnormal size and capacity, and should any sacks of similar size and capacity remain in the brigade, they must forthwith be returned to Ordnance.*

*Lt. Stone had gone ahead as billeting officer and had made all ready for our arrival. A more able pen then mine deals with these early days and it only remains to fill in one or two items.*

*The duty of the brigade was to provide artillery for the mobile defences of Plymouth. This necessitated a good deal of reconnaissance in which we were greatly helped by the generosity of gunner Price of the 3rd battery who took us round in his own car.*

*Conditions in Plymouth did not make for efficient training, and the C.O. got busy early to get us moved to Crownhill. Here we were under canvas and luckily the weather was kind. We really did some excellent work and undoubtedly, by the time we moved into winter quarters at Broomfield near Chelmsford, round which the rest of the 1st South*

## The Bristol Gunners

Midland Division were billeted, we were *highly efficient* – all ranks in all branches.

The most marked improvement was undoubtedly, [as we gunners say] "In front of the splinter bar." Under the eagle eye of the C.O., horsemanship and horsemastership improved beyond all expectation. Two incidents stand out in memory of Crownhill first the order to send some horses to France - 24, I think - perhaps someone will correct me. The C.O. picked out the best in the brigade - 18 of them were those we had for three years in our peacetime, stations, true field artillery type of horse.

There was great competition to be selected as the horse party to go to France; everyone looked on it as a certainty they would be kept to join some battery out there despite the order, which said the party would return after delivering the animals.

There were long good-byes "we will write in 2 or 3 weeks and let you know what it is like out there." "So sorry, old boy, you aren't coming too, but of course we can't all go." Born optimists and full of cheer but as yet quite unaccustomed to army ways. They all returned some 48hrs later very disappointed.

The second incident was the teaching of regular gunners to harness up a team of horses and drive it. It came about in this way. On mobilization, the siege batteries [6" Howitzers] were disbanded and the personnel transferred to other duties. But the war had not long in progress before the urgent need for 6" howitzers was realised, so the 1$^{st}$ Siege battery was hurriedly reconstructed and did so at Crownhill. New officers, new N.C.O.s - new men, all arrived to reform the battery. Most of them being Garrison men were fine strong upstanding fellows, many nearing 6ft, and accustomed to moving big guns about and loading heavy shell. To them arrived vat after vat of harness, in one vat dozens of breast collars, of breechings in another hundreds of straps, and so on.

Just imagine their bewilderment, hardly one of them knew what harness looked like and certainly few, if any, knew what to do with it.

Horses, too - heavy draught type, began to arrive and – "Heavens above, have we to water and feed them - and groom them too? Ye Gods and Little Fishes, what is the Garrison Artillery coming to?"

## The Bristol Gunners

*To cut the story short, the 1st South Midland Brigade came to their rescue - collected the parts from the various vats and made up their sets of harness, fitted it to the horses and generally mothered them, even to driving in some of their teams on the way to the station when ordered overseas as they very soon were.*

*Oh! And another excitement occurs to me "I say. You fellows, here's a dam' scandal - the Wessex Division say they are under orders to proceed overseas. "What! The Wessex? Why not us? It's perfectly scandalous." – "Of course it is; the South Midland Division is much more efficient." - "Well, why aren't we to go?"*

*Esprit de Corps was a very live thing and was shocked at this slight. We were no whit mollified when Dame Rumour said they were going further east than Flanders as they were drawing Khaki Drill uniform. If we had known that they would not get to the war in France as we eventually did, but spend the whole time on garrison duty in India, we should have been satisfied - none would have changed places with them.*

*In due course we moved to Broomfield where we were billeted all over the long straggling village and spent five dreary months of mug-fog-snow-rain-ice. Training was almost impossible and our standard went back from lack of practice. In our spare time we dug many gun positions near the east coast, from which to defeat the Bosche should he ever venture to disturb our rural retreat. They must have fallen in, in due course.*

*The cold damp foggy winter of our East Coast dragged slowly on. One might add, "only relieved by the weekly optimism of Mr. Hilaire Belloc." At that time every strategist, amateur, self taught or professional, purchased week by week a copy of "Land & Water" to enable him to argue who was winning and why and Mr. Belloc gave week by week a description and illustrated account of the actions on the Western Front.*

*At last the great news arrived that we were to prepare to embark for service overseas. Inspections became the order of the day - men by Medical Officers - horses by Remount Officers - guns by Ordnance Officers, and so on."*

As Captain Boyce briefly mentions, another West Country TF Division, the 43rd Wessex Division, were sent to India in late 1914, and spent the

entire war on garrison duty there, never being sent into action (though they did send drafts of men to reinforce other divisions fighting in Mesopotamia).

**The GVA leave their HQ in Bristol on mobilisation for war, headed for the railway station at Temple Meads, Bristol, on August 7th 1914.**

Before we move on to the brigade embarking for France I would like to add a little more detail to the early months of the GVA's war.

The GVA base in Clifton was used as a reporting centre for all kinds of former servicemen and reservists, men on leave, men with previous service but no obligation to serve, plus many other 'odds and sods' trying to get into uniform and out to France. All these had to be administered, documented, and redirected. It must have been a miracle that with this going on the brigade did manage to get itself ready and meet the train schedule for its journey to Devon.

Another problem that appeared was that while horses, stores, and ammunition turned up promptly, sufficient uniforms did not. In the normal way, each man and sub unit made the best job that they could and somehow dressed themselves in some semblance of uniform, though they must have been in what the military calls 'mixed dress!'

## The Bristol Gunners

They went by train to Plymouth firstly, where they were tasked to assist in the defence of the naval base there. Plymouth was also being used to assemble many units and individuals, and the 'organised chaos' of military life must have been impressive to see. Lieutenant Colonel Harold Essex-Lewis (at that time a trumpeter) describes the scene:

*"Plymouth seemed to be the allotted war station of half the mobilising Army. Its streets were full of the returning reservists and militia men all going back to rejoin their old regiments, many thankful for the prospect of a bed, board and pay as and when required after a none to successful bout with civilian life - "A man of five and twenty as 'asn't learned a trade, with "Reserve" as well agin' 'im, 'e's better never made."*

*Add to this crowd for at least three regiments of foot, the returned naval ratings of the Plymouth Division Reserve and the caught on leave soldiers and sailors, and it will be realised that Plymouth could have spared the 1st S.M. Bde. R.F.A. its appearance on the scene. Raglan barracks and the Brickfields stand out as the landmarks of that hectic period, with nights in the Plymouth streets and suppers at the fish and chip shops, or strolling back to barracks consuming the same fare from newspaper and crooning, "You made me love you, I didn't want to do it."*

*The warm, and mercifully fine, August days went far to help us shake in to soldiering, and at least once the battery took horses swimming."*

The brigade stayed in the Plymouth area until October 20th. One historical event that some in the brigade witnessed was the arrival of the first Canadian troops in Plymouth on October 14th. Canada, as ever, was in the forefront in supporting the old country and putting action ahead of words. These Canadian troops would arrive on the Continent ahead of the Territorial Force divisions, and become crucial to the outcome of the second battle of Ypres (April 23rd - 25th 1915) where gas was used for the first time in war. The GVA were just south of this area at that time and experienced the smell of gas. More of this later.

The Brigade was starting to adjust to the realisation that they were in the war for real, and a number of things were to happen before they were ready to set sail for France.

The commitment for members of the Territorial Force was for home service only, that is, to serve in Britain but not overseas. For TF soldiers

## The Bristol Gunners

to be sent abroad required them to individually opt for 'Imperial Service' (IS). Prior to the outbreak of war this issue had been raised and TF soldiers given the opportunity to opt for IS, and only around 10% did so at that time. The uncertainty over whether the TF would be available for overseas service was a part of Field Marshall Kitchener's decision to ask for his New Army Volunteers, it is reported that he did not altogether trust the TF.

In the event, a majority of the TF did opt for IS after mobilisation, though some did not, and this required some reorganisation of TF units to release those not opting and to absorb new recruits or returning soldiers. This occurred in the GVA shortly after their move to Crownhill, near Chelmsford, in late October 1914. Lt. Col. Essex Lewis:

*"At this point there arrived from Bristol the first draft of recruits to fill up holes. For, though at this distance of time the old discussions, objections and quarrels are dead, the brigade had been cleft in two by a refusal of certain of its members to serve out of England. Time has shown those who volunteered for Imperial Service, and wore the silver badge on the right breast, that they were no more free in their choice than whose who, on paper, refused to go overseas, but the cleavage left the batteries short of I.S. men and the vacancies were immediately filled from Bristol with men, some newly joined, some of previous service, and all ready to go anywhere at once."*

The Brigade also had to learn how to operate effectively as part of a larger formation. The various parts of the division (infantry, artillery, engineers, supply troops, medical) had to learn how to work with each other and to co-ordinate their activities. Their division, the 48th (South Midland) Division (TF) was concentrating in the Chelmsford area, in preparation for deployment to the Continent. While the brigade was well practised in gunnery, the full division had never before worked as a complete formation. The individual soldiers had to be properly equipped and administered. There were forms to fill, inoculations to be suffered, uniforms to be fitted and adjusted. The equipment and guns had to be maintained and brought up to full working efficiency.

The 48th division was entirely Territorial Force, with a leavening of individual regular personnel. It comprised three infantry brigades, each of four infantry battalions of around one thousand officers and men each. There were four brigades of artillery, one being the GVA (1st Brigade),

## The Bristol Gunners

each artillery brigade numbering around six hundred men. There were also other supporting units, Royal Engineers, pioneers from the Army Service Corps, veterinarians from the Royal Army Veterinary Corps, doctors, and attendants from the Royal Army Medical Corps, and many others. In total, something a little under twenty thousand men.

An infantry division, like the 48th, is the basic manoeuvre formation in any army (there were also cavalry divisions of horse mounted soldiers similarly organised). It contains all the arms and services needed for independent deployment and operation on the battlefield and was commanded by an officer of the rank of Major General.

Initially six regular army infantry divisions made up the BEF sent out in August. Further divisions of regular infantry and cavalry were formed and sent to France in the autumn of 1914. The Territorial Force divisions started arriving in France from December and this continued into the early part of 1915. Next came the Kitchener Volunteers, or the 'New Armies' as they were sometimes styled (ultimately reaching thirty or so divisions), arriving on the battlefield in late 1915 and into 1916. Their first major challenge, and also for some of the TF divisions, was to be the Battle of the Somme in 1916.

For the moment, though, back to Chelmsford, and the training needed to bring the 48th Division and the GVA up to the level of performance and equipment needed before being ready for active service on the Continent.

The Adjutant, Captain Boyce wrote:

*"On October 20th the Brigade was moved to join the Division at Chelmsford. We occupied the village of Broomfield and arrived in the early afternoon at this old-world village. Clothing had arrived and at last we looked a little more as we should.*

*November saw us attacked by ringworm among the horses. As each case broke out the horse was taken by a driver to a village called Little Waltham, which became, in fact, one huge sick line.*

*Organised training suffered in consequence and guards and flying pickets seemed to be the order of the day. This meant that the order "Right turn - stables" brought with it a walk of, perhaps, a mile to certain sub-sections.*

## The Bristol Gunners

*In December the first leaves came through and we returned to Bristol for a few days to sun our lean selves in the smiles of our old city. Christmas brought such festivities as our officers could manage, and they worked wonders, so that we sat down to a Christmas dinner such as is seldom imagined and never described.*

*March saw us free from ringworm and with stores arriving almost hourly. Rumour was abroad. Nor was the necessity for secrecy forgotten. One incautious corporal having been told that solar topees had been seen going into stores, led his sub-section in singing "Egypt my Cleopatra," and was rebuked by a zealous "non-com" on the grounds that German spies might hear him.*

*Prior to proceeding overseas, all artillery went to Salisbury Plain for a day or two's practice, and we duly went into that land of cold and chalky mud. Conditions were certainly very different from those at the Whitsun camp some nine months before. There had been big changes in the personnel of the Brigade too - officers and men - but it was the same 1st S.M. Brigade with the same cheery spirit.*

*Back again to Broomfield - final inspections, closing of equipment ledgers and pay accounts, and so at last to the great day - Sunday, March 28, 1915, when, with many farewells to all our kind hosts and friends, the Brigade marched to Chelmsford Station to entrain en route for the British Expeditionary Force."*

The attack of ringworm, which seems to have affected most of the horses of the brigade was possibly the result of needing to acquire a large number of horses from far and wide to meet the needs of a rapidly expanding army. Ringworm is not a worm but a fungal infection, and it is very contagious. It can be transferred from animal to animal directly, or via equipment, such as saddles and tackle. It can also be transferred between humans and horses.

It is likely that some of the horses brought into the military were not well looked after by their previous owners. Certainly, having a large number of horses together from a range of sources, and sharing equipment and tackle, and a large number of humans, could easily lead to a rapid spread of this disease.

## The Bristol Gunners

In the case of the GVA, it seems that after a while it was brought under control and caused no serious delay to training and the embarkation schedule.

The story regarding the alleged sight of solar topees going into stores may have had some basis in fact. At that time, February/March 1915, the attack on Gallipoli in Turkey was being planned and prepared. Two TF infantry divisions did, in fact, take part in the Gallipoli campaign, as did others in the campaigns in Egypt and Palestine, so it could have been possible that the 48th Division was being considered for use outside Europe.

The Christmas leave in Bristol must have been difficult for the soldiers as well as their families. The war had drawn to a stalemate of sorts in France and Belgium, and there seems to be no doubt that those in uniform wanted to get out and do their bit before it all ended, for there was still much optimism of an early peace, even if not by Christmas. For the families, just having got used to being without their sons, brothers, and husbands, to see them again and having to say 'goodbye, and fare thee well' yet again, cannot have been easy.

In the spring, the GVA was issued with more guns to bring them up to full strength of four guns per battery, a total of twelve in the brigade. These were still the outdated BLC 15 Pounder guns that they had been using since 1908. Field batteries of the Regular Army had been equipped with the newer and better QF 18 Pounder. As the Kitchener's New Army formed its artillery brigades they were also equipped with these newer guns. The Territorial Force artillery, though, continued with the BLC 15 Pounder, which, in the light of front line experience, would prove to be unsatisfactory. It has been said that Field Marshall Lord Kitchener, then Minister of War, had a low opinion of the Territorial Force and this led him to keep it on low priority for equipment, favouring instead his New Armies. The reason for this may well be due to his experience of TF men who volunteered for Imperial Service during the Boer War. When that war was won, most of them returned home to Britain, leaving Kitchener, then a junior general, short of manpower to do the clearing up and pacification of the populace. Kitchener preferred, it is said, to have troops with a longer term commitment to serve rather than the 'hostilities only' commitment of the TF.

### The Bristol Gunners

So the months passed, and March arrived. The pace quickened, movement orders arrived, dates were set. They were off to war - at last!

It is not always appreciated in the modern day how important the railways were to military thinking in the early twentieth century. The major Continental powers (France, Germany, Russia, and Austria) all had developed railway systems that were a central part of their military planning. Their decisions to mobilise were based, in part, on the time that they would need to mobilise their armies and get them to their frontiers ahead of their opponents. A good railway system was a strategic necessity, and most of the armies spent much time ensuring that they could get military advantage from them.

The Germans had planned, and were building, a railway from Berlin to Baghdad. Though this would not be complete until after the First World War this railway was a factor in the campaigns fought by the British against the Ottomans (Turks) in Mesopotamia and the Arabian Peninsula. The German intention for this railway was for Germany to be able to trade with the Middle and Far East without needing to use shipping, thus avoiding interference from nations with large navies – such as Britain and France.

The railway systems used by the enemy were also regarded as important targets. Disrupting the enemy's supply routes by capturing or interfering with key rail junctions was a vital part of military planning as it sought to limit an enemy's freedom of movement for supplies and reserves.

The British also relied on their merchant marine to transport forces for the defence of the Empire and to move the army to the Continent. The Royal Navy had the task of protecting the Empire and of necessity the merchant marine, both for defence as well as for commerce.

The armies moving from Britain to France (the main British allocated port of arrival was Le Havre) needed to travel by train from their bases to the channel ports, and then by sea to France. The French railway system would move them on to a railhead, normally Hazebrouck, in the Pas de Calais region, just behind the British held sector of the Front.

One can imagine the feelings of the officers and men in Chelmsford when the orders for France came through, excitement, mixed with

apprehension, and perhaps thoughts of 'what on earth have I let myself in for?' In the military, intense activity is the normal antidote to uncertainty, and no doubt the officers and NCOs stood to the task with a will.

On Sunday March 28th 1915 at 10 p.m. the GVA, along with the rest of the 48th Division marched out of camp to Chelmsford railway station for a train journey to Southampton, where they embarked on seven different ships the following day. At this time German submarines were operating in the English Channel and some ship losses had been suffered. The policy was for every unit to be spread across several ships so that one sinking would not destroy a complete unit. If one ship were sunk, or damaged, any unit would still be effective and could be brought back to strength relatively quickly.

Lieutenant E L Gedye wrote in a letter to his mother:

*"Wandered round the docks with Finley and inspected a Cardiff ship that was in the dry dock for repairs, having had a big hole made forward by a mine or torpedo. Quite cheering."*

This illustrates that the threat from the Germans was very real, and must have been quite sobering to see just before leaving port on a similar vessel.

The GVA set sail on the allocated ships at 6.30 p.m., escorted by two destroyers. No doubt many stood at the rails of the ships as they slid into the Solent, looking back at 'Blighty', wondering what lay ahead, and if they would see home again.

The journey across the Channel was uneventful, and the ships docked in Le Havre at 8.15 a.m. on Tuesday 30th March 1915.

Lieutenant E L Gedye described the disembarkation:

*"Anchor weighed at 7.30a.m, and 8.15 berth ship. Horses and vehicles disembarked under the direction of an extremely fussy little fellow, the A.M.L.O. [Assistant Military Landing Officer] who apparently marked me down as the most harmless O.C. on board and followed me everywhere repeating his instructions four or five times and varying the detail on each occasion. He told us he was formerly a rear admiral on*

### The Bristol Gunners

the retired list, and on the outbreak of war, applied for a job in the Navy. This was refused him [and no wonder] so he went to the war office and sat on the doorstep until they gave his present job with the rank of Lieutenant Colonel. From his entire ignorance of military matters, I can quite believe that his tale is correct.

He sent me off in his car to try and find the 1st Bty whom I discovered about a mile away. On my return, he told me that he had instructions to send us off at the first possible opportunity, and that accordingly, we were to entrain with the whole of 1st Bty at 5.30 that evening.

The horses having been disposed of and the vehicles parked by the quayside, we lunched in a large shed now occupied by the A.O.C. as stores. Here the interpreter, a subaltern from the 7th Regt of siege artillery, Yclept Migno, joined us. A very decent fellow who speaks English excellently. At 5 o'clock, we moved off from the quay en route for the station, Gare des Marchandises, Point 3.

Here we found the train divided into three parts at different sidings - horse trucks, vehicle trucks, and carriages. The horse trucks are much sounder than ours, taking the same number of horses [8] but the animals are entrained four at each end of the truck facing the centre where there is sufficient space for the harness to be stacked.

A couple of men were told off for each truck to act as piquet, and the remainder were put in 7 trucks - seventeen to each. This sounds rather close packing, but as a matter of fact they had ample room, the carriages being intended to take 36/40 men. There was a plentiful supply of straw in each carriage and I rather fancy that the men slept a great deal better then we did in our first class coach.

The entraining was a very lengthy job and when it was finished there was still further delay while the various parts of the train were joined up. At last, about half eight, we started.

We were all pretty well done up, and after a little grub from our travelling luncheon baskets, we made ourselves as comfortable as possible and were asleep within a minute."

The Brigade War History also mentions this phase of the journey:

## The Bristol Gunners

*"Entraining was rather exciting. This was active service, and whether one travelled in a passenger coach as an officer and hushed one's curses over the orders of the MLO - Military Landing Officer - with a thrill of delightful and imminent danger on reading the warning notice "Taisez-vous! Mefiez-vous! Les oreilles d'ennemis vous ecoutent,"* (Keep quiet, beware, the enemy is listening to you) *or, more prosaically debated whether, after reading the notice on your carriage "Hommes 40; Chevaux 8," you still reckoned in the Army as a man or the fifth leg of a horse, it was new it was exciting, and it was the Real Thing."*

For practical reasons the French railways used the same goods wagons for conveying horses, men, and stores. Used to being transported in the UK in passenger carriages it came as a surprise to British soldiers to be expected to travel in goods wagons, and the notice 'Hommes 40; Chevaux 8' (40 men, 8 horses) was noticed and mentioned in many personal accounts of the war.

The several trains carrying the 48th Division rumbled steadily across France, arriving in Hazebrouck.

Lieutenant E L Gedye describes the journey in a letter to his parents:

*"Woke up at 2 a.m. to find the train halted and a French soldier handing out cups of cafe au cognac, this was not too good, but warm and wet and better than nothing. So to sleep again.*

*Awake again at 6 o'clock. Bright sunshine and rather pretty country, through which we crawl along at a pace that could not have exceeded 15 miles per hour at any time.*

*Presently another stop at a small town or large village called Eu. [I think this is still sufficiently far from our final destination to permit of the name being mentioned] we get out to stretch our legs and the variety of costumes seems worthy of a photograph.*

*The next stop is Abbeville, there we water and feed the horses and drink much coffee at the buvette.*

### The Bristol Gunners

*Lane and Fullerton were nearly left behind here, as they had been left in charge of the train, while we went across to the buvette, and only had a couple of minutes to get their refreshments. They naturally lingered over this, and had to sprint across several lines of railway, one platform and between two or three trains. However, they easily caught up our old tortoise, Lane sustaining a bruised knee as a result of a fall.*

*This, with the exception of a five minutes halt at -------- (censored) was our last stop before reaching our destination station------- (censored, probably Hazebrouck). The first sound, which reached us there, was a chorus from a number of gamins of "Tipperary" and from a distance, the English pronunciation appeared quite good."*

Hazebrouck was the railhead, the main rail destination, for the BEF, and is just south of the border with Belgium, being well sized and placed to feed supplies and troops into the areas occupied by the British, at that time in northern France and Belgium.

The British sector extended from Ypres in Belgium down to Loos, a few miles north of Arras. The British were given a northern part of the front (though the section north of Ypres at that time was the responsibility of French and Belgian troops) as his area was closest to Britain, and it therefore made sense to keep supply lines as short and as straightforward as possible.

Since the battles of 1914 had been fought the Regular Army had held the line with little help from the TF or New Armies. The front they held, therefore, was quite short. In later times, as the British Army strength grew from a quarter million men to over a million, and ultimately to over two million, their share of the front lengthened.

In March 1915, the aim for the newly arriving divisions was twofold. Firstly, to release regular army divisions from the front line for rest and recovery. Secondly, to insert newly arrived divisions into relatively quiet sections of the front to enable them to become used to the conditions and gain valuable experience, to finally 'shake out' as a military formation.

The 48th Division had the task of replacing the regular army 4th Division in its position near the town of Neuve Eglise (now NieuwKirke) in Belgian Flanders, just to the west of the Messines Ridge. This area

would be the scene of a major success for the British in early 1917. However, at the time of the GVA's arrival it was a quiet sector, and ideal for settling them in to the ways of war.

At Hazebrouck station, they unloaded their horses, wagons, guns, and stores, and marched by road to their positions around Neuve Eglise.

Lieutenant Colonel Harold Essex-Lewis, at this time a Trumpeter, related:

*"As Captain's Trumpeter, the writer was the last to leave the station riding behind the Battery Capt. A. E. Stone. We trotted some little way when Capt. Stone turned in his saddle and held up a forefinger. We were hearing the first rumble of gunfire and felt that we were on Active Service at last.*

*Night saw us at Rouge Croix, a village behind the Messines front. It was Easter Sunday. On moving up towards the line, we passed our old friends the 4th and 6th Gloucesters on the march.*

*Late afternoon found the batteries in action in positions behind the ridge overlooking Messines. It rained hard, as it had indeed, all day, and we felt that this was the real thing. Guns were in front of Neuve Eglise village and wagon lines behind it."*

The handover from the 4th Division took three days, and on 4th April, the guns and other troops took their positions in the line, now fully responsible for the defence of the front. This was it, into action, at last.

Since the frantic battles of the autumn of 1914, both sides and all combatant nations had needed to reconsider their positions. The Germans had failed in their attempt to knock France and Britain out of the war. They had also failed to defeat the Russians. The Kaiser's promise to his army in August 1914 that "You will be home before the leaves fall from the trees" had proved to be false. Germany had feared a protracted war on two fronts, and this was now becoming a fact. They could not be victorious in both simultaneously. They must choose one front to defend, and one on which to attack. So, the Germans decided on defence in the west, and attack in the east.

The French had averted the disaster of Paris being occupied, but much French territory was in German hands. The reigning doctrine of the

## The Bristol Gunners

French Army was to attack, wars were not to be won by defence, especially if the Germans were in occupation. They must be thrown back and ejected. The French therefore decided on a policy of being aggressive.

The Belgians had most of their country occupied. Some of their army had escaped capture and were entrenched opposite the Germans on the extreme north of the trench line, but the Belgians did not have it in their power to eject the Germans, and feared taking serious casualties from a small and irreplaceable manpower pool. The Belgians decided on a policy of passivity.

The British were still a small presence on the Continent. The Regular Army had been severely bloodied, but it was unbowed. Britain's (and its Empire's) strength was slowly being built, some TF and Empire divisions had arrived over the winter, but it was to be many months before it could see its strength grow to the point where it would present a real threat to the German Army. Britain was a junior party to the French, and adopted a policy of growing its military forces while supporting any French actions.

Thus, as the spring of 1915 came the Germans had gone on to the defensive, building a series of fortified zones to give them the ability to frustrate any allied penetrations, and allow them to transfer troops to the Eastern Front in order to defeat Russia before turning their attention once more to the west.

The French wanted to attack whenever and wherever possible. The British wanted to show willing and prove their worth as allies, but lacked the strength for a major offensive.

The Belgians were determined to sit tight, not lose any more territory, and preserve their army.

Between February 1915 and September 1915 six TF divisions, and fifteen New Army divisions would be absorbed into the BEF. As a result, the British would be able to take over greater lengths of the front. In May, just after the GVA arrived, the BEF took over five more miles down to the town of Lens, and a further fifteen miles in August, taking them down to south of Arras in the Somme region.

### The Bristol Gunners

Immediately before the GVA arrival at Neuve Eglise, the offensive year had started with a British attack at Neuve Chapelle, on March 10th. This attack, thoroughly planned by General Haig, was initially successful, but later became stuck due to the basic features of trench warfare. This would be a familiar pattern in the years to come. It did serve to highlight some important shortcomings in British capabilities. Insufficient artillery ammunition, the difficulty in accurately and effectively destroying wire and trenches to facilitate success, inadequate communications, and the problems of reinforcing success by getting reserves forward and through any break in the enemy defences.

The GVA, however, were not to become involved in any major actions for over a year.

Shortly after their arrival, the GVA found themselves on the downwind edge of the first use of poison gas, at the second battle of Ypres on 22nd April. The Brigade War History describes this:

*"The second Battle of Ypres commenced soon after we were in action, and although this did not extend to the 48th Divisional front the sounds and signs of battle were quickly made familiar to the Brigade.*

*Their first acquaintance with gas took place on April 22.*

*It was confined to a smarting of the eyes, but some of the Brigade whose duty took them next day on the Bailleul road saw those terribly tragic victims of this form of warfare - ambulance after ambulance passing filled with men black in the face, gasping for breath. An unforgettable introduction to that side of war.*

*In those days gas helmets were unknown, but orders were quickly sent out for the provision of some form of respirator protection, and units had hints of what to do and were left to work out the details.*

*Now, nothing is so plentiful in the haberdashery shops of Belgium and Northern France as crepe, and therefore several funerals' - worth was procured, the earliest gas masks taking the form of respirators of cotton wool covered with crepe, which were placed over the nose and mouth and tied behind the head."*

### The Bristol Gunners

Thus, the front line troops had to improvise protection from the chlorine gas with locally procured materials. It is surprising at this distance that no official precautions had been prepared, as the potential use of gases of various types had been foreseen. As the war progressed, of course, more and better measures were introduced, and ultimately even the most noxious gases were seen as a nuisance, a 'neutralisation' measure, rather than a means of destruction. Nevertheless, this was an unwelcome development, roundly condemned in the Allied press, then quickly copied and improved by them. The British used it in an attack, at Loos, six months later, in September 1915.

Adjusting to life in the front line was a mix of terror, excitement, frustration, and exploration.

The terror of being shelled, and the fear of sniper fire even in rearward areas. The excitement of young men experiencing new sensations and situations. The frustration caused by inadequate food, insufficient shells, and fuses that failed, and the exploration of a new country and their own abilities.

The Brigade War History notes in regard to the terror element:

*"Artillery fire in those early days of 1915 was not on a heavy scale on either side. Those were the days when enthusiastic souvenir hunters rushed out in the middle of a hostile shoot to dig for a fuse that had just buried itself, happily regardless that another might be along in a second to make a similar ceremony necessary for the searcher.*

*It had not then been realised that the official idea of the soil of Flanders was that it existed to be lifted in small quantities and placed in sandbags.*

*Sniping and machine-gunning were, however, a constant source of danger. The trench system, as later understood, was totally inadequate when the Division took over.*

*Two strands of barbed wire, festooned with empty tins and jars to give warning of approach, were the average protection for the front line, and in that wet low-lying country the "trenches" were in the main composed of a very shallow trench with breastworks above the ground level.*

## The Bristol Gunners

*Two such lines with no adequate communication or support system were all that existed.*

*The quiet and peace of those early days were realised only in later comparison - at the time, everything was new - responsibilities seemed heavy, and life full of both danger and incident."*

Ammunition was a specific problem. Each gun was supplied with three rounds per day, and the fuses supplied had a very high failure rate. A shrapnel shell which does not explode at the right time ceases to be effective, and becomes essentially a large and inaccurate bullet. This was a problem throughout the army, not just with the GVA. The problem eventually led to questions in Parliament, and the appointment of David Lloyd George as Minister of Munitions, who then vigorously set about increasing the quantity and quality of munitions. GVA Lieutenant E L Gedye played a part in this affair. In addition, it came to be accepted that the BLC 15 pounder guns that the TF were equipped with were inadequate to the job, and would have to be replaced.

The Brigade War History records:

*"The firing of the Brigade was restricted - the acute shortage of ammunition was such that a court of inquiry would almost have been summoned had the day's ammunition expenditure ever reached double figures.*

*This was, perhaps, not an unmixed evil - the Brigade was still equipped with 15-pounder guns which had outlived their effectiveness. Modern conditions necessitated an accuracy of fire which the 15-pounder was incapable.*

*Regular brigades had 18-pounders, and the New Armies being formed at home were already being equipped with brand new guns as they became available from the armament firms.*

*The Brigade, while doing their utmost to obtain accurate firing from their old guns, knew them to be inefficient and, in close working with the infantry, liable to cause unnecessary casualties.*

## The Bristol Gunners

*Feeling very strongly on this question, an officer of the Brigade - Lieutenant E. L. Gedye - wrote home and secured the interest of a local Member of Parliament - Sir William Howell Davies in the matter.*

*Sir William interviewed Mr. Lloyd George then the all-powerful Minister of Munitions who promised to give the matter consideration and investigation.*

*Within a very few weeks, all the 15-pounders in action in France and Flanders were withdrawn and 18-pounders issued."*

The adequacy of the food seems to have been a problem in the Division. After some complaints the matter was corrected and the food supply improved massively. It is a generally accepted fact that the British soldier, above all other nations, was consistently well fed throughout the war, and it is a credit to the military supply organization that this was so. The diet, could be, and was, supplemented by local arrangements. Again, the Brigade War History:

*"The village of Neuve Eglise was on a spur of Kemmel Hill, the one piece of higher ground in that very flat country. Civilians were still living close to the firing line, and it was recalled later in the war to an incredulous audience that the observation post party would kick up no end of a row with madame if she failed to produce a really good lunch in the parlour or in the garden during the tour of duty."*

And:

*"Bailleul and Armentieres, though close to the line, were the shopping area of the Brigade, and the cafés and estaminets in each town knew great prosperity."*

There were other incidents worthy of note. One which maybe demonstrates the paranoia and ineptitude of the times, from Captain Boyce:

*"And then the Spies! We, like many others had spy mania. It must have been about 6 weeks after our arrival at Neuve Eglise that rumours went around that there was signalling going on at night. It was observed*

### The Bristol Gunners

*towards Kortepyp, about a mile S.W. of the village at about 9.50 pm and appeared to be coming from a farm.*

*This was observed several nights in succession and eventually caused some eager officers to investigate.*

*They approached the farm slowly and quietly, until one of them fell into a ditch in the dark with plenty of water in it and then sounds came forth that were neither French nor Flemish and were understood only by the tracking party - not by the Flemish watchdog who was within earshot and fairly raised the roof.*

*Still the signalling continued, something of vital importance must be in course of transmission. A rush with revolvers drawn was made for the front and back doors and the dog was silenced. Much searching and questioning of the four occupants followed one old man, his antique wife and two regrettably and incomprehensibly voluble daughters followed, all to no purpose and in due course the party withdrew defeated.*

*The explanation was, of course, perfectly simple. At about 9pm the one lamp was lit and as in those days there was no orders about not showing lights at night, no curtains or blinds were drawn and the occupants walking between the light and the small window gave the effect of Dots and Dashes."*

Many people, even those with only a casual knowledge of the First World War, will know of Bruce Bairnsfather and his cartoons based on the character 'Old Bill.' Bairnsfather served at this time with the Royal Warwickshire Regiment, part of 48th Division, and he had left some of his drawings on the walls of the farmhouse at La Plus Douve farm, which was in the front line and was the location for the night OP for the GVA. Captain Boyce:

*"The H.Q. of one of the infantry battalions in the line facing Messines was in a farm called La Plus Douve. On the buff-coloured walls were a number of pictures in coloured chalk by Bairnsfather [who was with a battalion of the Warwicks] and hundreds who had the good fortune to have to go there whether on duty or not enjoyed them. Two remain in the writer's memory, one a delightful head and shoulders of a gipsy woman, the other a splendid head and shoulders of a Spanish girl."*

## The Bristol Gunners

The 5th Gloucestershire Regiment were also part of the 48th Division and produced their own newspaper. Lieutenant E L Gedye, though of the RFA, wrote articles for this paper under his pseudonym of 'Emma Kew.'

The war in the Neuve Eglise area was relatively quiet. In July, the 48th Division were ordered to move southwards as the BEF took over positions from the French on the Somme. The division were now fully prepared and knew their trade as well as any other division.

Before we follow them on this journey we should hear again from Trumpeter Harold Essex-Lewis on the reality of life just behind the front line:

*"Spring came on us here. Primroses appeared almost on the battery position, and there were still enough trees in the country to collect birds' eggs. These were blown and given to the Major whose small daughter collected them. At a cottage not far away lived Madame Zeppelin, who, said rumour, pinched chocolate and cigarettes from our parcels out from home, and sold them to C Battery at war prices.*

*The evenings lengthened and as the nights became warmer, song parties used to gather and give tongue. One recalls how, when taking a message one evening to C Battery one saw the black silhouettes of the guns against a moon-silvered sky and heard the notes of a violin playing "There's an old mill by the stream, Nelly Dean." Presently the men joined in and sang with such fervour that they seemed to be wallowing in the most acute misery.*

*In June, a New Army division came in for a short period of training beside us, and our personnel withdrew to wagon lines where sports were held. The Major's groom, mounted on a mule, and fantastically garbed, was a splendid clown and kept the show in a roar of laughter."*

There was time for fellowship, laughter, and nostalgia. Throughout their four months in Belgium there had been no serious injuries or deaths in the GVA. It was not entirely safe, however, as we have heard. There is now a Commonwealth War Grave Commission cemetery at La Plus Douve farm, and it contains 37 graves of men from the 48th Division killed during their time in this position, including that of 2nd Lieutenant George Keith Savile, of the Gloucestershire Regiment, son of the first commander of the GVA, Colonel HBO Savile.

## The Bristol Gunners

Just before the 48th Division left Belgium a new commander was appointed. Major General Sir Robert Fanshawe. He was the youngest of three brothers, all of whom became generals and commanded divisions in the war. Robert was an infantryman, having been commissioned into the Oxfordshire Light Infantry in 1883. The eldest brother, Sir Edward Fanshawe was a Gunner and incidentally was born in 1859, the same year that the GVA came into existence. The middle brother, Sir Huw Fanshawe was a cavalryman, having been commissioned into 19th Hussars. Huw also rose eventually to the rank of Lieutenant General, commanding V Corps later in the war.

Robert Fanshawe had two nicknames, one obvious, 'Fanny', and the other needing a little explanation. He was known as 'The Chocolate Soldier.' He was very much a soldiers' general. He was frequently in the front trenches, making personal reconnaisances, and it was not unknown for him to slip out into no-man's land for a closer look. He 'dressed down' while in the front areas, covering his uniform with an old raincoat so as not to intimidate those around him. He also had a habit of handing out chocolate bars and cigarettes to soldiers that he met, and thus earned his nickname.

More importantly, as an officer of wide and hard won experience (as were most commanders at that time) across the empire, he favoured 'elastic defence.' This was a doctrine that was unpopular at first with some military and political figures, but which by the end of the war was seen to be the most sensible and effective method. In elastic defence the 'front' is a series of lightly held outposts with increasingly heavily manned and defended positions deeper back into the line. This allows enemy penetration to some extent, with minimal exposure to our own troops, but with the ability to conserve forces and push back at the critical time in the battle to expel intruding enemy forces, and provide the opportunity for rebound gains from the enemy positions.

The 48th were very lucky to have Fanshawe junior in command. Accounts of his exploits are told with much affection and respect. He would lead them through the most difficult battles up to the summer of 1918.

And so, in July 1915, the 48th division withdrew from the front, and trekked its way south.

The Bristol Gunners

A gun crew under Lieutenant Basil Fullerton in position near Neuve Eglise, in April 1915. The guns are the obsolescent 15 Pounder BLCs, soon to be replaced with more modern QF 18 Pounders. Lieutenant Fullerton, on the left, standing, was killed in August 1917 during the Battle of Passchendaele. His younger brother, John, died nine days later in the same battle. Sergeant Sherriff and Gunner Owen would also die during the war.

The Bristol Gunners

# Chapter 3  The Roses Are Blooming In Picardy.

The division moved out of their positions below the Messines ridge in late July 1915. This area would become famous two years later for a successful British battle that went according to plan when twenty massive explosions along the ridge destroyed German positions and allowed the British to capture all their objectives. Possession of this area allowed full observation into the German defences beyond with the advantage of height.

In 1914, during the race to the sea the Germans had been astute in establishing their defensive positions by occupying the high ground. This gave them tremendous advantage as it enabled them to observe deep into our rear areas and not only see what we were doing, but to interfere with our activities with shellfire. It also meant that the Germans could keep much of their activity out of sight from the Allies by siting their main defensive trenches and supply lines on the reverse slope, out of direct observation. Of course, this advantage was somewhat moderated by the use of aerial observation from aeroplanes and balloons. This in turn lead to the air war over the front involving aeroplanes defending or attacking the opponent's observation planes and balloons.

The British were somewhat slower to appreciate the need to occupy the high ground, and in large parts of the front were in possession of lower ground, under observation, and where groundwater made trenches more difficult to dig and keep mud free. In some areas, notably Flanders and where the GVA had been, near Messines, the 'trench line' was in fact not a trench, but a raised line of embankments or 'breastworks' totally inadequate for the type of warfare that was to develop later.

So, the period between the end of 1914 and the spring of 1915 had been used by both sides to re-appraise their relative positions, and work out what to do next.

The Germans had resolved to go on the defensive in the west, and build fortress like positions on their chosen ground. They had the high ground, they built massive underground refuges and barracks. They would allow the Allies to attack, and destroy them while they did so. They understood that for a while, and until the war in the east had been resolved, that they were going to carry out positional warfare.

## The Bristol Gunners

The French, the senior allied partner, resolved to attack, and expected to push the Germans out of France. Their positions were thought of as temporary, with no need for massively engineered fortifications. They would soon be out in the open again, chasing the 'Hun.' They were expecting to once again try to carry out manoeuvre warfare, to attack the Germans, break through, and then break out into the ground beyond the front and create flanks that could be exploited (though not every soldier and general believed this to be possible).

The British army was building its numbers gradually. The Regular Army was depleted, but intact. The TF divisions were arriving steadily, and New Army divisions were starting to arrive in France. In order to give room to the expanding British Army, and to allow the French Army to concentrate forces for attack it was agreed that the British would extend their line southwards and relieve French formations for further deployment. Thus, in the summer of 1915, the British were to take over the line as far south as the Somme River, in Picardy.

Other things had changed further afield. The Italians had finally come into the war on May 23rd, on the side of the Entente. Italy had been a member of the Triple Alliance, with Germany and Austro-Hungary, in the hope of gaining the Irridenta from Austria by negotiation and as a reward. Despite Austrian promises to discuss and resolve this issue, they had held on to the Trento region, Trieste, and Istria. The Italians optimistically believed that their best course of action was to take what they felt were theirs by right, by force. They declared war on Austria, and immediately attacked, with some early successes. However, the Italian Army lacked the ability to defeat the Austrians, and their campaign became bogged down and almost led to their own defeat.

French and British landings had been made in Gallipoli in order to knock Turkey out of the war and allow supplies to the Russians via the Black Sea. This campaign was to drag on throughout 1915 until the final withdrawal of Allied troops in January 1916.

So, the 48th division moved south into France.

Initially they 'trekked' (another terminological hangover from the Boer War) to a small village called Ferfay, near the railhead at Hazebrouck.

### The Bristol Gunners

They stayed there for three weeks, during which time some gun sections were sent to Mazingarbe, to support an attack. However, the guns did not see action, and returned to the fold after a few days.

The division then trekked to Lillers and travelled by train from there to Thievres, in Picardy. There the GVA and the other artillery brigades were re-equipped with what was the standard British field gun, the QF 18 Pounder. They were to keep that type of gun for the rest of the war, and for many years afterwards.

The old 15 pounders were not taken out of service, however. They were to remain in service in the more remote parts of the Empire until war's end. The decision to do this must be questioned. While there is no doubt that it made practical sense to keep the 15 pounder in use due to stocks of shells and spares, it did not make moral sense. It had been recognised that inherent faults with the gun and ammunition could easily result in casualties to our own troops.

An artillery gun is normally placed behind our own troops and fires over their heads. In this way shells have to pass over our troops on their way to the enemy. Obviously, anything that might result in those shells landing short, or exploding prematurely, would put our troops in danger. Shells fired from the same gun do not all land in the same spot. They land in an established pattern, in an elliptical shape. This ellipse is ten times longer than it is wide, and is lengthways along the line of fire. It is called the 'beaten zone', or sometimes just the 'zone' of a gun. For a 15 pounder, this may typically be two hundred metres long and twenty metres wide. Individual shells could land anywhere within this zone.

A shell fired at an enemy, therefore, with no pre-adjustment, could land two hundred metres in front of the enemy, where it is quite probable that our troops may be, especially in the attack. This means that artillery fire would have to stop when our troops were still some way off, leaving the enemy free to fire at us with rifles or machine guns without the risk from our shellfire.

In addition, the 15 pounders were mostly supplied with shrapnel shells. These had a time fuse that was designed to explode the shell in the air before it hit the ground. Many of these fuses were dud, in that they did not explode the shell, or faulty, in that the shell would be exploded some

time before or after the intended point. Thus, our shells sometimes exploded above our troops, causing casualties, or passed harmlessly beyond the enemy without exploding, reducing the effectiveness of the shellfire, and exposing our troops to the enemy small arms fire more than otherwise would have been the case.

This situation, having been demonstrated in the early part of the war with TF artillery in Belgium drove the replacement of the guns and ammunition with improved types. It made no sense then to expose other troops in other parts of the Empire to the same hazards.

The new guns had a more compact zone, and therefore were safer and more effective. The problems with fuses, though, would continue for some time, and would not be entirely solved even at the end of the war. The source of the faulty fuses was partly design and partly manufacture. Improved designs would be brought in as the war progressed, and quality of manufacture improved as munitions factories developed better trained workers and quality control methods.

The British were not alone with these problems, of course, and dud fuses and shells were also to plague all other combatants to a similar degree.

The time spent by the GVA at Ferfay was recalled by Trumpeter Harold Essex-Lewis:

*"The trek was a wonderful experience and seemed to put the seal on our indentures as soldiers. One felt that the Brigade was on real active service at last and up to its job. Various halts were made but the longest stay was at Ferfay outside Lillers*

*The Brigade was in a private wood with an open space in the centre and 4 clearings. Each clearing took one battery and the Brigade Headquarters. The men built bivouacs of twigs and groundsheets and some little ingenuity was displayed in the construction of these. Water was very scarce and had to be brought from a long distance away. The chateau housed the officers, and as each battery had collected at least two goats as mascots, a special line was erected for these against the chateau wall. In choosing the sites, no one seems to have remembered that directly above the line was the window of the Brigade Commander's room. At his urgent representation, the line was removed, and the mascots disposed of.*

## The Bristol Gunners

*During the stay at Ferfay, we saw our own Indian Cavalry and admired their physique and turn out, which contrasted oddly with that of the French Moroccan troops who were also in the district. Here too we spent an evening in an estaminet with the men from the French 75 battery and found that music forms a wider international currency than even beer! Both batteries rendered samples of their national songs, sometimes simultaneously."*

This was not the first contact with the French Army. Liaison officers had been available during the division's arrival back in April, and no doubt, there had been official and casual contacts from time to time. However, this is the first mention of French colonial troops, and also first contact with British colonial, or rather, Empire, troops. This was a sign of the growing scale of the war and of the scope and scale of both the British and French Empires.

The Germans started the war with a small series of overseas possessions, all of which in due course would be taken from them by the British and French, resulting in permanent confiscation. They had African colonies and Pacific Islands, all of which were divided up among the Allies. The British took German South West Africa (now Namibia) mandated to the South Africans, German East Africa (now Tanzania), part of Cameroon and Togoland, and the Solomon Islands in the Pacific. The French took part of Cameroon and Togoland. Belgium was given Rwanda-Urundi. The Portuguese took part of German East Africa. The Pacific islands north of the Equator (The Marshalls, The Carolines, the Marianas, Palau, and the German enclave of Jiaozhou in China) were taken by our allies the Japanese. The British took Pacific islands south of the Equator, and administered them via New Zealand and Australia (Samoa, German New Guinea, the Bismarck Archipelago, and Nauro).

It is worth noting at this point that the German forces in East Africa, though small in number and out of direct contact with Germany, continued to fight throughout the war, and were undefeated at the end. Their commander, General Paul von Lettow Vorbeck, was probably the most effective German General of the war, and was almost unique in being seen as a hero at war's end. He carried on a guerrilla campaign against the Allies with minimal resources, his objective being to draw in the maximum number of allied troops and thus weaken the Allies on the Western Front. In this, he was remarkably successful.

### The Bristol Gunners

Britain was not at war alone. Certainly, she had the French, and Belgians, as allies, with their colonies, and Russia as a co-belligerent also attacked by Germany. Britain had the British Empire to call on, and the response was quick and generous. Troops from every Empire nation served. There were also other states that allied themselves with the Allies, sometimes for selfish reasons (Italy and Serbia), sometimes for less selfish reasons (Portugal, Brazil). Some were reluctant allies, such as Greece and the USA, who took quite some time to realise that their best interest would be served by formally joining the Allied cause.

The Germans, therefore, were fighting against a growing coalition of states and their accumulated power. The Germans relied solely on internal sources of supply and communication (with some help from neutral nations such as the Netherlands and Sweden), which gave them advantages and disadvantages. Like Britain, the Germans were not self sufficient in foodstuffs and other key materials, and this fact alone would lead to severe problems as the war progressed, whereas the Allies had exterior lines of supply, vulnerable to attack and disruption, but potentially expandable and sufficient.

The GVA at Ferfay were clearly enjoying the fact of having new, modern guns. They were benefiting from a few weeks rest out of the line, and enjoying meeting and interacting with peoples from far off places through the common currencies of beer (and wine, no doubt), song, and shared experience.

Though the mix of nationalities was unique to the times, one can imagine the same scene occurring all over the world, even in the modern day. For soldiers, and young men, share certain characteristics wherever they come from, and wherever they happen to be.

In due course the General Staff decided that it was time for the 48th Division to take their place in the line again, and in late July the trains were loaded at Lillers and rumbled their leisurely way southwards to Picardy.

The area chosen for the 48th Division was opposite the German positions at Gommecourt at the most westerly point on the Western Front. The GVA took position at the southern end of this portion of front, just

outside the village of Hebuterne. When they arrived in the summer of 1915, it was a quiet location, and it would remain relatively quiet until the following summer and the Battle of the Somme. This battle would be, for more than just the 48th Division and the GVA, their first trial by fire.

On arrival, the first task was to take over from the French, who had been in position since the autumn of 1914. The ground conditions in this region of France are very different from those found in Flanders. The underlying rock is chalk, which drains well, and is suitable for digging trenches and underground workings. The only problems are the fact that any chalk is much paler in colour than the topsoil, so that any that is dug up, if dumped locally, identifies very easily where excavations are placed and how extensive they are, and when wet, chalk mud is extremely slippery and glutinous.

The French Army had established themselves in the area and had created a comprehensive system of trenches, strongpoints, and zones of observation. They also seem to have established strong contacts with the local inhabitants, as, though the village itself was very close behind the trench line, some of the locals still lived there and farmed the fields.

Lieutenant F S (Stanley) Gedye (younger brother of Lieutenant E L Gedye) describes the first impressions of taking over from the French, and seeing their 'soixante-quinze' (75 mm gun, equivalent to the British QF 18 Pounder gun) in action:

*"The Brigade took over this area from the French, we quite definitely enjoyed it. We had little French - they no English, but our conversation made up in ingenuity what it lacked in volume. Picture the walk to the O.P. with the French Lieutenant who had provided a superb and lengthy dejeuner. Reaching the end of the village, we jumped down into Papin, a trench that is the main traffic avenue from Hebuterne along the top of the forward slope towards the German line. Following the lieutenant, we began to have misgivings as to the ordinaire quality of the vin at dejeuner as the unmistakable sound of a bicycle bell is heard. There is barely time for a glance backwards at the amazed faces of the telephonists, which is somehow reassuring, before a Poilu appears round a traverse peddling madly on a French army bicycle. Of course! How French! How delightful! And of course how very sensible of us, not to have refused the second glass. We get to the O.P. to be known only too well every single night for*

### The Bristol Gunners

*the next eleven months as 'Central' and have the leading features pointed out to us trench points such as the Hook and The Point, La Louviere Farm and behind these Puisieux, Serre and in the distance Bucquoy and on the extreme left the belt of trees that form Gommecourt Wood.*

*The S.O.S lines are pointed out to us in a Gallic effervescence of soixante-quinze - 50 or 60 rounds in almost the same number of seconds ["Gawd" we think in our frugal way a "blinking bombardment."] So the novel experience goes on until, the relief complete, we settle in for a long period of goalkeeping.*

*The Hebuterne Plain was in country not unlike Salisbury Plain, it had more villages and tree lined roads, but somewhat similar gently rolling plain open, yet not monotonously flat. The battery positions, which were moved occasionally during the year, were in a triangular piece of the plain bounded by the roads Hebuterne – Sailly - Colincamps and on the third side facing the enemy was the reserve trench Papin just over the horizon."*

The Latin motto of the Royal Artillery is 'Ubique', which means 'Everywhere.' This refers to the fact that the Royal Artillery is always present wherever the Army serves. This motto is shared with the Royal Engineers for the same reason. Another feature of life in the artillery is that while infantry and cavalry units (as well as other troops) tend to be rotated into the frontline with regular periods out of the line or at rest, or in reserve, guns are generally always available, on duty. The Royal Artillery must always be able to respond when called, and respond quickly and accurately.

The divisional system in the army at this time was based on the concept that the primary arm (in most divisions the infantry, in cavalry divisions the cavalry) was the lead arm, and all others, the Royal Artillery included, were subordinate to them. The organisation was very straightforward, each brigade of infantry (at this time four battalions of infantry) would have a brigade of guns at their immediate command. Each brigade of guns was three batteries of four field guns (QF 18 pounders). Each battery was subordinated to an infantry battalion, and essentially became part of its defensive or offensive organisation. Communication between batteries tactically was very limited.

## The Bristol Gunners

Each battery commander (BC) regarded the infantry commanding officer (CO) as his immediate commander in the field, and took his orders from that CO.

Fire control, that is, telling the guns when, where, and how to fire at the enemy, was the responsibility of the BC. In open mobile war, he would place himself in a position to see both the battle and his guns. He would pass instructions to the guns by voice (or bugle, using his trumpeter), observe the effect of the gunfire, and make corrections as necessary.

As trench warfare established itself, it became necessary for military assets to be placed out of harm's way below ground or under cover. The BC was no longer able to position himself so as to be able to 'talk' to the guns, while observing the battle. This was overcome by establishing an observation post (OP) forward so as to see the front line, sometimes actually in the front trench, and lay a telephone line back to the gun position so as to be able to speak to them. This OP was ideally close to the command post of the supported infantry where observation of the front could be combined with easy and quick communication with the CO, but this was not always possible. A choice needed to be made sometimes between effective observation, and effective communication.

This raised certain problems that had to be solved in turn. Telephone cables are easily damaged or go 'U/S' (unserviceable, i.e. not working) for example by traffic or enemy shellfire. This would break the communication and result in no gunfire when needed, therefore the cables (at this time, of course, wireless communication was not sufficiently developed to be of use in the trenches) needed to be protected by burying several feet below ground. Special arrangements were needed to cross roads and tracks with cables. Even so, it was a regular occurrence (usually at least daily) for signallers to have to move around the position and repair cables. Additionally, fixed telephone cables were not of much use when advancing 'over the hill' and out of sight.

Another problem was fatigue. The BC had many tasks to complete as well as controlling gunfire on demand. If the OP was some distance from the gun position, typically one or two miles, the BC just could not be everywhere at all times. To alleviate this each battery officer took turns to man the OP, and obviously needed to be trained how to do this. Movement between the guns and the OP could be very hazardous, as in many of the early positions there were minimal communication trenches

to provide protection. Travel between the guns and the OP had therefore to be limited to proven approach routes and sometimes only at certain times of the day to avoid the OP party becoming casualties from shellfire or sniper fire.

As the war progressed, the army and the Royal Artillery considered the problems being thrown up by the new realities of war on the Western Front and came up with solutions. These solutions were sometimes very innovative, sometimes borrowed from other armies (including the Germans) and often devised and implemented very rapidly.

For the time, though, we will hear a little of what the GVA experienced in the months spent in and around Hebuterne.

Lieutenant F S Gedye records the situation regarding 'defence stores', the material and equipment needed to create and maintain a defensive position. RE (Royal Engineers) were responsible for supply of all defence stores:

*"The routine of the brigade settled down to a steady monotony that was seldom seriously disturbed. The wagon line officers at Coigneux had the usual round of fatigues to arrange, the stables hours, watering parties, drawing of rations and occasionally, ammunition [not often as the number of rounds fired was still very strictly kept down] and the main outing of the day was the dispatch of the G.S. wagon and water cart to the position, the former carrying rations, post, any general stores required etc. In addition to these duties the wagon line officer and the B.Q.M.S. were always engaged in a ceaseless struggle to procure, by hook or by crook, R.E. material for improving the horse lines and the battery positions, and in particular corrugated iron sheeting to make a waterproof roof for our dugouts. "By hook" included a flutter of indents, appeals to their better nature and reviling of the baser character, of the O.C. R.E. Dump and was a process that in the main produced only one result in "peacetime" days - precisely nothing.*

*"By Crook" was the more effective, the more fashionable and when successful, left a warm glow around the heart. It included scouting parties, mysterious departures of carts by night for an unnamed destination, and all the various methods by which dirty work is achieved at cross roads and other places.*

### The Bristol Gunners

*A third method by master strategists was guile, and the Battery Sergeant Major of B Battery could tell a wondrous tale of how, as winter approached and R.E. material was resolutely refused, the officers' mess contributed two bottles of whisky. These were then taken many miles to the ordnance depot and bartered for an incredible number of Coats, Warm, British, Mounted Troops for the use of, then recently introduced and quite definitely the 'Mode for Men.'*

*A beneficent Higher Authority had authorized their issue to certain units, but had not in his mercy included the personnel in charge of the R.E.'s dumps. Since one bottle of whisky equalled x number of "British Warms", it needs no strong imagination to realise that 2 x British Warms were equivalent to a muttered permission "bring your wagon after dark, and for Gawd's sake be quick about it" or put baldly, sufficient timber and corrugated iron to complete perfect winter lines for a four gun battery."*

At this time, the Germans were better at counter battery (CB) fire than the British were. Counter battery fire is usually carried out by the heavier guns of artillery as they have a longer range to reach enemy guns and a heavier shell, with more explosive in the shell for destructive affect. British army doctrine was to emplace guns in heavily reinforced pits with adequate overhead cover to protect the crews from HE or shrapnel. The problem with this approach was that the structures required (as the gun barrels needed to be above ground in order to fire) were very hard to conceal because of shape, size, and shadow, very easy for enemy planes to spot and report on. In time doctrine changed to concealment as the primary aim of gun site selection, that is camouflage over protection. F S Gedye again:

*"The Hebuterne battery positions were a shock for the book-trained gunner brought up to regard concealment as one of the vital principles. As one rode up from Sailly to Hebuterne there were half a dozen blots on the fair surface of the plain. These were the battery positions, each consisting of four large emplacements with smaller excrescences beside them [the dugouts]. Some of these were 12 feet in height with straight sides to cast maximum shadow, with wide, deep, unmistakable tracks leading up to them, passing the line of pits and circling back to the road, leaving no possible shadow of a doubt to the enemy planes as to their meaning. Yet in those peaceful live and let live days, the positions were*

## The Bristol Gunners

*practically never shelled, a state of things that ended forever on July 1st 1916.*

*At the battery position, the first parade of the day was usually about 9 am, when the officer living on the position held the usual inspection of turn out, arranged the work on the position for the day and then inspected the guns, ammunition, and dugouts. Prior to this, the guns had been taken off night S.O.S. lines, and re-laid on aiming posts, pits cleaned and everything cleaned and polished.*

*The Sergeant and the three members of the guard of the previous night became orderly Sergeant and aeroplane sentries. The sentry on duty of the latter was detailed off to look out for hostile aircraft and as soon as one was identified, three blows of his whistle meant that all movement ceased on the position, until a single whistle indicated "all clear."*

*The day's work depended largely on the condition of the position. If in good order, the days were easy, but if rain caused dugouts or pits or cave in, there might be strenuous days.*

*About 6 pm, the guard was mounted and an inspection made to check the laying of all the guns on their night S.O.S. lines, which were usually about midway across No Mans Land or just in front of the enemy wire. In those days there was no electrical equipment and a lamp was put on a single post in front from which each gun had its angle to the S.O.S. lines chalked up in the pit. The last duty of the O.P. officer before dusk was to fire on the battery datum point for the night corrector and a typical message would come down as "night corrector 145; drop50" this correction being applied to the setting of the eight fuses held in readiness for an S.O.S. and to the map range to the S.O.S. line.*

*On occasion, [depending on the weather and the belligerency of the officer on duty] the guard would receive the order during the night "Test S.O.S." and each subsection timed in getting in to action.*

*On the order, one of the guard doubled out to the night aiming post with a lamp of the policeman's or bicycle type that had a tin shutter that gave out a thin beam of light for the layers to get an accurate lay. A slack wire was laid from the pit nearest the guard dugout to the post so that he could double out in the dark without losing his way.*

## The Bristol Gunners

*There were lamps for the gunpits, which always blew out immediately on the gun firing, and the No1 had an issue electric torch which usually did duty first for the layer, then for the corrector bar and fuse setter and finally for a flash round to see no one was in the line of recoil.*

*Night time was also rat time on the Hebuterne plain and owing to a ruined sucrerie and natural perfection of French battlefields as breeding grounds, they were numerous and almost man-eating.*

*The battery commanders with generally one subaltern had a billet in Hebuterne; brigade H. Q. was also in the village. The "billet" consisted of what was left of a house minus, of course, windows, some bits of wall and lots of bits of plaster, but was generally chosen for its possession of a funk hole in the shape of a cellar or dugout for the less healthy hours. Each battery had its O.P. to man, and one officer from the brigade was on duty all night at "Central.""*

The 'sucrerie' was a sugar factory, where the locally grown sugar beet was processed into sugar.

As F S Gedye states, the gun positions near Hebuterne were rarely shelled, a position that changed during and after the Battle of the Somme in 1916. The gun positions were out of sight of the Germans behind a hill and at this stage of the war, their aeroplanes were few and far between. The village of Hebuterne, close to the front trenches and in sight of the Germans, was, though, shelled from time to time.

Unlike the British, the Germans did not use a standard map grid. As a result, often, German units working together would be working with different map systems with different datum points and significant survey errors. This led to serious problems for the Germans when trying to co-ordinate actions. One beneficial result from this for the defenders of Hebuterne was that the German gunners opposite must have been using inaccurate survey for their gun positions or inaccurate maps as their shells apparently aimed at the village always dropped short, F S Gedye:

*"The village was practically undamaged and it appeared that the Hun had it placed wrongly on his maps for he used to retaliate occasionally but his shots always fell about 200 yards short of the nearest point of the village. With their usual tact, however, a battery of 9.2s came and settled*

### The Bristol Gunners

*immediately behind the village and from that time on, our life was less serene.*

*I always remember the cold-hand and icy-feet feeling that came over me on the first day that 5.9s pitched up and down the street of our lovely billet and our mess windows began to shatter."*

As the British army built its strength and came to grips with modern warfare against a continental army, pressure came on many types of resource. One of these resources was space. In order to counter battery (CB) enemy artillery we needed heavier guns (such as 9.2s), mostly howitzers, which are better at destroying hard equipment and fortifications due to having high explosive (HE) shells and a plunging trajectory. Howitzers are different from field guns in that they can, and usually do, fire at a higher angle so that the shell at the end of its journey is travelling vertically downwards (as opposed to field artillery shells that are fired at a shallow angle and strike the ground at a glancing angle). As the targets for howitzers tend to be further back from the enemy trenches the howitzers ideally should be as far forward to our trench lines as possible when they fire to make best use of their range.

The British 9.2s mentioned by F S Gedye were placed close to the village of Hebuterne, and at that point were probably closer to the enemy than the GVA field guns. The Germans, in trying to destroy the 9.2s seem to have come closer to destroying the village instead with their heavy 5.9 howitzers. This increased danger also brought about some lighter moments, though for those involved at the time it probably did not seem very amusing. Captain Boyce records:

*"It was while we were at Hebuterne that the C.O. celebrated his birthday.*

*So, after breakfast, it was decided that he and the Adjutant should visit the wagon lines at Coigneux. This was done and they returned via Sailly where a purchase of "Boy" was made and carried home in a nosebag that "happened" to be available and otherwise empty. The bottles [Plural please, Mr. Editor] were placed on the only shelf in the building above the office chair. About 6pm, just as the Adjutant was busy making out his "Daily Lie" the Bosche elected to put a salvo into the village, one round of which fell on the pavé outside. The Adjutant ducked quickly - quickly enough to dodge the splinters, which came in through the place where the*

### The Bristol Gunners

*window had been, but not quickly enough to escape a shower of broken glass down his neck - that didn't matter, but what did was the precious liquid went there too.*

*Each bottle pierced about 1inch from the bottom and not one drop did we ever taste. Quelle misericorde! Quel dommage!!* (What mercy! What a pity!)

*Life there was generally very peaceful. Many an evening after mess a gramophone was turned on near the signaller's phone and plugged through to D.A. H.Q. behind, to battalion H.Q. up in the line and even on to Company H.Q., it was said. The batteries too, listened to the concert, which, it must be added, was "strictly forbidden.""*

The 'daily lie' which Boyce refers to was the daily ammunition return. In the military each unit has to record and report to the next senior headquarters a whole range of statistics and returns on a fixed schedule. One of these was the daily ammunition return, which stated how much ammunition had been fired, how much replenished, and stocks remaining. In the autumn of 1915 and spring of 1916, this return seems to have caused many problems in balancing the books. Captain Boyce again:

*"The only source of worry was the daily ammunition returns especially that due on Sunday, which was the end of the official week. At that time each battery was allowed 55 rounds per week, and Oh! the difficulties to account for them. Whether subalterns were keeping a few spare rounds for their next tour at the O.P. or not was never satisfactorily settled, but rumour was very strong on that point.*

*Certainly battery commanders were not strictly accurate and the Adjutant was always credited with a few rounds up his sleeve each week in case the B.C.s figures got out of hand and showed an over expenditure."*

It seems that 'creative accounting' may well have its origins in the Royal Artillery.

Soldiers have always needed a good sense of humour. One young officer, Second Lieutenant Ridler, was a cousin to Major C W Todd, the Battery Commander of 1st Battery. It seems that he was prone to 'tall stories', so one night, while he was fast asleep, some brother officers introduced a

## The Bristol Gunners

dud German shell to his bed. In the morning he woke to find the shell and told a fantastic story of how the shell had come through the roof of the house and how lucky he was. A 'Little Willie' was a shell from a German 77mm field gun, named after Kaiser Wilhelm II's son, Crown Prince Wilhelm. Lieutenant F S Gedye tells the story:

*"It was in the early days of February that Ridler's famous romantic episode with the Little Willie dud occurred.*

*He was at liaison with the 6th Gloucester's in Hebuterne village, as he swears, awoke to find his arms enfolding a dud Little Willie which had apparently entered his chamber with out any invitation from him.*

*The Infantry however, had a very different story to tell of it but, needless to say, they in their thousands would have been powerless to shake the smallest detail from Ridler's triumph."*

Though much of the time at Hebuterne was routine, some events stood out as being of note. The Battle of Loos occurred in September 1915. Though the actual attack area was a long way north of Hebuterne, the GVA were tasked with deploying two guns forward of their OP on the edge of the battle in order to carry out some form of deception firing to interfere with the Germans while the battle was in progress. The general opinion of the time was that putting guns that far forward was an insane thing to do as they would be in full view of the Germans and would come under immediate fire and would probably last a matter of minutes only. Fortunately, the order for this action was cancelled before the battle. F S Gedye:

*"Just in front of the O.P. a position for two guns had been dug the previous autumn and the guns were put in, not merely in the open, but clearly in view on the top of the ridge that dominated the Bosche lines. The idea was to cut wire and assist in making a display during the Loos show.*

*All was ready and the ranging of the guns was timed to take place at 2.30 on a certain afternoon. The position was so obviously suicidal that the battery had had several heavy bets that no shots would ever be fired from the position.*

*It must be pointed out in extenuation that the unit was still comparatively new to active service and still had the absurd ideal that orders were issued with some sound underlying motive: later in its career, few, if any, of its members would have been guilty of so a theory.*

*However, for once, innocence triumphed, and at 2.25, an urgent telephone message stopped the shoot. Had the guns been fired, there seems little doubt that the battery would not have waited until June 24th 1916 to enrol its first name on the Roll of Honour - that of Gunner Jenkins, a recent recruit from the 3rd line."*

We will return to the fate of Gunner Jenkins a little later. He was not, in fact, the first GVA man to die on active service in France. That unfortunate honour goes to Bombardier Phillips, as recorded in the 240 Brigade War History:

*"It was in the autumn of 1915 that Bombardier Phillips was the first man of the Brigade to make the supreme sacrifice. He was hit by shrapnel while working in a chalk pit just in front of Hebuterne, and died of wounds."*

Gunner Jenkins was the third man to be killed, on 26th June 1916. The second was Shoeing Smith G Milton who died in December 1915 and whose cause of death is not mentioned in GVA records. He appears to have died at base hospital in Rouen, whether from injury or disease is not clear. In his role as a shoeing smith it is most likely that he spent his time in the wagon lines attending to the horses. It is most likely, therefore, that he was injured in an accident, or stricken by disease, and died while being treated at the hospital.

Gunner Jenkins had been in the 'third line' that is, he was recruited in Bristol after the GVA was mobilised and trained with what became 305th Brigade RFA and which served with 61st Division. The War Office had determined that to expand the army quickly it would task TF organizations to form firstly a second identical unit once the peacetime unit had been mobilised, and this occurred in the autumn of 1915. Once this second line unit had marched out to serve, the TF were required to form a third identical unit. This third brigade was formed in early 1915, and Gunner Jenkins was recruited to this. It seems that he had arrived at Hebuterne to join the GVA only a very short time before his death. The Brigade War History:

*"In May, 1916, a brigade formed from the third line of the 1st South Midland was sent out to the Division.*

*In the winter of 1914-15 a second line which became a duplicate of the*

## The Bristol Gunners

*1st South Midland Brigade had been recruited. This latter formed a unit of the 61st Division and proceeded overseas in 1916.*

*In April, 1915, Major Walter Swayne, a former battery commander, was given the task of forming a third brigade at the headquarters in Bristol. This acted as a draft-supplying unit to the 1/1st and 2nd /1st SM. Brigades for some time, and then was sent out to the 8th Division in May, 1916.*

*The arrival of this brigade heralded the reshuffling on a big scale of the units.*

*Originally the artillery units of the Division had been;*
*1st (Gloucestershire) Brigade of three field batteries and a brigade ammunition column.*
*2nd (Worcestershire) Brigade of three field batteries and a brigade ammunition column.*
*3rd (Warwickshire) Brigade of three field batteries and a brigade ammunition column.*
*And a howitzer brigade of three batteries of 4.5 howitzers.*

*In the reshuffling, the 3rd (Warwicks) Brigade became an army brigade and left the division. The brigades, to their sorrow, lost their Territorial description - South Midland and were given numbers, becoming 240 Brigade (Glos.), 241 and 242, and a new brigade was formed - 243.*

*The howitzer brigade was split up, one battery coming to each of the other brigades on May 17, 1916, and the brigade ammunition column was abolished and divided between the batteries and the division ammunition column. The new brigade was formed on arrival of the third line, and each 240th battery gave up a complete sub-section to form A/243, the personnel of the third line filling up the gaps in 240 batteries."*

Individual and groups of soldiers from the second line and third line units were often posted to the 1st South Midland (now 240) Brigade to maintain numbers when necessary. Gunner Jenkins seems to have been very unlucky, as he was killed in circumstances experienced by just about every other member of the GVA from time to time. Lieutenant E L Gedye wrote in a letter to his parents:

### The Bristol Gunners

*"I had rather a disturbed night chiefly owing to the guns just behind us that loosed off on an average every half hour. About midnight Stanley rang up to say that they had had two casualties - one killed and one wounded, I was, of course, very sorry to hear this but at the moment my chief feeling was one of annoyance at having been disturbed just as I had got to sleep.*

*I am not due at the O.P. until noon, the Bosche is much quieter today, and one can walk over the plain without much fear from that side. The chief danger from walking above ground is from prematures from our own guns, every road and track being enfiladed by at least one battery. It appears that the two men knocked out in the 1st battery [I can't bring myself to say A battery - it sounds too much like the New Army] were victims of the Fresh Air Habit. I count myself a fairly strong devotee of the F.A.H. but I'm hanged if I would sleep in a bivouac on the outskirts of Hebuterne especially at a time like this. I am awfully sorry for the two poor fellows but really they ought not to have expected much else."*

A premature is a shell that has a faulty fuse which causes it to explode too soon, in this case while still travelling above our own troops, who it seems were sleeping out in the open, possibly for comfort (this was on June 24th so the weather may have been warm) rather than in a bunker or cellar.

The Brigade War History also notes the dangers:

*"Although the Brigade casualties were amazingly small prior to the battle of the Somme, the general atmosphere was not always as healthy as this would suggest. There was always a good deal of machine-gunning of the cross-roads in Hebuterne, and "Stuttering Sam," the machine-gun which operated in enfilade from the Gommecourt salient, used to throw many a tired bullet during the hours of darkness and maintain a healthy spirit of haste in those whose duty took them along the road.*

*Somewhat ominously, it led to the cemetery as well as to the trenches.*

*And on the warmest of spring days a sudden salvo of "Little Willies" falling unreasonably near you would remind you that, despite the spring*

### The Bristol Gunners

*feeling you had imagined a moment earlier, the ground was still very cold to the feet."*

Lieutenant E L Gedye refers in the extract above to 'First Battery' and 'A Battery.' These in fact were the same unit, but in June 1916 a comprehensive reorganization in the RFA had taken place, with new names, numbers, and organizational structures, as detailed in the previous extract from the Brigade War History.

The whole of the Royal Artillery was re-organised at this time to reflect its growing size, and to reflect the hard won experience from previous battles.

Prior to this reorganisation an infantry division had three brigades of field guns (18 Pounders) and one brigade of howitzers (4.5 Inch Howitzers), equivalent to one artillery field brigade and one howitzer battery for each brigade of infantry, with some (mostly Regular Army) divisions also having a battery of heavy guns (60 Pounders) manned by the Royal Garrison Artillery. In the reorganization the divisional howitzer brigade was split up, each of its batteries was then grouped (brigaded) with each of the field brigades, so that a field brigade then comprised four batteries, three of 18 pounders and one of 4.5 inch howitzers.

The 48th Division, being a TF division, started out in 1914 with three brigades of field guns, each brigade of three batteries, each with 4 guns (total twelve guns, 15 pounder BLC) and a howitzer brigade of 4.5 inch howitzers, but no heavy battery. In July 1915, the field batteries were re-equipped with 18 pounder QF guns. In the May 1916 reorganisation, each field brigade received a howitzer battery to form a four battery brigade, but still with only four guns per battery. This would rise to six guns per battery early in 1917 with a consequent rise in manpower.

The other part of the reorganisation related to the ammunition columns. In 1914 each artillery brigade had its own ammunition column. This comprised the wagons, horses, and men needed to carry and resupply ammunition to the gun batteries. In May 1916 all the ammunition columns from all artillery brigades in the division were formed into the Divisional Ammunition Column (DAC), primarily for efficiency and economy of effort. Later, the DAC was divided into two echelons, A & B, A being the wagons and men who moved forward on a daily basis to

resupply the guns positions, while B echelon was those men and equipments that largely stayed to the rear and were involved in collecting ammunition from central stocks, maintenance and storage.

As a result of this reorganisation, some old unit titles disappeared and were replaced with a more unified numbering system and titling. The old title, 1st (South Midlands) Brigade RFA (TF) became 240th Brigade RFA (the other artillery brigades in the 48th Division becoming 241st, 242nd and 243rd brigades). Batteries changed from 1st, 2nd and so on, to letters, so A Battery, B Battery and so on. Thus A Battery of 240th Brigade would be referred to as A/240.

The Brigade in which the GVA found itself, now titled 240th Brigade, gained a new commander, Colonel Lord Wynford. The previous commander, Colonel Balfour, had been in command since mobilisation in 1914, and is credited with turning the GVA from gifted amateur gunners into an effective and efficient brigade. The Brigade War History:

*"Shortly after settling in at Colincamps, we lost the CO., Colonel A. M. Balfour, D.S.O., who, left us on appointment to a Home Command. He was succeeded by Colonel Lord Wynford, D.S.0.*

*To Colonel Balfour lies the credit for taking, in August, 1914, a civilian brigade, and duly delivering on the quay at Havre on March 29, 1915, an efficient and soldierly unit.*

*In this work he has always paid full tribute to the splendid work of his adjutant, then Captain E. Boyce, but as C.O. his was the guiding hand at the helm, and very thoroughly his work was done.*

*Having with the maximum of success put the fear of God and the C.O. into every man at home, when the address became B.E.F. he allowed the other side of him, that was the secret of his popularity, to appear more freely, and it was to the deep regret of all ranks that he left the Brigade.*

*Lord Wynford remained with the Brigade until the middle of 1917."*

Each infantry division had a staff officer known as Commander Royal Artillery (CRA) in the rank of brigadier. His role was not to command the field and howitzer brigades, but to advise the divisional commander

on artillery matters. The field batteries were commanded by their commanding officers, and were in direct support of their infantry units.

Where a heavy battery existed in the division, it was tasked with Counter Battery (CB) fire and came under the direction of the CRA as it was seen as a divisional resource rather than a brigade resource. As the war progressed, and new weapons were developed and deployed, such as trench mortars these came under command of the CRA.

At the next level of command, the Corps, there were also two artillery Brigadiers titled Brigadier General Royal Artillery (BGRA) and Commander Heavy Artillery (CHA). The BGRA's role was to co-ordinate divisional and corps artillery plans to fit with the corps commander's overall plan. The CHA's role was to command the heavy artillery (generally guns of larger shell size, weight, and range) in its role of CB and other more strategic bombardment tasks.

Munitions and equipment were arriving in increasing quantity and variety. The weight of artillery available to Army and Corps commanders provided new opportunities. Heavier guns of up to 12 inch bore were used to reach behind the German front and destroy or disrupt important locations.

A range of trench mortars had been developed, which could supplement conventional artillery. Trench mortars are as their name suggests, deployed and fired from the front line trenches, and have a shorter range than an artillery gun. A mortar is different from a gun in that the barrel is smooth (not rifled with grooves) and has a closed end, that is, has no breech for loading the projectile. In some ways they are like cannons, in that the projectile and propellants are loaded into the muzzle of the mortar. In another way they are like howitzers, as they are fired at high angles, which means that their projectiles impact the ground at a steep angle, useful for reaching behind obstacles. A mortar is much smaller and lighter than an artillery gun, and therefore can be used in places inaccessible to larger and more weighty weapons. Mortars could also be used for specific tasks such as destroying individual strongpoints, or to discharge gas and smoke. Smoke was of use in 'blinding', that is obscuring either your own troops so that it was harder for the enemy to aim accurately at them, or to deal with enemy strong points by making it hard for them to see what was happening. Trench mortar batteries were

operated by RFA gunners, that is, they were organisationally part of the artillery, though they necessarily spent much of their time in close contact with the infantry.

The Germans also had trench mortars, and the mortar bombs were very much feared by all soldiers in the front trenches. They had a high ratio of explosive to total weight, making them very destructive. Their slow speed also made their approach visible to the intended recipients. Seeing a large lump of high explosive and steel fly up from the trench opposite and apparently intent on coming to join you in your trench must have been a very distressing experience. Both sides would retaliate vigorously when they identified an enemy trench mortar position, and casualties in trench mortar batteries were higher than in gun batteries in consequence.

Trench mortar troops were unpopular with their own side as well. Having a trench mortar detachment turn up to share your trench could mean only one thing, that the enemy would retaliate and blow the mortar and you to kingdom come in a very short time. This was not a welcome prospect.

There was also artillery co-ordination at Army level. All this was in contrast with the arrangements existing at the outset of war, where batteries were in effect subordinated to their infantry battalions and essentially independently commanded by their battery commanders. It was now understood that artillery needed to be effectively planned and co-ordinated to achieve specific tasks before the infantry could be free to carry out their mission. In addition, ammunition supply was calculated and pre-dumped, rather than being replenished on a daily basis.

The effects of this on the GVA, as in most other batteries and brigades of the Royal artillery was for more manpower to be brought over from second and third line units that had formed in UK, and for some individuals to be posted between batteries and the DAC, thus diluting the pre-war TF element. Most of those posted out from UK were men who had joined the army as volunteers after August 1914 and largely did not have length of service, but made up for this with enthusiasm.

As the war progressed, the army grew dramatically in numbers. The original regulars and TF soldiers became a small minority in the ranks. New Army volunteers initially were organised into new units, but some were posted to regular and TF units as reinforcements (a military

euphemism for replacements – that is, generally to replace casualties). Up to 1916 injured soldiers were usually returned to their own unit after recovery. From late 1916 onwards this system started to change and recovered casualties would be 'pooled' and posted back to the front in any unit of their arm (infantry, artillery, cavalry) which needed them. Thus, over time, the GVA had fewer and fewer Bristol volunteers with them. Ultimately, with conscripted men arriving at the front from late 1916 onwards, some unusual postings occurred, with Scottish regiments receiving many Englishmen, and vice versa, for example.

The artillery also grew not only in size, but also in its proportions relative to the total army. Gunfire, and lots of it, was increasingly seen to be the key to unlocking the trench warfare of the Western Front, and the proportion of men engaged on serving the guns grew as time went by.

Another event of note at Hebuterne occurred soon after the 48th Division had arrived in the summer of 1915. Summer rains turned the whole position into a quagmire resulting in many problems for the British and German occupiers. The Brigade War History tells the story:

*"The great floods arrived while the 1915 summer was still in evidence to lessen the misery of them. The trenches were so deep in water that infantry discarded boots and socks, and even trousers were omitted from the toilet of those who moved in the mode of the moment.*

*Bombardier Grant, of the 1st Battery, probably held the fancy dress record for appearing, amid delighted applause, garbed only in a cap, round which was draped a handkerchief for sun-protection, a shirt, and as a delicate tribute to the proprieties - an all-important safety-pin."*

Rain would cause problems again the following year, when the British attacked, in their first major campaign, the Battle of the Somme.

The Bristol Gunners

## Chapter 4  The Battle of the Somme.

Before the arrival of the British Army on the Somme it had been a quiet sector of the front, with both the French and the Germans happy to live and let live. The British, however, were determined to change all that.

The reasons for this change were several. Firstly it is an important part of British military doctrine to dominate the battlefield, which basically means making such a nuisance with the enemy as to make him respond to us, to take the initiative. Secondly, so far most of the fighting by the Allies had been carried out by the French and Belgians; the British had only taken a minor part, and now wished to demonstrate that they had the wherewithal to play a full part. Thirdly, the British needed to find out who they were facing, and how good they were. So, capturing prisoners, provoking responses from the Germans, examining how they respond, is good military practice. The final reason, though, was more important. In February 1916 the Germans had launched a major attack at Verdun, a strategic fortified city on the Meuse in Lorraine, north eastern France, close to the German border. It sat astride the route to Paris taken by previous Prussian invaders. For logical reasons, the Germans predicted that the French would defend the city at all costs. It is generally accepted that the German commander, Erich von Falkenhayn, proposed a massive attack with the intention not necessarily of capturing the city, but of forcing the French to pour in massive numbers of troops that his army would destroy. He would 'bleed the French Army white.' The Battle of Verdun was the first deliberately attritional battle of the war.

The battle raged on through the spring and into the summer, with no clear result except the slaughter of hundreds of thousands of French and German soldiers.

In order to take the initiative and relieve pressure on the French at Verdun it was decided for the Allies to attack further north. If done on a large enough scale this would force the Germans to move reserves to meet this new attack and to halt their attack at Verdun and this would relieve the pressure on the French Army.

The original plan was for the attack to occur at the junction of the French and the British astride the River Somme with broadly equal numbers of

## The Bristol Gunners

troops from each army. In due course the plan was altered so that the British took on the larger role, though it remained a joint attack.

It was also an opportunity for General Haig to use the greater number of troops that were now joining the BEF from the New Armies. As ever, he was looking for the decisive blow that would break the stalemate of trench warfare.

Thus, from March to June 1916 the British front from just north of Hebuterne (the Gommecourt salient, known as 'the Nose') south to the junction with the French near Maricourt intense preparations began in order to be ready for the attack at the end of June. Everyone was determined to show just what the British Army could do.

The 48th Division occupied the area around Gommecourt, from Fonquevillers down to south of Hebuterne, a front of about three miles. As new divisions were fed in to the area ahead of the attack the 48th divisional area was reduced to about one third of this distance, on the right of their former line. Their left was now Hebuterne, and it extended to their right limit a kilometer south stopping just short of the position opposite another village, Serre.

For the GVA, this did not require them to move, and they continued in the same areas as before, except that they were joined by progressively more and more troops and guns until the whole area swarmed with activity.

The German and the British lines in this sector were about five hundred meters apart. The Germans, had built massive bunkers and strongpoints, especially in 'the Nose' as from this position they could fire down No Man's Land in both a southerly and northerly direction. They had built three wide bands of barbed wire in front of their trenches, making the whole position one of the most well defended locations on the Western Front.

The British were to attack Gommecourt with two reinforced divisions. The 46th (North Midland) Division north of Gommecourt, and the 56th (1st London) Division to the south. Both of these were Territorial divisions. The role of the 48th Division was to support the 56th Division, but not attack directly. The Gommecourt attack was subsidiary to the main attack,

designed both to take out a vital German position, and to confuse the Germans as to where the main thrust of our attack was to be.

The role of the field batteries of the artillery was wire cutting. Though ammunition quantity started to improve in the spring of 1916, the quality was still poor (many duds) and they were still overwhelmingly shrapnel shells. The job of the OPs was to control the fire of the shrapnel shells such that they burst above the belts of barbed wire and the hope was that the shrapnel balls would cut the wire to permit the infantry to pass through unhindered. Results in this were mixed.

The role of the howitzer batteries and the heavy batteries was to fire on known strong points, bunkers, and trenches in order to destroy them, and to fire into the rear of the enemy positions in order to disrupt activity and destroy as much as possible.

As part of the early preparations for the battle, the infantry were tasked with carrying out night raids on the German trenches, to probe for information, and if possible, to capture prisoners. Prisoners were a potentially valuable source of information, both by identifying their units from the badges they wore, and by interrogation.

The Brigade War History describes one of these raids:

*"The most thrilling event of the 1915/1916 winters was the successful raid by the 6th Gloucester's on Gommecourt, which seemed to fix at last in the minds of the multitude in the home county that the local Territorials were actually in action.*

*As they were only about eight months behind the times in their discovery, this was considered a most praise worthy effort on the part of the Bristolians."*

Trench raids worked in both directions, of course. The following description is by F S Gedye. The role of the field artillery, when they are not firing is to have their guns loaded and laid on a designated 'SOS' target. An SOS target is decided between the infantry commander and the battery commander as being the area where the infantry would be most at risk if the enemy attacked unexpectedly. This can be very close to friendly troops, and rounds can be fired very quickly in order to disrupt any sudden attack.

### The Bristol Gunners

"*The next really notable evening that comes to memory is March 19th, when the front woke up suddenly to a very noisy raid by the Bosche on the 6th Gloucesters. A very heavy bombardment for those days opened the show with our first unpleasing ration of gas shell. Our S.O.S. barrage came down within a minute of the start of the show & the C.O. [Col Nicklem] was very complimentary, saying it was a most excellent and accurate barrage, shutting the first wave in our lines, and preventing the 2nd wave from crossing No Man's Land, among whom it caused very heavy casualties.*

*The raid was "Successfully repulsed with only light casualties to our troops" as Comic Cuts invariably lied."*

In addition, another in May:

"*The Bosche made one big raid on the 4th Berks, then Commanded by Col Clarke, in May after which the Brigade was again thanked for an excellent barrage.*"

For artillery to receive complimentary remarks from their infantry colleagues is praise indeed.

Throughout the spring preparations for the big attack progressed. More troops and supplies arrived in the sector. New equipment was issued, including the new 'shrapnel helmet.' F S Gedye:

"*The first issue of tin hats was made to the battery, seven of these attractive pieces of the milliner's art being sent in just before the Somme show began.*

*We had first seen them worn by the infantry in April or May, but this was the first time we had a chance to "try on." We were, long afterwards, told a scurrilous yarn by a vet [so that no reliance should be placed on its authenticity, Vets and Padres were the natural Os/S of the Ananias* (thought to refer to a biblical character) *department of the rumour factories throughout the entire war] of how the tin hat contract was made. The contractor, having submitted his tin [or hat], was commanded to appear at the War House.*

*He went, intending to state that his price was 15/- [£0.75p] per hat [or tin]. However, after being kept waiting a long time, a small and thoroughly inefficient young captain, gorgeous to behold with scarlet and*

### The Bristol Gunners

*gold covering all possible positions of his attire, arrived and, silencing the manufacturer with a wave of his hand, told him that it was useless for him to mention or discuss his idea of price, the government would pay £1-1-0 per hat and that if he objected, his factory would be taken over by the government.*

*This story is worth setting down because even if untrue in this instance, it was surely applicable to many Government contracts during the war."*

Ammunition was plentiful, and being delivered in previously unimaginable quantities. F S Gedye:

*"....for the first time in our lives ammunition came up in hundreds instead of tens and we realised when we heard that each gun was to have 1,000 rounds on the position, that the day had passed when, to balance the weekly ammunition return, one fired 2 rounds of "Ac" [Shrapnel] and then entered them as "4 Ax" [H.E. or High Explosive]."*

Lloyd George, as the Minister of Munitions has taken the credit for the improvement to the quantity of ammunition and guns that were now flowing onto the Western Front. However, it is likely that this is more than generous as the credit should surely go to all those industrialists and workers who actually made things happen. The politicians, Lloyd George included, had starved the army of money and modern technology for many years, and it is not right that they then gained the credit for making the funds flow when there was a crisis.

In the spring of 1916 several events occurred that were significant for the battles that the GVA and the British Army were about to enter.

Food was becoming scarce in Germany, both as a result of the Royal Navy's blockade and due to poor weather the previous summer. There were food riots in Berlin – cities suffered more from food shortages than the countryside.

On May 31st the Royal Navy's Grand Fleet and the German Imperial Navy's High Seas Fleet met at the battle of Jutland. The outcome was a tactical defeat for the British – they lost more ships and men, but a strategic defeat for the Germans – they never again felt able to emerge to challenge the world's most powerful navy.

## The Bristol Gunners

Field Marshall Kitchener, Secretary of State for War, originator of the New Armies, and possibly the most prescient of soldiers and politicians, died by drowning while en route to Russia in the Royal Navy Cruiser Hampshire. This was a great shock for the country, but his legacy survived him. The new Armies, fully manned, growing, and well equipped were his bequest. He was not to see the full flowering of their abilities as they changed the face of warfare over the coming months.

It is arguably the fact that the New Armies were a true volunteer citizen army, full of men from all works of life, with all the skills of a functioning modern democracy. They had a vigour and determination that overcame many of the shortcomings of being recent recruits. Many of the techniques and improvements to tactics that the British Army would develop and hone over the coming months derived from the infusion of civilian pragmatism and innovation.

The Battle of the Somme is sometimes used by those with a bare knowledge of the First World War as a demonstration of the horrible conditions of war and its futility. The truth is somewhat different.

There were parts of the battlefield that became a morass of 'mud and blood.' Both sides suffered greatly, there were many men killed and injured. The results of British attacks were poor, initially. However, the main objectives of the battle were achieved, attack methods improved very rapidly, innovative tactics, equipment and weapons were introduced, and the Germans became aware that they could not win the war.

The objectives achieved were that the German attack at Verdun was halted; the British Army had demonstrated that it could hold its own as a Continental army.

The first attacks on July 1st 1916, the first day of the Battle of the Somme, resulted in a casualty rate that made this the worst day in the history of the British Army. The tactics used were inadequate to the task, the results were disastrous particularly on the northern sector – the southern sector was much more successful and achieved most of its immediate objectives. Within a month, new methods had been introduced and, as we shall hear from the GVA, attacks became more and more successful as the autumn came along. New equipment was used, most notably the first use of tanks in September. By the end of the battle the British knew how to plan and execute a successful attack in the conditions then prevailing.

### The Bristol Gunners

The most important outcome of the battle was, though, the realisation by the Germans that they were not going to win the war. The Germans called modern industrial warfare the 'Materialschlacht', or Material War, and it was clear that they were losing it. As the war was progressing the Allies were getting stronger, better equipped, better fed, the Germans were getting weaker, more poorly equipped, and food was getting short. Though the debate within the German Army would go on (there was no superior functioning civilian government in Germany) as to whether they could and would win, the Somme marks the point of inflection where optimism turned into increasing pessimism about the war's outcome for the Germans.

Though 1st July 1916 is taken as the first day of the Battle of the Somme, in reality it started many weeks before that date. The flow of materials increased to fill the dumps of ammunition, food, and all other supplies. The planning effort by the Staff, the movement and training of hundreds of thousands of men. All this took time.

Many of the troops who were to 'go over the top' at the battle were newly recruited. They had received a good basic training, but did not have the accumulated knowhow of the experienced soldier.

In previous, smaller scale, attacks, the army had identified barbed wire obstacles as a major impediment to successful attack, and therefore they had to be removed before the attack could begin. The field batteries of artillery, such as the GVA, were tasked with degrading these wire obstacles. The weapon they had at their disposal was the 18 Pounder gun with its mostly shrapnel shells. The technique used was to fire at the belts of wire, exploding the shells above the wire and hoping to cut it with the hundreds of lead balls that were projected. This proved not to be an exact science, especially in view of the factors of dud fuses that did not explode, inaccurate fuses that exploded too soon or too late thereby missing the wire, more wire than could be destroyed, wire that was not visible, so that results could not be observed. In addition, of course, the Germans would try whenever possible to repair or strengthen their wire defences when artillery was not firing.

Then there were strong points, not all of them visible from our lines, and not all of them identified. Heavy artillery could destroy them if their shells could land close enough, but there was no confidence that they could all be eliminated. Tunnels had been dug over many months beneath

### The Bristol Gunners

some strong points where we knew of them, and distance and soil conditions were suitable. Explosives had been placed under these strong points to be exploded at the start of the attack.

Many more methods, both conventional and innovative were to be used. Gas, smoke (for blinding or obscuration), trench mortars, long range machine gun fire, aeroplanes for observation. Communications were seen as a problem to be solved. The commanders needed to know where our troops were during the attack and what was happening so that supporting fire or more troops could be effectively deployed.

June was when preparations for the battle came to full voice, and the GVA were in the thick of it. E L Gedye wrote to his parents in an optimistic but realistic tone:

"Sat. 24/6/16.
My darling Mother,

*I told you this morning that I would put down the happenings of each day and send them on to you when I had accumulated enough matter to make a respectable letter. As a matter of fact, I shall not be able to send this off until events have moved so far; that the information I give will no longer be of use to the enemy.*

*Well, the day for which we have waited and, incidentally worked is almost at hand. Today is the first day of bombardment and within a week I hope we shall have pushed the German line back considerably. I am not such a blind optimist as to think that we are going "right through" and finish the war, but I do think that we ought to make a big dent in the Bosche line and possibly even break it temporarily.*

*Certainly a great deal hangs on the success or otherwise of this push of ours. If we can make a real good thing of it, it ought, in conjunction with the Russian successes and the un-comfortableness of life in Germany, to go a long way towards making the civilian Bosche think that the sooner he gets out of the war the better.*

*The Colonel brought home a cheering piece of news last night. It is estimated that we are putting into the fight on this Army front alone about 10 men to every single Bosche at present against us. And that at the outside, the enemy can only bring up sufficient troops to make the*

difference just over 2 to 1 so that, if we do get beyond their trenches we ought to go some way before we have to stop.

After dinner yesterday, I went up to the O.P. to superintend the final preparations, chairs, tables, petrol cans with fresh water, numerous anti-gas appliances, lights, provisions, primus stove oil, and a hundred other things necessary to the proper conductance of war. We loaded the Doctor's cart with all the items and started out, 5 beside myself. It began to rain just after we left Sailly and I don't think it stopped for the rest of the night, except for a few hours while we were in the O.P.

The Observation Post

The O.P. is in a very shallow trench on the forward slope of our crest. It is really a portion of the trench covered with iron pails, corrugated iron and dead grass and floored with concrete. In the centre is a horizontal slit divided by window frames into three. Each frame consists of four outsize pieces of wood with wire netting nailed across; the netting is threaded with grass both real and imitation.

The whole thing can be raised or lowered at will by means of a thick piece of wire fixed to the centre of the frame and bent at the other end to fix in a notched piece of wood, so that the height can be regulated. As a matter of fact the window is never raised more then three or four inches, as with that one can get a beautiful view of the German lines. At one end of the O.P. is a perpendicular shaft 25 feet deep; leading to the signaller's dugout, which also is our funk hole in case of necessity. A ladder is nailed on one side of the shaft, but the journey up and down is a very unpleasant one as there are only the rungs to hold on to and they are usually thick with mud.

When we got up there, the Sappers had not quite finished and after carting our stores as far as the O.P. we had to wait for their party to get out before we could start to pack our things away, the corporal in charge assured me he would only keep me 10 minutes. At the end of half an hour he thought it wouldn't be much more than 10 minutes longer, but at 1am - 2 hours after we had got there he got a little less optimistic and thought that it might take the best part of a quarter of an hour.

## The Bristol Gunners

*However he got clear eventually and we woke up and got on with our job. I don't like to think of the walk back - it rained the whole time and for about 10 minutes a good deal harder then that. None of us had coats and I fell down 3 times - once in a full shell hole and twice in the mud! By 3 o'clock I was in bed asleep.*

Start the War well

*I started the war well this morning - breakfast at 11.30a.m. The bombardment of course had already started, but it was not very strenuous.*

*At 3 o'clock I started off to relieve Benson at the O.P., the Bosche were dropping a number of 150mm Hows. just in front of a French 75mm battery that has come down - so they say to fire a new shell, full of gas more poisonous than any even the Bosche has yet invented, as the shells were falling uncomfortably close to our track we slid over into a communication trench and ploughed our way up through that.*

*Soon after we reached the O.P. the Bosche started shelling a quarry beside of us, which, he appears convinced, is used as an O.P., it used to be.*

*The bursting shells were quite close enough to us and made a terrific din and showered pieces of metal over our little shanty. After half an hour's gazing, I discovered, in front of Puisieux, rings of smoke rising from behind a crest. And every time a ring was blown up, a 6-inch shell started on its journey towards us. Reported accordingly by wire - "smoke rings from 150mm battery shelling quarries visible at Gr------." Of course they may be fakes, but I don't think so, as a battery has been discovered in action there before.*

*Nothing else of interest to see to day except two ammunition wagons or a gun and wagon that I spotted on a road 8 to 10 miles away. Owing to this confounded Day-light Saving scheme, observation is possible up to 9.39 pm and I have to stay here until then, before I can start on my homeward journey.*

*Sunday 25/6/16*

## The Bristol Gunners

*....While at the O.P., I was delighted to see one of our heavy batteries tackle the battery I had spotted the night before. For twenty minutes the place was completely obscured by smoke and dust, and I doubt if we shall hear from the same guns again, certainly not from the same position.*

*I had had a very good view of the 1st Battery cutting wire during the afternoon. It was in front of the German Third line and no one could have wished to see better shooting. Hardly a round was wasted, at the end of the shoot, a complete gap some 20 or 25 yards wide had been cut through the wire and a loophole or machine gun emplacement behind had been smashed up.*

*Monday 26/6/16.*

*Sausages, Airplanes and Smoke*

*More good news to-day, shortly after I had left the O.P. yesterday afternoon, our airplanes attacked the three enemy observation balloons opposite us with incendiary bombs and succeeded in destroying all three. They were seen to descend in flames, that means a lot to us gunners, as the sausages have been locating our battery positions very accurately lately. It must have been a pretty difficult task for our machines, as the sausage is usually hedged round with Archie's; also he lives some way behind the lines. In spite of Mr. P. B. I don't think we need worry about air supremacy just yet.*

*Our balloons have moved up much closer to-day and I should say they must be within gun-range. Probably as a result of having no balloons to help them, the German Hows. were making very poor practise against the 3rd Battery this morning. As I went past about half past seven, they were sending over a large number of 150mm shells, all two or three hundred yards plus.*

*Quite an interesting morning at the O.P. At ten minutes past ten after a heavy bombardment of the Bosche trenches we discharged a cloud of smoke followed five minutes later by another and larger cloud of gas. I don't quite know what the object was probably to put the wind up the Bosches and find out how many guns he has got. It was rather a horrible sight. From 20 or 30 different points in our trenches a thick white cloud oozed out, changing to brown when the gas was turned on; well, the*

### The Bristol Gunners

devils over the way started it, but I think they will wish they hadn't before we finish with them. It is the first time I have seen gas being discharged, although at Plugstreet we saw the first cloud as it drifted down from poor old Wipers.

We have shifted all our Soda water [and other] bottles into the new dugout to day. I expect poor Sailly will get it in the neck when we start on their billets.

The civilians were moved out on Friday and were very sad to see them go, our landlord a great sportsman with the single defect of getting drunk once a week; he was so sad at having to go that he overstayed the time and did not leave until Saturday morning. He bade me a fervent "au revoir", and hoped it would be the last time we should have to do battle with the Bosche and expressed his intention of trying to get permission to come back for a little while the next day.

His wife who was resplendent in black with bonnet to match and all shimmering with beads, was equally enthusiastic and said the old man was dying to take a hand in the battle himself. Then they mounted the farm cart which contained the whole of their possessions, including, I regret to say, the fowls on which we have relied for breakfast eggs, and drove off to the accompaniment of much waving of hands and lifting of caps.

Bad luck

Tuesday 27/6/16

Here's rotten luck! I was smitten last night with a sudden and violent attack of the Flu and have been in the throes of fever all day. At about 8 am the Bosche started to shell us with a heavy gun, one round every 4 or 5 minutes and after one had fallen about 50 yards away I thought I should be better off below ground, so I got Harris to shift my bed into the dugout.

Wednesday 28/6/16.

I felt too seedy to write yesterday, as a mater of fact there was very little worth noting, except that four or five 8 inch shells fell quite close to

## The Bristol Gunners

us; one being within 50 yards or so. It did not worry me very much though, as I was far too miserable to be upset by anything the Bosche could do, short of putting a round actually on the top of my bed.

The dugout, in which I am now living - sharing it with Weill, the interrupter, is of the type known as a "Elephant house." If you can imagine a length of about 18ft of tube railway removed from its surroundings and placed in a square hole some 14ft deep, entrance is through a long mined passage one end and a shaft for ventilation and light the other, you will get some idea of our funkhole. The interior is semi-circular, 6ft high in the centre and pitch black except for a pallid light that filters down through the shaft. It is quite roomy when illuminated by a lamp and two or three candles it becomes almost cheerful. I am quite happy down here, as I know I need not run out when the Bosche starts to shell the place, as he has done two or three times a day. Benson came down about 8 o'clock this morning with collar and tie in his hand. The morning hate had caught him in the middle of his toilet, which he thought would be better completed below ground.

The Colonel has just looked in to say that the show has been put off for a day or so no reasons given.

This is better than I deserve, for I should most certainly have missed the great day if the original programme had been carried out.

Friday 30/6/16.

Awaiting the Day

Nothing of interest has happened during the last two days.

Tomorrow is "Der Tag" and the four battery commanders are dining here tonight to receive final instructions. As far as can be gathered, the 4th Army attacks on the line SERRE-RIVER SOMME. The 48th Division is in the Corps reserve of the 8th Corps, on the left flank of the army. At the same time we are holding a portion of the front line and have two Brigades of artillery taking part in this bombardment our job in the first phase of the attack is to hold and maintain the flank of the attacking troops against counter attacks.

## The Bristol Gunners

On our left again, the 3rd Army is attacking but between their right and the 4th Army left is a small stretch of ground, which we have to keep intact. No attack as yet is being launched over this portion and we do not know what is intended after tomorrow is over. Sufficient unto the day!

While we were at dinner, a telegram comes in from division it read as follows;
"Sir Aylmer Hunter-Weston sends his greetings to General Fanshawe and every officer, N.C.O. and man in the 48th Division. He rejoices to be going into battle with so fine a Division as the 48th as his Corps Reserve. He knows that, when the time comes to put them into the fight he can rely on the men of the SOUTH MIDLAND to bear heavy losses from artillery, rifle, and machine gun fire and to stick it out and to win though in the end."

Very nice, but I think the last few lines might have been put differently I don't quite like the idea of being "relied upon to bear heavy losses."

The view from our O.P. has altered considerably during the three days I have been off duty; the village of SERRE is quite un-recognizable. It used to consist of a wooded belt through which two barns only were visible. Today there were no trees left; even the hedges had been almost cleared away, and in their places had been substituted a scene from the "Last Days of Pompeii." I have never seen such wreckage, except on the screen. It is a tiny little village with only one street and is quite close to our lines. In the last few days it has had guns and howitzers of every size and description turned on it, from the 18pr field guns to the 15 inch How.

All the buildings are in ruins.

One or two roofs have been lifted off and are leaning drunkenly against the walls that used to support them rather more respectably. The only building left which can boast a roof has lost half of the only wall that we can see and has apparently had a shell burst well underneath its foundations at one end, for the whole barn has been tilted up and now stands at an angle of about 20 degrees to the horizontal.

"Zero Time" - the minute at which the first wave of infantry starts across No Mans Land tomorrow is told to us after dinner, it is 7.30 am. The Colonel and Wyley are going up at half past five to watch the final

### The Bristol Gunners

*bombardment, Paul Weill and I are going to run up before breakfast to see the assault and I have then to come back here and do one or two jobs before going up to relieve Wyley.*

*Benson, odd man out, has been given the job of superintending ammunition supply for the batteries."*

His voice speaks eloquently across the years. The Brigade War History also informs us:

*"Major Chester Todd knowing how monotonous the wire-cutting job was, used to send down a sort of unofficial "Reuter, Press Association and Central News" bulletin. Once the section was on its line, the wheels well sandbagged down, and the orders after a time would be something like this [the guns would probably be at "section fire 45 secs" for an hour at a time].*

*"No1. Very good - only three more stakes left. Well done No2 you got one of 'em. No1 not so much as 2 1/2 minutes more right - just a touch. No2's last shot was damned hopeless - what the hell is Sergt ----- playing at. Well done No 1 you've bent it" and so on."*

Major Todd had been with the GVA for many years, and was held in high esteem by all those who knew and served with him. He had a brother and at least two cousins also serving in the GVA. He was appointed as Battery Commander shortly after mobilisation, and would remain with the GVA until his death in 1917. Lieutenant E L Gedye would die sooner, within two months of writing the letter above.

The first day of the Battle of the Somme has gone down in history as the worst day for the British Army, and it is usually seen as a massive defeat. In fact, accepting that casualties were extremely high, higher than expected, the day ended with some notable successes.

**Major Chester Todd DSO, much respected Battery Commander in the GVA.**

### The Bristol Gunners

The subsequent months of the battle saw the army improve its tactics and performance, with a number of highly successful actions to its credit. The British Army ended the battle in November on a rising tide of confidence in its abilities, while the Germans ended the battle almost totally exhausted, and with a strong understanding that they would never be able to win the war. German manpower losses broadly equalled those of the French and British. German losses in materiel and morale were more severe, and more serious, especially as it would prove far more difficult for the Germans to replace them.

The Battle of the Somme was the first major assault carried out by the British on the Western Front, it was the turning point of the war and by the end of the war in 1918, the British Army would be the only force in the field with the ability to win the war.

The first day saw the British explode a number of large mines under German strong points, then thirteen British and eleven French divisions (each around 18,000 men strong) climbed the parapet and went 'over the top.' The Germans knew an attack was coming and had made their preparations. The attackers' progress varied depending where in the line they were. South of the central axis, the Albert - Bapaume road, objectives were taken and in some instances exceeded, however north of this road almost no ground was won, and most of the casualties were suffered in this sector.

The two divisions north of the 48th Division (46th North Midland and 56th 1st London, both TF divisions) attacked the Gommecourt 'Nose' and took a terrible beating, recording 7,000 of the total of 57,000 casualties suffered by the British that day. The infantry of the 48th Division did not take part in the assault (apart from two battalions loaned to 56th Division), though the artillery did, including the GVA. The 48th Division were thus spared most of the carnage of that first day.

**Lieutenant E L Gedye, elder brother of Lieutenant F S Gedye, both of whom kept diaries and letters which appear in this narrative.**

### The Bristol Gunners

Between 48th Division and the Albert – Bapaume road were six British divisions, 31st (a New Army division), 4th and 29th (Regular Army divisions), 36th (Ulster) and 32nd, (New Army divisions), and 8th (Regular Army). These divisions also had a torrid time, failed to gain their objectives, and suffered a very high casualty rate.

48th Division were lucky to be placed in a short sector of the line where the infantry did not have to be exposed to that trial by fire that others had to endure. Lieutenant E L Gedye described his experience of the first days of the battle to his parents:

*"Saturday July 1st 1916.*

*"Der Tag"* (The Day)

*It is 6.30 am, just time to write a few lines before we leave.*

*The bombardment has already started and will increase steadily until about 7.20, when it will reach its height and will slack off a little as the attack is made.*

*We had quite a lively night. Wyley and Benson were twice driven down into the dugout between two and three by a bombardment apparently directed at our billet but probably meant for the 6 inch How's just behind. I see the garden wall of the house opposite us has been blown down and the Iron Gate has been lifted across the street and is now resting against our wall.*

*9 a.m. Just seen the first lot of infantry go over. The sky was cloudy when we started, but the sun was trying to break through and there was a delightful freshness in the air. "A morning for victory" Weill said as we walked up, I hope so.*

*We found Major Browne's O.P. [Central] deserted when we got to the crest, so we immediately took possession of it. It was at first almost impossible to make out the hostile trenches, the sun of course was against us and the cloud of shell smoke and dust hung all over the valley. About 7.15 am the sun came out and we could just see No Mans Land, the last 10 minute's bombardment, during which smoke was discharged, must have been absolutely hellish. A continuous succession of big shells beat*

## The Bristol Gunners

down on the German trenches and on SERRE, covering almost every inch of ground.

I saw several points of light twinkling in the sun and focusing my glasses on them, I saw a long line of men forming up, as if for an inspection, in front of our own wire under cover of the cloud of smoke. Then at a slow double, they went forward and almost immediately, another line began to form up in their places.

The German artillery had been replying fairly vigorously to our bombardment and I dreaded to see them get right amongst our fellows. The Bosche was also putting a stiff barrage on our communication trenches and most of the men found it safer to "go down over the lip" i.e. above ground in twos and threes, I don't think many of these were hit, but I saw one little group of five or six hit by a big shell, there was a cloud of smoke, fragments of earth and God knows what else and as it blew away there was no longer any party there.

I waited for 20 minutes to see if anything could be seen of the assault on the 2nd line, but only a few shadowy figures could be picked out, poised for a moment on the parapet with a bayonet twinkling in the sun.

As I came back, wounded men in parties of two, three or more were straggling back across the plain. These of course, are the walking cases only. Their wounds are inspected and dressed at regimental aid posts and if sufficiently lightly hit, they are sent back to the Field Ambulance in charge of a very slightly wounded NCO or an unwounded man.

The other cases are packed off in motor ambulances from the advanced dressing stations, which are usually in dugouts on the outskirts of forward villages like Hebuterne.

And so to Breakfast, for which I manage to raise an enormous appetite.

I am afraid a lot of men must have been knocked out before they reached the German wire and trenches for the Bosche barrage was very severe and strangely enough even before fellows got over the parapet the Bosche artillery was concentrated on the part of the line from which we were going to attack. A little north of the point of exit there was a patch about 200 yds long that was getting no shells at all.

### The Bristol Gunners

It's wonderful how the enemy seem to know just where we are going to do.

Saturday evening.

When I went to the O.P. at 11o'clock this morning, there was no sign of an infantry battle although the guns on both sides were still plugging away. No messages or signals were received from the assaulting party but the Bosche was shelling SERRE and his own trenches in front, so that presumably our fellows have achieved their objective.

We have heard that on our left the London [56th] Division had taken GOMMECOURT and SERRE and were as far forward as ROSSIGNOL WOOD.

Tonight we here are sad rumours flying about, it is said that both GOMMECOURT and SERRE have been retaken while some say that we still hold SERRE, but that the Bosche has got the trenches between us and it.

I was right about the German barrage on our infantry I counted 200 bodies laying in No Mans Land this afternoon. The swine were sniping at any who might not have been killed; the position of the bodies is a wonderful tribute to the gallantry of the attacking force. A lot are quite close to our own wire, others part way across, but the great majority are right against the German parapet and between their first and second lines, showing that although our fellows got into the thick of it right away, they did not give way but went steadily though it and on with the job. Of course, I am not an expert in these matters, but it seems rather a remarkable thing to send an assaulting party over at 7.30am and not to send a single reinforcement either of men or ammunition for the rest of the day, not even a reconnoitring party to find out how things were going.

I imagine it could have been done quite easily in small detachments, there would certainly have been losses, but they would have been comparatively slight to those sustained in the original attack.

Sunday 2/7/16.

## The Bristol Gunners

*Snipers*

My turn to be early at the O.P. the usual few shells came over at us during the night. One demolished a barn in our courtyard and another burst three yards beyond the dug out. Everyone slept below last night so we were not disturbed. After a cup of tea, I bicycled across the plain as far as Prideaux's position whence by trench to the O.P. getting there at 7 o'clock.

The Colonel, who slept up there last night in case of any sudden development has no news except that a sergeant of the 31st division is reported to have come through the German lines with a message to the effect that there are over a hundred of our fellows holding a portion of SERRE still.

I don't know if there is any truth in the tale I should say not. The Germans are undoubtedly in their original front line; because I saw several of them go past a point where the trench has been practically levelled. There is a remarkable quietness. Neither side is shooting, probably because neither side knows quite what has happened or what is going to happen next. We hear that our attack further south and the French below the Somme have been successful and that we hold the German Fourth line and a number of villages including the important one of Thiepval. All rumours though and nothing official can be heard for love or money.

*Monday 3/7/16*

The Bosche fairly put the wind up us last night at tea. Wyley, Weill, and I had just started when I caught a familiar whistling sound. I put up my hand and said, "Here they come." Almost as I said it there were four appalling crumps, two on either side of the house. We opened the window and were nearly choked by the dust and fumes that had drifted in as with one accord we made a dive for the dugout. As we reached it four more 6 inch shells came over and after a minute's interval some more. All told, I think, there were 16.

Net results, one barn pushed over, one house bent a little at one end a big hole in the road and three round our dug out. No one was hurt but our tea was rather spoilt.

## The Bristol Gunners

*Tuesday 4/7/16*

I am writing this in an O.P. It has rained hard since 10 o'clock this morning and it is with difficulty that I can keep dry in this rottenly built place. I wish Clissold were up here for the afternoon just to show him how badly Sappers can work, when they make up their minds to it. There is a heavy bombardment in progress some way to the south of us, about Thiepval, I should say. We discovered a wounded man in No Mans land yesterday. We could see him clearly through the telescope. He spent most of the afternoon turning his water bottle upside down hoping to find a drop of water left that he had not discovered, poor devil. I was so perturbed about him that, after locating him on the map just where he was, I went down to the battalion H.Q. covering that part of the line.

The colonel, who seemed quite overwhelmed to think that a gunner of another division should have taken so much trouble, gave me a guide to take me down to the company commander, to whom I offered my services.

However, when I described the position of the wounded man he said that they had already seen him and were going to bring him back in as soon as it got dark enough. Twenty-six men had been rescued the night before, three of them in broad daylight. As a matter of fact, this particular fellow was not brought in until 10 o'clock this morning. I suppose they must have missed him in the dark, but it is a plucky thing to go into No Mans Land and bring a fellow in broad daylight. The devils of Bosche were sniping him yesterday, one swine got into a shell hole just outside their wire in order to get a better shot, I rejoice to say, though that one of our 18 pdrs sniped the sniper during the afternoon and after that our man was left in peace.

We are not manning the O.P. after today, tomorrow evening the stores will be carted back to Sailly and presumably we go back to the normal routine of trench warfare. We have still to keep open the gaps of wire out through the enemy's wire, so that possibly we may take up the offensive again later, if things go well enough down below. But, for the time being, anyway, the great push as far as we are concerned, is *"Na Poo Fini La Guerre."* (This is not the end of the war).

### The Bristol Gunners

It took a couple of days for the full truth of the failure to be recognised for what it was. Though the GVA were not part of the main attack, they played a part in it and witnessed many of the results. Before the war was won they would witness, and be part of, several other major actions.

The British generals responded positively to the results of the first day. It was clear that progress in the north would be hard, and that the south offered better prospects. Consequently, more attacks were launched over the coming weeks and months. The fighting never really stopped, rather each attack was followed by a series of more limited actions to recover a position or to consolidate gains.

In mid July it was decided to move 48th Division further south to take part in the attacks just north of the Albert – Bapaume road, towards Ovillers and on towards Pozieres and Mouquet Farm. Initially the artillery of the division were left in place at Hebuterne to support the Welsh 38th Division when they relieved the 48th Division. After a couple of days the artillery received orders to move out and rejoin the division in the Ancre Valley just outside Albert. The 38th Division had been involved in the fighting for Mametz Wood where their divisional memorial stands today. Lieutenant E L Gedye, at this time working at brigade headquarters:

*Wednesday 12/7/16.*

*Wire Collecting*

*The colonel and Wyley have gone down to the wagon lines for a rest, leaving the Doctor and myself up here.*

*My job is assist in clearing the Divisional area of disused telephone wire, of which there must be quantities. We are nominally attached to the 242nd Brigade [late 3rd South Midland Bde] with whom we are going to dine. Our other meals, we shall have here and I can foresee that we are going to have quite a pleasant time.*

*Saturday 15/7/16*

*Our part in the battle may not yet be over after all. The infantry are in the process of being relieved by the 38th Division and the two brigades in reserve have already started south. We are all hoping we shall be*

### The Bristol Gunners

*allowed to follow them and I don't think I am exaggerating when I say that the infantry hope so too but at present it rather looks as if though we might be left. We are all heartily sick of 16 months "Goalkeeping" 12 out of the 16 between the same posts. It is much worse to be inactive when others so close to us are in the thick of it.*

*The Division, which is relieving us, or rather, whose infantry is relieving ours, already thinks itself fit to look at us a little disdainfully in spite of the fact that we were in action probably before they had fired their musketry course. Still, they are fresh from the Mametz district and have had a pretty strenuous time, so we shall have to make allowances.*

Monday 17/7/16

*The C.R.A. has told us today that we are to join the Division, down south. We don't know where and we don't care very much. It is enough for the time to know that we are to do something.*

Thursday 20/7/16.

Going South

*We go south to-morrow. We were relieved this afternoon and are sleeping tonight at the wagon lines*

*Quite by chance, in the course of conversation with the orderly Officer of the Brigade relieving us, I discovered that his adjutant was an S.Q. - G P Thomas, a Welshman. I went round to his H.Q. after ten & had a few words will him. It is over 7 years since I saw him last but I could almost imagine it was yesterday he has changed so little, another surprise was waiting for me when I got back, Hitchings W. H., he is in the same division as Thomas [38th].*

*We have to breakfast tomorrow at 4.30.am so I am for bed.*

Saturday 22/7/16

*I was too sleepy yesterday to write anything in my dairy I could not have had a better day for moving. The country was looking perfect and, though it hardly seemed possible that we were really moving at last, I*

The Bristol Gunners

think there were very few regrets. I went down by motor lorry together with a few of our H.Q. and a number of "D" Battery officers & men. Our mobus broke down just outside Bouzincourt, and we had to disembark & wait until one of the others had made the journey and could come back and fetch us.

After an hour's wait we started off again, but had the misfortune to fall in at the tail of a long motor convoy and for 30 disgusting minutes, we were breathing and swallowing the greater part of the dust which had accumulated during the last two or three months on the Albert road. At last, we got clear of the convoy and saw in front of us the buildings of Albert, surmounted by the cathedral with the famous leaning statue of the virgin and child. The town itself did not appear very greatly knocked about except just round the cathedral, which had evidently been the central point of all the bombardments.

We left the lorry just outside the town at one of the many bridges over the Ancre and went on foot.

On the way, we met Colonel Langham of the Sussex very cheery and voluble old boy who detained us for about 20 minutes in order to tell us all the very latest news. Just here, we parted company. Major Fowler and his party going off to discover his new battery position. My way lay through a wood, and in the middle of which, I discovered our H.Q. The Colonel & Wyley, who had ridden down, were, I found, already on the scene, as were Colonel West and his staff. We are still working on the Group system that is to say, one Colonel in charge of two brigades for tactical purposes.

Colonel West is running our Group, although we are all going to be up here to lighten the work.

The H.Q. is in a really charming spot. The dugouts are on both sides of a broad ride through the wood, which is sufficiently small timbered to give any amount of light & air. Looking down the ride we get a glimpse of the river, which is at present in flood, and on the side of it a building, which is, probably, called a chateau. Between us and the river is a fairly broad space of marsh, also flooded, and spanned by a wooden bridge optimistically labelled "To Bapaume, Cambrai, Courcelette & Berlin."

### The Bristol Gunners

*A number of telephone wires run across the marsh and there is an old rowing boat for the convenience of linesmen. In this Selby-Lowndes [Col West's Orderly Officer] and I lazed for an hour or so this afternoon.*

*I wish the war could be run like that always. It was rather strange rowing gently in between the tall trees which grow right across the marsh while time shells of all sizes were whistling, overhead on their way to the Bosche.*

*The Colonel of the brigade is sleeping here tonight so I'm dossing in with the doctor Davidson and his dog who ought to keep the rats out at any rate.*

*This division has a system of code names - most of them Christian names - for the various units. A message was given to me after tea, reading "Report by wire as soon as the relief of Doris has been completed." This I handed on to Davidson, as it seemed to fall more within his department than mine.*

*There is a very objectionable habit here it seems of keeping an officer on duty at night. I had the last shift last night & had to get up at 4.30am (Saturday) morning I believe it is popularly supposed that sunrise is a magnificent spectacle but after having seen it on two successive days, I am beginning to lose my enthusiasm.*

*This morning Wyley, Davidson and I paid a visit to one of our forward O.P.s in Ovillers.*

*A few maimed tree trunks mark the site of the village. There is no vestige of a building left, the whole village having been literally flattened. As we went over the old German front line trenches we saw bricks and rubble here and there which looked as though they might, at one time, have been the foundations of houses, but I am not exaggerating when I say that there is not a fragment of a wall above ground level.*

*The whole place is honeycombed with trenches and bits of trenches and wherever there is no trench, there are shell holes the ruin and havoc is beyond description.*

## The Bristol Gunners

*The German dugouts are the only things that have survived and most of them are now sheltering our own Infantry and Artillery observers. Over some of the dug-outs are placards bearing the names of its former occupants, others have simply a title. Various articles of equipment, German and English, but mostly German, are scattered along the trenches and in the dug-outs.*

*I salvaged a Bosche smoke helmet and Davidson secured a pair of white overalls for the cook. Everywhere there are bombs, some blind, some not used. These we avoid as there have been several men injured as a result of stepping on an apparently dead bomb, shells and bits of shells also lie in profusion and there are a number of huge 9.2 shells that have failed to explode.*

*In one trench we came across two "petrol can throwers" of which you have probably seen descriptions of in the papers. The barrels are made from 3 or 4-inch boarding bound with galvanized wire and they throw a petrol can about 2ft long by 1ft in diameter full of explosive. We also passed one dead Bosche; he was not a pleasant sight to behold. We had a look at the country from the O.P., it was strange to see our telephonists working on the steps of a dug-out labelled "Oloffbereitschaft."*

*On the way back, we passed the time of day with two or three infantry officers, one of whom accused me of playing against him at hockey. I did not remember him but he assured me it was so, his name is FIELD of the Imperial. I also met Phillen going up with his platoon.*

*There were parties collecting material in the open between Ovillers and La Boisselle quite un-molested by the Bosche, who must certainly have his tail between his legs. La Boisselle is distinguished in having two walls standing about 6 feet high, I am told that this is the church! A few more maimed and scattered trees on the crest represent Pozieres, which I suppose is the next objective.*

*We called at infantry Brigade H.Q. on our return journey, where I met Andrews. He told me that Gilbert Castle had greatly distinguished himself in the last attack and is likely to be recommended for the D.S.O.*

*There is to be another attack tonight. The 6$^{th}$ Gloucesters are going over in front of us with the Australians further on our right. The aim of*

## The Bristol Gunners

the latter is to take that part of Pozieres south of the Bapaume road. Our job is to try and capture one line of trench west of Pozieres. I am not on duty tonight, but there is little chance of my getting a full ration of sleep owing to the bombardment.

Sunday 23/7/16

I was quite right about the sleep. There is an infernal battery of soixante-quinze just behind us, which fire directly over our heads.

Apparently the detachments stand easy for quarter of an hour, at the end of which they remember there is a battle on and spring to the guns for the next five minutes they fire like the devil, loosing off as only a French 75 can loose off, and then, having exhausted all the ammunition within easy reach, drop off to sleep again for another 15 minutes.

These people, together with a battery of 60 pounders and what I imagine to be a 6 inch gun, effectively prevented me from getting any sleep until after 1.30 am.

The echoes round here, by the way, are quite remarkable. The valley, the water and the trees each contribute to the production, or rather reproduction and reflection of all the many sound waves that are continually being set in motion. An 18pdr shell travelling through the air gives a very passable imitation of the Cornish Riviera [name of a railway train] passing through Taunton station, while quite a small Bosche shell pretends to be from a very large gun.

This afternoon I went with Colonel West to Browne's forward O.P. on the Ovillers - Pozieres road. After going some distance on the road to Ovillers, we struck off right handed across what used to be No Mans Land.

From here onward, we were in full view of the German present lines, but apparently, the Bosche is either too scared to look, or else too tired to shoot. Any way, apart from a few stray shells that wander up and down the valley at intervals there is nothing to hurt one.

This particular hollow is known as Mash Valley, a name which conveyed nothing to my mind until I saw that the next dip in the ground is

called "Sausage Valley," probably from its outline which might be said to resemble a Wurst.

There was quite a lot of shelling just ahead of us. The Bosche may have been counter attacking on the S.E. of Pozieres: he certainly was not on our side of the village, or he may have been merely demonstrating his dislike for us; en tout cas (in any case), I was not at all sorry when I caught sight of Browne sitting on the parapet of a sometime Bosche communication trench the barrage was much too close in front of us to be really enjoyable. Selby-Lowndes and I were left in a shell hole, to avoid having too large a party at the O.P., which like everything else, is fully exposed to German view.

We are comparatively happy there until the wind shifted around a point or so then we made haste to refill our pipes. I think for everybody's sake parties should somehow be raised to get these remnants of the first attack decently and inoffensively interred. To my mind it is horrible that a men who has fought and died gallantly, whether he be Bosche or British, and the majority of them are our own fellows, should be left to become a nuisance and possibly a danger and an object of repulsion to all who cross the bit of ground that he helped to win or defend.

We came back through Ovillers. I find I was wrong in my description of the place yesterday; there are two or three fragments of wall still standing on the Eastern side of the village, but not sufficient to afford any evidence of ownership. We passed the time of day with Todd at his O.P. and after having prospected for other likely spots in the neighbourhood hurried home for a well earned and much overdue cup of tea.

Morgan, from Browne's Battery, has been selected for a job of work on the Corps staff; this will give me a chance of getting some battery work temporarily. Even the Colonel can hardly fail to see that, apart from my 3 hours duty at night, I am absolutely wasting my time. There are two adjutants to divide the office work; Colonel West's orderly officer is naturally in charge of wires and I am left with nothing to do but look pretty.

## The Bristol Gunners

*In any case it is not the sort of job that I am suited for, and as the battery work is pretty stiff even for 5 officers, it is not right that there should be an officer out of a job.*

*Later. The colonel has given me permission to work with the battery by day, but will not allow me to go there altogether because "I must be up here for night duty," subject, of course to his better opinion, I should submit that 2 x Adjutants and an orderly officer, not to mention 2 x Colonels, could get through all the work at H.Q. both day and night, with out any undue strain. However, I am grateful enough for the concession. I can, at any rate, feel that I am doing a little to help on the show, even if it's not a wonderfully important little."*

Lieutenant Gedye had been working as part of the brigade commander's staff at brigade HQ. His decision to ask to be sent back to the battery to help out would have serious consequences for him.

To this point, the GVA had suffered very few casualties, despite the fact that they had been subject to German counter battery fire throughout their time in Hebuterne and especially during the run up to and early days of the Somme attacks. This could have been due to the fact that they had been able to construct substantial underground shelters for the guns and the men, some in the basements of houses in Hebuterne. Now they were in a new area, and as the attacks during the following months allowed the front line to move into what was previously German held territory, they would be using gun positions and OPs wherever they could. They would not always be able to construct secure accommodation, and with the intensity of the fighting, the casualty rate would rise.

On 21st July, the battle had moved to the area north of Ovillers. The Somme campaign was partly to wrest the high ground from the Germans so as to remove that advantage from them and place it in our hands. The highest point on the Albert – Bapaume road was at Pozieres. There was a prominent windmill on the north east side of the village, and the attack and capture of Pozieres was the first time that the 1st Australian Division went into battle in France, and the village is now the site of their memorial.

The fight for Pozieres lasted from 23rd July through to 7th August. The Australians were tasked with assaulting the village from the south west,

### The Bristol Gunners

while their left flank was taken by the 48th Division, assaulting up from Ovillers towards the left of the village of Pozieres.

Lieutenant EL Gedye wrote a passage on the death of Captain A.E.Stone. He had come out to the Continent as second in command of 1st Battery, though had been posted to another battery (A Battery 243 Brigade, also in 48th Division) earlier in 1916. He was a long term and enthusiastic GVA man, and had volunteered for Imperial Service during the Boer War:

"*Monday 24/7/16.*

*I have spent the day at the battery position getting hold of how things are done, every officer and certainly every battery commander, has certain things that have to be done just so, and it is best to find out at once what these things are.*

*We are all rather cut up this evening. Capt A. E. Stone was killed about 4 o'clock while on duty at the O.P. the one we saw yesterday in Ovillers. I am awfully sorry. Old Stone was one of the very best and although he left the brigade some time ago now, when the new battery was formed, we shall miss him badly. He has a long record of service, longer than anyone else out here with the brigade dating back to the old volunteer days. He has always been a very staunch upholder of our Volunteer and Territorial traditions.*

*A great thing in these days when the principal object of those set in authority over us seems to be to make us forget that we were ever anything else than the 240 Brigade RFA. I remember how frightfully sick he was when this new numbering was adopted. It was even worse for him than for us, because, being with a newly formed unit, he had not even the excuse that we gave for calling ourselves in defiance of all regulations 1st, 2nd or 3rd Gloucester Battery, instead of A & B or C/240. At mobilization, he was quite the keenest man for Foreign Service in the Brigade and it seems hard that he should be the first to fall. Still, I think he would have chosen to go the way he did, in a pukka show, on duty and on territory just captured from the Bosche.*"

The 48th Division continued in action in the Pozieres area until the end of July when it was withdrawn from the front and moved out to rest further south. The days in the Ovillers/Pozieres area were not without further

The Bristol Gunners

action, as described by Lieutenant EL Gedye; his description gives a good feel to how conditions were at that time:

*"Wednesday 26/7/16.*

*Both yesterday and today I spent the greater part of my time at the O.P., it is not a place I should select on the score of either comfort or safety.*

*It is situated in the narrow trench behind the late Bosche 3rd line or to be more accurate, on the trench.*

*The only method of observing is to sit on top of the parapet, where the Bosche can see you a great deal easier than you can see him; the parapet, moreover, is composed of lumps of chalk of various sizes, which even a wad of sandbags does not do much towards softening. Heaven forbid that it should rain, for the place would become quite untenable. As it is, however, I get along quite well, for once I start gazing at the country, I forget the several disadvantages of the position.*

*Our great difficulty is to decide on the exact points where our line ends and the Bosche begins. The position here, on the extreme flank of the attack is rather curious. The Flank line that we hold cuts across his [German] system at right angles, so that both parties share the same trenches.*

*In the sketch, I have marked the line held by us in red and by the Bosche in blue, the shaded portions being the trenches actually held and consolidated by either side. The blue dots are strong points usually trench junctions out of which we are endeavouring to bomb the enemy by clearing the communication trenches forward in the direction of the arrows. Hence, at any minute of the day our fellows may get to a point which, as far as the gunners know, is in German hands, and unless the infantry get a message back pretty quickly, they may possibly get some of our own shells in their backs. As a matter of fact they always tell us when they are starting out to bomb and what their objective is, but it is very difficult for us to find out how far they have succeeded. Also, of course, the Bosche can counter attack in the same way with bombs and it is more likely that we shan't know until it is all over. In default of anything else*

## The Bristol Gunners

we keep up an irregular fire on the Bosche communications and to make the provision of ammunition and rations as difficult as possible.

They gave me a bit of a fright this afternoon. There was a working party on the road in front of the O.P., and I thought it would be rather a good idea to fire a couple of salvoes over the Bosche trenches to prevent anyone getting his head over the parapet and seeing our fellows, which I did. But no sooner had the two parties gone out of sight safely than some confounded Bosche seized hold of a machine gun and fired at me! He couldn't do any damage of course, unless his first round was a bull, which is not likely at that range but I don't want to have to observe in the intervals of dodging machine gun bullets. Also he may tell his gunners about us, which would be more uncomfortable still.

However, I got upon the parapet again after having allowed about half an hour to go by, and as I was not troubled again, I am beginning to hope that he was really aiming at something else in the same line as myself. If he really has discovered us then I shall have to find another O.P.

*Friday 28/7/16.*

As I rather feared, we had to find a new O.P. yesterday. I got up there as usual about 11.30 and found that nothing untoward had happened, and accordingly we continued to observe from the parapet.

There was a gunner from the 25th Division with me, who was prospecting for a new O.P. for himself. Suddenly there was an appalling Whizz-Plump close to us and we collapsed gracefully into the trench, we saw a little wisp of smoke rising a yard behind where we had been sitting. I am not quite sure now; how it was the shell did not pass though one of us on the way; fortunately it was not a timed shrapnel or I doubt if either of us would have been much more use to His Majesty.

We beat a rather hurried retreat down the trench, which is not only narrow, which is an advantage - but also in places, shallow - which is decidedly the reverse. After we had covered about a hundred yards, we lay down in a fairly deep trench and for twenty minutes listened to the shells flying around us at the O.P. They were bursting them in the air now, just too late from the Bosche point of view.

### The Bristol Gunners

*I rang the Major, who told me to select another O.P. and that he would bring up some more wire to connect up to it when he came up to relieve me.*

*I found quite a good place lower down where the trench became dead white [chalk] fairly close to where our wire ran. I camouflaged my tin hat by chalking it all over by utilising two of the signallers with me as orderlies managed to make it a working concern. I fired one or two registering rounds just to make sure I knew the country from my new point of view and then proceeded to strafe all the Bosche trenches I could see. It was naturally rather a slow process, as every order had to be passed down the trench, partly by hand and partly by voice, but it gave me a great deal of satisfaction.*

*When Browne came up at six o'clock he brought with him a Captain to whom he introduced me by saying "Captain [something or other] who is relieving us tomorrow." I was then told that the Brigade whom we relieved 6 days ago was now to relieve us.*

*I am now [Friday morning] sitting outside my dugout basking in the sun. It is a perfectly beautiful day, the best we have had since we have been here, and as we have to sleep in the open in the wagon lines tonight, it is just as well. Still, I am very glad I have not to trudge up to the O.P. this morning; I am afraid it will get very odorous in this weather.*

*Tomorrow we start early for Ampliers, near Doullens and the following day we make for St Ouen, where rumour has it we rest for a week. After that, no one knows what we do or where we go. I shall take advantage of the rest to have my second inoculation. I have seen enough in this last week to make me think it may be necessary."*

The 48th Division marched out of the line and took time to rest. Their commander, General Fanshawe, allowed them to relax a little more than perhaps was usual, for he was a personal dynamo. Lieutenant F S Gedye wrote of him:

*"Fanshawe, the GOC Div relaxed for ten days as far as we were concerned his appalling energy, which used to cause him to start his day at 3am and only end it after he had seen himself setting out on his day's*

### The Bristol Gunners

work next morning; his orders were for complete rest for everyone and I think the whole Division thoroughly appreciated his leniency.

There were no inspections, no tactical exercises - we just put our house in order, did a little mild open warfare practice to exercise the horses, pulled tails and cleaned harness and generally got ourselves in good order. On August 9$^{th}$ we again took to the road and marched back to Ampliers, which we made our headquarters until the 12$^{th}$.

We had a great evening in Doullens on the 11$^{th}$. Todd, Lane, Ridler and myself went in during the afternoon and after booking dinner for our selves Pride-Jones and Prideaux at the Bon Enfant, Ridler delighted us by visiting a hat shop in the absurd hope of finding something to fit his colossal cranium. He and Lane insisted on trying on every type of hat in the shop, from the small boy's green cap with a button on the top to the Poilu's blue Tamoshanter, which caused Ridler to indulge in a highland fling. His final admonishment to the proprietress on finding that she didn't stock his size sent us out into the street almost helpless with laughter."

The other Gedye, older brother EL Gedye, writes about the same events:

"Saturday 29/7/16.

Here we are at Amplier, out of the sound of gunfire at last. I went on in advance of the Brigade as billeting officer. It is much pleasanter than going down with the push, as we are not compelled to travel at a slow walk, which prolongs the journey well into the heat of the day. The country here is quite pretty, but the village, following the custom in this part of the world, is featureless. Wykeham the Staff Captain R.A., met me this morning and showed me the accommodation for the Brigade, which I had to split up and allot to the batteries. I secured a charming billet for myself, a little cottage with a rose garden attached, belonging to a delightful old couple.

The old gentleman, who looks rather like Mr. Pickwick, greeted me as "mon garcon" while his wife bustled round and showed me my room, quite large, cool, and spotlessly clean. She assured me I could rest as much as I liked, as they had no children, no cows and no poultry, nothing that could make a noise.

## The Bristol Gunners

*I had to go back then and meet the batteries, when they were settled in, I procured some lunch at the mess and then went back to my billet and got a bath and got in to bed. I didn't wake till nearly six, when I had a bath and a shave, after which Weill and I bicycled into Doullens for dinner.*

*Sunday 30/7/16.*

*We were away a little later this morning 7 o' clock instead of 6, the old people came down to see me off and made me promise to come and stay with them if I were ever in Amplier again either during the war or afterwards. St Ouen is a busy and dusty little place something like Taunton only smaller.*

*The horse lines and men's bivouacs are in a small portion of a long park which has avenues of tall trees running across the breadth of it every 40 or 50 yards. It is about 300 to 400 yards broad, bounded at the top by the River Authie and at the bottom by the railway.*

*The 1st Battery officers are going to live in the park but the rest of us have billets in the town. Most or them are going to occupy billets from choice, I from necessity; the extra 10 minutes in the morning being more than I can afford with an early bird like the S.O.*

*Wednesday 9/8/16.*

*I have not written in the log since we have been out, as one day has been so much like another that it would make even duller reading than before. We are on our way back to the war again now, and are spending the night in Ampliers; as billeting officer I was able to collar the same billet that I had on the way down.*

*We had a perfectly delightful holiday. On the first day, we received a bundle of congratulatory letters, General Fanshawe, in which he expressed the wish that we "Should enjoy the rest which we so well deserved." Hence, as no one seemed to expect us to do any work, we made no pretence of doing any. The weather all the time was perfect and we filled up the afternoons and evenings [most of the morning went in stables] with competitions, rides and idleness. Two days we had the divisional band discoursing music in the gun park while another two days*

### The Bristol Gunners

were absorbed by boxing contests. I had one day in Amiens with Davey. He borrowed a trap from the senior Padre, McNulty, and we started off from St Ouen about 9.30 am.

It was one of the best of the many glorious summer days and the drive across country was really beautiful, we spent the day eating and shopping, left at half past ten and got back to the lines shortly after 1pm.

We had to tie the nag up by his head collar, complete with blinkers, as there was no sign of a stable piquet. The old Runt, as Davy affectionately called him must have felt an awful rake the next morning when he woke up and found he had been put to bed in his blinkers!

Tomorrow the colonel has invited us [H.Q.] to dine with him in Doullens, as this will be our the last night out of the line, I could rather wish I were going in somewhat less sedate company, but I expect we shall meet a good few of the others in there.

Friday 11/8/16.

Had a great time in Doullens yesterday. I went over in the afternoon, via Beauval, where I hoped to see the dentist. They told me, over at the hospital that he was out visiting an ambulance and would not be in until after 5 o' clock. Accordingly, I bicycled on to Doullens, intending to get a dentist of another C.C.S. to have a shot at me. I went in to one, Number 19 C.C.S. I think it was, and the dentist man told me I ought to have my teeth done at Beauval "I have been there already" I replied "but they told me the tooth professor was visiting a field ambulance, I don't believe he really was though." "You were quite right" he replied with a grin "he wasn't - he is right here" and so he was, just behind me. Apparently he had come over to Doullens to get his own teeth doctored. He accepted my apologies amiably, and arranged to meet me about half past five at Beauval.

I then went to get some tea and purchase a hat, the latter in deference to the frequently expressed wishes of the C.O., who has a strong distaste for the "Gorblimeys." While engaged in the selection of a chapeau, I was informed that "Le Roi d'Angleterre vient a Doullens a quatre heures et demi" (The King of England is coming to Doullens at half past four). It was then only a quarter past, so I went to get tea with two other fellows I

### The Bristol Gunners

*met and just as we were sitting down, we heard someone call out "here he is." We dived for the door, and got out just in time to salute the old Gentleman, who gave us a very gracious salute in return.*

*This was not the last excitement of the day. I started off for Beauval about 5o'clock, and as I spun round a cross road, whom should I espy coming down the road but Corfield! Quite regardless that he is now a Major, I hailed him loudly by name and we fell on each others necks and wept, he was as cheery as ever, I promised to try and see him again after dinner.*

*When I got back later and found Todd's party dining in the same pub as us, I telephoned Corfield and got him to come down and join them. Then when the C.O. went back rather early, I also added myself to the party and we had a very merry evening talking over old days."*

Though not stated, this may have been the last time that the Gedye brothers were able to enjoy each other's company out of the line.

At 08.40 on 12th August, the brigade marched out from Ampliers back towards the front. The officers' party, having seen the King in Ampliers, were to come across him again on the march. At that time, Lieutenant F S Gedye was with the ammunition column and describes an incident that must have been a frequent event in those far off days of horse drawn wagons:

*"After about hour on the road we passed through a village where the infantry were lined up for the King to inspect them. Not a quarter of a mile outside here, the mess cart had a fiasco. The lead horse was blind in the right eye and refused to answer the rein; the whole thing swung round and I saw the poor beast lying on the bank. No damage was done to the horse or the cart but he had finished with the "Officers" for that day and after trying both the Q.M.S.'s horse and my own in the lead with no success, I sent the farrier sergeant on to bring back a spare wheeler from the battery. Finally, after enduring agonies of apprehension least H.M. should shout "Off with his head" as he passed me nestling forlornly by the side of the mess cart, to say nothing of the contemptuous smiles of the other batteries and brigades whose mess carts were still in action, we got a good wheeler back and set off."*

### The Bristol Gunners

It is not easy for us in the modern day to understand how important the horses were to the soldiers of the brigade. They were vital for war work. They brought up supplies, food, jars of rum, articles of war, and articles of comfort. They were also companions, loyal and hard working. There is no doubt that officers and men were both immensely attached emotionally to their horses, and very keen to secure the best horses when remounts (replacements) were needed. Lieutenant FS Gedye tells the story:

> *"There was also a gigantic row over the distribution of remounts between Ridler and Hurndall, who at that time had the right and left sections with Matthews and myself attached to them. This was no unusual thing - for some unknown reason the distribution of remounts was always stormy and the most severe of tests of friendship between rival Section Officers."*

Friction could also develop between individuals and units over resources. F S Gedye again:

> *"Still more famous was the row, or rather opening of hostilities between A/ 243 Bty, and ourselves over their incinerator, which abutted on to our alfresco mess, which constructed and lit by BSM Blackman, nearly smoked us out. After a somewhat heated interchange of words; the situation was rendered more delicate by Ridler's energetic act of dowsing the fire with the contents of our water cart, and Todd's personal appeal to his cousin's better feelings one day at lunch time from which he returned almost [but by no means entirely] speechless with indignation.*
>
> *I know that when we met the Todds in the street at Doullens on the trek back we had to look round surreptitiously to see that our Major was not in sight before we dared to cross over to speak to them."*

The battery commander of A Battery 243 Brigade was Major Chester Todd's cousin. There were others of the Todd extended family in other batteries of 243 Brigade. It seems that though they were related, and had previously enjoyed very good relations, the episode of the incinerator burned more than just waste; it also burned up some of the goodwill between them.

The 48th Division moved back into the area that they had occupied in late July in the Ancre Valley, outside Albert. They were there for two months

## The Bristol Gunners

and took part in the attacks on Thiepval and the Leipsic redoubt, some of the fiercest fighting of the whole battle. Casualties increased, including a number of officers who had been with the brigade for many years.

A former peacetime member of the GVA was Captain WHB Savile, who had been posted to 70th Brigade RFA, serving with 15th (Scottish) Division, a New Army division. He was killed on 14th August during the fighting north of Delville Wood, in the area around High Wood. He was a son of the Colonel HBO Savile, the first commander of the GVA.

240th Brigade was in action again on 18th August until 26th August, involved in supporting infantry from the 48th Division in attacks on the Schwaben trench on the Thiepval Ridge, just southeast of Thiepval village. Lieutenant FS Gedye describes some of the action:

*"Everything was much as before until our big daylight attack on Friday the 18th, when the division really came into its own down here. I went up to our sap in Coniston Street with Todd and Lane and it was a wonderful sight to see our barrage open.*

*At 5pm there wasn't a burst to be seen on the first trench objective of the infantry, but within 10 seconds the square formed by the front and second Bosche line and the two communication trenches was a mass of bursting shrapnel.*

*After about 5 minutes our view was obscured by the smoke candles, which were lit from Leipsic to hide the Bosche machine gunner's view of Thiepval ridge.*

*For three hours until the light went, we were busy with glasses watching the prisoners coming back-the bursting of grenades as the infantry bombed up a hundred yards beyond their new trenches to erect barricades etc.*

*The region of our O.P. was stiff with the gilded staff that day - even the Army Commander was there and we got fed up with greeting such common fry as Brigadier Generals. Matthews, who was on duty at the battery that night had a restless time, all the telegrams of congratulations flowing in - Army Commander, G.O.C. Div and General Birdwood of the Anzac corps on our right.*

## The Bristol Gunners

*We had two more successful daylight attacks and improved our gains there, and then Thursday 24th the 48th Div. Arty. were lent for an attack on the Hindenburg trench from Leipsic.*

*This entailed crossing 200 yards of open space uphill as usual the infantry got out as our barrage started and walked up the hill and ensconced themselves in shell holes close to the parapet until the gunners' barrage lifted.*

*It was one of the most wonderful sights it is possible to see of an attack. Colonel West told us there were over twice as many guns employed as in Friday's attack and we certainly saw more from the O.P. of the show. Our infantry could be seen from the moment they lined up in our trench until they jumped down into the Bosche's.*

*We then saw big groups of prisoners coming back - the place must have been stiff with Huns. Here is at least one incident to show how indifferent the Tommy is to shellfire.*

*It occurred about half-an-hour after "zero-time"[4.10] when the Bosche was putting a fair amount of stuff into the groups between our lines at Leipsic and the Hindenburg. A party of Bosche prisoners escorted by a single Tommy were fairly haring across the open and flinging themselves into shell holes when they heard another shell coming.*

*Not so Tommy, who kept serenely on until just before he reached our trench, he stopped, and went over to another man who was going the other way - after a minute they went slowly on their separate ways, apparently quite unconscious of the shells all around them."*

After the disaster of 1st July, the British Army had learned quickly how to improve their methods. A typical attack now was more limited in scope and scale. Typically a section of German trench was selected, bombarded by artillery until the moment our troops rushed the last distance to jump down into it before the defenders could emerge from their dug outs. The artillery fire would then switch to isolating that occupied stretch of trench, with shells landing either side and behind it to prevent Germans from counterattacking or moving around. Smoke was used to obscure ('blind') German machine gunners and observers in enfilade positions while the attack was taking place. The artillery fire continued while the captured trench was secured and prepared for defence against counterattack. This

was the use of artillery in the true meaning of 'barrage', that is, it formed a barrier behind which our own forces were protected. These attacks were more like a surgical excision of an enemy position than the previous sledgehammer approach. Over the coming months until the end of the battle, the method would be repeated and refined. The British had learned the lessons of war, and they had learned them well.

On the night of 23rd/24th August Lieutenant EL Gedye was killed while at the battery position. He died in an explosion resulting from a fire in an ammunition dump, a constant hazard at a gun position where by this time large quantities of ammunition were stored to enable the guns to keep firing. His younger brother, Lieutenant FS Gedye, was also with the GVA at this time with the ammunition column, but, strangely, does not mention it directly in any of his diaries or later writings. There was a third Gedye brother in uniform, the eldest, George, who served as an infantry officer with the Gloucestershire Regiment. George was wounded at some point during the summer of 1916, but again, the youngest Gedye fails to mention this fact at all. George Gedye would go on to serve in British Military Intelligence, and become a journalist based in eastern Europe between the wars. He served with SOE (Special Operations Executive) during the Second World War.

The 48th Division moved about two miles from the Ancre Valley north westwards. The artillery of the GVA went to Mesnil Chateau on 29th August. Mesnil Chateau stands at the top of the hill overlooking the Ancre Valley north of Aveluy Wood (Bois d'Aveluy) facing eastwards across the valley to Thiepval Chateau, the scene of possibly the most intense and continuous fighting of the battle. The guns were emplaced in the grounds of Mesnil Chateau on the reverse slope, out of sight of the Germans across the Ancre Valley.

Though out of direct observation by the Germans, the village and chateau were the subject of bombardment. Lieutenant FS Gedye describes the scene:

*"Three or four days after I got down, the battery moved to Mesnil and I rode over to see how the guns and ammunition were to be brought up. Mesnil is one of the most remarkable standing [no, tottering is the better word] ruins I've seen.*

## The Bristol Gunners

*It stands on the side of a hill, which overlooks the Ancre and Thiepval wood. The village is not on the Bosche side of the hill, although the eastern end is quite visible to them - in fact; Lane fired for the night corrector one night and observed from the chateau "windows."*

*As usual, the church has suffered most considering its strength, but there isn't a building that would stand against anything. It is still shelled daily and is not a nice place to get six - horse teams through. It took our drivers all their time to steer round the shell holes that had fallen half way across the road.*

*I always went up when there were more than two wagons to see there were not two in the village at a time. I have seldom seen any place where everyone was so keen on getting away.*

*The guns were in the open in an orchard there, with a sandbag wall for protecting the detachments, and camouflaged over the top to conceal the gun from the air.*

*After being in action three days, they got a direct hit on "A" gun emplacement and messed the gun up thoroughly blew away the lower shield, splintered one wheel, chipped the slides and bulged the muzzle. Fortunately, the detachment were not there at the time, but next day we had three casualties, one being my senior No. 1 Sergt. Derrick, and another who was very badly hit was Shapland who used to be QMS to the 3$^{rd}$ line.*

*They used to have a lot of trouble through the Bosche's love of gas shells, although fortunately, we did not suffer any casualties through this."*

Mesnil was an unhealthy place to be, though that could have been said of almost any position within two miles of the enemy at that time. Sergeant Derrick and Sergeant Shapland survived their injuries, but Shapland was to die a year later in the fighting around Ypres in the Battle of Passchendaele.

The GVA were in action here throughout September in support of a number of other divisions who were gradually reducing the German positions on and around Thiepval Ridge across the valley. Though not

stated in the diaries, there is an interesting development in what is called in military terms '3C', or Command, Control, & Communication.

At the beginning of the war each battery was required to take instructions (Commands) from one supported battalion of infantry (or regiment of cavalry). Switching priorities for targets was decided by the battalion commander and communicated to the guns by the BC. There was little system for batteries to be able to switch command during a battle as communications were not capable of enabling this, though undoubtedly ad hoc methods were used from time to time, such as co-locating OPs so that BCs could speak to each other and agree to share targets. Batteries generally fired only in support of their own infantry brigade, and within their own divisional boundaries.

By this stage of the war, two years in, it was recognised that to win battles, especially in the attack, artillery fire needed to be concentrated when and where it could have its maximum effect. Systems started being developed to ensure higher levels of co-ordination between artillery brigades and divisions.

During their time at Mesnil Chateau, the GVA mostly fired in support of other divisions in their attacks around Thiepval, and this could only have been possible with improved 3C methods, especially better Communications.

At this time battlefield communications relied heavily on traditional methods. Field telephones relied on line (telephone cable), but this was vulnerable to damage by enemy fire or own troops movements. Carrier pigeons were used, but obviously, these were vulnerable to shot and shell, and only worked in one direction. Runners – specially nominated soldiers whose task was to literally 'run' between forward troops and headquarters to physically carry written messages. Runners had probably the highest casualty rate in the war as they had to traverse the battlefield more often than other soldiers did. Flags and other signalling devices could be used to indicate where troops had reached during an attack. Heliographs were used, but were not effective at night or in smoke and fog. The Royal Flying Corps could observe and report back, but not immediately, as they have to either fly back and drop messages, or land to report. In many cases, poor communications led to missed opportunities and complete ignorance of the situation. Many brains were

## The Bristol Gunners

working on how to improve communication methods to increase the effectiveness of officers' ability to control the battle.

One of these improved methods was wireless. In 1901 Guglielmo Marconi had successfully proved that wireless communication over long distance was possible. By 1916, though the equipment necessary for wireless communication had been improved, it was still far from compact enough to be portable on the battlefield. The military did use wireless communication, notably during the siege of Kut in Mesopotamia in early 1916. General Townshend used wireless communication to exchange messages with his commander's headquarters throughout the siege and eventual surrender.

In July 1916, the newly arrived Australian 1st Division had been tasked with the capture of Pozieres. During this battle, wireless was used for the first time in the field during the attack. Wireless equipment was carried forward as part of the attack and used to send messages back regarding progress. While results were not wholly positive, it was a first step towards better equipment and methods. By the end of the war, wireless was much more widely deployed in the field, some sets even being small enough to be used in aircraft. In 1917, wireless was used in tanks, not so much for them to 'talk' to each other tactically, but rather to make wireless available on the battlefield so that local commanders and runners had somewhere close to the fighting to be able to take messages and transmit them back to the rear.

On September 15th the British used tanks for the first time in battle, in the attack on the villages of Flers and Courcelette. The GVA were not present at this battle. However, it is notable in that it demonstrated yet another instance of innovation and application of new technologies by the British.

The GVA were in support when the Thiepval Ridge was captured by the British at the end of September. During this period the Germans were suffering from a shortage of fresh troops and equipment, though were still capable of stiff resistance and the ability to inflict losses. Lieutenant FS Gedye on an incident on 28th September:

> *"Rumours of a move forward to night reached the wagon line and I rode up with Ellerton to see what orders were issued, and was told to go forward at dawn, one section to remain in action, until the other is*

*registered in the new position. This means an early morning, as we shall have to leave the wagon lines at 5.15 in pitch dark*

*We lost our group commander today Col West; he had just left Todd at the position and ran towards his horses, which were waiting on the Pozieres road. The Bosche was putting 5.9s on the road a few hundred yards nearer Pozieres and just as the Colonel got to his horse, they started to lengthen and before he had gone far down the road, a shell burst close to him, killing him and both horses and seriously wounding his groom.*

*He was a most gallant man; at times he took what seemed greater risks than he should take. He would go anywhere and expected everyone under him to do the same.*

*At 9.30 I went up to group to arrange for a trench bridge for the following morning and found everything cancelled, at any rate for the present. What a life.*

*The major had a remarkable escape yesterday. He went up with Constantine to the Zollern redoubt, which had been captured in Tuesday's advance, and on the way up got mixed up with a Little Willie shrapnel burst and felt a sudden blow in the ribs on his right side, he says he knew at once he was hit and undid his tunic to find, to his great mortification that there was no hole in his shirt! After a thorough examination, he discovered that the shrapnel bullet had gone into his breast pocket, smashed two pencils in half, passed through the corner of his leather cigarette case, torn the corners of about 20 leaves of his note book and then dropped peacefully to the bottom of his pocket. So the net result is a big bruise and a most priceless collection of souvenirs."*

At the end of September the GVA pulled out from Mesnil and into rest again. One aspect that developed during the war was that when artillery units were relieved by another, the usual system was to exchange guns to minimise the effort needed to move one set out of their pits and insert another set. It also meant that the guns were 'on call' throughout the relief, just exchanging crews. This caused a number of issues. The guns in the position had usually been firing and needed maintenance to keep them efficient. In good batteries, the crews took great pride in the condition of their guns, and often when relieving another battery felt that the guns needed more than a reasonable effort to bring them back up to

## The Bristol Gunners

'scratch.' The other result was that, apparently, under this system, many guns probably never went into action, being purely dragged from one position to another only to be exchanged again. Lieutenant FS Gedye:

*"In the afternoon I rode over with the Major to see about taking over guns from the other division as we are handing over ours to the incoming battery.*

*The swapping of guns is a familiar game to us all now.*

*Until we left Sailly to come down to the war, the only change the Brigade had made was from 15 pounders to 18 pounders, but we handed over ours then to the relieving division. We brought their guns down to Bouzincourt and handed them over to the battery we relieved. And so it has gone on ever since. Practically every time we move, unless it is to advance our position, we hand over. It was pretty rotten luck for our artificer [Betty] when went back to St Ouen, the guns we took over had come from Mametz wood and needed the hell of a lot of overhauling and after 10 days solid work on them, we trundled them back to boozy and once more they changed hands.*

*There must be quite a large number of guns whose share in the G.P. [great push] is to be lugged along the roads of France and taken to and from rest camps"*

During this move Lieutenant FS Gedye had the opportunity to visit his brother Len's grave at Aveluy, and here he reflects:

*"Tonight, just as it was getting dark, I went over to see the cemetery via crucifix corner and all the past few weeks came vividly before me. There were some more of our Brigade buried there since my last visit.*

*First, as I walked along the path, I passed Sergeant Price's grave, he was the 2$^{nd}$ battery N.C.O. who was killed in the earlier explosion of August 23$^{rd.}$ Next but one to Len lies poor old Bill Wyley, and just behind him, Geoffrey Browne. Two great pals who crossed over together. Close to Browne's grave, Stone is resting. I felt, as I stood there, that although tomorrow takes us away to some other district, we are leaving a big part of the spirit of the old original 1$^{st}$ Gloucester Brigade behind us.*

## The Bristol Gunners

*Len, Browne and Stone were Territorials of the best and keenest type - so many new officers and men are with the first line now who know nothing of all that the original Brigade did in peace time that fitted it to become one of the best shooting brigades out here. I feel that, although to my constant regret, I never went through the ranks in peace time, I know something of the splendid keenness they all put into it, and although enthusiasm takes, sometimes, a bit of working up out here, it is only for the battery to know they have some special job given to them in order to have it done well.*

*And the old spirit is on top in a minute. And now we have to move to action and leave behind us three of the best of those who knew, worked for, and made the Brigade the splendid unit it has proved itself to be. I am sure the officers will never forget Aveluy and what it means to us all."*

Lieutenant F S Gedye had joined the brigade from the University OTC where he had started with the rank of officer cadet. His older brother, Len (Lieutenant E L Gedye) had joined the GVA as a Gunner in 1912 and had therefore spent some time 'in the ranks' learning some basic gunner skills and some understanding of what is possible. Most Regular Army officers had not spent time in the ranks, joining their regiments directly as commissioned officers. The family spirit of Territorial units is largely derived from the fact that nearly everyone has the shared experience of having started their military life in the most junior ranks and the understanding that this can bring.

F S Gedye also comments that the brigade now had a significant proportion of its strength made up of men who had not been Territorials before the war. Some Territorials had not opted for foreign service, some new men had been recruited as early volunteers, some had come along from later recruitment phases form the brigade second and third lines, and, no doubt, some men had been posted in from other batteries and brigades during the re-organisation of early 1916. Some also had been sent to the brigade to replace casualties, both deaths and injuries. During the Battle of the Somme (June to November 1916) 240 Brigade lost some five officers and six other ranks killed. Bristol recruited men who served in 2nd and 3rd line units, and died elsewhere in the Royal Field Artillery amounted to two officers and fifteen other ranks during the battle.

The GVA trekked out of the line and through the town of Albert, forever linked with the British Army on the Somme. The cathedral in the town

### The Bristol Gunners

was adorned with a statue of the Virgin. During German bombardment the statue had been displaced and, though still on its plinth on the roof, was hanging at an angle, as if ready to fall. The myth grew up that if the 'Virgin and child' were to fall the town would also fall – to the Germans. This myth held such sway that the Royal Engineers were tasked with shoring up the statue to prevent it falling. The statue did in fact fall, in 1918, when the Germans captured the town during the 'Kaiserschlacht offensive' (Kaiser's battle – Kaiser Wilhelm took personal control of this attack).

Once again we rely on Lieutenant F S Gedye to describe the next phase:

*"Yesterday was one of the days it will be difficult to forget. It opened just as all the recent glorious days have-misty, with a promise of sun later. As I had hoped, the turn out was ripping. During our recent moves, every one had learnt the value of carrying a minimum of kit, and consequently the wagons looked very neatly packed. Harness, wagons, men and horses all looked clean and smart and the arrival of Peter [Lens charger, which the C.O. had allowed me to take over] very much all there, tossing his head and pawing the ground, white head rope and burnished bit just put the finishing touch to the picture. Major Fowler made very complimentary remarks to Major Todd as we marched out.*

*He was acting C.O. until the little man rejoined us here last night.*

*The battery was halted in the square at Albert to let a battalion of P.P.C.L.I.* (Princess Patricia's Canadian Light Infantry) *go by, headed by six pipers. They have one company of Canadian Japs who made a quaint contrast with the magnificent type of men the P.P.C.L.I. manage to keep up."*

The division moved back into its old area opposite Gommecourt arriving in the early days of October, and would spend over seven weeks in the area just to the north, near the village of Fonquevillers – nicknamed 'Funky Villas' by the British. This part of the front was much quieter now than the situation of July 1st. The British line had been thinned out, so that the 48th Division held a part of the line previously held by three divisions.

While in this position, each battery was increased to six guns (from the previous four). This needed some expansion of manpower and movement

of individuals and crews between batteries. The brigade found that the facilities that they had taken over were in some need of improvement, and spent much time and effort on doing this with a much improved flow of defence stores.

There was time to let off a little steam. It was announced that Major Chester Todd, BC A Battery, had been awarded a DSO (Distinguished Service Order medal) and a party was held to celebrate this:

*"Last night we heard that Major Todd has been awarded the D.S.O. We are all bucked that there is a decoration for an officer of "that Ack Battery" at last. This was the Colonel's remark at Doullens. When our mess is united and out for an evening's enjoyment, we can make as much noise as anyone out here and a great deal more then his Lordship appreciates. Corfield was with us, and his re-appearance that night was being celebrated in the usual way. He, Todd and Ridler were doubling us up with glorious yarns of the Crownhill and Broomfield days and after one particularly good roar, the C.O. who was "hosting" H.Q. Staff in the next room said "Hark – what a noise those fellows are making; Oh, of course it's that Ack Battery.*

*I don't know what he thought when; a few minutes later two of the H.Q. staff joined us - Len and McConnell, and the Doctor, the din then became really terrific. Corfield is a delightful man and kept the house in one continual roar."*

It was a quieter interlude in the war. While the battle continued further south around High Wood where the British were gradually rolling the Germans back toward Bapaume, the GVA spent their time looking out towards No-Man's Land, not seeing much, mainly due to mist, but also because the Germans were not doing much of a war-like nature either.

One way to overcome the autumn mists was to use observation balloons, which could rise above the mist. A basket below the balloon held two observers capable of communicating with the guns and controlling their fire. The balloons were part of the Royal Flying Corps (RFC). F S Gedye describes his impressions of them:

*"The Kite-Balloon section is going to register some points for us which we can't see - such a treat for them! It is a quaint branch of the service*

## The Bristol Gunners

*and one of the most delightfully mannered-people chiefly with the type of "K'nut" that Basil Hallam portrays.*

*Of course it's an amazingly comfy job, the luxury of kite-balloonists is amazing - her Majesty of Sheba would have stared some, I reckon, if she had seen anything like it in her day. Of course they are very much looked down on by the R.F.C. proper and they feel a bit neglected and consequently they love to be used by the gunners and get in to the limelight. Their keenness to observe for you is often pathetic in its intensity and if you want to go up in their gas bag they'll come down anytime and take you up. I haven't been up yet but I'm awfully keen to do so on a fine clear day."*

The Basil Hallam referred to was a music hall star who had joined the RFC and became a balloon observer. He created the character 'Gilbert the Filbert' in his music hall act, the K'Nut referred to above. He described himself as 'The Kernel of the Nuts.' Hallam died on 20th August 1916 during the Battle of the Somme, not by enemy action, but by accident. His balloon lost its moorings and started to drift towards the Germans. In attempting to bale out, he died when his parachute failed to open.

Balloons were hydrogen filled. Hydrogen is extremely flammable, and many other observers were killed when their balloons caught fire and they were not quick enough to jump out. Balloon observers were the only RFC soldiers supplied with parachutes – it was felt that if aeroplane crews had them it might encourage them to abandon their aeroplane too soon.

There was some shooting for the guns, but on a much smaller scale. F S Gedye:

*"Great sport in the O.P. this morning. As soon as the light is good in the morning, we fire on a datum point for the error of the day, this can be a distinct point in a trench or on a track. It is done to find the variation from the map range, the guns always shoot under map range unless there is a very strong wind blowing, but this drop varies with the temperature wind etc and it is necessary to find out how much it is each day.*

*When I arrived this morning, it was too hazy to get this accurately and I decided to wait, after about half an hour I saw water being chucked out*

## The Bristol Gunners

*of a trench in the front line [last night was a soaker] I gave "No 2 Action," plotted out the point on the map, gauged the drop and deflection, and fired. A lovely shot right on the parapet but about 30 to 50 yards on a flank. Immediately the baling ceased, but I made my correction and fired a couple more just to show my dislike.*

*There was no more baling on my field of vision again, it is a topping sensation after an early rise to harass the Hun and know you are annoying him."*

Another change to gunnery that was beginning to appear in the Royal Artillery, and which would continue throughout the rest of the war, was that it was becoming more technical. It had been realised that surprise was important. As with the man baling out water from his trench, if you did not hit the target with your first round, then men had the time and opportunity to take evasive action. Getting a first round hit was important. Also, if preparing for an attack, adjusting fire gave away how many guns there were, where they were, and what the objective was. This allowed the enemy to assess our intentions and interfere with our plans by counter bombarding our batteries before or during action.

It was realised that it was important to have more information about how artillery fire can be more accurately predicted, that is, firing data to be calculated rather than relying on firing adjusting rounds.

Strangely, all the techniques required to do this were available well before the war started, but were not used by Field and Horse artillery. The Royal Garrison Artillery manning our coastal guns knew all about predicted fire. It was a standard part of their craft, but 'field' gunners were loath to take advice from, or learn from, what they regarded as a more junior part of the artillery.

However, a number of innovators were abroad within the ranks of the field artillery. The most prominent was Herbert Uniacke, a Regular Army officer, who rose eventually to be Lieutenant General. He advocated better methods and systems for 3C, and the use of calculation to enable predicted fire to become more accurate. These calculations used survey, meteorological data (temperature, air density, wind speed and direction, barometric pressure), barrel wear, shell weight (shells do vary by small amounts), and propellant temperatures. With the correct data, the first round fired could be placed with more accuracy and certainty.

### The Bristol Gunners

As the technique of accurate predicted fire improved, it enabled the British to bring in more guns prior to an attack and protect them from CB by not using them until they could deliver an accurate 'hurricane' bombardment. This allowed the infantry to carry out a 'surprise' attack, preventing the Germans from knowing what was intended and taking them off guard and therefore making them more vulnerable.

This ability to use predicted fire, plus increasing numbers of guns and ammunition resulted in the British Artillery becoming the most effective and feared part of the British Army.

Though the Gommecourt part of the front was generally quiet, there were occasional busier times. F S Gedye describes one:

*"The only event that really interested us yesterday was the shelling of our position by the Hun. About 12, a Hun plane came over and observed the effect of about a dozen shrapnel bursts, and after a short interval, they started throwing over at about 30 seconds interval, 4.2s and towards the end, in a continual steam at 10 seconds interval. Fortunately, although their range was good, they all fell to a flank, the nearest being 50 yards from the officer's mess. I was at the O.P. at the time, and was trying to spot the batteries firing; one 4.2 in and another 5.9 in."*

Another he describes could be described as an 'own goal':

*"On November the 5th the battery held a most wonderful orgy of hate, at the beginning of the week the Major had said we must have a few rounds spare to boost off on the 5th and told us to enter in the daily situation reports and ammunition returns a few more rounds than we had actually fired. This was done only too well, for on the morning of the 5th we counted our ammunition and found we had 250 rounds to spare.*

*It was made the occasion of the battery dinner.*

*W.A. Todd who was coming up to the gun-line came up with a joint of pork and sundry other delicacies and Ridler, who was to replace him at the wagon lines stayed up for the night and went down next morning.*

*About 9.15 p.m. when our meal was ended, we all padded across to the battery in very great spirits and Todd procured a megaphone and gave "Battery Action." We had at this time a wonderful list of targets*

*numbered from A to M which covered all the principal roads, farms, and tracks in our zone. He had selected a few of the best - Essarts village, Rettemoy farm etc, and proceeded to give a wonderful half hour of rapid fire on successive targets - wonderfully varied fire, rounds of battery fire 1 second, battery salvoes six rounds gunfire etc. Amidst the greatest delight and enthusiasm, he then lined the detachments up and told them what the whole show was, dismissed them and so ended our most successful Guy Fawkes Day.*

*The only mistake we made was that our position was plainly visible from the tops of trees in Essarts village and the Hun, being rather rattled at having such obvious hatred shown him without rhyme or reason on a quiet night, must have clambered into his look-outs and taken most damnably accurate bearings on the flashes of our guns with unpleasant results that are detailed elsewhere.*

*There is no note of this "Do" in my diary but the incident can be vouched for as the whole show was quite unforgettable and ranks with our greatest battery achievements. It was probably omitted purposely, as there would have been a most unholy strafe if it had ever come to the ears of the higher command."*

The Germans, having located the battery by flash spotting, had proceeded to shell the position on and off for three days and nights. Fortunately no casualties were apparently caused by the German retaliation, but a lesson had been learned – do not act alone, do it in company.

F S Gedye was returning to his battery position a few days later when he narrowly escaped joining the role of honour:

*"The Hun is a rotten beast and with no sense of humour. On Monday when I got back from Col. Cossart's lecture at Souastre, the Hun was putting Time - HE at long intervals over the battery position so I decided to get in between a couple of bursts but just as I got there, they increased the rate of fire and I first flatted myself against a pile of sandbags, then on to No 4 pit and finally to our dug out, but found everyone had cleared out earlier. I was alone on the position with the exception of a couple sheep, which the Brigade has, bought with the absurd idea of fattening up for Christmas. As we have the richest pasture round our position, we have been appointed shepherds. With singularly tactless and thoughtless action, however, we have appointed as chief shepherd, one Blackmore*

### The Bristol Gunners

who is in civvy life a butcher, and the first touch of his professional and appraising hand on their backs must have put them into a permanent state of slaughter - shock for although they consumed quantities of grass they remain lean.

To return to the affair of the moment, as it seemed to be pretty harmless stuff, I decided to wait and do a bunk if it got hotter. It stopped after a bit and in about 10 minutes, the others returned and the water cart rolled up. They hadn't been back 5 minutes when we heard the well known whistle of a distant 5.9 shell and a couple of seconds later the first one arrived, not 10 yards from the team and yet the horses barely looked round. [The water cart horses were my pride and joy; they were attached to "B" sub and were a truly grand pair of bays]

We sent the team off at once and before they had moved a dozen yards another arrived. As they were falling close to the officers' mess and dug out, we decided to leg it and did so with more speed then grace, throwing ourselves flat every time a fresh one came over. Splinters and lumps of earth were whizzing all round us and we were really lucky to get off so lightly. We watched the show from about 500 yards away, sitting on an old plough in the moonlight. They finished soon after six and we were glad to get something to eat about eight. They had the range nicely and had popped plenty round the position, doing particularly well on No 5., scoring a bull on the right front of the pit and chipping the range drum and telescope."

Another German bombardment two days later:

"Yesterday was quite quiet but today when I got back about 4.30 I found they'd been through it thoroughly since about 11.30. I went round with Lane to see the wreckage. First, the cookhouse which was the scene of our only fatality where two kittens were killed and the dinner distributed over the surrounding countryside. Then I visited the star turn No 5 gun, a shell had pitched right under it and had blown the whole gun right over so the muzzle was pointing towards the pit - both wheels were blown off it and the shield was in fragments, some of them 50 yards away. The only articles serviceable from the whole gun were two spanners, a fuse key, and an oilcan.

The "sleeping" position to which everyone retired when they started shelling also more or less caught it in the neck but, luckily for the men

*inside, didn't get a direct hit, although there were several holes within ten yards of the dug outs."*

So, though the war was largely being fought elsewhere, Fonquevillers was still a dangerous position. It was not even totally safe during the night time:

*"....it was a wonderful light moonlight night and about 7.30, just as the last ammunition wagon was being filled we heard an aeroplane overhead and it was such an exceptional night and the plane was so low that I was able to see it. I didn't think it could be anything but English until it got over Fonquevillers and dropped two lights - that absolutely put the wind up me and I got the wagons away as quickly as possible nothing happened but it was a suspicious bit of work."*

The brigade was in action on the morning of 19th November in support of 63rd (Royal Naval) Division in its successful attack on Beaumont Hamel, during which Bernard Freyberg won his Victoria Cross. Freyberg was a New Zealander who would later be Governor General of New Zealand, and was one of the most decorated men of the First World War:

*"It was very cold there and there was a thick and dripping fog. We shook our heads over the job and predicted muck – up in such mist. We fired merrily on their 1st line lifting to the 2nd and 3rd, after which we sniped any likely points of roads etc down which they might send reinforcements. It turned out afterwards that it was a huge success on the right – the centre about Serre did not get their objectives and that the left had got their objectives but owing to the lack of support on their right, had to give way to the counter attack."*

In the last week of November the brigade were relieved and trekked down through Albert to take up positions in the area of High Wood, east of the Albert – Bapaume road, where the British were slowly pushing towards Bapaume.

As well as improving our abilities at predicted fire, other improvements were being developed in identifying enemy targets. The Germans had used 'flash spotting' to identify the GVA on their Guy Fawkes' night celebrations, and by triangulating bearings had been able to retaliate, discomforting the gunners. The British were also honing their skills at this technique, and developed 'sound ranging.' In this technique, it was

not necessary to see a gun being fired, but by careful use of sound directional equipment from two or more locations the target could be triangulated with some accuracy and the gun be counter bombarded. By the war's end the British would become very good at these techniques and used them to suppress enemy artillery. The brigade War History records:

*"Flash-spotting was a great occupation for the night OP party and taking bearings on to an active battery would help to fill in the sometimes interminable night hours of watching."*

The ground and weather conditions in November 1916 in the Somme battle area were terrible. There had been much rain, and autumn fog, and as the British were now operating on the former battlefield the ground had been shelled into a quagmire. Any kind of movement was difficult, and eventually the attacks would peter out, both due to these difficulties and the fact that the British had reached the final high ground in front of Bapaume, the so called Butte de Warlencourt. From here they could prevent the Germans having a dominant view into our rear, while putting their transport hub in Bapaume under threat from our positions.

Lieutenant FS Gedye describes something of the results of the deteriorating conditions:

*"The battery had an appalling time at High Wood and in the neighbourhood of the Butte de Warlencourt and the O.P.s in Rutherford Avenue and Le Sars and an organized strafe known as little wood concentration have been immortalised in those classical examples of W.A. Todd's delicate art of embroidery.*

*These tapestries are verbal goblins in the mastery of their execution and mass of detail.*

*The life of the horse in those winter months reached the depths of misery. The ground was so appalling, that ammunition wagons could not be pulled over it and all ammunition had to be taken by packhorse and mules. The sight of these unfortunates with the mud of days caked in hard lumps on their coats and long chunks on their tails was most pathetic. It was too hard and clayey to be removed easily and washing, the only real way was prohibited and of course dangerous to the health of the animal under those conditions.*

The Bristol Gunners

*So life dragged muddily on until the Brigade came out of action at the end of December."*

Embroidery was a popular pastime of soldiers in the brigade, and it seems from the comments in the previous section that Lieutenant WA Todd was very good at it.

1916 had been a year of transitions. The British started the year as the minor party on the allies side, but ended the year having helped halt the German attack on Verdun, developed their methods and materiel so that they were definitely on the up. The Germans had started the year hoping to bleed the French Army white and knock them out of the war. However, they had been forced call a halt to their attacks and respond to a series of serious blows from the British, and had started to realise and accept that they were not going to win. The French had started the year under severe pressure at Verdun, and ended the year still in the fight, yet with much of the enthusiasm having gone out of their army.

The year end found the GVA coming out of action to rest at Corbie, where they would spend a month out of the line. 1917 was to bring more action, and more loss.

**GVA signallers laying telephone line. Such men had a dangerous and difficult job keeping communications working under fire.**

The Bristol Gunners

# Chapter 5  1917, A Year of Changes

On being withdrawn from the front around the Butte de Warlencourt, and the misery of High Wood the GVA went with the 48th Division for a month at Behancourt where they could sort themselves out and bring their kit back up to scratch. The artillery were lucky, Behancourt was behind the old British lines and in relatively good shape. Much of the rest of the 48th Division were quartered in sections of the battle area that had been shelled and fought over throughout 1916 and conditions there were very poor. The battlefield had not yet been fully cleared of debris and bodies, so that for most of the infantry life was a struggle.

In the first week of February, the division moved further south, to Corbie, a town on the Somme River a few miles from the major rail centre of Amiens. This was the main logistical centre for the British Army during the Somme battle, and a number of training centres and other military establishments were in that area.

Lieutenant FS Gedye remembers his time there in billets:

*"We had an absolute joy-week there, the best billet we ever had, very little work and a huge variety of food [daily we used to go down to select the very best and fattest oysters!]*

*It was frightfully cold there but the house was warmed with hot pipes and fires so we were in real clover. I find that my diary omits the mention of one person who deserves to be immortalised and alas, I have forgotten her name! She was dearest of Irish nuns belonging to a Belgian nursing sisterhood and was nursing our billetee - a retired coal merchant. She mothered us all and in particular spent much time in providing me with every sort of cure for a nasty 'acking cough that was my legacy from the 'Flu.*

*Every night, she arrived with hot milk and kirsch, which I had to take and when we left, she begged me to take it always and gave my batman many instructions as to how to look after me. After we were in action, I received from her a letter full of sound but unpractical advice and a box of special lozenges. [Bless her very dear old heart]"*

All the quotations in this chapter are from the personal diaries of Lieutenant FS Gedye, except where noted.

The lessons learned from the previous six months' fighting had been used to develop new ideas and methods that needed to be passed on to the formations of the British Army. Many officers from the division spent time at these training establishments, including some from the GVA.

As far as the artillery was concerned, the training increasingly focussed on standardising methods and drills across the whole army. Gone were the days when individual batteries could do things their own way, officers were now expected to follow 'SOPs' (Standard Operating Procedures). The flow of ammunition was improving, greater quantities being produced, and fuses were becoming more reliable. During the year the 106 graze fuse would be introduced. This fuse was an improvement in that it meant that the shell would explode on the surface even in mud, better for wire cutting and against troops in the open, rather than bury itself deep in soft mud or soil before exploding. New types of shell, and a changing mix of shell types, would be introduced. New shells included types of gas shell, and smoke shells. Though the 18 Pounder had high explosive (HE) shells previously, the proportions of these being supplied increased.

Though artillery was still regarded as being secondary to the infantry, it was increasingly being seen as critical to success. The new fuses and shells allowed wider options to commanders, especially in the attack. HE shells with graze fuses could clear wire very quickly and permit surprise attacks, rather than give clear warning of our intentions by firing at wire for a week or more with shrapnel.

Counter battery (CB) fire was seen as more important also, both to destroy enemy artillery positions, or, to 'neutralise' them, that is stop them firing temporarily at a critical time. CB plans had to be a part of any successful attack, and equally important in diminishing the enemy's attack power. Counter Battery Staff Officers (CBSO) dedicated to co-ordinate and control CB plans for the division were appointed in each division. It was recognised that TF and New Army artillery units were every bit as efficient and reliable as Regular Army artillery. Divisional artillery was also reorganised, two mixed (field and howitzer) brigades per division, plus Army level field artillery brigades which could be concentrated and allocated to the section of the front most in need.

CB is only effective if you have known targets, that is, you know where the enemy has placed his guns and therefore where to shoot at them.

## The Bristol Gunners

Improved methods of identifying enemy batteries were helped by flash spotting and sound ranging, as well as by aerial survey and photography, both from balloons and aircraft. Air supremacy was hotly contested, and favoured each side from time to time, with rapid developments in technology and quantities of aircraft and capabilities. Though the Germans gained local air superiority from time to time, increasingly the air war was being dominated by the British and French.

Better survey methods, use of meteorological data, and increasing attention to other variables, such as shell weight and barrel wear would lead to a much better ability to fire accurately at 'predicted' targets, that is, those that have not been adjusted by fire. This so-called 'silent registration' would permit more tactical options to commanders. Guns could be brought up to the front and used to good effect without giving away their positions until necessary. This was especially valuable where surprise attacks were planned, to disguise our intentions, and protect our guns from German CB activity.

The early part of 1917 brought changes elsewhere than in Picardy.

The winter of 1916 to 1917 gave severe weather, cold and wet, the worst for many decades. The British blockade of Germany was effective and food was short for the German Army and civilian population. That winter was dubbed 'the Turnip Winter' in Germany. Food riots broke out in Berlin in April. Later in 1917 the German Navy (Kriegsmarine) would experience mutinies. The flow of munitions and other vital supplies was never enough. The Somme battle had severely damaged the German Army, and forced a change in German leadership. Erich von Falkenhayn had gone, to be replaced by Erich Ludendorff and Paul von Hindenburg. They now controlled the German war effort more pragmatically, but made some decisions that turned out to work against German interests. They scoured the Fatherland for more manpower and planned to convert more of the economy to war production.

They declared unrestricted submarine warfare in January, which meant that any ship, even neutrals, sailing to or from Britain or France would be a 'legitimate target.' This would lead to the sinking of American ships, which in turn would lead to the USA declaring war on Germany in April 1917, a mistake that increased the threat significantly rather than diminishing it. The American Army mobilised and the first division took its place in the line before the end of the year.

### The Bristol Gunners

The German losses in 1916, notably at the hands of the British, but also at their failed attack at Verdun, meant that the Germans had to accept that they were in a war of attrition, which they could not win. Hindenburg and Ludendorff (they were joint leaders) decided to shorten their Western Front by some 50 kilometres and enable them to transfer 13 divisions to the eastern front. In great secrecy, they constructed a new, straighter, defensive line up to 40 kilometres to the rear, on better ground, and defended on a more economical basis. More concrete, deeper lines of defence, and fewer men in forward trenches. This was to be true 'defence in depth', and they thought that it was impregnable. They called it 'The Hindenburg Line.'

Russia was in chaos. The army had not performed well, largely due to the tribal nature of command – for example the artillery refused to take orders from the infantry, and often seemed to be fighting different battles altogether. Russian industry could not supply the army effectively, nor could the allies, especially due to the failed operations in Gallipoli (the 'logic' for which was to open a supply route to the Crimea). In February, the Tsar abdicated and a period of confused government ensued. Eventually, in late 1917, the Russians would exit the war as a belligerent nation, allowing the Germans to transfer most of their forces from east to west.

The Italians and the Austrians continued to batter each other on the northeastern Italian border. Both these countries had entered the war totally unprepared for a long conflict and neither had the industrial capacity to sustain their efforts. Politically also, they were both confused and irresolute, though the Austro-Hungarian empire was in decline, while the Italian state was in the ascendant. Much would happen in the Italian theatre of war that would impinge on British and French military planning.

Therefore, while the 48th Division, and the GVA, were recovering near Amiens, actions and decisions were being taken in many places that would affect them.

In order to help the French Army recover from the effects of Verdun and prepare an attack further east on the Aisne the British took over some of the French positions south of the Somme.

## The Bristol Gunners

In this part of the battle front, the attacks of early July 1916 had gone well. The French had been able to advance pretty much to plan, and had pushed the Germans back some 10 kilometres on the south bank, to a position opposite the town of Peronne. In early February, 48th Division trekked up river from Amiens to relieve the French in this area, on the hill above the small village of Biaches.

Once again, the differences between the British and French armies were noted by FS Gedye:

*"The roads were packed with transport of all sorts but mainly English. Just outside one small village we halted to let two battalions of Les Poilus [Hairy Ones] through. They had just come from the trenches and although they were, as usual grubby and somewhat unshaven, they marched well and looked a fine lot.*

*The change from Khaki may have made the difference, the Poilu's uniform of blue is certainly very effective and becoming [a strange word in the third year of war] and with the French pattern helmet was a relief after our drab kit. All the same, when Bosche shrapnel is about I wouldn't change my headgear for French or Bosche. The brim alone gives you the power of control over your lower limbs.*

*The interest on both sides was intense but where as we had seen "Froggies" before, they evidently had never seen an English battery on the road.*

*The strangest sight of all is the French transport. I have described before the ragtime appearance of the tail end of our column with our unauthorised transport, well it pales into insignificance beside the French transport. To begin with harness and vehicles are never clean - yet their results are wonderful."*

The positions they were taking over had been occupied by the French since the previous July, and were in range of the German artillery behind Peronne. The Germans had fortified the area before the French had captured it, so that many deep well constructed dugouts were available, though exposed to view by the Germans and therefore liable to well aimed shellfire. On arrival, they were to notice this immediately, especially as the Germans now tended to use harassing fire with a mix of shell types (HE, shrapnel, and gas):

## The Bristol Gunners

The German losses in 1916, notably at the hands of the British, but also at their failed attack at Verdun, meant that the Germans had to accept that they were in a war of attrition, which they could not win. Hindenburg and Ludendorff (they were joint leaders) decided to shorten their Western Front by some 50 kilometres and enable them to transfer 13 divisions to the eastern front. In great secrecy, they constructed a new, straighter, defensive line up to 40 kilometres to the rear, on better ground, and defended on a more economical basis. More concrete, deeper lines of defence, and fewer men in forward trenches. This was to be true 'defence in depth', and they thought that it was impregnable. They called it 'The Hindenburg Line.'

Russia was in chaos. The army had not performed well, largely due to the tribal nature of command – for example the artillery refused to take orders from the infantry, and often seemed to be fighting different battles altogether. Russian industry could not supply the army effectively, nor could the allies, especially due to the failed operations in Gallipoli (the 'logic' for which was to open a supply route to the Crimea). In February, the Tsar abdicated and a period of confused government ensued. Eventually, in late 1917, the Russians would exit the war as a belligerent nation, allowing the Germans to transfer most of their forces from east to west.

The Italians and the Austrians continued to batter each other on the northeastern Italian border. Both these countries had entered the war totally unprepared for a long conflict and neither had the industrial capacity to sustain their efforts. Politically also, they were both confused and irresolute, though the Austro-Hungarian empire was in decline, while the Italian state was in the ascendant. Much would happen in the Italian theatre of war that would impinge on British and French military planning.

Therefore, while the 48$^{th}$ Division, and the GVA, were recovering near Amiens, actions and decisions were being taken in many places that would affect them.

In order to help the French Army recover from the effects of Verdun and prepare an attack further east on the Aisne the British took over some of the French positions south of the Somme.

## The Bristol Gunners

In this part of the battle front, the attacks of early July 1916 had gone well. The French had been able to advance pretty much to plan, and had pushed the Germans back some 10 kilometres on the south bank, to a position opposite the town of Peronne. In early February, 48th Division trekked up river from Amiens to relieve the French in this area, on the hill above the small village of Biaches.

Once again, the differences between the British and French armies were noted by FS Gedye:

*"The roads were packed with transport of all sorts but mainly English. Just outside one small village we halted to let two battalions of Les Poilus [Hairy Ones] through. They had just come from the trenches and although they were, as usual grubby and somewhat unshaven, they marched well and looked a fine lot.*

*The change from Khaki may have made the difference, the Poilu's uniform of blue is certainly very effective and becoming [a strange word in the third year of war] and with the French pattern helmet was a relief after our drab kit. All the same, when Bosche shrapnel is about I wouldn't change my headgear for French or Bosche. The brim alone gives you the power of control over your lower limbs.*

*The interest on both sides was intense but where as we had seen "Froggies" before, they evidently had never seen an English battery on the road.*

*The strangest sight of all is the French transport. I have described before the ragtime appearance of the tail end of our column with our unauthorised transport, well it pales into insignificance beside the French transport. To begin with harness and vehicles are never clean - yet their results are wonderful."*

The positions they were taking over had been occupied by the French since the previous July, and were in range of the German artillery behind Peronne. The Germans had fortified the area before the French had captured it, so that many deep well constructed dugouts were available, though exposed to view by the Germans and therefore liable to well aimed shellfire. On arrival, they were to notice this immediately, especially as the Germans now tended to use harassing fire with a mix of shell types (HE, shrapnel, and gas):

## The Bristol Gunners

*"I set off at 4.30 p.m. the next afternoon with the right half of the battery. Just before we passed through Herbicourt, we all felt a slight smarting in the eyes but I could smell nothing and put in down to the wind, which was bitter.*

*However, once past Herbicourt on the way to Flaucourt, which was practically my destination, there was no question about it - lachrymatory gas [tear gas] was strong and we began to weep a bit.*

*The road was being shelled at fairly long intervals with this gas muck so I opened out the column and halted on the peacetime portion. We had met several drivers who had been sent back without their vehicles who told me that the battery positions were being shelled "something crool" with lachrymatory, so I decided to leave the column in charge of the senior sergeant and wander on with my guide to see Lane. The dugout was in a sunken road and the gas was very thick there so I outed my helmet* (gas mask).

*I found Lane and Ridler and the French Lieut, sitting in the dugout crying quietly and cursing softly. The battery was in action on barrage lines although they didn't know whether the Bosche were raiding us or only bombarding our trenches.*

*I arranged with Lane to send back when it was possible for my column to come up and then went back to the road.*

*After about ¾ hour I got a message to come on, a sub-section at a time, at 15 minutes interval, we got in without trouble and things had become very quiet, but I hear a lot of the drivers were sick on the way back to the wagon line.*

*The dugout was rather gassy but we cleared it to a certain extent with some patent tack of the Frenchman's, which he lit in a tin and afterwards upset nearly burning down the dugout."*

The weather when the division arrived was cold, and would remain so for some weeks. This was a mixed blessing. While it could be uncomfortable while above ground or exposed to the elements, the deep dugouts were able to be warmed and provided a degree of comfort. The frozen ground and frosty weather (it remained below freezing for all of February) prevented any digging, or the disposal of dead horses.

## The Bristol Gunners

*"They cleared off early the next morning [the 6<sup>th</sup>] leaving us a bon supply of fuel, huge numbers of dead horses lining the road and a fair number of smashed wagons.*

*The horses looked most unattractive by day. There's poor old Horace, close to a gun pit who still wears his harness. He has been there so long that he is now almost part of the scenery. One of the first jobs when he thaws will be to give him a decent chlorinated burial, or at any rate a little overhead cover."*

During the handover from the French, there was some discussion on the relative merits of British and French equipment and tactics:

*"Owing to the gas, the French had not fetched their guns away during the night and we had to turn one of them out of its emplacement for Lane to register our guns.*

*The French Lieutenant was loath to shift it but finally gave way and put it in action in the middle of the road.*

*We have rather lost our admiration for the famous French 75's while we have been taking over. Bar speed, they have nothing to boast of over the 18 pounder.*

*To begin with, the sous-officer told us they never fire on the Bosche front line and their S.O.S. lines were between the first and second lines. [This is possibly an unfair and ignorant comment] we realised afterwards that the French were miles ahead of us in the use of machine guns for a protective barrage in No Man's Land and used their field guns entirely for putting down a concentrated barrage to prevent the bringing up of reserves.*

*When you contrast that with our barrage which is placed across No Man's Land - obviously the place where it is needed and realise that they won't trust either their guns or themselves to shoot within 200 yards of their own lines, I reckon out little toy is one up. [Oh Ignorance, Oh Bliss!]*

*Their star line is speed and quantity. They fire an enormous amount of ammunition. When lane went up to the O.P. the sous officer showed him their barrage lines by boosting off about 60 rounds where two or at best six, would have been ample."*

## The Bristol Gunners

Due to the rapid advance by the French in July, the villages behind the position had not been as badly smashed about as the villages further north:

*"One of the first things that impresses you here is that the French, at any rate round here, have no idea of what the Somme battle really was. Herbicourt and Flaucourt still have many walls left standing and are still unmistakably villages.*

*If you think of them in comparison with La Boiselle, Pozieres and Fricourt or Contalmaison, it is absolutely obvious that the struggles and losses that every inch there cost us is a thing unknown to the French except perhaps at Verdun. They have French graves within 800 yards of our present line of men who fell on July 9/15 at that time we were still fighting on the outskirts of villages that were originally in our front line, or close to it. The French told us that for two miles they marched with slung rifles apparently the Bosche hadn't the slightest idea that the French were going to push and it took them by surprise. What an advance it would have been if we had the same conditions!"*

During the Battle of the Somme the British were used to having superiority in aeroplanes, the Germans generally did not have freedom of movement over our lines whereas the RFC operated in force and had the advantage. South of the Somme, though, the Germans were in the majority:

*"The trenches on our zone have been very difficult to pick up in frosty weather but in the heat of the day today, there was a wonderful light and we were able to pick up something of the zone. Unfortunately, owing to hostile balloons and aircraft, we were able to do very little shooting, though.*

*Our R.F.C. and A.A. [Ack Ack] don't seem to have found their feet yet. We had Bosche planes over all day and very often not a round was fired at them, at one time Lane counted 17 over us."*

In the conditions as found in February 1917 movement around the position was difficult. Not only was there danger from observation and shellfire from the Germans, but the ground conditions also made any form of movement difficult:

## The Bristol Gunners

"Before I forget all about it I must try and write of our experience of the 19$^{th}$. Colonel Cossart, who is our Brigade Commander, rang up to say, in the morning that one section would move forward that night to a position suitable for wire cutting. The right section, little Stanley in charge, was detailed and went over in the afternoon to reconnoitre.

I was not favourably impressed by the position. It was only about 200 yards from the road but the place was simply pitted with shell holes, there was only one way in without danger of losing a vehicle and that was a winding way among the shell holes with nothing to mark it in the dark.

We set off, 2 guns and 4 wagons, about 9 p.m. from the battery and got to the point where we left the road for the position just before 10.30 the first gun was our worst trouble. As was almost inevitable, it got off the track and we had a two-hour struggle before we got it into position. There were enormous shell holes everywhere, and once or twice when the gun stuck in one the muzzle went right into the mud, 3 or 4 inches deep. However once "A" sub was in position, we got on better and the last wagon was clear just before 3.30 a.m.

I went out and gave the guns their line and after a cup of tea and rum, made by the cook, turned in for an hour's sleep or two.

Next morning there was a fine driving rain and we had the pleasant job of moving up the ammunition from the corner of the position, where we had dumped it on trench boards, into the gun pits over about 100 yards of filthy slush, a rotten job.

On the 20$^{th}$ the 4$^{th}$ Gloucesters did a raid and the section was in action. We heard later that the ground was so hopeless that they only got part way across. Just as well, I think for if they had got into the Bosche trench, they would certainly never have got out.

Yesterday, I went up to the O.P. and the transformation since the rain is tragic and terrific. The mud is every where a foot deep in Albert [the trench that leads to our O.P. in Iglau] and is caused by a wholesale collapse of the sides. In places where it is very liquid it isn't so bad but in the sticky places, where every move practically wrenches off your boot, it is pretty awful.

### The Bristol Gunners

*I got up to the O.P. in a horrible state of sweat after being 40 minutes over a ¼ hours journey, and then mainly owing to the excellence of my thigh-boots.*

*The heavies were shooting busily and did some nice work on a couple of trenches – clouds of chalk and muck flew up and there were some good bursts plunk in the trench."*

By this stage of the war the soldiers found it easy to identify who was shooting, and what was shooting. They had become very familiar with the signatures of each piece of equipment. The Brigade War History records:

*The next few weeks were comparatively uneventful and give an opportunity to pay tribute to one or two of our competitors. Of these, the four most regular features and "stars" were the "Minnie," the "Little Willie" the "4.2" and the "5.9."*

*The Minnenwerfer was, of course, confined-thank God-to the front line system. It could be seen-when the eyes were not blinded with terror - loping slowly over.*

*One of the battery telephonists, telling his mates about it in our earliest encounters with it, said "You can see the---coming after you. You've time to run round a couple of traverses and then you find he's had time to turn round and come after you."*

*To give any adequate idea of the explosion is impossible. Imagine a roar too loud to be true, a deafening, shattering, earth-tearing and head-splitting detonation that left every nerve rocking to and fro - then picture a section of trench that had been neatly revetted and sandbagged, with one or two men sitting and smoking on the fire-step a second before, turned into a hellish shambles, with everything torn, split and shattered, Multiply this many times over to compensate for the inadequacy of words-and there you have the "Minnie."*

*The "Little Willie," a 77 mm. field gun, was a foot-chiller - sudden, snappy, and apt to come just when it was most unreasonable that it should, and seldom alone.*

*Twins or quadruplets would crash on you as you were walking back to*

## The Bristol Gunners

*the battery thinking of a cheery evening with, for once, no night duty and feeling that life was, perhaps, not too bad.*

*In one second, "Little Willie" altered all that - it was.*

*You glanced round quickly to see that your telephonists were unhurt, the pace quickened, and the sun went in.*

*The 4.2 was, in the main, strangely lacking in character. Close acquaintance was nasty - very - but it somehow kept to the open spaces more than the others.*

*It was very popular with the Germans as a "woolly bear" - a high burst with thick yellowish or pinkish smoke, and a lateral burst of Time HE., instead of the nasty whipping forward cone of shrapnel. It was, of course, a swine - everything they hurled at us was that - but a lesser swine.*

*The 5.9 was different; very, very different. To every field-gunner, the 5.9 must have been a dominating life influence.*

*It was a howitzer, and the quality of the shells from a purely German standpoint was superb. Duds were practically unknown, but such was the "five-nine" character that even a dud was effective.*

*There was no feeling of rejoicing when one didn't burst. It was sinister; it rocked the ground and shook your dug-out, and you felt that the next would be doubly appalling.*

*They typified the methodical German character, there was no sudden salvo and then peace.*

*Suddenly, into the calm of a peaceful day, you would hear a long way off the distant "plop" of a gun firing - a matter of ten or fifteen seconds at the outside and a swish in the air that grew to a sudden, terrifying, rushing roar came straight out of the sky, above, down, down, down, definitely on to your head this time, anyway, and a column of earth would shoot into the air 50 yards ahead.*

## The Bristol Gunners

*A pause of perhaps a minute - or a lifetime - for correction, and again the distant "plop."*

*This time, the rush becomes louder, more sickeningly on top of you, and this time a bush would fly into the air 50 yards behind you.*

*A few more ranging rounds at irregular intervals, and then a steady regular battering at half-minute or minute intervals would stream over for perhaps an hour or more, until you felt that you could never again think for more than 30 seconds without having every idea blown out of your mind.*

*With every burst, if you were in the ordinary English type of dug-out, the candle would go out, your lungs would be deflated like a forcibly-closed bellows, and a dry, airless feeling filled the dug-out.*

*Nothing shattered life in the battery like the 5.9. It was regular, relentless, and the picture of it ever present. There were other "swine," such as the H-Vie (High Velocity), which chased you along a track.*

*First, you would find a spray of earth hurled over you, then you heard the explosion, then the rush of air of its approach and finally the sound of the gun firing.*

*It was extraordinary and really happened like that. Owing to its flat trajectory, it did little damage except by a direct hit. It was a gun that seemed to fire backwards through the looking-glass - a Cheshire Cat gun.*

*First, the grin, then the head, and finally the cat itself. It never left time for more than a muttered "Oh-my-God" - a quick-gasping "swine."*

*Then the 7.2-inch or biggest thing they had that was fired from a railway mounting - and probably recoiled from Belgium to Berlin and came back ten minutes later to fire one more-that rushed overhead, practically every time-again, thank God to bury itself in the heavies or a town behind, like 14 express trains rushing abreast through a tunnel-lifted the roof of your shack, O.P., or dug-out at least six inches as*

### The Bristol Gunners

*it passed, and let it sink back again with a sigh of relief as a large percentage of France dashed into the sky and turned somersaults.*

*So much for our competitors. We all cherished one ambition that was never fulfilled to about-turn a battery of "five-nine" and push its loathsome metal into the tender and retreating back portions of its owners."*

One of the most complicated phases in war is the withdrawal in contact, that is, to voluntarily disengage from the enemy and fall back to a more advantageous position. The Allies had done extremely well when they left Gallipoli, no casualties and the Turks not knowing they had departed.

The Germans also needed to match this feat when they decided to withdraw to the Hindenburg line. The Allies did not know that it was going to happen, and it was all but complete before the Allies realised that something had happened and the Germans had departed the scene.

In mid March, probing patrols started to find empty positions opposite our lines. On March 18th an attack was launched on a farm directly below the British positions:

*"Yesterday was a wonderful day for us all – no one had ever experienced anything like it before. Our attack met with no opposition at all - the party at la Maisonette captured 12 prisoners but beyond that, there have been practically no traces of Huns. Quite early in the morning, we had cleared Biaches and the first three lines of trenches and on our right the 1st Division occupied Barleux and pushed on for the river.*

*I went up to relieve Todd at the O.P. about 11 - it was a glorious day hot and spring like and I strolled all the way up over the open ground. We, by this time were in possession of the whole of the high ground east of La Maisonette and although, as far as we know, the Bosche were still in Peronne and Mont St Quentin, he was doing no firing."*

There had been signs – burning buildings in Peronne, but these were thought to be due to shellfire from our guns. In reality, the Germans had withdrawn and were carrying out a 'scorched earth' campaign. Anything that could be of any use to the Allies was being systematically burned, destroyed, poisoned, or booby-trapped, depending on whether it was stores, buildings, wells, or anything else.

## The Bristol Gunners

The British started to advance, cautiously at first, then with increasing confidence. They could see villages burning in the distance, the Germans were gone, but there was still danger:

*"The whole retirement is a marvel of organisation - there is nothing of value left behind. All the river bridges are blown up and a few dugouts destroyed, all water poisoned in the wells and traps everywhere to catch the advancing force. Nearly every casualty we have had, and they are remarkably small, has been caused by bombs in the barbed wire, bombs with trip wires in the dugouts – in short whatever you touch has a sporting chance of going off.*

*It is all so wonderful that it seems as if I could write forever about it.*

*For the first time we've absolutely lost the Bosche, we don't know within a thousand yards where our infantry are. They are going steadily on and we get messages from time to time to say they have gone so far and are pushing patrols on to so and so.*

*Consequently at the moment, we seem quite unnecessary.*

*The effect on everyone is marvellous. We have ceased to be fed up with the war. The monotonous show has provided an utterly new sensation and a pleasant one at that.*

*The old regular type is perhaps the happiest of all, a part battalion of the – division went over in extended order yesterday just on our right. The infantry is living in a world of piquet's and outposts in fact the training manuals are coming to life if for a day or two.*

*And just as things are really interesting here and were looking forward practically to a pursuit, there comes a rumour that the division is moving north almost immediately to take part in the real advance - i.e. Making the Hun retire, not watching him do it.*

*Eh bien (Ah, well), we must be grateful for this one touch of novelty."*

After a time bridges were built over the Somme and roads improved so that the artillery could catch up with the advancing infantry. When they got into Peronne itself, they found out that the last Germans had left two days previously. Contact with the Germans had been broken.

151

### The Bristol Gunners

The British then decided to 'advance to contact', a standard phase of war which entailed moving forward until the enemy are contacted again, but always ready to be able to deploy and attack so as to keep the enemy moving.

The following weeks involved a series of movements from one village to another, one ridge line to another, staying balanced but seeking out the Germans. Cavalry troops were out in front reconnoitring, with two of the brigade's batteries with them forming a 'flying column.' The German rearguard was very effective, giving some response when British cavalry were spotted, forcing the British to deploy, and mounting a deliberate attack. While this was happening, the Germans melted away to the next village or ridge. In this way, the Germans successfully slowed us down and gave themselves time to concentrate in their new positions.

Not all was good news, though. The booby traps caused some casualties, sometimes days or weeks later, as the Brigade War History tells us:

> *"Trap bombs caused very heavy casualties until the troops realised that nothing could be touched safely - a footbridge would blow up when crossed, a doorway had a loose wire, which when touched detonated a bomb - and so on.*
>
> *One battalion, 6th Gloucesters - H.Q. used the cellar of a house in Tincourt, and many days after the Germans had retired, a time fuse caused the complete wrecking of the cellar, killing practically the whole H.Q. staff."*

Eventually the British came up against the German Hindenburg Line. This was a very strong position, and varied from past practice. It consisted of many lines of trenches in depth, with the front only being held by a line of outposts in strong points. This was based on the concept of 'elastic defence', a concept that General Robert Fanshawe, GOC 48th Division, also believed in and had been practising for the previous year.

It had become clear that to attack successfully infantry needed artillery. Once infantry advanced out of the range of their own artillery they became vulnerable as defensive fire could not be supplied reliably, and the Germans could counter attack without fear of their rear areas being shelled. The Hindenburg Line was designed to take advantage of these facts. Their outposts were on ridgelines, with main positions on reverse

The Bristol Gunners

slopes behind, out of direct observation. Thus, if the British attacked, to an extent they were attacking 'blind.' If they passed through the outpost line they would be uncertain what lay behind the crests and did not have the ability to engage targets with artillery 'on call', that is, unplanned. This was because the artillery still did not have effective and reliable communications that were portable and could maintain contact with advancing infantry. In the dead ground beyond the German outpost line would be the main belts of wire and other obstacles, and all the ground would be in the beaten zone for the defenders' weapons, who would have the advantage of good observation, and artillery in range.

The advance to the Hindenburg Line was the first taste of open warfare for the British in two and a half years. The cavalry were able to be used in their normal role for the first time since the autumn of 1914, with a number of sharp actions by them pushing back German rearguards, and demonstrating that well handled cavalry could outsmart defenders with machine guns.

At the end of April, it was decided to move the 48th Division out to rest, and then send them back northwards. The GVA remained in the area east of Peronne for another three weeks, supporting another division in a series of minor actions, and enjoying the spring weather which was a pleasant contrast with the cold winter and the rains of March.

While the GVA had been pushing up to the Hindenburg Line, others had been busy elsewhere. The British and French were planning a coordinated series of attacks to knock the Germans off balance, and force him to waste time and effort in moving his reserves from position to position. The first act was at Vimy Ridge, north of the city of Arras. Four Canadian divisions attacked on 9th April, emerging from tunnels dug in the chalk hills to overwhelm the Germans and push them back off the ridge and onto the flat ground below. This removed the German observation of our movements in and around Arras, and enabled us to observe deep into German held territory including the coal mines and rail system around the town of Lens.

The British at the same time attacked from Arras and pushed the Germans back from there as well. Both these assaults, really part of the same battle, used the improved methods and technology that had been developed. Tanks, highly effective CB, silent registration of targets, graze

fused shells, creeping barrages, and new platoon level tactics all played a part. The northern end of the Hindenburg line was just south of Arras. Some good gains were made against the old front line position in Vimy and Arras, but progress was not good at the Hindenburg Line due to it being better for defence than the older sections of front line.

The Vimy and Arras attacks were a preliminary to French attacks on the Aisne at Chemin des Dames, between Rheims and Verdun, a week later. The idea was that the Arras attack would cause the Germans to move their reserves north to the Arras sector, so that when the French struck there would be fewer German reserves to counter attack. It was hoped that the French could execute breakthrough and end the war quickly. Robert Nivelle had replaced Joffre as head of the French Army. He predicted that the battle would end the war in two days. However he was too optimistic, and the Germans were aware of his plans. When the attack was launched they were ready and the attack failed, at huge cost to the French.

One result of this was that mutinies started in the French Army. Nivelle was sacked, and Petain was put in charge of the army. Petain was careful to listen to the complaints of his soldiers, and brought in many measures to improve conditions for them. Mutiny was, however, unacceptable, and in units that had mutinied men were selected at random and executed 'pour encourager les autres' - to encourage the others. From this point on the French Army had in a way been neutralized, its appetite for attack had been diminished, and it had to increasingly rely on the British to display aggression and keep the Germans on the hop. Though the Americans were now in the war, it would be a long time before they were an effective force.

What the Americans would supply was increasing numbers of newly recruited fit and healthy men. Their training would need finishing off when they arrived in Europe, and they would need all their heavy equipment, machine guns, artillery, aeroplanes, transport, to be supplied by the British and French. The Americans were to be commanded by General Pershing, who had a firm views on what he wanted. He would allow individual units of his Americans to be sent to the trenches alongside the French and British for familiarization purposes, but when it came to attack, the American divisions must fight as an American force, not sent piecemeal to reinforce their allies.

The Bristol Gunners

May 20th found the GVA arriving at Hermies, east of Bapaume and on the west side of the Canal du Nord. They were relieving Australian troops who set a good impression:

*"We got there about 10 a.m. and found the Anzac Major just having breakfast. It was a splendid position on a fairly steep terraced slope and there were plenty of shacks and corrugated iron huts about. The Anzac's were a very good lot - their guns clean and they themselves much smarter than the casual crowd they were once considered."*

The guns found a good position near Velu Wood with plenty of fresh grass for grazing their four legged comrades, though it took a little time to find a good position for the OP that could see the allocated zone:

*"We went up to see two O.P.s in Hermies one in a delightful garden [where afterwards I discovered asparagus beds] and it had only a view of Havrincourt. The battery zero line was on the chateau but our zone is further north so it is of no use to us.*

*We then wandered on to a ruined mill and found a fairly good view awaiting us but one can only observe by periscope.*

*The Bosche has chosen his position with great cleverness. There is absolutely no place with a commanding view and all our observing has to be done from our crest line by periscope, if we get any further forward, our view of the canal and the Bosche present front line is obscured by a spur."*

After some reconnaissance, they found a better OP position:

*"On the right, just the other side of the valley lies Havrincourt, which is behind a sort of annexe to the Hindenburg line, but the real thing runs behind it; then left of that are the trenches running behind the Spoil Bank which is a huge heap of chalk from the canal, with Flesquieres in the rear.*

*In the distance about 8/10 miles from here can be seen Cambrai, two or three spires standing up quite clearly. A lot of railway traffic goes on there and the factory chimneys still smoke busily. Among the interesting things I have seen during my many tours of duty here is a visual signalling station which the Hun with frightful nerve, use both day and*

*night. Strangely enough, the O.P. is directly in line with the station it sends to and we can get the messages, which are mostly in code.*

*I thoroughly enjoy these O.P.s with a big view and can seldom tear myself away and leave the N.C.O. to look out when the light is good. First of all the general view through glasses and the correct fixing of distant villages and copses has to be done and then to our high-power telescope which in a good light is simply wonderful.*

*At any thing up to 3miles away you can tell whether a Bosche has a soft or tin hat on and whether he has a pack on or not."*

The area that they could see would become the site of a tank attack, the Battle of Cambrai, that would be fought in November that year.

By this time, it seems that wireless had started to appear and be used by both sides to improve communications, as described in this description of an incident:

*"The Bosche have recently taken a fancy to shelling our valley and worry us three or four times a week for about an hour with 8 inch and 5.9's.*

*The Major came into the mess this morning and told us they had registered his dug out by aeroplane at about 8.30. He has of course a wireless station and picked up the observations "one plus" "one minus" and then "one washout." The Hun then shut up and went home. Sound rangers and an aeroplane have fixed the Hun's position [matter of fact we saw the flashes also from the O.P.] and it also is in a sunken road. It is estimated that he is firing pretty well at extreme range on us and fortunately the 6 inch can reach him with the three new guns that they have. They shut him up three days ago."*

An indication of how new technology (wireless, sound ranging, flash spotting, predicted fire) was not only coming into use, but being co-ordinated and used to good effect.

Another incident was recorded that shows how quality issues with ammunition, though diminishing, could still be serious:

## The Bristol Gunners

*"We had rather a nasty accident at the guns when I was on duty the other night. The base of a cartridge case was faulty and a certain amount of explosive blew back; the flames were forced out through the gas escape channels and burnt the No 3's tunic through and scorched his back. I got lanolin to the rescue but he has had to go down the line. He was jerked off the gun and was, I am afraid, injured internally."*

The 'No 3' refers to a gun crew number 3, whose duties were to lay the gun for line and fire the gun. It is not recorded whether the unfortunate number 3 recovered from his injuries.

Even in a relatively 'quiet' sector danger was ever present. On 5th June 1917:

*"The second battery, has lost another officer. Two days ago their position was badly shelled about 8 a.m. and it set fire to some ammunition, the Major and two of the subalterns who had just finished clearing the men off the position, went over to see if it could be put out and a 5.9 landed about five yards from them. The force of the explosion threw them down and when they got up they found Baines had taken a large splinter through the lung just under the heart. He lived for 2 days and died at Grevillers yesterday, he was one of the very best."*

Second Lieutenant Henry Burgess Baines was 26 years old when he died. He was the middle son of three, with two older sisters. His mother was widowed soon after the birth of the youngest son and both she and Henry were employed in the pottery industry in Stoke on Trent.

On June 7th the British opened the Battle of Messines. The battle was fought to clear the Germans off the Messines Ridge, which, ever since 1914, had given the Germans observation into the British rear areas around Ypres to the north. The British were preparing a big attack out from the Ypres salient later in 1917, and needed to have their rear areas free of German interference before they could launch that offensive.

The battle opened with the detonation of 19 huge underground explosive mines, which destroyed the main German strong points on the ridge and in doing so killed perhaps ten thousand German soldiers. The attack was possibly the best executed attack of the war so far. The British had planned it well, using all the range of technology and organisational changes they had to their advantage. Heavier, more accurate artillery fire,

tanks, aeroplanes, better control of artillery at army level, all contributed to success.

The GVA were not a part of this battle, and its successful conclusion, but were called upon to assist from their current location towards the end of the fighting:

*"We have really moved into this position to make ourselves look like masses of artillery and we have a lot of firing to get through. The idea is to simulate the opening stages of a bombardment to prevent the removal of too many Hun guns northwards but whether the Bosche is going to be deceived by occasional outbursts of hatred by 18 pounders and 4.5's remains to be seen. Just at present we fire about 4,000 rounds in a 24-hour period of which 240 are fired at certain irregular intervals during the night on roads and tracks."*

It seems that this local action was intended to keep the Germans guessing about where the next attack was to be delivered, to encourage them not to move reserves to Messines but leave them where they were.

The reality was that the next attack was going to be to the north of Messines, at Ypres, to be officially called 'the Third Battle of Ypres', but more commonly known as 'Passchendaele.'

The 48th Division were to have a front line role in this new battle, and were to be withdrawn from the line, rested, then sent north. The area chosen for their rest was, though, less than ideal:

*"The Brigade remained in this area until June 23, when the Australians again relieved us. It was, on the whole, a peaceful tour - the weather was glorious and the wagon lines at Velu Chateau put up a very fine horse show, which drew great praise from the C.R.A.*

*The Practical Joke Department then saw fit to take us from this area, which was in very delightful unspoilt open country that had seen little hard fighting, and send us back to rest.*

*There must have been many areas in the rear that would have been utterly delightful in summer for rest and preparation for the Ypres mud and bloodbath, but the department selected Montauban.*

## The Bristol Gunners

*Exactly twelve months before, Montauban had been one of the shambles of the Somme. Every foot of ground had been contested bitterly, and the shells of both sides had torn and shattered the whole area. Roads had been partially re-made, but the battlefield on all sides was untouched.*

*No trace of buildings or trees remained, of course just a sea of weed-grown shell holes. Into this foulness the Brigade was thrown for rest, "A" Battery having the particular honour of being billeted in the Prisoners' Camp still surrounded by barbed wire.*

*The smell hanging over the camp was indescribable and unforgettable. We buried 3 horses that had been lying dead for six to nine months within a couple of hundred yards of the camp - and before we left to trek to Ypres, on several days when the wind was in a favourable quarter, it was almost possible to draw a healthy breath without being nauseated. So much for rest in that year of grace, 1917."*

The old battlefields were desolated. The debris of battle still lay around, with dead horses and men unrecovered. Salvage teams were at work, but the area was so big, and the amount of work so immense, that it would take years to fully recover everything and restore the land to 'normal.' Even today, almost 100 years after the event, relics from these battlefields are being uncovered, and the area remains very dangerous.

Lieutenant F S Gedye did return to the area to the rear of the old positions near Albert to visit his brother Len's grave at Aveluy, and remarked on the recovery of that area which had not been fought over, but which had been in the battle zone:

*"Up at 4 a.m. this morning and bicycled to Aveluy, which is only 4 or 5 miles away, it was very cold at first and I was a bit doubtful about the light but just as I left the cemetery, the sun came out and threw a beautiful light over the country side. It never looked better and I took a good many photos, which I hope will give you some idea of the district. My way back lay through Martinsart. Last September it used to be my place of assembly for the teams after delivering ammunition to Mesnil and I always heaved a sigh of relief to get the teams through the risky portion of the journey without casualties.*

## The Bristol Gunners

*Today I stopped to have a cup of coffee with one of the local inhabitants who have returned this year. All the area behind the Ancre is being cultivated busily this year."*

Before we follow the GVA northwards, Lieutenant F S Gedye records in his diary interesting comments which point out how artillery methods had improved:

*"Practically all our night firing is done entirely by map and atmospheric corrections are made from a telegram that comes round from "Meteor" six times a day. [Meteorological - Army Officer] This gives six groups of figures for six times of flight from 50 seconds to 7 seconds. The ones we use are chiefly in the 10 and 20 second groups. These double groups consist of one group of four figures and one of five, thus 2055 11250. This means that at 20 seconds time of flight the temperature of the air is 55deg, the rate/speed of the wind is 11 foot seconds and the bearing of the wind is 250 deg.*

*The system of making our corrections from this information is wonderfully accurate compared to the old days before the telegrams were sent to us.*

*Last year on the Somme it would have made a wonderful difference to us when most of our firing was by map and it was almost impossible to recognise points on the ground to range on. And nowadays, if the wind changes in the night, there is no need to worry as to whether you have added too much or too little. Your last meteor message comes over the wire about 11 p.m. in time for night firing and at 2 a.m. the first for the day arrives."*

Many of the improved methods had been in use by coastal artillery for years, but the field branch was slow to accept their methods, but when they did, the progress was very rapid. British artillery was on the way to being the most effective arm of the army, and intensely disliked by the German Army.

The 48th Division trekked northwards into Belgium, arriving near Pezelhoek to the west of Ypres in the third week of July. Preparations for the Third Battle of Ypres (also known as 'Passchendaele') were well advanced, and the Germans knew what was coming, and did their best to interfere.

## The Bristol Gunners

Those who were there in almost any capacity, and at any stage during the battle, write about the same common experiences, the rain, the mud, the constant enemy shellfire, the gas, and the carnage.

Ypres is situated in the middle of Flanders, a region that comprises much of western Belgium and north-eastern France. It is low lying, and in ancient times was a bog, maybe much as the Fens in East Anglia were, or the Somerset Levels. Drainage works over the centuries had turned Flanders into a productive agricultural area. The complex system of drainage ditches and coastal flood control gates together allowed the amount of water on the land to be controlled, in a delicate balance between the rain, the sea, and the soil.

In 1914, when the Germans were invading, the Belgians had opened the sea barrier gates and allowed the northern part of Flanders, from the coast down to just north of Ypres, to become flooded by the sea to prevent the German advance. During the two battles fought in the Ypres salient in 1914 and 1915, much of the normal drainage systems had become damaged, or at least not operable. The massive bombardments of the Third Battle of Ypres in 1917 completed the destruction of what drainage remained functioning, and the land reverted to bog.

August 1917 was also a notably wet month, with higher than normal amounts of rain falling, from the first day of the attack, with occasional violent thunderstorms thrown in for good measure. With the ground repeatedly torn up by shell fire and troops, horses, and vehicles moving across what had been open fields, with few good roads, the earth turned to mud, sometimes several feet deep. Movement on the roads was dangerous due to enemy shell and machine gun fire. Movement off road was dangerous through the risk of drowning in water-filled shell holes or in mud.

The battle had been conceived to address a number of objectives, military as well as political.

German submarine warfare was having a serious effect on British trade and supply of food to Britain. The Belgian coast was being used by the Germans to base their submarines, at Zeebrugge and Ostende. The original intention of the battle was to capture Zeebrugge and remove this menace by a further advance up to the Netherlands border, thus forcing German submarines to operate from Germany itself. There were also to

have been amphibious landings and a general advance along the coast. Political objections by Lloyd George (now British Prime Minister) and Marshall Foch to these attacks led to a diminution in the scale of the attack. The main German rail centre at Roulers was thought by General Haig to be a worthwhile new objective, to disrupt German supply. Since the Second Battle of Ypres in April 1915, the Germans had occupied the high ground to the east of Ypres and could fire into the town and our defences more or less at will. By pushing the Germans back over the ridge at the village of Passchendaele they would no longer have the advantage of observation, and Ypres would be largely out of range of the German guns.

The reasons for the offensive, the political situation, and the conduct of the battle are subjects for discussion even now with no absolute consensus as to whether it was the right battle, fought well, or not.

Almost immediately the 48th Division, and the GVA with it, were in action:

*"I found the wagon lines this morning on my return from leave about 3 miles north of Poperinghe, and I am going to the guns in a few minutes. The battery and also the whole Brigade has had rather bad luck since it came up. We had one damn good old chap, Bombardier Grant killed and Matthews, the Sergeant – Fitter, Betty, and about four men sent down with gas poisoning and one man wounded.*

*There is a great deal of night strafing of back areas and "B" battery had 9 horses killed and 23 men wounded last night.*

*Altogether, the general effect is not too cheering on the freshly returned from leave.*

*The roads are packed with transport of all kinds and the traffic regulations are very involved, only certain roads being open at certain hours to the different units that require them.*

*I passed a wood that was concealing about 30 tanks and I believe there are plenty more in the district. The country is utterly different to that which we have just left, very flat and close.*

*The hedges have grown very high and afford plenty of concealment.*

## The Bristol Gunners

*Every hedge and bush seems to have its heavy howitzer and as I came up, there was, every few hundred yards, an ear splitting roar close to me."*

Virtually all supply and movement had to go through the town of Ypres, and this caused much congestion. The roads leading out of Ypres towards the front were largely under observation by the Germans and subject to their artillery firing from three directions converging into what was known as the 'Ypres Salient.' This salient curved round the east of Ypres from north to south in an arc, around two or three miles from Ypres. At this distance, all the salient was essentially prone to artillery fire from any of the German positions. While this was a problem for those fighting the battle, it was one of the logical reasons to push the Germans back and out of range.

In order to concentrate the mass of troops, equipment, and supplies to start the battle, the salient had to be packed to capacity. Virtually every acre of the salient had something military within it, and thus the Germans could shell at will, at any time knowing that they were certain to hit something, or make life very unpleasant for someone.

The use of British artillery had changed. It had been recognised that field artillery with 18 pounders had shells that were not effective at destroying enemy constructions and wire. Medium and heavy guns were being used mostly in the preparatory bombardments, to smash up German trenches and bunkers and their artillery batteries. The role of the 18 pounders was to form barrages around our own troops as they advanced and consolidated any captured trenches to prevent German counter attacks, and to fire shrapnel at any enemy troop concentrations that were seen in the open.

18 Pounder batteries were put into position as close to the front trenches as possible so as to be able to maintain range cover for the assaulting infantry while they were advancing. The GVA position was at Hill Top Farm, just behind the hill crest and out of direct observation. The hill on which the farm sat is not a hill as we would understand, but a rise in the ground, but sufficient in that part of the country to qualify. The guns were within 800 metres of our front trenches, very close, and very vulnerable.

Lieutenant F S Gedye describes the situation during the last few days before the infantry went 'over the top':

## The Bristol Gunners

*"The bombardment has been going on heavily for about 10 days and there are still about four more to go, and still the heavies are rolling in and fresh batteries come into action every night.*

*The waiting for "Z" day is getting on everyone's nerves [although more on the Bosche's than ours] and a lot of the men are suffering slightly from gas, which they rain over every night in shells. The front line is comparatively peaceful in these days for the Bosche has learnt something from the Somme last year and knows the value of back area strafing.*

*In fact, it seems as though, not having enough shells to do all he wants, he is dropping a few all over the ground behind, tracks, batteries, villages and wagon lines, this sort of shelling is very effective for you never know where the next will drop you or how many are coming. He has apparently all his heavy guns here up to 17 inch.*

*We are preparing a forward position some 400 yards from the front line to which we move after the first two objectives are captured, or approximately, 4 hours after "Z", and we have been dumping ammunition there each night, taking it up by pack horses.*

*Last night the party got caught on a semi-circular barrage of 5.9's just before getting to the position and had to dump the ammunition in pairs. By a miracle, we had no casualties, but it was a hot show.*

*The row each night is really awful. Days are the reverse of quiet, but both sides begin all out at dusk, we have got our little shelter pretty well gas proof by blocking up this ventilator and letting down a gas blanket which fits closely round the entrance but it gets frightfully stuffy at night.*

*Still, as they start shelling at all hours of the night, we do it, and it also keeps out a bit of the din. We have had rather a trying time today. Our guns have been more silent than usual and at about 10, the Bosche started a hate. He first of all went quite mad, putting H.E. and "Woolly Bears" [a mixture of H.E. and Shrapnel bursting in the air with a thick yellowish-white smoke] all over the place with delightful indiscrimination, and incidentally put up one of our small S.A.A. dumps and started a small fire somewhere else.*

*Then he started a pukka hate on the road between our dugout and the 5.9's and 8inch, as we have no cover that would stop more than Little*

## The Bristol Gunners

*Willie [and that with luck], we evacuated with more haste than dignity, to a field in the rear and wandered about as the "Hate" moved for an hour until it appeared to be over. We had barely got back when they started again and put one within 10 yards of the sergeant's shack and off we rushed again. The afternoon was devoted almost exclusively to Bosche hates of various districts around about, until just after tea, they crept close and finally landed one close enough to bring showers of earth and muck onto our roof and entrance and we cleared the battery out at the hell - for - leather canter. We had no casualties, the only damage being the bustification of one sandbag wall and two big holes in the gun wheel. We are remarkably lucky not having to fire from our present position until "Z" day.*

*Last night we had a warning that we might have to move forward. The Bosche are believed to have retired, but infantry patrols who went out, found they hadn't, so we are as we were. Today as been quieter bar two terrific hates of ours at 5.15 a.m. this morning and the other as I am writing this at 7 p.m. they are more or less practice barrages for "Der Tag" but although the heavies do not fire on them, the row is paralysing. I was talking to the artificer when this evening one started, and, after about four efforts to finish my sentence, had to give it up as a bad job.*

*It was such a glorious morning and fairly quiet [as I have learnt to understand the word here], the Major proposed an alfresco breakfast and we ate it on the roof of the dug out. It was really great, there was a heat mist going but the remains of Ypres Cloth Hall Tower, about a mile away, was clearly visible with the sun shining down on the one side that remains.*

*Meanwhile, the bombardment goes on. We are at "W" day and on the 31st "Der Tag" arrives. I think we shall all be thankful when it does. We shall know then what sort of share ours really is in this big bit of war.*

*Price gave us an interesting bit of news at midday. The Guards on our left had a stunt yesterday and found the Bosche front and second lines empty and went on to the next and had a scrap. Later on, one of their officers saw a brother sub, badly wounded trying to crawl back to the lines along a canal. He called the two nearest men to form a covering party and went out and brought him in. This officer reported the Bosche 1st and 2nd lines still evacuated and our patrols went in and occupied it. There they found a Divisional order that the trenches evacuated without*

### The Bristol Gunners

*orders were to be counterattacked and captured at once. This counter attack apparently took place about 9.30 p.m. tonight. There was a terrific din anyway.*

*Just after it had died down, Lane's servant came in to say, "The tanks are going up, sir." We are about 30 yards from one of the main traffic tracks [called Queens Road] and when we got to the top of the steps, we saw four forms on the track coming along at a great lick. These low black forms moving without a sound or so it seemed with the racket going on, occasionally showing up every detail against a gun flash, looked very sinister and formidable opponents.*

*They are much faster than last year's and seem more compact. The turret on each side has practically disappeared and the pair of wheels in the rear has gone. They are faster, being able to do between 10 and 12 miles an hour as against 3 or 4 miles last year but it is the idea of silent speed that impressed me most standing at the top of the track watching them coming towards us with lights showing through the port holes. They certainly looked like some prehistoric monster; rumour has it that there will be something like 1000 here in action this time."*

The Germans had applied with vigour their new policy of 'elastic defence.' They had also provided their outposts with concrete bunkers or 'pill boxes.' They knew that to put their men into forward positions in great numbers would result in a high number of casualties, so kept the minimum numbers forward, and protected as many as possible in deep concrete shelters, even evacuating sections of their front positions from time to time, relying on counter attack to regain possession.

The British were bringing up their latest tanks. The use of these had improved over the nine months since their first use in September 1916. The ones seen by Lieutenant Gedye were probably Mark IV versions, first used at Messines in May of 1917, where they did well, advancing faster than the infantry, destroying, and disrupting German defences. They would, however, not do well at Passchendaele, due to the boggy ground conditions. There would not be a thousand of them, and a speed of 10 miles per hour was still optimistic, especially over rough terrain. Of course, Gedye can be forgiven for accepting British propaganda as truth.

There were many dangers around, some obvious, others more subtle. Three days before the assault was to start an immense explosion, bigger

## The Bristol Gunners

than any experienced before occurred at the howitzer battery belonging to 241 Brigade that was located alongside:

*""X" day and very nasty at that. We had a great deal of shelling all round us during the night together with a fair amount of gas, but it didn't keep me awake. But during the night the Bosche put over eight of the most terrific shells I've heard, at intervals of about 40 minutes.*

*As they came over, the air was filled with an extraordinary loud rushing sound and although they were all duds, and did not explode, they hit the ground with a terrific dull thud, and one or two of them rocked this little dugout like an earthquake - well, to be brief, they upset us. I had just finished my toilet and Todd was up washing when there was a huge explosion he leapt down into the dug out and the force of the explosion shook things down all round the dug out and put out both candles. It sounded just outside but afterwards was found to be a good 100 yards away. We can't decide what it was, it made a crater a good 20-25 foot deep and more across. It landed between two 4.5 Howitzers and blew them both over sideways scattering the ammunition far and wide. We have several of them lying round the shack as Todd says, "To see the crater is really terrifying and if they've got a gun that will do that I give them best"- I don't believe a 17inch could do it.*

*We really had the wind up over it, until breakfast had worked its soothing influence.*

*Later, to our intense relief we found it was not a mobile ammunition store that blew up, but "D" 241 Brigade's ammunition dump."*

In preparation for the attack, large quantities of ammunition had to be stored at the gun positions. Resupply during the battle would be difficult because the roads would need to be kept clear for reserves coming forward and casualties going rearwards. These ammunition stores presented a significant hazard, as we saw in the last passage, and as we shall find out later.

The infantry went 'over the top' on July 31st. The last day and night before were busy as the assault troops passed by the guns on their way to the attack trenches:

### The Bristol Gunners

*""Y" night was horribly unhealthy; the Hun was chucking stuff all around us, every now and then a heap of muck would land on top of the dugout. Just before 12, they landed a shell in No 5's pit and blew up about 200 rounds. We found it quite impossible to get any sleep so lay in bed and smoked and yarned until 2.30 a.m. when we shaved and had breakfast. Parties of infantry who were going up to the line and took temporary shelter from a near burst frequently invaded our shack.*

*I went out about 3.15 a.m. to see everything was ready and found it pitch black. Number 5's gun crew was busy clearing its pit for action and managed to be ready in time.*

*It was still dark at 3.50 a.m., when the show opened with a terrific crack and roar.*

*All change of targets were being done by whistle and I found that I had to use my whistle through a megaphone at each gun pit to make it heard and although Plowman was helping me on the position, it took some running about."*

240 Brigade's task was to provide a creeping barrage, that is, a protective wall of shells ahead of and moving forward at the same speed as the advancing infantry. This had been tried at the Somme a year earlier and the speed was too optimistic. A gap had opened up between the barrage and the infantry. This gave the German defenders time to emerge from their dugouts, set up their machine guns, and shoot down our infantry. This time the speed was slower, the movements or 'lifts' smaller, and by doing this, in many attacks, the infantry were better protected. However, where they were held up, by enemy action, by ground conditions, or just the 'fog of war' the barrage sometimes still moved too far ahead of the troops.

The following months were spent by the GVA in supporting a series of attacks, gradually the front moved closer and closer to the ridge line on which was situated the village of Passchendaele, until, in November, the ridge was in British hands and the battle drew to a close. The brigade were quite static during this time, there were moves of position, but they were relatively small, and confusing not only to those who were there, but also to any student of the battle trying to work out where units moved and for what purpose.

## The Bristol Gunners

There have been many accounts of the battle, and the conditions. In this account, we will rely on the eyewitness account recorded by Lieutenant FS Gedye in his personal diaries.

On the first day of the assault things seemed to be going well:

*"I shall never forget the extraordinary sights we saw on the way up, long columns of vehicles, parties of prisoners and a continuous stream of British and Bosche wounded helping one another back. One couldn't help marvelling at it all. An hour or so before we couldn't make it too hot for them and now we were seeing British with their arms around the Bosche helping or being helped along. We saw one ambulance that had just been filled with about 6 Germans and 2 of our boys. The Tommies produced cigarettes and handed them around, then matches, and the ambulance set off with a very cheery little domestic party."*

Right from the start the weather deteriorated and became a major factor in the conduct of the battle:

*"31$^{st}$ July: The teams got up and away without shelling which was lucky as "A" sub gun leaders fell into a crump hole full of water and it took half an hour to get them out.*

*The men had first to dig out the emplacements, which had been blown about some, and then we gave the guns their line. By the time this had been done, rain started to fall.*

*1$^{st}$ August: Next morning I was awakened at 7a.m. to find I was lying in a puddle of wet mud and we had to bale hard to keep the place from being flooded out. My fleabag and most of my kit bar the odd clean change in the head of the valise was absolutely sodden. It continued to rain all day, and all day we had to be out on the position baling water out of the pits and unloading ammunition from the packhorses.*

*By midday we realised that timbers would have to be put right across the floor of the pits if the guns were to remain in action and even then we nearly lost "C" gun, which, after an S.O.S. in the afternoon, sunk in up to the axles. Every man in the battery had to man the drag ropes to pull it up on its platform of logs.*

## The Bristol Gunners

*The next day, August 2$^{nd}$, same sort of thing a steady fine rain and very low clouds. By this time things were pretty bad. No one had a dry stitch; the mud was ankle deep everywhere and much worse on the tracks.*

*Boots and socks were miserably wet and muddy. We were still getting up ammunition [we have to have 5400 in total = 900per gun]. The Bosche hadn't used any gas shell since the 31$^{st}$, but stray shelling had occasionally proved to be damn sight too close for real comfort.*

*Meanwhile the wagon line had many troubles besides the rotten journeys with ammunition. On Aug 1$^{st}$, the stream by their new wagon line rose about 9 feet in a few hours and flooded acres of country. The horse lines were two feet under water and the men who were out on duty at the time lost most of their kit. All the shacks were flooded in fact they had the wetter time, if possible but not so "Metallic."*

*August 3$^{rd}$ was just the same all over again except that the ammunition was up to establishment and by this time we were muddy to a most monstrous degree.*

*On the 4$^{th}$ it stopped raining and except for two heavy showers we were able to get about in the dry. My fleabag had its first airing and the Major was suggesting that a bath all round and especially for me, as the sharer of his blankets was really to be desired. In the morning, the Major went forward to try and register but the light was too bad and he had to give it up, in the afternoon he, and Major Wilson went down to the wagon lines for a bath and two night's sleep and Lane came up."*

The rain would come back on and off for the rest of the campaign, and the mud became worse and worse. It was bad for the artillery, which had to operate the guns, move them from time to time, bring up ammunition, and live out in the open. For the infantry, who had to move forward, under shell and machine gun fire, and fight to the death, face to face and hand to hand, with the Germans, it was truly a nightmare.

The Germans, aware of the nature of the ground, and wishing to operate an 'elastic defence' with an eye on economy of manpower, had constructed many concrete strong points (pillboxes). Their men could shelter in these constructions, and even fire weapons from them. Not all German troops were accommodated in these pillboxes, but many were, especially headquarters and communications (signals) sections. They

provided protection to a degree from British artillery. A direct hit from a small calibre shell would not be serious for the occupants. However, they generally only had one entrance, at the rear (facing east). Larger calibre shells landing close to the pillbox were likely to tilt them over, especially as the battle continued and the ground became more and more saturated. The mud was unable to support properly the foundations. There were many examples where a pillbox tilted over, the entrance sinking in to the mud, and the occupants became trapped inside, to drown.

Many of the pillboxes were overrun and captured by the British, the problem for them being that the entrance faced the Germans and was therefore exposed to observation and small arms fire, making the use of the pillbox a hazardous occupation.

The British constructed many wooden track ways across the mud as they advanced, but these were subject to German artillery and machine gun fire. Many men and horses slipping off the tracks, injured, overburdened, tired, could only get back onto the harder surface with much difficulty. Many died by drowning, as did the infantry in attack, falling wounded or sheltering in shell holes, and being unable to get out again.

For artillery to be an effective support for the infantry several things are necessary. They must, of course have guns and ammunition, but just as important they must be able to get to a position to identify targets, and to be able to see those targets whenever they need to fire. The wet weather and mud made moving to an OP position very difficult. The autumn mists and rain made observation difficult or impossible when the OP was reached. In addition, when visibility was good, every battery OP tried to make up time by firing their guns at identifiable registration points, meaning that an individual observer was not sure whether he was observing his rounds or someone else's:

*"I set off just before five with two telephonists to find the O.P. in a pea soupy of a mist. One of them was supposed to know the way to a test box about two thirds of the way. Of course when we got well out, he didn't and the early hours making me somewhat terse with one, I sent him back to the battery for someone who did.*

*Thus passed a cheery hour in the mist, finally we found the test box tried the line and found it OK. From there, there is a ground line to Canopus trench and the O.P. and we patrolled it on the way up; if we*

*found 200 yards of continuous line we thought ourselves lucky after a bit. We mended between 20 and 30 breaks and in several cases had to put in 50 and 100 yards of wire, the original line having vanished. About 8.15 we finally arrived at the O.P., still in a thick mist. Later the light cleared and I was able to register all our guns and was just observing for "D" Battery when the line went. The area round the trench was being badly strafed so I decided to get under. The O.P. had reinforced concrete emplacements in the trench which you could only get in to on all four's and then sit down hunched up between the roof and three inches of dirty water on the floor a distance of about 3ft 6inches. Still, the 6ft of concrete overhead was enormously comforting.*

*Although my telephonists went out several times on the wire I could not get communication again and as the Bosche was playfully following them round with time shrapnel, I decided that as I'd finished our registration, the game wasn't worth the casualties."*

Later:

*"After half an hour at Hill Top Farm, Major Wilson and I set out for the O.P. As I had expected every B.C. was flooding out the O.P.s, and nearly every one was firing on my point, the only possible one in the whole zone. We each got three guns done but it was frightfully slow work; one had to repeat so many rounds to be sure one wasn't confusing one's own round with those of another battery."*

The communication between the guns and the OP was still by 'line', telephone cable. This was obviously easily cut by shell fire or troops moving around. It was not unusual for signallers to be constantly moving up and down the cable, from the OP back to the guns looking for breaks and repairing them. As this had to be done in the open, there was great risk to the individual, and many signallers were wounded or killed.

## The Bristol Gunners

**Photo taken from an observation balloon of the battlefield in front of the GVA position at Hill Top Farm before the battle began. The GVA gun position is at the bottom left of the photo, marked as 'A/240 Guns.'**

The Ypres salient was very congested, and there were few roads leading into it from the rear. The town itself was fortified in earlier centuries with strong walls and a moat. A canal joined the town with the coast, running just on the western side and extending to a moat which enclosed much of the eastern side of the town. In July 1917 there were just three bridges and roads leading out of the town eastwards. The British had built several temporary bridges across the canal to improve the road capacity, but Ypres was very much a bottleneck and keeping the traffic flowing smoothly through it was a major task for military police. One major junction just to the south east of Ypres was nicknamed 'Hellfire Corner', which tells all you need to know about conditions there. Gedye describes one incident:

*"When I got back, the orders for the longed for relief were waiting, we had to be at the position at 9.30 a.m. pull the old guns out, and take them to the wagon line.*

### The Bristol Gunners

*I set off once again the following morning with the limbers, one spare team in case of accidents and the G.S. wagon. When I got just beyond Ypres, I met a lad of the 241 ["C" battery; MacLeod's] on his way back and he told me the traffic control wouldn't let us through. I told him no one would put off our getting out of action and plodded on.*

*A little further on, up bobbed some ANZAC traffic subaltern who motioned me to halt, which I did, but after seeing several parties of pack horses allowed to pass me, I thought it was time to chip in. I rode up and very nicely and politely I am sure asked him to let me move on as I had urgent orders to move my guns forward, I thought that sounded better then moving back - at least, to the traffic control. He calmly told me no wheeled traffic would be allowed further than this point between 6 a.m. and 6 p.m. without a signed chit from the A.P.M. Ypres. Internally, I always boil when I have to ask favours from these traffic birds and at that I simply bubbled over.*

*After a short but pointed conversation, I rode straight to Brigade H.Q, which fortunately was only a few hundred yards away.*

*The Adjutant rang the A.P.M. who said orders had been sent out and that it would be all right and that it would be would be all right by the time I got back to the road.*

*I took a chit from the Adjutant to this effect but the little swine on the road told me he wouldn't recognise it but that he would let me through if I went back to Ypres and got a chit from the A.P.M. That absolutely capped it and I lost my hair. I asked him if he thought I was out for a ------- joyride and that I had nothing better to do than ride 1.1/2 miles into Ypres and back; also if he realised that he was trying to stop the ------- war for a ------scrap of paper. He got rather haughty at that and once more I went to Brigade this time the C.O. got rather worked up and phoned the APM that he'd dam' well have to turn out and put things straight.*

*This was quite a triumph and I remained at the corner till the immaculate A.P.M. rolled up in a car and told the youth that all transport of the 48th and 66th Divisions were to be allowed through all day.*

*After that, I got on pretty well, but I didn't get to the battery until 11. We had an absolutely putrid job getting the guns out. The position was*

### The Bristol Gunners

*500 yards from the road along one of the most hopeless tracks imaginable.*

*On that day it was a liquid mass of mud almost up to the axles throughout and of course shell holes, which were deeper still were absolutely invisible. I passed two "C" Battery horses which had been all in and they were just moving lumps of mud solid from the ears to hoof. We only got two guns stuck badly and those we managed to get out. I arrived back in the wagon lines with the last team at 3 p.m."*

One of the stories of the campaign was that Staff Officers in the rear areas were not fully aware of the conditions faced by troops in the field. Whether this is true or not is debatable, but one can understand why the front line troops thought it was true could have been due to this type of incident:

*"To improve matters, the Corps commander has sent round a paper drawing attention to the apparent apathy of officers and men to the number of derelict cartridge cases and rounds of ammunition on all roads east of the canal, and announces that if this is not cleared by the 20th inst, all leave of officers of the Divisional Artillery and Heavy Artillery will be stopped until he is satisfied that his instructions are being carried out.*

*This may be all very simple but if these elegant individuals would only come up and live in the battery areas under corrugated iron for a few nights in this district, they would perhaps realise the particular hell that has fallen to the lot of the gunner on this front. There can't be many batteries whose positions have not been shelled out more times then they can remember and as often as not, come back to find the position strewn with charred empties and damaged rounds. The net result of the order is that wholesale burials are in progress and thousands of cartridge cases are being hidden from the sight of the men!"*

From time to time artillery batteries were pulled out of the line for a few days rest, to clean up horses and maintain equipment. Soldiers were not the only people in the area. While Ypres had been largely evacuated of its civilian population, the rest areas to the west of the town still contained farmers and other civilians, and operating in these areas required co-operation between the military and the civilian. Relationships were not

always smooth, as apart from language difficulties, both groups found it hard to accept the other's standpoint:

> "We had had to set out in all our Ypres mud and the horses were still caked with it. While we were grooming, the farmer, a surly old Beast, who would only let us put our horses on a putrid bit of ground, turned on one of his stable drains which flooded down over my section lines.
>
> We were just in the mood to deal with this sort of thing and promptly moved the section lines on to his best bit of ground. That stopped his monkey tricks, but from an over heard scrap of conversation next morning, I believe the Sergeants Mess took a couple of his fowls that night in retaliation."

Sometimes persuasion was preferred to retribution:

> "We had a good billet with a dear old soul, who at first didn't want to take even one officer, but after a stilted conversation, which included my special sob - stiff appeal for L'Entente, les Allies etc, I did her down for three officers and a mess and she was an absolute trump afterwards."

The GVA as part of 48th Division were involved in the battle of 'Third Ypres' from July through to the middle of October. During that time many men were injured, and two officers and twenty five men were killed. This proved to be the most dangerous period in the history of the GVA.

Some of the dangers were obvious, and some less so. Probably every single man in the brigade during that time had a near miss story to tell. Lieutenant FS Gedye recounts those that he was present at or aware of, and there surely must have been many more:

> "After we had had a look at our position, which by the way was truly crumped. I went back to meet the guns and show them the track way in. Just as I got off the position, the Huns started shelling it with 5.9's and the Major had to clear his advance party off.
>
> One shell burst about 100 yards behind me and landed a fairly hefty splinter full on my back stud, there was no force left in it but it just served as a reminder that there was a war on."

### The Bristol Gunners

The back stud that Gedye refers to is the stud at the back of his shirt which was used at that time to secure the shirt collar. Later:

*"They shelled around practically the whole day, but we sped homewards in a more or less peaceful lull. I got back looking forward to a hot meal as, bar a cup of tea at 4.45 am, I had had to rely on sandwiches, but alas it was not to be. The battery was full of many crump holes and I found them just trooping back to the position, having been a little way away, watching the 'appy 'ome go sky ward. As a matter of fact only two shacks had been outed but as one of them was the officers servants' home and kitchen, our rations had gone with it. Once again did we consume much bullied beef and I, in a fit of rage and abstraction, consumed two pickled onions which as we are sleeping in close, oh very close billets, must have been rather peeving for the Major and Fullerton.*

*The last two days [7th & 8th] have been fairly uneventful, except that the Bosche has developed a reprehensible habit of bursting low shrapnel over the position at unexpected and irregular times during the day."*

A little later in the battle:

*"We had a rough time on the 21st, at 9 a.m.; the Bosche put down a barrage on the original No Mans Land and caught several batteries in action there and searched back behind us with shellfire.*

*There was a devil of a row he seems to have every gun going, from little Willie shrapnel to 8inch and simply pumped it over.*

*The men had to clear out of the position and about 9.30, we had to clear out of our trench and nip out to a flank. They also put an 8 inch shell on the road and put up the ammunition dump behind No 3 gun, the cordite and N.C.T. charges exploded in the heat and blew several rounds out on to the position but the shells didn't go off.*

*Just before I reached Buffs road, an 8 inch shell landed about 50 yards behind the guns quickly followed by another, which pitched among the shacks where the men had just got back I dashed over and found two men kneeling over my "A" sub Sergeant, Rivers, who was about 2 ft from the burst. A quick look showed that he had passed over and as there was no one else badly hit, I cleared everyone off the position at the double.*

### The Bristol Gunners

*We were remarkably lucky not to have lost more heavily but we had one more, Sergeant Baker, wounded in the head through his shrapnel helmet."*

Sergeant Baker survived this wound, but died soon after the war back in Bristol.

The dangers were also to the horses, as they did not have the benefit of dugouts to shelter in. After his brother Len had been killed in 1916 Lieutenant FS Gedye had asked that he be allowed to take over Len's horse, Peter. On 27th August, Peter became a casualty:

*"I went down to the wagon line to clean myself up on the 25th. On the 27th. my groom Blanning came up to tell me that little Peter was badly hit.*

*A shell had pitched in the lines some 10 yards from him and one splinter had broken his thigh. Poor little Peter he was one of the best horses in the Brigade and certainly the most interesting, intelligent and affectionate. I feel half the attraction of the wagon line has gone now, without him."*

No doubt the loss of Peter was all the more difficult because he had been Len's charger.

Gas, shell fire, and machine guns were not the only hazards created by the Germans. At night, German aeroplanes would fly over the salient and drop bombs:

*"On the 17th the battery came down to the wagon lines for three days rest, the wagon line is by no means the place of peace it might be. Long-range guns tickle us up. Every night a few parties of bombing planes come over and we generally have to finish dinner and turn in without lights.*

*The battery people had only been down an hour when an H.V. fell in the next field about 100 yards from the mess, this was a good start and they followed it up by two bombing raids. The searchlights found two of the planes but they got safely back to Hun land. Still it was quite a spectacular little show."*

And another:

## The Bristol Gunners

*"On the 25th we had a very rough house. About 7, the Bosche shelled around the men's bivvies and they cleared over the road to our trench. We had just had the roll checked to see that every one was present when we heard some planes coming over and as they seemed pretty low, the Major started to get the men into the various little corrugated iron shelters in the trench. Before the first party was in, there was a heavy Crrrrrump, followed by four more bombs, the swine!*

*There was a wonderful simultaneous rush for cover; about 12 others, and I who didn't want to be killed in the rush, crouched in the bottom of the trench close to the side. I could see the flashes of the detonations and two pitched one side of the trench and two the other, none of them 50 yards away - it was one of the nearest things I've had and splinters and clouds of earth came singing over the trench.*

*We soon packed in to the trench shelters and waited events, but only for 5 minutes for then there was a nasty rushing sound and an 8inch shell landed about 40 yards away."*

The Battery Commander of A Battery at the start of the battle was Major Chester William Todd. Todd had originally joined the GVA in 1896, retiring in 1912. On the outbreak of war he had rejoined, and quickly rose to become BC of A Battery. He was a very popular officer, much respected. On 9th August he was killed, along with Lieutenant Basil Fullerton, another long time GVA officer. Both were killed by the same German shell while on the gun position.

Gedye's comments at the time:

*"I've been at the wagon line since the tragedy of the 9th. We can't get accustomed to the realisation that we have lost Major Todd and Fullerton. It is of course only natural that our thoughts are mainly of the Major; it was so great to have him back and despite the beastly hole we are in, he has been so splendid through it all.*

*It has caused a big shock to everyone in the division. A Q.M.S. of one of the R.E. companies came round specially to ask if he might have the privilege of making the crosses as he had a great admiration for the Major. And every man who knew him has showed the same feeling."*

The Bristol Gunners

Casualties in this battle were the most severe that the brigade would experience throughout the war. As well as deaths, there was a high rate of injuries and wounds. The Brigade War History records the need for promotions to fill the gaps in the ranks:

*"One battery made 16 promotions through casualties one Wednesday. The following Saturday, during a visit to the wagon-lines, the B.C. found he had to make 21 more to fill the gaps, and this was the rule and not the exception.*

*Gun-lines and wagon - lines suffered equally. The misery in the line was shared by the flooded conditions of the wagon-lines at Vlamertinghe; the shelling by the gun personnel and the never-ceasing ammunition parties from the wagon-lines, night firing and bombardment at the guns by aeroplane bombing raids that took place most nights and killed hundreds of horses in the Brigade lines during the two months."*

On October 14th the brigade pulled out of the salient and was sent a little south, to Vimy, a little north of Arras. There they took over positions in Vimy village, at the base of Vimy Ridge facing east towards the Germans. This area had been captured by the Canadians in April 1917.

The Canadians were being sent into the Ypres salient to take part in the final push to capture Passchendaele, which they did on 6th November when the village fell. The Canadians had ejected all remaining Germans from the Passchendaele ridge by 10th November, when the battle formally closed.

British losses had been severe – a quarter of a million men killed, wounded, or captured. German losses had been greater, maybe twice as high.

240 Brigade, however, had finished with Ypres and the salient for good. They spent a month in the positions in Vimy town, a time of relative calm in the French region of Pas-de-Calais, a few miles north of the city of Arras.

On his way to Vimy, F S Gedye stopped off to visit Sister Jennings at Number 33 CCS (Casualty Clearing Station). A CCS is the place behind the lines, out of artillery range, that casualties are sent to after their first aid treatment in a Regimental Aid Post (RAP) or Advanced Dressing

Station (ADS). The function of the CCS is to decide whether a casualty should be sent to hospital, evacuated, or can be sufficiently treated to be returned to duty. They are generally situated next to good rail and road communications so that casualties can be moved efficiently to hospital or to the coast for evacuation back to 'Blighty.' It is not clear the exact nature of the relationship between Gedye and Sister Jennings, as he does not mention her before these comments. Mabel Jennings was a pre war Territorial in the Territorial Force Nursing Service, she would later win the Military Medal for her service during a critical action in December 1917. It is likely that Gedye had known Sister Jennings before the war as she was also a resident of Bristol and he clearly enjoyed her company and was willing to make an effort to see her:

*"I set off with Fisher in the Padre's trap for Bethune, which was only about 4 miles off and I knew that Sister Jennings was to be found at No 33 C.C.S. there. We got there about 5 p.m., and although she had just turned in to rest before night duty, like the sportsman she always was, turned out at once, gave us tea in the matron's room and after a delightful hour, we made off with many invitations and promises to return if possible."*

FS Gedye records his observations on their arrival at Vimy:

*"You cannot realise until you see it, quite how marvellous the capture of Vimy Ridge was. It absolutely dominated the whole area north of Arras and the whole country round Neuville St Vaast, St Eloi, and Souches was under observation. But from our point of view it was even more wonderful.*

*On the enemy side the slope is more pronounced and although Vimy village makes a bit of a false crest, the extent of the view is simply marvellous.*

*Lens, Avion and Mericourt lay in front of us and, miles of Hunland stretched out behind. I have never seen anything more wonderful in natural O.P.s.*

*The only drawback is that the battery is entirely cut off from traffic by daylight as the Bosche has the road taped off to a yard and nothing can go there except over the ridge and it is only safe to send small parties of four or six dismounted men at a time.*

## The Bristol Gunners

*The next morning, I took out the third section up to relieve and after a bit of wandering round, found the position. They were all living in cellars of semi-ruined houses just outside the village of Vimy and seemed very comfortable and happy.*

*The gun pits were well camouflaged but rather awkwardly placed and owing to an alteration of the zone, the guns were firing right across the pits.*

*The Canadians have put in some wonderful work here."*

The Canadians had been in this position ever since they had captured the Ridge in early April, and had made good use of their time in consolidating the defences. As Gedye states, all supplies had to come forward over the ridge line, and any movement on the ridge, or on the forward slope facing the Germans was open to observation and shellfire. The supply situation was, though, very good due to a narrow gauge rail system installed by the British of the type used in many places up and down the front:

*"The Decauville railway system is priceless and all ammunition and R.E. material etc, is delivered practically to your door by these light trains. The roads are wonderfully broad with a topping surface and the main road from Arras to Lens up to within 300 yards of the ridge is like the Bournemouth roads, broad, dry and with a surface of yellow gravel. In addition to this the wagon lines have got nearly all their winter standings up we have only to add the finishing touches and make a few rubble roads around the lines."*

The Decauville referred to was a French manufacturing company which supplied the track and rolling stock for these light railway systems, based on designs that had been in use in many countries since the late 19th century.

The position in Vimy was so good that Gedye was moved to make a full description of it:

*"The officers, telephonists, and cooks live in the cellars of some houses about 300 yards from the Vimy Station. A few stairs lead to our mess cellar, which is a roomy affair with a big table for meals, a topping fireplace where we daily burn the houses of Vimy, an office corner and a*

### The Bristol Gunners

*store cupboard. A hole in the wall leads to our bedroom, another cellar with three wire beds. I fixed up a wire grill in the fireplace, which we call Piccadilly, which is very excellent for toast, cheese, bully, herrings and other little chef's stunts.*

*The gun position was about 200 yards from the mess. The six gunpits are made of elephant hutting and about 3ft below the surface. There is a trench in the rear connecting the pits and a dug out in the centre.*

*The position when we moved into it was well camouflaged, but needed a lot of improvement. We first deepened the trench to 6ft and revetted it with X.P.M. and pit props, all the earth dug out was sandbagged, put on to a truck and run three hundred yards down the railway line and emptied into shell holes. 1500 sandbags were dealt with this way. The trench was covered with half sections of elephant hutting covered over with turf and the floor was trench boarded.*

*From 200 yards away, when we had finished, it was almost impossible to see that there was anything there at all and from the air, it must have been absolutely invisible.*

*The gun pits themselves were magnificent; as we only had four guns in action there, the two end pits were used as section messes.*

*Each pit had a wooden platform and an arc made from an old wheel used to keep the gun steady, and a trail board, made in most cases from an old wooden sleeper.*

*These were oiled until they looked like oak and they had brass fuse covers nailed on to them to show the 5-degree switches in direction.*

*Each pit had a green painted store cupboard, which was made from three ammunition boxes; these cupboards were used to keep cleaning material in. The box also had a brass knob on the door and three brass clips to hold the men's rifles.*

*The 250 rounds of ammunition were polished and stacked in racks at the back of the pit. A target board was fixed up on the right hand side showing the switch, angle of sight and range to each target and the S.O.S. lines.*

### The Bristol Gunners

*All the painted parts of the gun were oiled over each morning and the brass work polished and the general effect was simply priceless.*

*It is far and away the finest position I have ever seen and the corrugated iron kept pits and trench absolutely dry what ever the weather.*

*The Gun detachments and telephonists slept in a mined dug out between No. 3 and 4 gun pits. The whole thing was so much more practical than the old type of position. In the old days; we used to build great square gunpits for the guns with rows of logs on top that could be seen for miles and rotten little dugouts for the men. The new idea is invisibility first, really deep shellproof dugouts for the men, and if the guns have splinter proof cover, that is good enough*

*It is very sound because, if the position is really well camouflaged and you haven't to fire much, the chances are you won't get shelled, and if the Bosche spots you and gets really annoyed, he can always push over any old gun pit with an 8 or 11 inch shell, so that really shellproof cover for the personnel is the important thing."*

It is interesting that the men seemed to have gone to extremes with the 'spit and polish' of the gun pits, and this may well have been a natural reaction to the previous three months living in the mud of the Ypres salient where it was impossible to keep anything clean.

It seems that nothing violent occurred in their month at Vimy, as confirmed by the Brigade War History:

*"A peaceful month followed - it was an admirable ordered, quiet sector, and we appreciated the relief of it. As a reaction from the squalor and horror of Ypres, something approaching a sergeant-major's dream of a corps-general's spit-and-polish ideal took place."*

In mid November, the Canadians had completed the Third Battle of Ypres, and were to be returned to Vimy to clean up and repair their losses. The 48th Division were also to move, but at this time to where was not known. The answer to this question, when answered, came as surprise to everyone in 240 Brigade.

*"Nov 15 1917*

## The Bristol Gunners

*I must make a few notes tonight, as we have the first definite news of what we have been prepared for some days. On Saturday, my leave warrant was sent round for the 11th that is to leave that night and cross on Sunday. Two hours later, I sat in the mess in all the glory of a brand new pair of "Harry Halls" the latest and daintiest line in gent's breech wear, waiting for my horse to carry me to the railhead, when the phone buzzed and the Adjutant had rang up to know if I was there. I vehemently assured him I had left some hours previously and was even now taking all known seasickness remedies preparatory to crossing the channel but it was useless. All leave was withdrawn and no officers were to proceed on leave that had not been in the country [France] for 18 months since last leave.*

*This afternoon there was a B.C.'s conference and Lane has just returned with the news.*

*We are being relieved on the 17th and 18th and on the 19th we march to Aubigny and entrain for an entirely unknown destination. In the meantime we are to complete our stores and train as far as we can, for open warfare.*

*Our instructions are that if anyone asks us why we are doing it, we are to state that the Bosche are expected to retire shortly further south.*

*Nothing is known by anyone, but the reduction of kit and general shaping up is to be done by everyone. Of course, everyone mutters with hushed breath "Italy" but other inventive minds counter with Ireland, Soissons and Macedonia.*

*Anyway my leave is "Off", and we are sending away, as quickly as possible, all men who have been in the country for 18 months without leave, but we have been warned that we, very possibly, shan't see them again."*

### The Bristol Gunners

Lieutenant F S Gedye was not the only disappointed man. One Field Marshall Luigi Cadorna had just been thoroughly defeated in battle by the Austro Hungarians at Caporetto and had been dismissed as Chief of Staff of the Italian Army.

GVA Sergeants and Warrant Officer behind the lines near Ypres, probably at Vlamertinghe in autumn 1917. The post battle strain can be seen in the faces of these men, or maybe they have been posing for the photograph just a little too long. Sergeant Fitter Betty, mentioned in some excerpts is the man on the far right, standing.

The 48th Division, with five other British infantry divisions were to be sent to join an Allied force including six French divisions to assist the Italian Army and prevent northern Italy from being overrun by the Austro Hungarians.

Gedye visited his friend Sister Jennings again as the brigade left Pas-de-Calais en route for Italy:

*"Yesterday was one of those memorable occasions that must be noted. I set out at 9, and rode into Bethune routed Sister Jennings from her lair and we had a cheery little lunch. After that I had a busy rush round doing some shopping. I paid the horrible price of 70 francs for a primus stove and returned in the dark, laden with nosebags containing oysters, mushrooms and walnuts for dinner."*

## The Bristol Gunners

In future, he would be swapping his francs for lire, and his vin blanc for vino bianco.

The Bristol Gunners

## Chapter 6 Andiamo in Italia!

<u>(Let's go to Italy!)</u>

As the 48th Division were withdrawing from Vimy in November 1917 events were unfolding elsewhere which would affect the outcome of the war.

In Russia, the interim dual power system of government between the Kerensky Provisional Government and the Soviets finally collapsed in revolution with the Bolsheviks and their Red Guards taking control. They reached agreement with Germany at the Treaty of Brest-Litovsk to cease hostilities and exit the war. Russia descended in to civil war between the Red and White Russians. The main result for the Allied Powers was that Germany was now free to transfer the bulk of its troops from the east to the Western Front, where it could go on to the offensive early in 1918.

In the Middle East, the Allies were making steady progress against the Turks and the Germans. In Palestine, Beersheba and Gaza had been captured, leading to the capture of Jerusalem in December, ending 673 years of Turkish rule, and marking a major point in the decline of the Ottoman Empire. In Mesopotamia, modern day Iraq, the British Indian Army had consolidated in Baghdad after its capture earlier in 1917. There they prepared for further advances northwards in 1918.

In the Austro-Hungarian camp things were deteriorating. Dissatisfaction with the war was growing, as little progress was being made, and food was becoming scarce. This would lead to riots in many cities, including Vienna and Budapest, in January 1918.

In Britain, the last Zeppelin raids had been carried out in October, though the Germans had moved to bombing raids using their Gotha heavy bombers. The Prime Minister Lloyd George had fallen out with Field Marshall Haig over policy on the Western Front.

The British Army had attacked at Cambrai on November 20th, on a position that had been only weakly held by the Germans. The attack was fought on a different basis than previously. The was no extended barrage, a mass of tanks was used, aeroplanes were used in direct support of ground troops by machine gunning and bombing. It was the first 'blitzkrieg' type attack, though that name would not be in use until two

decades later. The Germans were taken by surprise, the British advancing deeply into occupied territory. However, the British were also taken by surprise at the extent of their advance, and were not properly prepared to take advantage of their success.

One German artillery battery in the village of Flesquières had been commanded by a sharp-witted commander, who had practised his men in using their field guns in a direct fire role against tanks. In this village, the tank attack was brought to a complete halt for many hours, while the battle flowed around on either flank. One tank even reached a position whereby it could fire on a German ammunition train stopped at the rail station in Marcoing. The advance in one day was further than made throughout the whole Battle of Passchendaele that was then coming to a conclusion. The British also failed to appreciate how well the battle had progressed, and did not have reserves available to exploit the gains and turn it into a breakthrough. Many lessons were learned, but unfortunately others were not. The Germans were to develop their attack methods further, and use them to good effect in 1918.

The 48th Division were not the first British troops to be sent to help the Italians. Until October 1917, the war in Italy had been focussed on the Irridenta. The Italians had been engaged upon eleven battles in the region of their northeastern borders, on the line of the River Isonzo, trying to force the Austrians back into what is now Slovenia, but without significant success. Their army was poorly supplied with heavy artillery and General Cadorna had asked the French and British for the loan of heavy batteries to help him deal with Austrian artillery and other tasks.

British General Robertson, and French General Foch, had visited Italy in early 1917 and reported that there were several problems in the Italian Army in addition to its shortage of heavy guns. Contingency plans were put into place for transfer of British and French forces to Italy. Ten British heavy batteries were sent to Italy in April, another three in July, on loan until October. Cadorna requested more artillery from the Allies in September in anticipation of the transfer of German and Austrian troops from the eastern front. No more artillery was sent, however, and in October the batteries that had been sent started to be withdrawn from the front preparatory to returning to France.

The Austrians, with the help of German divisions that had been transferred specially, attacked the Italians on 24th October. The main

## The Bristol Gunners

thrust was around the town of Caporetto from which the battle takes its name (now Kobarid in Slovenia). They used new 'storm trooper' tactics, which were very effective, and would be used again by the Germans the following spring in France. In fact, the new tactics were so successful that the Austrians were to advance all along the front, from east of Lake Garda in the Dolomites to the Adriatic near Gorizia. The penetration at Caporetto split the Italian Army, and it was unable to seal the breakthrough. A withdrawal rapidly turned in to a retreat, leading to some units being routed. Chaos occurred in the rear areas as a mass of troops tried to withdraw across limited numbers of bridges over a series of river lines.

As soon as the attacks started, Cadorna asked for help from France and Britain, who both immediately despatched divisions to Italy using the contingency plans previously set. The first left France before the end of October and arrived in Italy to the west of Venice on 16$^{th}$ November, and these were complete and operational in position by 26$^{th}$ November, about the time that 48$^{th}$ Division started its move south.

The Italians had, in fact, established a new defensive line, on the Piave River, to the east of Venice by 10$^{th}$ November, without the help of the divisions arriving from France. Though the Battle of Caporetto is normally seen as a major disaster for Italy, the reality is that some aspects of the fighting were skilfully carried out by parts of the Italian Army. The Austrians had not prepared for such an advance and quickly outran their supply lines, and errors by some of their Generals prevented them from pursuing the Italians effectively.

Cadorna, as head of the Italian Army, was held accountable and was sacked, with General Diaz taking his place. Cadorna had not been popular with the army or the government so his leaving was not regretted by either party.

The route taken by British and French troops from northern France to Italy was through Paris, down the Rhone valley to Marseilles and then along the French Riviera, crossing into Italy at Ventimiglia, thence by several routes eventually to the Vicenza area. Some French divisions crossed into Italy by road across the Alps at Modane and re-entrained at Susa.

## The Bristol Gunners

The GVA entrained on 21st November and started their long rail journey. Many saw it as an adventure, and preferred to the alternative, which was to return to the trenches and mud of Flanders, Pas-de-Calais, or Picardy.

The Brigade War History summarises the journey:

*"Guns and horses were entrained, a meal cooked at the station, and by 11 p.m. the last battery was all aboard and en route for a new and interesting world.*

*Our route lay through the outskirts of Paris, Lyons, Avignon and, marvellous good fortune, Marseilles and the Riviera.*

*Each day there was one long halt of two hours or more during which horses were watered and fed, the men had a chance to wash and shave at wash-houses and have a hot meal at the camps which had been established for troops.*

*The journey was slow with occasional halts in the open country for anything from a couple of minutes to a couple of hours, and there was always a rush of canvas buckets to the engine driver to beg for hot water.*

*It took five days to amble across France to the Italian border, and the 24 hours between Marseilles and Ventimiglia were glorious. It was leisurely touring in brilliant sun, and the men sat out on the flats among the guns.*

*For two days we wandered along Italian railway lines with no idea of our destination.*

*Finally, detraining was effected at Bovolone and Cerea on November 27. When completed, each trainload of men was lined up on parade in the station and the detraining officer read out an Army order, solemnly warning all troops of the potency of Italian wine, which was far more intoxicating than French vin ordinaire and was extremely heady.*

*The look of incredulous rapture on every face was a thing not to be missed, and the sad tale, read out as an illustration, of one of the first units of another division which had to be practically swept up from the gutters after their first experimental night on the dangerous vino rosso, was definitely received as one of the most charming fairy stories anyone*

had heard since the days when Herren Grimm and Hans Andersen had pitted their inventive minds in fantasy."

They arrived in north eastern Italy on 28th November, the journey having taken seven days. Some of the flavour of the scenes on the train journey can be gained from the comments recorded by Lieutenant F S Gedye, something akin to a holiday outing:

*"The train journey was an extremely delightful experience consisting as it did of a very leisurely ramble through France via the Riviera to Italy."*

*"We halted at Ville-Franche, to water and feed the horses and get bacon cooked for the men. We are now nearing Lyons along the valley of the Saone and it is making us realise, almost for the first time in two years why this country is called La Belle France.*

*I must tell you how we are messing on the way down, our mess is in the next truck. There the batmen live and cook, and of course, our feeding hours are ruled by the halts or slow-downs en route. We are doing very well - I laid in a good store of tinned goods and we vary the 14 days' ration of bully and biscuit which we drew, by tins of sardine, steak and grouse pudding, fruit, tomatoes etc.*

*We get out and rush into the truck. There we have a table and seats fixed up of packing cases and as the rattling makes conversation almost impossible, we sing instead and very seldom any two are singing the same song so it makes for variety.*

*When I woke up at 7 a.m. this morning we were halted at Avignon, from there the scenery has been topping. Just before midday, one silly ass of a driver of mine fell out of his horse-box and was last seen running madly along the line in pursuit of us.*

*An A.S.C. [Army Service Corps] officer gave him a lift and we found him waiting on the platform at Miramas. We got into Marseilles about 8 p.m. and the bay looked perfectly lovely.*

*It has been a perfectly wonderful day I woke at 8 just as we were leaving Toulon and all the morning we have been passing through the most glorious country. Lines of hills on both sides, the crests swathed in*

## The Bristol Gunners

*blue mist, the green of the palms, pines and fruit trees, the red brown soil of the vineyards and here and there brilliant patches of autumn colouring have made a series of unforgettable pictures.*

*Then at last to the sea at St Raphael and from there the scenery was a dream of perfect delight. We saw Cannes just before daylight turned to moonlight [there was no real dusk]. There were a lot of small booths where we halted and I made a lot of useful purchases such as oysters, fresh fish, cooked chicken, nuts etc, which provided us with a six-course dinner which absolutely astounded a French officer we picked up at Cannes and took us to Monaco. He pointed out the places of interest to us. Nice, Beaulieu [and the Hotel Bristol built over a tunnel and owned by a Bosche]. He said there were 23 hotels in Menton owned by Germans at the outbreak of war, who left at once and resumed their commissions in the German army."*

*ITALY! We got to Ventimille at 10.45 last night, and were then told it was 11.45.*

*Our first Italian halt was at Berdighera just after 12. Matt and I, anxious to record the name of our first halt rushed to the window and were in the act of writing down "USCITA" when some instinctive caution made us hesitate lest it should turn out to be something embarrassing - a request not to spit, instead of the name of an Italian town and thus we learnt our first word of Italian on the spot.*

*At 9 am we were at Genoa for 40 minutes and now we are at Arquata.*

*11.30 p.m. We stopped at Vorghara about 3 and went over to a small bar just outside the station for entente vermouth. The girl spoke a little English and told us she thought the English were beautiful, but after a glance at the assembled multitudes of her fellow countrymen, we decided this was not a compliment but merely justice!*

*We have spent the entire day wandering round Italy. We haven't seen an R.T.O. all day and at one halt the stationmaster who, mercifully spoke French, asked us our final destination, as he hadn't the faintest idea what to do with us. As our destination station is altered at least once a day we couldn't help him. We are now rushing, apparently aimlessly up a single line to one station, back along another to another station and we are now*

### The Bristol Gunners

*on a third system at the end of which, Bovolone, our destination station, we believe, is said to be.*

*Nov 28/17.*

*We got to Bovolone, our detraining station at 8 o'clock last night. Detraining was a very slow business as only three trucks could get up to the platform at a time, and after these had been unloaded, the whole train had to be shunted out to get rid of the empty wagons."*

The GVA were not the only people interested in finding out where they were going. Throughout the war espionage was carried out extensively by all sides, and the Germans and Austrians were anxious to work out what was happening. F S Gedye recounts one episode as they skirted round Paris:

*"On the 22nd we passed through Chantilly. Spent a long time skirting around the suburbs of Paris. At 3.45 we passed through Noisy-le-Sec and saw the French gendarmes nab a spy as he alighted from the train. The R.T.O. [Railway Transport Officer] told us the line is infested with them, all trying to find out where we are going."*

Whether this was a real spy, or just an innocent French citizen taking an understandable interest is not known, but this type of event was not uncommon. Similar spy scares occurred in Britain as well.

So the GVA (240 Brigade RFA) arrived in Italy as part of 48th Division. Other British and French divisions were also arriving. The 48th was the fourth British Division to arrive, out of the five actually sent. The total British force was organised in two Corps, XI Corps, and XIV Corps, under General Sir Hubert Plumer. The divisions sent were 5th & 7th Divisions (Regular Army), 23rd and 41st Divisions (New Army) and 48th Division (TF). A sixth division, 21st, a New Army division, was originally intended to go to Italy, but the orders for this were rescinded during the Battle of Cambrai and the 21st remained in France. Six French divisions in total were sent to Italy.

Initially the British forces did not go to the front on the Piave River. The Italian Army had been able to reorganise and establish a strong defensive line there without external assistance. It was felt better to place the British and French troops further to the west of Verona to cover a

### The Bristol Gunners

possible Austrian attack from the north in the area of Lake Garda, an attack that did not, in fact, occur. Placing British troops so far to the rear was thought to be somewhat disconcerting to the Italians, so small groups of liaison officers from British divisions were sent to the forward areas to demonstrate commitment to co-operation with the Italian forces.

After concentrating, two divisions of the British forces went forward into position in late November to take over from Italian troops in the area of the Montello, on the River Piave. The Montello is a low hill overlooking the river, on the west bank, a few miles north of Treviso. The 48th Division, was kept in reserve, with the two remaining British divisions to cover both the British advanced divisions on the Montello, and also Italian forces to the north on the Asiago plateau.

The General Staff had used their comprehensive contingency plans well; however, the situation on the Italian railways caused many problems. Trains arrived at the wrong locations, troops arrived with no orders, maps, and unable to communicate in the Italian language. Road transport was short. The British Army, though, in its usual way, coped admirably with the chaos and all units arrived at their intended destinations by one route or another.

The behaviour and performance of the British Army impressed many Italian civilians and soldiers. The British had need of buildings, property and fields belonging to Italians, and generally treated these with care and respect. A passage in Military Operations in Italy quotes a report from an Italian officer to the British Ambassador in Rome on the behaviour of British troops:

*"They are marvellous. I am not speaking of their discipline, which is perfect, but of the singular delicacy of feeling which distinguishes officers and soldiers. When they leave a billet which they have occupied not a chair is out of its proper place. Their cleanliness is so great that you would not find a straw on the ground. So also with their camps, where hundreds of wagons and quadrupeds have stopped; they do not leave any trace of their passage. No one even takes a glass of water without leave."*

Of course, the Italian officer may have been more used to the behaviour of Italian troops, which by comparison may have favoured the British, but it is cheering to know that our men were so well thought of.

### The Bristol Gunners

There were, of course, many new things to see and comment on for the GVA. Lieutenant FS Gedye recorded his first impressions:

*"We moved off at 9.30 this morning on a four-mile journey just to break in the horses [poor old sods, they were as stiff as pokers last night when we walked them up and down] and are spending tonight in Oppeano. The first actual impression of Italian villages is very favourable, the streets are very broad and clean and the food, if one only knew how to ask for it, good and very cheap. Today, for instance, we had two excellent chickens for lunch - 9 Lira [a lira is worth about 6d] In France; we should have done well to have got them for 14 francs.*

*The Italian men are, almost without exception, evil looking, dirty and unshaven and wear very weird kit, but many of the women and girls are very good-looking, some really handsome and all very much more attractive then the average French peasant.*

*The kits of the Italians are very interesting to us; we have seen very few of the feathered Bersaglieri that one imagines are so plentiful. The majority wear a light blue green uniform with very ugly caps that fit very closely and have a big peak.*

*On most of the stations there were two or three weird looking fellows with grey felt Napoleon - like hats and dark blue cloaks, a sort of guard, evidently [Apologies for my ignorance, O Carabinieri, most attractively garbed of police].*

*Cloaks are THE things for gents to wear and all the old jigs trot about in tweed homburgs and long dark capes and more ostentatious put a bit of their pet goat or retriever around the collar. Makes them all look like the brigand chorus from the "Maid of the Mountains" and they are a fearsome sight at night."*

The Brigade War History also records initial impressions:

*"The change of conditions had a marvellous effect on all of us. The climate, the country, the billets, people, food, everything was new and intensely interesting.*

*Nights were intensely cold and frosty, but by 10 a.m. the sun had*

## The Bristol Gunners

*warmed up everyone, and as we trekked coats were discarded and the hours of daylight were delightful.*

*The country was very flat and the fields were divided into long narrow strips that looked like small holdings by what we later learnt were almond trees, to which wires were strung. Between the trees vines were planted and trained along the wires.*

*The main crop was maize, which was ground by each farm into a yellow flour and made into a sort of heavy batter called polenta. This, with the wine, made from the grapes grown alongside it, formed the staple diet of Northern Italy.*

*All the farms and houses were of stone and of an attractively simple type. There was an arched open store-room on the first floor where maize stalks were dried and stored. Every cottage had its poultry and hens; guinea-fowls and turkeys roamed in and out of the houses, and when we first arrived eggs and poultry were amazingly cheap.*

*The people interested us. The man of the house was usually undeniably dirty and unshaven, apparently bone-lazy, and ambled about to direct his womenfolk in the work of the estate, dressed in a black slouch hat and black cloak, with a bit of goat or retriever on the collar.*

*In those pre-Wallace days we likened him to a bit of brigand chorus from musical comedy.*

*His wife and daughters were generally handsome, very poorly dressed in black, and did all the work of the home, the farm and the land, trudging through mud in wooden, heelless sabots, which remained on their feet by a miracle or long-life skill."*

Lieutenant FS Gedye records another occasion:

*"Tonight I found an A.S.C. Sergeant very much the worst for wear lying in the gutter, on my way back to the billet, and as there were a couple of villainous looking old dagos with black cloaks hovering round I turned out the Sergeant of the guard and had him put in the guard room for the night.*

## The Bristol Gunners

*Our billet is not very pleasant as I found the largest line in "kronks" climbing out of my bed just now, and his wife are taking too intelligent an interest in our belongings. We have therefore taken everything to our room for the night and are sleeping on valises on the floor.*

*On the 2$^{nd}$ we marched to Pressano, which turned out to be a topping little place. The billet includes two really beautiful daughters, the married one being a French edition of Phyllis Dare."*

Phyllis Dare was a popular British music hall actress and singer.

Communicating with their Italian hosts caused temporary difficulties, and at times, much mirth. There were some Italians who could speak English, and some British who had some Italian. Interpreters were made available, but generally only at headquarters locations so that most soldiers had to improvise. F S Gedye again:

*"On the next morning I went forward billeting and overtook Ryan, Prideaux, and Brooke-Taylor. At 10, we met Morgan at Vincentina Noventa. He told us the billeting area allotted to the brigade was the worst he had ever seen and so it turned out to be. After 2½ hours rushing about, we found a school that would accommodate one battery, 2 farms that would take another: we lumped all the outlaying billets together for the third and for the fourth, the still unreconnoitred area.*

*I drew the latter and only just as the battery was arriving, I did find a farm that was outside the area but offered sufficient accommodation.*

*My vocabulary for billeting consisted of about ten words, the only ones I found useful being "Soldate Inglese dormiente" [and in light of later knowledge, how the devil those helped, I can't imagine].* (Soldate Inglese Dormiente does not make sense in any one language, but was probably intended to mean 'British Soldiers Sleep')

*It is absolutely unbelievable that they have dumped this brigade down in this country, with a language none of us can speak a word of, and left us without an interpreter and an English-Italian dictionary is unobtainable!*

*The people of this billet were gentlemen farmers and the family consisted of a white haired mother, the son and his wife and two middle-*

The Bristol Gunners

*aged and three youngish women. They were all delightful people and anxious to do all they could for us. We sat by the fire in their kitchen and with the aid of the French-Italian dictionary, my photos of Ypres and Matt's of this family [which, by the way, has been a huge success at each billet] managed to have a very cheery evening. They described by actions and much derision, the recent actions of the Italians at Caporetto which as far as we could gather, mainly consisted in a dash for the back areas - anyway at one time, the whole family except Mother, were engaged in a panic- stricken rush across the kitchen.*

*We were convulsed with mirth, yet at the same time as it seemed to be a bit of history of our newly met allies, tried to preserve a sadly sympathetic demeanour, and doubtless succeeded in looking completely paralysing idiots."*

Nevertheless, the GVA did adjust to their new environment. Other new experiences included getting transport lifts from Italian Army drivers and finding their way around unfamiliar cities:

*"Yesterday was a rest day and in the afternoon Lane, Matt, Pepper, and I went into Padua. It was bitterly cold and we weren't able to start until just after four.*

*After walking about one and a half miles we were picked up by an Italian Flying Corps lorry. Ye Gods! The speed we went at, we covered the five miles in about six minutes. We missed everything by inches and sometimes a great deal less. People, cattle, vehicles, signposts and even buildings, wiped the dust off the lorry as we flew past.*

*Padua is a most interesting place it has a walled city and as soon as we got inside the gates and walked up a street it was just like a scene from Shakespeare brought to real life. The narrow roadway with foot traffic under the archways of overhanging buildings was just like "Act One, Scene One, a Street in Padua." It was all very old and interesting.*

*It was dusk when we arrived so we couldn't see a lot of the place but we wandered around and under archways and through innumerable squares for an hour, making small purchases and then about 6.45 went and had a nice little dinner for 10 lire apiece.*

## The Bristol Gunners

*Our horses met us about halfway home [by the way it is quite a science to get out of the place, every street is so exactly like every other one and all are badly lit with these arched pavements]."*

While the GVA were adjusting to Italy, the war continued. The front had stabilised after Caporetto, but the Austrians were still seen as a real threat, especially from the north, east of Lake Garda. It seems that there was some discussion as to the best way to use the three British divisions that were in reserve on the Venetian Plain west of Padua.

Italy had been poorly prepared for war, and the civilian population was short of many basics, including fuel. The staple food was grown locally, and conditions were less than perfect for the locals, as Lieutenant FS Gedye describes:

*"The nights are frightfully cold now and the Italians seem to have no idea of comfort. Most of the rooms have no fireplaces, coal is unknown and the only fuel we can buy is light wood - willow branches and that type of stuff and they know how to charge for that too. The more luxurious and self-indulgent villagers, when there is a really bitter night, treat themselves to a small earthenware pan of charcoal which gives about 2 candle-power of heat, but the great Majority don't believe in coddling themselves to this extent.*

*We have been able to look around a bit more and observe the habits of the people. They are very unlike the French - the men are a dirty unshaven looking lot of villains but the women are usually spotlessly clean and often very good-looking.*

*They wear the most extraordinary footgear – a wooden slipper with no heels. Whether this is on account of the shortage of leather or some other form of economy, I don't know, but they look miserable as they slop along these muddy roads with a good layer of mud between stocking and clog, and how they manage to get along without losing the clogs absolutely beats us.*

*For food, they seem to live on Polenta - a very heavy insipid stodge that is a sort of mixture that would result from a cross between stodgy batter and coarse mealy bread which is made from maize flour. This and red wine, most of which tastes like cheap vinegar, is their main diet*

### The Bristol Gunners

*which I suppose they vary occasionally with the poultry and pigs that are kept by every country cottage.*

*The country just round here is all vineyards and maize fields. The vines grow very differently from those I have seen in France and Switzerland. Here the vines are planted against some small variety of tree [these afterwards turned out to be Almond trees and the picture in spring when the fields for miles were massed with the beautiful pink of the almond blossom was simply delightful] and the leads are trained along wires from tree to tree.*

*The result of miles of these fields on dead flat country is to make training for field work almost impossible. If we succeed in finding a position, there is no O.P. unless one scales a neighbouring church spire or if available, a telegraph pole.*

*I hope we shan't have to fight in this sort of country If we do, the only way we shall know where the enemy is, will be seeing them enter the field we are in - a most unpleasing thought."*

By late December, the threat from the Austrians near Lake Garda had not developed and it was thought that the 48th Division should take over position in the hills above Bassano del Grappa. Reconnaissance parties were sent up to examine the Italian positions just north of the small hamlet of Rubbio with a view to relieving the Italians there. The Brigade War History describes this reconnaissance:

*"Immediately after Christmas a series of mountain reconnaissances took place in the Rubbio area. Parties were taken up by 30cwt. lorries in perishingly cold weather to reconnoitre an area it was expected we should take over from the Italians.*

*It took a couple of hours of furious Italian driving to reach the Italian mountain trenches, and the plains were often full of frosty fog, but after a hair-raising drive into the mountains, one reached powdery snow with a clear, sun-bathed air.*

*The Italian drivers were brilliant, but reckless - their way of getting round the innumerable hairpin bends on the ice-covered mountain roads was to rush at them at 40 to 45 miles an hour, jam on all brakes and skid round.*

The Bristol Gunners

*An error of judgment might mean a sheer drop over the edge of the road of anything from 100 to 1,000 feet, and on some of the more dangerous bends the wreckage of one or more lorries could be seen hundreds of feet below.*

*The Italian trenches, blasted out of solid rock, were marvels of engineering and the front line, facing a ravine or valley with a few crevasses near, might be thousands of yards from the Austrian line on the mountain opposite.*

*This, with the whole area thickly covered with pine trees, showed us that we would have to learn a new method of warfare.*

*On one of these mountain reconnaissances, our C.O. had with him all his battery commanders, three captains and an adjutant.*

*We asked permission to walk down the mountain to the next village on our way home to get warm after a very cold day, whereupon he suddenly thought it would be amusing to go straight home to the Brigade, some 30 or 40 miles away and leave everyone to find their own way home.*

*He proceeded to do so. The stranded senior officers clambered down to Marostica, a really wonderful old walled town at the foot of the mountains, held a council of war and decided that, as it was impossible to find a "lorry-hop" to our very rural area, they had earned a night in comfort.*

*So all lorry-hopped into Vicenza, the nearest big town."*

The war in the mountains, part of the Dolomites, was fought on a very different basis from that on the Western Front. The countryside was undulating, with very deep and steep sided valleys. The underlying rock, limestone, was close to the surface with little soil, and the area was heavily wooded in places with tall pine trees. The Italian Army had used their considerable engineering skills to create extensive trenches, tunnels, bunkers, and roads in the hills as part of their defensive positions. Pre-war the Italians had been very advanced in developing hydro - electric power generation in the hills using the multitude of rivers and streams and most village houses had electrical power connected, something that

was not so back home in Britain. This electrical power was used extensively by the Italian Army to power cable lifts that were used extensively to convey supplies between the Venetian Plain and positions in the hills.

Italian Army doctrine in defence was still based on methods used at the start of the war. The front line trench was substantial and cut into the rock, but no support lines or communication trenches had been provided. This meant that the positions had little depth, and movement into and out of the front line had to be 'over the top', exposed to observation and hostile fire. The British were impressed, though, with the engineering prowess and fortitude of their Italian comrades.

The weather was also to become a factor. Conditions on the plain could be very different to the higher ground; one could be shrouded in fog while the other was in bright sunshine. Days could be bitingly cold, or mild and damp.

The division spent all of January on the plain between Padua and Vicenza. Time was used in training and visits between the various nations (Italian, French, and British). The Italian military bands played music, football matches were played between neighbouring units. Mock battles and other exercises were carried out, with varying degrees of efficiency, and the weather often interfering. Due to winter conditions, the war in the mountains had reached a low level of activity.

In the wider world, though, events continued to unfold in early 1918. Conditions for the Central Powers (Germany and Austro-Hungary) became harder. Food riots broke out in Vienna and Budapest in January. Russia had stopped fighting, and the Central Powers were able to move considerable numbers of divisions from the east to the west and south. American forces were starting to enter the front lines on the Western Front, their numbers growing strongly as the year progressed, but they were not yet able to fight independently. American forces needed to gain experience and training. Their heavy weaponry and logistics were provided by the French and British. General Pershing, the senior American in Europe, resisted attempts to integrate his forces with the French and British, insisting that they fight as an American Army, under his command.

## The Bristol Gunners

In Italy, a token American force of one regiment of infantry arrived to help defend the Piave line. Italy was short of everything needed to progress the war. Food was becoming scarce, and coal for fuel extremely so. Italy had no coalfields of her own. The supply from France had reduced as the Germans occupied the coalfields in Flanders. Supplies from Britain were restricted by shipping shortages. Italy lent 100,000 men to France to help with munitions and other war material production. Without Allied assistance, Italy would have succumbed and exited the war, allowing more Austrian troops to be sent elsewhere to help the German cause. Consequently, Britain and France were determined to keep Italy in the fight.

The enemy engaged on a campaign of night aerial bombing of the Italian towns behind the front, which made trips to town for recreation a dangerous prospect for men of the GVA. Lieutenant F S Gedye mentions this in his diaries:

*"I rode into Treviso, which is about 6 miles away and is a most depressing place.*

*It is bombed nearly every night and is also within gun range. From what I saw of it, it is only slightly damaged but practically all the civilians have cleared out and only about four shops are open so it feels rather like a city of the dead. The streets are absolutely silent and felt horribly cold although it was a glorious afternoon. Water is the great difficulty here. There is practically none at all and so our clever staff have billeted four batteries and the crush at watering parades is really chronic.*

*Practically every night, we have Austriaco planes over bombing Treviso and villages around although they haven't visited us yet.*

*The Italians have some A.A. guns but putrid searchlights - we have no A.A. and apparently neither of us have any planes that can get up and scrap at night so each battery has to arm the picket with rifles. They have to wake the orderly officer if planes come over and fire in defence of the village. Oh, Futility!"*

In fact the bombing aircraft were not Austrian, but German. The Austrians were not in the habit of bombing towns or cities, but this change in behaviour is attributed to German squadrons being sent to help

### The Bristol Gunners

the Austrians, and the Germans holding a different view as to the sanctity of built up areas. They had been night bombing towns and villages in the rear areas on the Western Front since early 1917, and had been sending Zeppelins and Gotha bombers to bomb London and other places from early in 1915.

48th Division remained out of the line, in reserve, throughout January and the early part of February, while the High Command decided what to do with them.

On 23rd February orders arrived. The 48th Division was to move forward to relieve the 41st Division in its positions on the Montello overlooking the Piave River. In the event, the orders contained an error, and they actually relieved the 7th Division, also on the Montello, but on the southern side of the hill.

Lieutenant Colonel GH Barnett describes the position on the hill in the book 'With the 48th Division in Italy':

*"This is an oddly-shaped hog's back hill, some eight miles long and averaging three miles in breadth. It is a sort of excrescence on the uniform flat of the plain, and is probably of volcanic origin. The centre of the hill is a ridge, which is about 1,000 feet above sea-level, and the slopes are steeper on the northern and eastern sides than on the southern and western. About twenty parallel roads, not more than 1,000 yards apart, run right over the ridge from north to south; there is a lateral road, which runs along the top of the ridge, and another making a complete circuit of the base. The story is that originally the Montello was densely wooded with heavy trees, and that these were felled and used for the piles on which Venice was made.*

*The soil is of red sandstone, the roads are unmetalled, and consequently a comparatively small amount of rain renders them almost impassable. The terrain is fairly closely cultivated, with isolated farmhouses and cottages dotted about. There are some spinneys and a good deal of undergrowth, but no large trees now.*

*To the north the hill is bounded by the river Piave, which emerges from the mountains at Pederobba, curls to the south at Jacor, and leaves the eastern end of the hill in a south-east direction at the ruined village of Nervesa, which was in the front line. The Piave here consists of a*

riverbed over half a mile wide, and, normally, the water flows through various channels from ten to thirty feet in width with a depth of four to six feet. The melting of snow in the mountains or heavy rain may, however, turn this collection of small streams into a huge turbulent river; hence it can be easily seen that any operations conducted with a view to crossing the river are attended by the gravest risks."

This was the first time that the division had been in the front line since their time at Vimy in early November, three months earlier. Observation into enemy territory on the far side of the river was good, though positions on the Montello were also prone to enemy observation and interference by artillery, it being at a bend in the river and therefore open to two sides, to the north and east.

There were limited crossing places on the Piave, the bridges having been destroyed, and positions for assault bridging limited by the width and variable state of the river flow.

The Montello was a key position in the line, both for defence and attack. It would become the scene of intense attacks by the Austrians later in the year. However during the two weeks that the division was there hostile activity was very subdued, and it was noted that casualty rates were very low.

Lieutenant Colonel Barnett comments:

*"Taking it all round, it was the most quiet and comfortable sector ever held by the Division during the war. Hostile artillery action was negligible, the weather above the average, observation splendid, and there was plenty of opportunity for recreation. The artillery had a view second to none, with pleasant quarters, and gun positions which were excellent in 'peace' warfare of this kind."*

Lieutenant FS Gedye accords with this view when he describes his move to the Montello to take over positions from another artillery brigade:

*"The Major and I were bound for the position and Fisher came up to guide the teams back. It was a topping morning for the road; a bit cold to start with but about 8.30, it was glorious. We came up through Castagnole and Pozana and got to the wagon lines of B/76 Bde about*

The Bristol Gunners

*11.30. After lunch, the Major took six mounted men up to the position and six of the working party came back.*

*I set off at 5 with the guns. As the Huns have a nasty habit of coming over in planes at dusk and machine-gunning the traffic, we opened out to a good interval and had some rifles ready for any rash aviator that came too close.*

*I got to the position about 7. Couldn't see much of it last night but found our quarters quite de luxe. Bar a few men in dugouts, the battery is billeted in a big farm called Casa Freschi, just outside Arcole and about 200 yards from the guns.*

*The servants cook and sleep in a big entrance hall affair and we have our mess and bedroom in a room leading out of it. There is a deluxe bath and toilet saloon upstairs.*

*Yesterday morning I had a look round the position - it is quite excellent - an old Italian 4 gun position in a hedge but the Austrians discovered it and sent over about 20 rounds and rumour has it that the Italians were last seen going all out for Padua.*

*The country here is rather extraordinary - dead flat all round until you get to the Montello, which is a long low mound, rather like a very much elongated Brean Down, two-thirds of which is on this side of the Piave and is held by us and the other third is on the other river bank and is, of course, Austrian. Although far from being a mountain, it overlooks the whole area here; from all positions you can see it and a huge white building at the south of it called San Salvatore. The place has hardly been touched - I was looking at it yesterday and thought I spotted a hole in the roof otherwise it looks perfectly sound. Our heavies are dealing with it on DerTag [the day] I hear. The country is even flatter than Flanders and all the roads near the front have to be screened, sometimes on both sides.*

*The quiet on this front is simply too amazing for words, for hours on end there isn't even a rifle shot to be heard and if more then 20 rounds came over it would mean an S.O.S. Our heavies cough up a few weary rounds after breakfast and lunch and the Bosche sends over an occasional round of their combined shrapnel and H.E. 4.2, and generally lands in the middle of an empty field.*

### The Bristol Gunners

*It is weird stuff - bursts in the air with a white puff and then part goes on and bursts on the ground - H.E. Both bursts look fairly feeble."*

Though things seemed quiet in Italy, plans were afoot on both sides. The Germans had transferred their divisions from east to west, and would launch a massive attack on the Western Front, starting on March 21st. They would make extensive use of 'stormtrooper' tactics, using small groups of highly trained soldiers to infiltrate through our lines with minimal artillery bombardment. This offensive was to be known as the 'Kaiserschlacht' (Kaiser's Battle), and it would throw the British and French back many miles and almost achieve a critical breakthrough to end the war. The British held, though, and the German offensive would run out of steam and come to an exhausted halt in July 1918.

In Italy, the Allies were planning an attack across the Piave, to start in early March, but this was cancelled when heavy rain caused the Piave to swell and prevent any crossing. Lieutenant F S Gedye comments on this in his diaries:

*"The rain arrived on March 1st., detonating the proximity of a British offensive. It really leaves no doubt about the matter at all. The powers above do not work for us in the matter of weather. It has been getting steadily wetter for some days and now the Piave, which could be waded when we came into action, has risen three feet and is swirling down carrying with it the preliminary foundations of the bridges that the R.E.s were preparing for the show. The attack, after several postponements, was to have come off at dawn to-morrow, but we heard at midday that it has all been postponed.*

*The barrage, which we worked out last night was a bit of a brute. The general scheme was that at 7 p.m. on "Y" night, two battalions were to cross in boats, one at Casa Trentino and the other at the railway bridge and lie under the dam on the other side until Zero hour. They would then advance and capture their objectives.*

*As soon as they had consolidated these positions and were assembling to push on to their final objectives, a daylight parachute rocket will be sent up which opens disclosing the French flag. As soon as this is seen, the C.R.A. will fix "X" hour. That is, the moment for our barrage to start to cover the final advance.*

### The Bristol Gunners

*This will be recognised by the attackers by the increased rate of fire and each battery will fire one round of percussion before going on to the usual low airbursts.*

*When the final objectives [which are not a mile from the river bank] have been taken, we lay our guns on a S.O.S. line all round the captured ground and our people hold the ground for 8 hours.*

*They then return to our side of the river again. The whole of our show is merely a diversion for an Italian show which is to clear the Austrians from the bank of the river further south.*

*It is a big show and on the day, a barrage will open from the Vigor on our left to Venice - a distance of 80 Miles.*

*That is the scheme as it stands [postponed] at present. Owing to the extraordinary idea of fixing the offensive at a time when the wet season is, apparently, always in progress here, every stream and ditch is filling rapidly and it looks as though the whole show will definitely be off."*

British senior officers now clearly understood the need for flexibility and control of artillery during attacks, and from the passage above it seems that much thought had gone into working out how to communicate (with parachute flags and use of percussion shells). One wonders if this scheme would have worked, especially looking out for an aerial French flag from some miles in rear. Perhaps it was fortuitous that this particular plan was not put to the test as the 'fog of war' would almost certainly have reduced the plan to chaos.

British Military Intelligence in London had received some warning of the impending Kaiserschlacht attacks, and it was decided to thin out the British (and French) presence in Italy by returning some of the divisions back to the south of France. They would be held as reserves there, being able to be sent north to the Western Front, or back to Italy, when needed in either place. Some Italian troops had been sent to serve on the Western Front, to gain experience and justify the 'mutual assistance' relationship between the Italians and their allies. It was felt that though the Western Front would need all the divisions that could be found, if all British and French troops were recalled from Italy then the Italians may well recall their divisions to Italy. General Haig, commanding the British on the Western Front was asked if he would like to receive two British divisions,

### The Bristol Gunners

or four Italian divisions. He chose to receive the two British divisions, and thus 5th and 41st Divisions withdrew from the line and started to move back to France.

The British forces in Italy then comprised three divisions, and this required only a single corps headquarters. Therefore, General Plumer and his Army HQ returned to France, leaving the remaining troops to be commanded by General Cavan. His XIV Corps, comprised 7th, 23rd, and 48th Divisions.

Lieutenant F S Gedye mentions this in his diaries in March:

*"We are now wondering what it all means and whether we go back to France instead of the division we were about to relieve or whether the much-talked-of Hun offensive in the west is not coming off and the real show will take place here.*

*Of this, there have been some vague rumours lately and the Italians are preparing for a big Bosche drive from Lake Garda. The Italians are on the south of this lake but the Austrians hold the northern portion and if they could drive down over the narrow strip of plain and reach Genoa, Italy and all of us would be cut off."*

It was decided that the British would move from the Piave front around the Montello to take up positions on the Asiago Plateau. This was a mountainous area, just west of the positions near Rubbio that had been reconnoitred in December. This change of position would require some training and re-equipment of the British forces. The Corps was sent back to do this in the area just west of Vicenza in the first days of April 1918.

On 9th April, the 48th Division was visited by the Duke of Connaught (then Governor General of Canada and a son of Queen Victoria) who inspected one of the infantry brigades (144th). Lieutenant Colonel George Barnett mentions this in his book, illustrating one of the problems of operating with allies:

*"On the 9th April H.R.H. the Duke of Connaught inspected the 144th Brigade. The review went off well, although the salute was somewhat spoilt by Italian airmen from the aerodrome at Castel Gomberto, who insisted on doing 'stunts' about twenty feet above the heads of the troops."*

## The Bristol Gunners

The GVA were billeted in the village of Montecchio Maggiore, the Brigade War History notes:

*"At the beginning, of April the brigade moved to Montecchio Maggiore, a village in the foothills, our own particular hill being surmounted by two ruins that rumour ascribed to the Montagues and Capulets.* (The warring families in Shakespeare's Romeo and Juliet.)

*We learnt later that twin ruins are generously allotted to the Montagues and Capulets in Italy as are four-poster beds to Elizabeth, or skulls to Charles I in this country."*

During early April working parties went up into the mountains on the edge of the Asiago Plateau to prepare positions for a planned offensive later in the spring. During this time the weather improved, as described in the Brigade War History:

*"Spring came suddenly to the plains, and in the space of two or three days the whole district was transformed into a fairyland of pink and white almond blossom, mingled with the pale green of young vines and crops.*

*Spring in Italy was a marvellous experience - a gigantic contrast to the awful thaw of Peronne in '17.'*

On 24th April preparations in the hills were complete, and the division marched up into position near Monte Langabisa.

The Asiago Plateau was a critical location, and it is worth reading the description it in Lieutenant Colonel George Barnett's book:

*"Some description of the Asiago Plateau position is necessary for the reader to understand the sector taken over by the British forces. The Venetian Plain extends northwards to a line running roughly from east to west through Marostica, Breganze, Thiene, and Schio. Just north of this line, the ground rises abruptly to an average height of 4,000 to 5,000 feet. The Asiago Plateau is a sort of natural basin in the Alps, and is some seven miles in extent from east to west, and three miles from north to south.*

## The Bristol Gunners

*The central point of the plateau is the town of Asiago (3,000 feet), a well known pre-war winter sports resort. The plateau is bounded on the south by pine covered mountains of a depth of about 4,000 yards to the point where the mountains slope steeply down to the plain. To the north lies a higher and deeper range of mountains guarding the Southern Trentino, and merging back gradually into the high Alps. At the western end the plateau narrows down to the gloomy ravine of the Val d'Assa, where the opposing front trenches are close to one another on each side of an impassable gorge some 2,000 feet deep. To the east, the plateau again ends in the rugged heights on each side of the Brenta* (River Brenta).

*The plateau itself consists of undulating cultivated land freely sprinkled with villages, and perfectly adaptable for ordinary military operations.*

*The importance of the position may be judged when the point is grasped that this was the only part of the whole Italian mountain front where the operations of ordinary attack were possible."*

The Val d'Assa, the valley of the River Assa, is steep sided and a strong natural barrier. The poet, Dante, is thought to have visited the valley and used it as his inspiration for the Gates of Hell in his work 'Divine Comedy.' The Brenta is one of the rivers that run from the mountains to the sea across the Venetian Plain, emerging from the hills at Bassano del Grappa.

The plateau was important because an Austrian attack in this position threatened to penetrate to the Adriatic coast west of Venice and thereby cutting off the bulk of the Italian Army facing east on the Piave River. Similarly, it was realistically the only point where the Allies could attack the Austrians on the mountain line with any chance of success. The border with Austria ran just north of the plateau, Trentino being at that time an Austrian province, but which is now part of Italy.

## The Bristol Gunners

**B Battery gunners relaxing outside their hutted accommodation having helped to win the war. The man standing at the far right of the back row is Corporal Henry James Shakespeare, on whose camera this picture was taken.** (photo Peter Shakespeare, Corporal Shakespeare's grandson)

In the positions that the British would take over, two divisions would be in the front line, with one in reserve. The three divisions would rotate, each taking a turn in reserve.

The weather on the plateau, though it was now spring, could be fickle. Bright sunshine could raise the temperature, though snow could fall as late as June. Extra warm clothing and sleeping bags were supplied from Italian Army stocks. In those days, British soldiers normally used blankets; a sleeping bag was new and unusual technology at that time.

Lieutenant F S Gedye describes visiting the mountain positions:

*"Yesterday Lane took B.C.s up by lorry to see how the battery positions were progressing. It was a jolly interesting day. We went up via Vicenza, Thiene and Chiuppano and then, at Caltrano, began to climb the mountains.*

## The Bristol Gunners

*It was the usual type of winding road, but the scenery was much finer than on the Rubbio road. We passed into the area of pine forests which was really lovely.*

*Our position is at Boscon, just in front of a large quarry and right in a pine forest, a lot of the trees have been cleared away in front and we are virtually in the open and the pits look right down on the Asiago Plateau.*

*The gunpits are made by cutting down the lighter pine trees and fixing them on to other growing trees to form an overhead framework. Then branches are laid across the top and round the sides which makes a very excellent camouflaged cover. The men are living in rough shacks and we have a big cave in the quarry for shelter in time of need."*

On another trip, a few days later:

*"I came up yesterday to spend a couple of nights with Fisher on the position, we lorried up and got here about one. As usual, it was raining, it practically always is up here. You leave the plains in a cloud of dust and get up here to find it either raining or hailing and after spending a day slopping about in the sludge you get back to the plains to find it as dry and dusty as ever. Yesterday afternoon, after looking round the position with Fisher, we went up to an O.P. on Kaberlaba that has a fine view of the plateau from this western edge of Asiago to Albaredo.*

*It was most interesting to get a panoramic view of the whole area. This morning we went down to have a look at the road forward, we called in at Battn. H.Q. and got a pass to go out in front of our own wire and strolled out into No Mans Land.*

*It is the most amazing thing in the world this war in the mountains. There are a few shell holes and the road is in perfect condition. It is camouflaged up to a certain point by us, then there is a gap about 100 yards and the rest is screened by the Austrians.*

*We went up to a farmhouse called Bassastoc, which is just this side of the Austrian wire. It is held by them at night or was until a few nights ago but we found it empty when we got there.*

## The Bristol Gunners

*It was very disappointing as regards view - No Mans Land is a succession of bumps and lumps and there was a little crest in front that prevented our getting a good view.*

*On the way back, we meet Major Corsan and Carter who were going about with hands on revolvers as the Company commander told them the Austrians had been mooching about last night. It was really rather funny, because although we had our revolvers, it would have taken at least a minute to get at them and by that time I don't suppose we should have needed them."*

Conditions in Italy were very different from the Western Front. It seems that both sides could walk in to No Man's Land with little fear of being fired at by the other side. On the Western Front merely raising one's head above a trench would result in a sniper's bullet or shell fire. Here things were almost peaceful, a 'live and let live' situation.

48th Division was taking up position as the right hand division in the area allocated to the British, facing to the North across the plateau. The Italians occupied positions to the west (left) and the French to the east (right).

The positions had been built by the Italian Army, very much on old concepts of line defence. The British felt that this trench line was too thin, and proceeded to develop the position based on defence in depth and elasticity. They put outposts deep into No Man's Land to both give early warning of enemy activity and better observation into areas of dead ground - areas where observation is impeded by hills and hollows in the ground.

The trenches had been cut into the limestone rock by the Italians, but were deemed unsuitable for a number of reasons. Firstly, they were deep and had no fire steps, so engaging the enemy from them was not possible without improvement. There were limited communication trenches, so front trenches had to be entered and left 'over the top.' There were only limited support trenches (second and third lines of fighting trenches) to give fall back lines of defence. Logistics were difficult, due not only to limited roads, but also to the elevation and weather. Mules and ponies used for resupply quickly became exhausted and needed special facilities. Water was short, for animals and humans, and special pipelines had to be installed.

## The Bristol Gunners

Some of the gun positions were placed in quarries and other natural dips. This gave some protection from shellfire and observation, but coupled with the tall pine forests also gave cresting and clearance problems when firing. The QF 18 Pounder gun had a very limited maximum elevation of 18 degrees, so any obstruction (quarry wall, tree, building) in the line of fire could be very limiting as to which targets could be engaged. Later, in June, during the Battle of Asiago, a battery of heavy guns in a quarry fired at night without checking crest clearance, resulting in shells exploding on the quarry wall, killing and wounding several men. Lieutenant F S Gedye refers to this problem in his diaries:

*"Last night I was at night O.P. on Kaberlaba and it was the first fine day since we came up here. I was in great luck for although it got very cold, it remained dry - no small consideration when you spend half the night in an open trench looking out and the rest under three sheets of corrugated iron in the same trench.*

*Dawn was a very fine sight - the snowy mountains that lie beyond the western end of the plateau and are I believe, the Dolomites, were lit up by the still invisible sun to a wonderful shade of rose which was well set off by the dark green of the fir trees.*

*I have had a dull job the last two days, finding out what each gun can fire, owing to being in the midst of a forest, although we have cut down some of the trees, we can't cut down the lot, and consequently we have to be awfully careful that the guns are not pointing actually at the tree trunks."*

The main British trench positions were placed in forests, which gave good protection from observation, but limited visibility for artillery observers who needed the best possible field of view. Later we will read an account by Lieutenant FS Gedye who, during an Austrian attack and under fierce shellfire, had to control artillery fire from an OP ten metres above ground in a tree at the top of Monte Lemerle, and vulnerable to splinters and bullets. Not an ideal position for any soldier. Gedye describes a similar OP in quieter times:

*"The O.P. is marvellous - perched at the top of three very tall fir trees and nearly at the top of the mountain. A wonderful view but give me terra firma when the wind blows. I believe it is perfectly safe - the Italians generally make a good job of these things but there are horrible creaks*

*and groans during a storm. I had an amusing day there today. The Bosche had left a motor lorry on the road nearly out of our range and I spent a happy half hour trying to do it a bit of no good."*

Faced with inadequately prepared positions the British set about improving things with energy and the benefit of their Western Front experience.

Another habit brought in from the Western Front was that of activism. The Austrians opposite were used to the Italian habit of 'live and let live', there being little in the way of active or aggressive actions on either side, until, of course, the British arrived.

The artillery observers set about identifying as many actual and likely enemy positions as possible and then proceeded to fire at them. The Austrian trenches were half way across the plateau, and their supply lines were open to observation from the hills on our side of the open ground, so the targets seen and shot at were many and varied. This provoked a degree of retaliation from the Austrians, but their doctrine seemed to be to shell almost at random with no apparent pattern.

The British infantry immediately moved to dominate No Man's Land with active and energetic patrolling.

Soon after arrival the winter snows thawed, and revealed the accumulated detritus of three years occupation by troops with limited attention to field hygiene. This was also put right by all units until the position started to take on the semblance of an effective and efficient military operation.

Troops not in the front trenches were accommodated in wooden huts or underground dugouts which were on the whole efficiently heated and comfortable.

Lieutenant F S Gedye describes his first impressions of the position:

*"The whole place is pretty cheerless. Our quarters are very extraordinary - the position is about 150 ft below the top of Monte Longabisa and in the midst of the pines.*

## The Bristol Gunners

*Our hut is built on the ledge of a ravine - to get to it you descend ten deep log steps and along a narrow platform to the hut which is about 20ft by 6ft.*

*As you walk into it, there is about a yawning ravine about 12 to 15 feet across and at least 100ft deep. The mess is built on the side narrow ledge with a frame work of logs and the ravine side is walled with split logs. The other side is neat rock and it is roofed with red tiles. The whole thing is a triumph of Italian building but looks and, at first feels, most uncanny.*

*The whole place leaks abominably. The tiles are badly laid and far from waterproof, snow, hail and rain pour down the rock side and the place is filthily cold and draughty.*

*Fisher and I are sleeping in a little hole in the rock off the mess which also leaks badly - in fact the floor of our bedroom has a hole about 2ft deep and the water that drops from the roof onto the Macintosh sheet which covers my valise drains down on to the ground, into this hole and provides us with washing water.*

*It hailed solidly all yesterday afternoon and snowed all night. This morning after breakfast, the sun came out and the general view was priceless; but it is simply beastly to be back in winter conditions again in the line with day O.P., and night O.P. and liaison three nights out of four. Already we are fed up to the neck with the Asiago Plateau; it is an amazingly cold, wet, and cheerless place."*

Being on duty at another OP was not much better. FS Gedye:

*"My turn for the O.P. this morning and I left the battery at 7 a.m. The snow is about 6 inches deep and still falling intermittently mingled with sleet and hail. The O.P. is a hole in a trench covered with two sheets of corrugated iron, which drip continually, and it is unpleasantly cold sitting still in gumboots.*

*At the moment it is sleeting and the plateau is obscured by mists and clouds. Our zone is left of Asiago in the neighbourhood of Roana and the view would be interesting if one could look at it in anything like comfort.*

### The Bristol Gunners

*The cave leaked such bucketsful on to my bed that I cleared out the last night and slept in the mess and it was a vast improvement. Poor old Matt had a putrid night last night at Group Night O.P. - 7p.m. to 7 a.m. in an open trench with absolutely no cover and it rained without pause until 3a.m.*

*We have a working party on it to-day - the people we relieve seem to have no idea of how not to do things.*

*We have never taken over worse quarters, worse registrations and worse general arrangements. And it all looks like sheer incapacity, as we are steadily settling in and making everything quite reasonably comfortable."*

All three British divisions were substantially under strength at this time. When they were withdrawn from Flanders their battle and other casualties were not replaced, and new drafts of reinforcements were directed to the Western Front where it was felt that they were more use in view of the expected German spring attacks. In addition, a flu epidemic had occurred, with a proportion of troops being non effective on each day. This was a precursor to the Spanish Flu epidemic that in 1919 would kill more people worldwide than had been killed in the war. The overall effect was that no unit was up to full strength, and many were at half strength for much of the time.

Supply was another difficulty. Main supply dumps were established at the base of the mountains, at the edge of the Venetian Plain. From this position, there were only limited numbers of roads up onto the plateau, and return journey times between the dumps and the forward areas took the best part of a full day. Some lorries were available, but most transport was made by mules or electric cables lifts (called 'teleferica.') The British Army had become used to an extremely efficient and beneficent supply organisation on the Western Front. In Italy the supply situation was more difficult, with supply stretching all the way back to UK for many items, and some resources in short supply in Italy generally.

On the plateau itself, there were few roads and flat areas suitable for supply dumps. New tracks had to be built to facilitate troop and supply movement between the rear and the forward trenches, as well as laterally, across and to the rear of the front to enable equipment, troops and supplies to be repositioned in case of attack.

### The Bristol Gunners

In one part of the position, behind the mountain of Monte Lemerle, this lack of suitable facilities was to lead to severe problems during an Austrian attack in the summer, when ammunition and other stores in a dump were set on fire by Austrian shelling. All the main routes to and from that part of the front became impassable due to the heat and danger from exploding ammunition. Add in the fact that an important headquarters was also in the same area, and the battle was almost lost due to the confusion and inability to move counterattack forces to repel the Austrians.

The British were also aggressive and assertive in the air war. Lieutenant FS Gedye describes one brief event:

*"It's beastly late - in fact 12.15 a.m. to-morrow, but I must make a note of one or two things.*

*First, a most priceless aeroplane show I saw from the O.P. Just after 2, three aeroplanes came round the corner from Kaberlaba spur not more than 100 ft up and skimmed over the Hun lines. They then flew to the Val d'Assa, a ravine like pass that runs from the Plateau right back through the Austrian Mountains. They dropped a couple of bombs on a battery position near it, flew up the valley and dropped some more and then came back machine-gunning trenches and roads.*

*The whole thing didn't take more than 4 minutes but the Austrians never fired a round. I've never seen anything like it and the background of towering mountains made it all the more spectacular."*

In mid May 48th Division were relieved and went back into reserve on the plain.

The British and French were planning an attack to advance across the plateau, pushing the Austrians back into the mountains beyond. In reserve on the plain, preparing and training for the attack, the GVA found the weather had changed dramatically since they had trekked up into the mountains six weeks earlier. The summer had arrived, and everyone changed into more suitable clothing, including topees, referred to as 'Egyptian helmets' or 'pith helmets.' Changes were needed to routines, and road movements became the stuff of night time. FS Gedye:

## The Bristol Gunners

*"We completed the relief and lorried down to the W.L. on the 22nd. The heat down there was very great after the mountains. In the evening we lorried into Thiene for dinner - a merry little party of seven.*

*On the 23rd, we set out at 8 a.m. and trekked to our first halt, a big field near Novoleco. It was terrifically hot and dusty on the road and we were glad to get there although there was a great scarcity of shade.*

*The next morning we moved off at 4 a.m. in the pre-dawn for our billets in the Montecchio area. We had a good trek - glorious weather and delightfully cool until about 8.30. The scenery was wonderful and the whole country is absolutely transformed since we were last on the Plains.*

*Our billet was at a big farm called Oltr'Agno, about 2 miles out of Montecchio.*

*We only had one night there and moved off at 9 a.m. for the school. [Gunnery H.Q School at Palazzo Forte, Montemerlo]*

*Glow worms and fire flies made their appearance after dusk and sleeping in a tent in the evening and wandering about this delightful country in the cool of the evening was a delightful experience.*

*We had a jolly good turn out and the battery looked well as it moved out.*

*Prideaux came to see us off and some of Brigade H.Q. staff came to wish us luck as we passed. It was a perfect night and about 10.30 p.m. it was as bright as day. It was comfortably cool on the road and practically no traffic or dust.*

*We stopped about 1a.m., just outside of Vicenza for water and feed and we had cocoa and biscuits. The sensation of trekking along the silent roads on these cool nights after hot and trying days is rather wonderful. There is the jangle of harness, the delicious odour of wheels on the gravel and overall the delicious odour of horse mingling with the fragrant night air. The general effect is one of silence or at any rate isolation and you go slowly along the road wrapped up in the most pleasant thoughts without a care on your mind.*

### The Bristol Gunners

*This trek became bit monotonous though about 4 a.m. and by 6.30 a.m. when we reached our resting place Longare, we were all very sleepy. The worst of horses in this hot weather is they have to be watered about every two hours and it means continual parades for the men. We arranged to move on for the School at 6 p.m. and once again although there had been a lot of work and very little sleep, the harness looked perfect.*

*This time our luck was utterly out, it started to rain just as we set out and developed into a series of heavy thunderstorms that lasted through our three hours on the road. Result - everyone soaked through and the harness ruined. When we got in, it was more or less dark and the accommodation regards horses and harness, very indifferent."*

As things turned out, the attack by the British and French was postponed. Military intelligence had deduced that an attack was to be launched by the Austrians along the whole front, but when and where was not clear. Orders were issued to put the positions on the plateau into strong defence, and 48th Division were tasked with climbing back up there, this time taking over the position immediately to the left of their former position, from the Regular Army 7th Division. Unfortunately for the 48th Division, and especially Major General Robert Fanshawe, this area had not been as fully improved and hardened as they had done at their previous positions to the right. In time, this would lead to serious problems for the division. Lieutenant F S Gedye describes the arrival of orders to return just as they had trekked through the summer heat and rainstorm to set up an artillery training school:

*"We heard on the evening of the 28th (May) that we were to be relieved here on the 31st by the 106th battery, 7th Div. It really is a damnable shame that the staff should work with absolutely no consideration for the units. We have had four days of hot, tiring trek down here and long hours of cleaning up to be ready for the re-opening of the school next Monday and now the whole thing is washed out and we have to trek back into action.*

*We are all feeling absolutely fed up, not only at missing what should have been a very delightful month, but at this eternal messing about and muddling that is part and parcel of the British Staff.*

## The Bristol Gunners

*We left the school at 8.45 a.m. on the 31st. it was the first really fine day since we had arrived there and the day before, every man had been issued with the new drill jacket and pith helmet. When we arrived on parade at 8.15, it really looked jolly smart.*

*The gunpark was in a big field and all the harness was in priceless condition and the sunshine showed the whole turn - out up to the best advantage.*

*My section was in the rear on the march and as I watched the battery move out in column of route, I nearly forgot myself and shouted "Ooray" - it looked such a ripping good show.*

*We had to halt for water and feed and arrived in Vicenza about 4.30 p.m. The horses were put on lines in a street just outside the old walls of the city and we had a billet next door to the Hotel Roma.*

*During the evening, which Matt, Little and myself made into quite a historic occasion, we met a very interesting Yank officer who is attached to the Italian army.*

*We taught him quite a lot, or at least he said we did. The next morning, I set off at 6.30 a.m. to come up in advance to the position and have a look round. The guns are only about ½ mile from our first position in the mountains.*

*The Major of this Bty is Abell, whom we have met up here before. The officers' quarters, which I arrived at first, are very comfortable. I sleep very soundly in a wood-sided cubicle on a wire-mattress and the mess which is at one end of the same hut, is quite baronial.*

*The draw back is that there are rather a lot of duties. Owing to the fact that the guns are about 800 yards from the mess, one officer has to stay on the position and sleep there: we have to man the O.P. all day from dawn to dusk, liaison comes every other night and night O.P. every sixth. Not really very strenuous but not quite so good as the wonderful convenience of the last. The night O.P. and Liaison are both nearly an hour's walk away downhill [which means a beastly trudge back at the end of work]*

### The Bristol Gunners

Extra guns were required to defend the area, and an Italian battery was sent up into the area occupied by the GVA. FS Gedye describes their attempt to get into position in the difficult steep and wooded country:

*"It has been rather interesting day. Yesterday, an Italian battery up by our detached section, about 5000 yards away, went out. [Came out of action] Their guns were prehistoric weapons – without buffers and muzzle-loaders. Today another battery came in [or tried to] with fairly modern guns [105mm]. They arrived about 8.30 and camped outside our mess. About 3 this afternoon, they started to get the guns up the steep rough track that leads up to the position.*

*They had 8 horse teams of poor little thin beasts that, incidentally, had not had their harness off or been watered since they arrived. The row as each gun moved off was simply deafening. The officer in charge yelled out "Avanti, Presto" (Forward, quickly) and every gunner instantly burst into shrieks and yells as he pulled on the dragrope; the drivers joined in at the same time lashing and spurring and the poor little horses either leapt forward or back as their degree of fright affected them.*

*By 8.00 p.m. they had the four guns as far as our battery position [the easiest part of the journey] and then they called a halt. The other event of the day was a rather successful shoot by Lane on a motor lorry which ended in setting the lorry and a dump of ammunition on fire. The finale was the explosion of the lorry which was scattered to the four winds of Heaven and ended, like the hoss shay in a cloud of smoke."*

The hoss shay referred to by Gedye was a form of one horse carriage in a poem by an American poet, Oliver Wendell Holmes, which worked perfectly for 100 years then fell to pieces spectacularly in an instant.

Lieutenant F S Gedye describes the OP that two days later he would occupy during the Austrian attack:

*"I am now perched in the tree O. P. that we use for the night work. It is rather a unique place on the top of Monte Lemerle. It is built between three trees and has a little flight of steps leading to a small platform and finally, at the top to the O.P. itself, there is also a reception-cum-boudoir hut at the bottom.*

## The Bristol Gunners

*Lemerle has a broad belt of absolutely dead fir trees from the summit down the northern slope towards Bosche land. History states it is the result of the Austrian attack in 1916, when apparently there was a bluggy fight here.*

*There are rumours of the much-delayed and mucked-up show coming off soon in a moderated form. Anyway the 7th, whom we relieved 10 days ago are up in action in forward positions and we expect orders to move in to ours any day."*

'Bluggy' was a euphemism for 'bloody' in use at that time in polite society.

The position of the OP was at the peak of Monte Lemerle which was still showing the signs of an intense battle there between the Italians and Austrians two years previously.

General Fanshawe had identified a number of weaknesses in his new divisional positions. The improvements that he wanted and needed were put in hand immediately, but there was insufficient time to complete the arrangements before the Austrians launched their assault. Telephone lines were the main means of communication, and as the position was on rock, most of it was laid on the surface and vulnerable to being cut. Observation was limited by the lie of the land and the trees. Trenches were deep, but there were not enough of them to form defence in depth.

The rumours of a renewed British/French attack were wide of the mark. The Austrians would strike first. Their attack was launched on June 15th, and was generally a failure. However, there were minor penetrations. They attacked along the entire front, from the Asiago Plateau round to the Adriatic Sea.

To the men on the ground it came as a surprise, but they responded immediately. Lieutenant FS Gedye describes the action well from his perspective:

*"June 15th 1918 is a day we shall remember all our lives. On the evening of the 14th, we had a chit from Brigade to say that the Austrian offensive was opening the following day. Rather a disturbing message but there had been a previous false alarm in March, so after seeing all was in*

## The Bristol Gunners

*readiness, we turned in as usual. Little was on duty at the battery. Rook at liaison and the Major and I at the mess hut.*

*At 3a.m., the Austrians opened up and in 2 minutes the air was thick with shells. We hopped into gumboots and I slipped into breeches and a British warm over my pyjamas and taking tin hat, smoke helmet and gas suit, we set off for the battery.*

*It was a very bad journey - 800 yards of stiff uphill track and shells were simply raining over - a certain amount of gas with the H.E.*

*When we had got about 100 yards on our journey, a hut which contained a petrol dump about 300 yards away blazed up lighting up the whole area. Half asleep, with gas tickling our throats, we staggered up the slope and got to the guns absolutely whacked.*

*All communication was cut in the first five minutes so we hadn't the remotest idea what was going on and could only keep a sharp look-out for the S.O.S. rocket.*

*Meanwhile, the Hun was keeping up a very heavy bombardment of our whole area. Bar cross roads and roads, no particular targets seemed to be engaged, but the whole was a gigantic area strafe with every calibre and with assorted H.E. and gas shell. A bombardment in these districts is pretty beastly; in addition to the shell fragments, there are falling trees and lumps of boulder flying about and the row of the explosion is magnified.*

*There was a thick mist hanging over the whole Plateau which lasted until 10, so we sent every man except one per gun pit into the dugouts and kept a sharp look-out for the S.O.S. rockets.*

*The Major went up to the O.P. about 7, although it was impossible to see anything. About 8, I went down to the hut for a shave and Webb [Officers Servant] gave me some breakfast. It was fairly quiet down there, but as I came back, they reopened on the track and I had to beat it into the wood on one side and scramble up over the rocks to the position.*

*From there, I went on to the O.P. about 10 to relieve the Major. I stayed there the rest of the day, resolutely declining to be relieved - it was far too interesting, and had a most amazing day.*

## The Bristol Gunners

*Soon after the Major left the mist cleared and I saw some Austrians get out of their lines. I got to what I estimated as to companies and did them a bit of no good.*

*From then on there were targets practically the whole day. Parties of Bosche in no mans land, batteries in action in or near the trenches, on roads - in fact he seemed to have got guns everywhere and plenty within range.*

*One position I cleared the gunners out of - they rushed into dugouts in the railway embankment. After an hour they came back and I cleared them out again. This time they cleared right away and didn't return. Nearly all our batteries couldn't keep communications with their O.P.s owing to the bombardment and those like ourselves who had only a short line had more than we could tackle.*

*The Bosche came over in bigger numbers about 4 p.m. and I got splendid targets as they came over and as they, later, went back. Meanwhile, the heaviest shelling subsided about 11, although a good lot came over during the afternoon and evening.*

*From my tree O.P. I saw the terrific effect of their 17inch bursts, They were shelling the road in front and below us and after some of the bursts, I saw as many as three fir trees spinning in the air at one time in addition to huge lumps of rock.*

*Our telephonists were simply magnificent all day. They were out repairing wires for 21 hours right through the shelling and they kept the O.P. wire going all day and the visual station to Brigade.*

*When I took over from Lane in the morning the Hun had just removed one rung from our tree ladder and all day one had the Bairnsfather feeling that if another and more successful round came " How the H - - L are we going to get down?"*

*Our only casualties were five men wounded in the mule wagon-line close to the mess.*

*The general events of the day were that the Bosches got into our front line about 8.30 a.m. In the Cesuna area on our left flank, he penetrated*

### The Bristol Gunners

*about a 1000 yards on a 2 ½ kilo front, but by the morning of the 16th, our front and outpost lines were restored.*

*Our [A Bty] position is rather a long way back for a field battery - about 3000 yards from our own front line - so we were miles out of the way of the Austrians but some of the batteries who had moved forward to their forward positions for our offensive, had an exciting time. 'C' battery had to take their breech blocks and clear out and help the infantryman in the support line.*

*When they got back to their guns yesterday morning [16th] they found the Austrians had not scuppered them, but an Austrian had turned in with his boots on, in Leslie's flea bag and put on a pair of his socks, leaving his own behind.*

*"D" Battery under Graham [Major Anderson was wounded early in the morning] took on the Bosches in the open with open sights at 700 yards. Not bad for a Howitzer battery.*

*As far as we can find out the Bosches got it hot here. We took over 400 prisoners and the area in front is strewn with their dead. In addition to some M.G s, we have captured three small mountain Howitzers.*

*A captured dispatch-box, revealed a map accurately marking, among others, all the 240 Bde positions, also a paper showing their first day's objectives were Montes Lemerle and Kaberlaba. Altogether they had a damn bad day of it - of course, we had a lot of casualties, but summing up the whole affair, the balance will be well in our favour. But I have no desire to face another hurricane bombardment in the mountains. There is a nasty feeling of hell about it."*

One can imagine his feelings being twenty or more feet up in the trees with bullets, shells, splinters and pieces of rock flying in all directions! It took real courage to stay there and continue observing and calling down artillery fire.

There are a number of interesting points raised by this last piece. The attackers were not 'Bosches' (Germans) but Austrians, at least on this part of the front. Communications were lost very early on as telephone lines were cut by shell fire and falling trees. The Austrian artillery had

been very quiet for the two weeks before the attack to avoid the British identifying their positions and counter bombarding them.

The Austrian artillery seemed to be remarkably lacking in enterprise. They shelled almost at random, whereas they should have concentrated their fire at the most vulnerable spots, which they could easily have deduced from the map as supply routes and positions for dumps and HQs were quite limited.

Gedye mentions that he had to pass by a fire started in one of the huts on his way up to the battery. It is not clear where exactly this was, but the limited areas of flat ground suitable for storage led to one major problem for the division. A key track junction to the rear of the OP position on Monte Lemerle, called Handley Cross, not only had to carry most of the traffic to and from the trenches and laterally across the position, but was also the site of the main ammunition dump for the artillery. This was hit early in the battle and the resulting fire seriously interfered with movement in the area all day, and presented a major hazard to other HQs and stores in the area. The Austrians had learned from previous attacks, and the success of the Germans during the Kaiserschlacht attacks earlier on the Western Front. Their bombardment was short and intense. Their attacking troops first came on using stormtrooper tactics, that is, infiltrating around known strongpoints to penetrate the defensive positions and then destroying each strongpoint in turn from the side or rear. They started well, but lacked the means to exploit their small initial gains.

The Austrians failed to make any significant penetrations of the position, except in the centre of the 48th Division positions. The extreme left (west) of the division's position was on the southern side of a very deep river valley, the Ghelpac, and it was almost inconceivable that the Austrians could cross this obstacle. However, where the river was shallower to the east the Austrians managed to cross and overcome some of the British outposts there. These were badly sited out of observation of each other and therefore unable to support each other with enfilade fire. One GVA battery, 'C' Battery, was forward in the area penetrated and had to withdraw, leaving their guns behind, having removed the breech blocks to prevent the Austrians being able to turn them round and fire them at our troops. The area of the penetration was enclosed by partly prepared switch trench lines, and the Austrians were halted on these trench lines. Gunners from 'C' Battery fought with the infantry in these switch

trenches under a GVA officer, Major Corsan, who was awarded the DSO (Distinguished Service Order) for his leadership in this action. Some of them also helped another battery, 12 Battery RFA, to manhandle howitzers forward and fire over open sights at the enemy during this action. As Gedye tells us, 'D' Battery, the howitzer battery of the brigade, fired at the attacking Austrians at a range of only 700 metres over open sights, which for artillery is a very close range engagement.

Major General Robert Fanshawe, commander of 48th Division, had correctly identified the dangers to his position in this area, and in the days before the attack had practised his reserve troops in moving forward and counter attacking from these trenches. On the day of the battle, this practice paid off. Exactly as rehearsed they move forward from the rear, occupied the switch trench, and then counterattacked, throwing the Austrians back out of the position. By the following morning, the British were back in their original trenches.

Major R A Corsan MC who won a DSO at Cesuna for his prompt and effective leadership during the battle of 15th June.

Fanshawe had long been a proponent of elastic defence. He had been given responsibility for this new position a bare two weeks before the Austrian attack. The orders given to him had been confused, prepare for both attack and defence. His formation was under strength, with around one third of the established numbers actually able to fight, due both to overall shortages of manpower, and influenza, which was particularly rampant at that time.

Nonetheless, he had made preparations as best as he could, and in the event, things turned out well and the Austrian attack was halted and repulsed.

Despite the successful defence Major General Robert Fanshawe was sacked from his position as GOC 48th Division over the performance of his division during the battle. It is likely that his dismissal was more of a

political move than a real statement of failure. Most other parts of the ninety kilometre front from Asiago to the Adriatic had repulsed the Austrian attacks with some ground being lost, to be recovered just as quickly as at Asiago. Fanshawe's commander, Lieutenant General The Earl of Cavan, though, was a believer of the old, rigid, defensive methods and it is possible that Fanshawe's use of more elastic methods fell out of favour with Cavan.

Lieutenant Colonel George Barnett, who served under General Fanshawe throughout his time in command of 48th Division describes the general:

*"On 19th June Major General Sir R. Fanshawe was ordered to hand over the command of the Division and proceed to England for duty there. The news was received with the greatest consternation by all ranks. It was certainly the heaviest blow to the Division which it received during the war. Sir R. Fanshawe had commanded since May 1915, and had been the soul and inspiration of his command during the whole of his three years.*

*He had that rare and indefinable personality held by some but not all great leaders, which inspires blind confidence and belief in those under him.*

*A man of intense purpose, and of an almost fanatical sense of duty, of total disregard for personal safety and comfort, he was an unflinching and severe taskmaster. But combined with these qualities he had always an unfailing consideration for his officers and men, an extraordinary insight into character, and a knack of getting the best out of every one under him.*

*He was rather eccentric – most great men are - and the men used to laugh at some of the peculiarities of "Fanny," as he was nicknamed. But there was not one who would have refused to go straight into the mouth of hell if he told them it was the right thing to do. His character has always appeared to the writer to be somewhat similar to that of the great Confederate leader, Stonewall Jackson. What General Fanshawe did for the 48th Division only those who served in it will ever know. His excessive modesty and somewhat nervous manner with strangers entirely hid from them the real nature of the man. It was probably given to him to have as large a share in the wearing down and defeat of the Germans as any one*

*individual similarly placed. Such, at any rate, is the opinion of his old comrades of the 48th Division."*

A general being sacked like this, despite having done a very good job, was not uncommon. His eldest brother General Huw Fanshawe was sacked from divisional command in 1916 after a failed attack, but went on to serve in Mesopotamia with promotion. The middle brother, General Edward Fanshawe, was also sacked in 1918 from commanding a corps during the Kaiserschlacht attacks, but continued to serve in the Army until 1923.

Lieutenant F S Gedye echoed Colonel Barnett's words:

*"Everything is still fairly quiet although there are rumours that the Bosche is preparing for another smack here.*

Major General Robert Fanshawe KCB DSO, GOC 48th Division from 1915 until he was unfairly sacked following the June 15th attack. He was the original 'chocolate soldier' and much respected by his peers and subordinates. (photo Wikimedia Commons)

*Poor old Fanshawe has gone home over this job. One of the battalions was absolutely caught napping on the day of the show. He has had the division practically from the time it first went overseas and there is no doubt his is the credit for a lot of the reputation that the 48th has.*

*He worked his division hard, but not harder then he worked himself, and the old man was a familiar sight in the trenches at all hours, complete with chocolate and soup squares, which he used to distribute if he went home to a meal earlier than he expected. The whole division was proud of the old fireater and he was a very fine type of British Regular soldier."*

Robert Fanshawe was replaced as commander by Major General Sir H B Walker, a commander with a wide experience, having commanded the 1st Australian Division in Gallipoli, and on

the Western Front, notably during the capture of Pozieres village. Like Fanshawe he was a respected and very able commander.

The only significant success that the Austrians achieved during the June attacks was to occupy part of the Montello position on the Piave River, a sector held by the Italian Army. Within a week this was recaptured. In total, the Austrian offensive was a failure, and in the following months the Austrian Army progressively became unable to continue fighting, and eventually surrendered.

Before this happened, though, the GVA as part of the 48th Division had a number of tasks to fulfil.

Immediately after the battle, in the latter half of June, the defensive positions were put back into order. The injured were collected and sent back down the line for treatment. The dead were collected and buried. Much material had been captured from the Austrians and this had to be sent back down the supply system.

The division was relieved by the 7th Division on 26th June, and returned to the Venetian Plain, where the new commander, General Walker joined them.

The artillery, though, remained on the plateau. They were in support of 7th Division, including providing artillery fire to cover a raid on the Austrian positions. There were also other changes in personalities. Lieutenant F S Gedye:

*"Firstly, Colonel Rudkin has gone - ostensibly on a month's leave, but we hope and believe, for good and thus goes one of the most amazing characters we have met in the war. It is an almost impossible task to criticise him. Brilliantly quick and perhaps, also, very clever, he was entirely inefficient, he has inspired many stories that have gone the round of the division, in which he was a universally known figure.*

*How else, for no two officers of the brigade could be together without some new exploit of his being discussed. Just one story must be related to show his very unorthodox method of conversation. Just after pith helmets were issued [and the effect on almost any well known face was not as a rule very becoming] Will Todd heard someone shouting "Hi" several times very loudly, from a car, not thinking it could be intended to attract*

### The Bristol Gunners

*his attention in the summary way he did not at first turn round but finally, seeing no one else about he stalked up to the car with much outraged dignity to find Rudkin ensconced therein "Oh Todd, its you is it" he remarked adding quickly "I did not recognise you, you look such a damn fool in that hat!"*

*His successor, Col Russell, is an awfully nice fellow and from what we have seen so far, a capable one.*

*There was a small raid by the 7th Div at Canove two nights ago in which we took part, 5 prisoners and over 30 killed, mainly by our barrage. The raider's casualties were two slightly wounded - not even hospital cases.*

*The 48th D.A. were covering the 7th infantry and they simply overwhelmed us with compliments. The Infantry Brigadier paid a special visit to the C.O. to tell him that the barrage was perfect. The O.C. raiding party's expression was "Every round was in the right place."*

*The 7th Div C.R.A. sent a signed letter to each battery taking part in the show to say the barrage came down at 11.30 to the second and lifted exactly to programme. The raiders found over 30 killed and wounded by the artillery fire and the accuracy and steadiness of the barrage put great confidence into many of the party who had not gone in under barrage fire before. Very nice of another division to go out of its way to acknowledge our work.*

*We have just heard the sad news we are moving out of here tomorrow, the 30th and July 1st and exchanging positions with the 7th D.A., who are coming back to cover their own infantry. It is very sickening the just as we get towards the end of work on a position, we are moved.*

*We shall be attached to the 23rd Div [with whom we don't get on too well or didn't under Rudkin] and our position which is further right than we have been before is probably only half built."*

The 7th Division was a Regular Army Division, and it was a significant compliment for a Territorial Force unit to be so praised, especially as many infantrymen were wont to call the artillery 'drop shorts' from the habit of some batteries to be somewhat loose with accuracy. The GVA

batteries were at this time as good as any in the army, and better than most.

It was not clear at this point that the Austrians had given up hope of further attacks or victory. There were a number of rumours and minor actions which the GVA were required to support, but no further attacks by the Austrians. There were signs, however, that make sense in retrospect, that the Austrians were not as aggressive as they had been. Lieutenant F S Gedye again, in early July:

*"Our staff is surely the most credulous in the world. Officers leave was stopped because some mangy Hun said the offensive was about to be resumed. Well, the other day, another deserter came in who said that numbers of others would desert if our continual gunfire ceased occasionally. Result - a silent period was ordered - and commenced the night before last. As no deserters have yet come in it is being prolonged for another 24 hours.*

*The deadly silence both day and night is absolutely uncanny yesterday the Hun got so nervy about it that he put over quite a lot of stuff early in the day, but finding we were not retaliating, he shut-up and has evidently decided to be thankful for the temporary respite. But for the fact that we still have to man O.P.s it would be very delightful for us. The effects are rather quaint though the infantry, who generally curse us for stirring up trouble, have the wind up to the back teeth ever since we shut-up and spend most of their time standing - to for a raid."*

The Austrians still could make life unpleasant. They had a very large gun, a 17 Inch (425mm), nicknamed 'beetle', which they used to shell somewhat at random, presumably in the hope of hitting something of military value. The arrival of these shells was somewhat spectacular. They would also fire at the British trenches if they saw movement or soldiers out in the open. Lieutenant FS Gedye:

*"I had quite an exciting day yesterday - twice while I was at the O.P. they shelled that part of the trench and cleared me out.*

*Of course we thoroughly deserved it - the whole trench is stiff with artillery and infantry O.P.s and the trench is very exposed with everyone observing over the top.*

### The Bristol Gunners

*As if that weren't enough, we get coveys of brass hats who come and wave maps about on top and point down with walking sticks and shriek "Oh yes, there's Asiago."*

*In the code of the moment, we are not allowed to refer to the Austrian's fearsome 17 Inch gun by name, but have to refer to "Beetle." Hayley arrived at the O.P. the other morning looking a little wan and I enquired what was wrong and he said in a most pathetic way "Why, I was only just sitting down to my breakfast, when Beetle came and settled on me.""*

On July 17th and 18th 1918 the Russian Tsar Nicholas and his extended family were killed by the Bolsheviks, bringing to an end any hope of restoring him to his throne. The Russian civil war fighting between the Reds (Bolsheviks) and the White Russians (Anti-Bolsheviks) would continue through to 1923.

The 48th Division returned from the plains in late July and took over the right hand divisional area, and the GVA moved across to join them. New tactics were being considered. Early in the war it had been realised that guns needed to be sited in dead ground in the rear of a defensive position so that they could not easily be observed by the enemy. The successful use of guns in direct fire during the recent Austrian attack must have set someone thinking. D Battery of 240 Brigade, had fired their howitzers directly at attacking Austrians with impressive results, as mentioned earlier during the big attack on June 15th. Also, it may have been thought that the Austrians may use tanks in any future attack. An order was issued to prepare gun positions near the front trenches that could be used for direct fire at the enemy, either infantry or tanks. Lieutenant FS Gedye:

*"We are probably moving the section in a few days. The C.O. has chosen a silent position for defence which is at the top of the hill from our O.P. The guns will be on the fringe of the wood just out of sight of the Bosche although without flash-cover.*

*They will not fire except in an Austrian offensive, but if the Bosches get out in the open, they would be manhandled about 100 yards forward and use open sights.*

*In addition to that, Matt and I have to take under our wing a position for an anti-tank gun down in front of Kaberlaba which the pioneers are*

building. As this can only be worked on at night, and we have to go down most nights to see things are going on correctly, the C.O. is going to take us off night O.P. and we are frightfully bucked about it."

And a few days later:

"Paid a joint visit with Matt to the anti-tank position last night. The pioneers really have made a good job of it and I will try to give you some idea of it.

It is an old disused Austrian trench on the forward slope of Kaberlaba, about 200 yards behind the front line.

Kaberlaba is on the treeless heights here - at present the grass is about two feet high on its slopes. This old trench is only about 2ft deep anywhere, and the soil is very usual one for this district - alternate layers more or less, of flat chalkstones and earth. The appearance of the trench before they started was a very white parapet, a brown and white surface to the bottom of the trench and a green parados fairly well sprinkled with chalk stones.

The first thing the pioneers had to do was to dig down to about 3 ft 6 in and make a platform for the gun so that the muzzle would be just clear of the ground level. The bed for the trail had to be dug two feet into the parados.

When we went down last night [incidentally I had paid a 4.30 a.m. visit from night O.P. that morning] we found the gun-emplacements themselves practically completed, the platforms of small logs closely fitted together being camouflage with chalkstones – the trail bed for which the rear of the trench had been cut back in a semicircle of about 3ft radius had a false surface of wire netting threaded with dyed raffia that made it absolutely invisible from a few yards distance.

The parapet, where the gun muzzle will be, was built up for about 9 inches or a foot – just enough to hide the muzzle from ground observation – with a false parapet of chalkstones that could be knocked over in two shakes if the gun had to come into action."

And getting the guns into the new position:

### The Bristol Gunners

"We took the two guns from the section position here down to the anti-tank position last night. We pulled them out of the pits about 7, and they were manhandled down the hill to the road where two eight-mule teams took them to a point just off the road where Matt and I who cut across country met them and guided them in. We had to pass through three belts of wire and two trenches in the support line system which the Pioneers had filled in or opened up for us as the case might be

We got in very easily and took the teams right up to the trench where we had a party of 18 men ready to manhandle them in.

Then we had to cut lengths of wire netting to cover the guns, partly to conceal the outline but also to prevent a dark shadow on the trench. We then sprinkled some white chalkstone and tufts of grass to harmonise with the general surroundings.

We tied canvas on the wheel rims to prevent the sun glinting on the iron tyres, we also camouflaged the mule tracks by throwing white chalkstone over the more noticeable places and had finished about 1 a.m. and the whole thing is I think a good imitation of invisibility. The C.O. went down just before dawn and thought it quite a good effect."

The likelihood of tanks being used in this area was extremely low, the ground was just too broken and unsuitable, and guns placed in such an exposed position would quickly be destroyed by enemy artillery as soon as they came into action. Luckily for them, they did not need to be used.

There were a few trench raids by both sides, the British getting the better of it. An Austrian raid was neutralised before it really got going. Lieutenant Gedye:

"I reported to Brigade on the way down and the C.O. told me that there might be a raid on the Villa Dal Brun; a house in No Mans Land, during the night.

The previous night the French had done a dam' good raid capturing 119 men and an Austrian Colonel and this miserable old devil had blabbed that they were going to do a raid on Villa Dal Brun as they thought we had a post there. He said that it was to take place on the night of the 2/4th and that 200 Sturmtruppen were coming up to do it.

## The Bristol Gunners

*At 11.30 the Bosche put down a barrage and at 11.35, in response to a red verey light [pre-arranged signal with the patrol that was out looking for the Bosche] our S.O.S. was put down. The whole thing died down about 12 and our patrols could find no trace of the Bosche, but from a prisoner since captured it appears that 70 Storm troops came over.*

*As their artillery were firing short, they fired a red verey light as a signal to the S.O.S., I guess they wished they hadn't.*

*Their casualties were 16 killed and 36 wounded. Not too bad for their first stunt since June 15th."*

It seems that the Austrians and the British had by coincidence decided to use the same colour flare to signal to their respective artillery. The Austrian signal to stop firing was seen by the British observers and assumed to be a call for SOS fire to protect their own infantry. So, the Austrians accidentally brought British artillery fire down on to themselves.

British raids were more successful:

*"On the night of the 8/9th there was a big raid by our division and the 7th on our left.*

*One whole battalion and two companies from each division entered the lines at eight different points. Our division captured 145 prisoners and a couple of machine guns - the 7th got over 200, including 7 officers, 4 trench mortars, some machine guns, a searchlight and a complete ration party including 5 mules and a fat quartermaster-sergeant.*

*Our people found a lot of pack ponies and four mountain howitzers in a quarry which they couldn't get away so they had to shoot the ponies and bomb the guns - great pity.*

*I was taking the shoot from the battery and the guns opened beautifully to the second with a terrific crack. The Huns were terrified and shoved up every sort of verey light he had, but his batteries couldn't do much - our heavies were attending to them.*

*The 6 inch batteries each had four hostile battery positions as targets and to each they gave 40 gas shells per hour.*

## The Bristol Gunners

*On the night of the 9/10th we repeated our bombardment on a smaller scale and the French sent 6 companies over on Sisemol and fairly swiped them again bringing back about 250 prisoners, trench mortars and machine guns.*

*The poor old Hun has been suffering from Vento Verticale* (wind up – nervousness) *ever since."*

In mid August the rumours started about the possibility of the Austrians withdrawing. The German attacks of the Western Front that had been launched in March (The Kaiserchlacht) had ground to a halt in July, with their final assault on the French on the Marne River being thrown back. On August 8th the Allies launched their counter offensive, referred to as the 100 Days Offensive. This was to push the Germans back continuously for three months and end in the Armistice on November 11th 1918. August 8th became known by the Germans as 'The Black Day of the German Army.'

It was becoming clear that the end game was coming on the Italian front as well. Lieutenant F S Gedye:

*"This morning the mountains north of the Plateau had a thin covering of snow on them - a very sinister sight.*

*Some half-baked deserter has come in and said that the Bosche is preparing to retire to a line that he is making about 2000 yards in the rear of his present one at the foot of his mountains. If he does go back, we are sure to be fools enough to go forward and occupy the ground that we have steadily crumped since March and is in a horrible state. We should then hold Asiago and one or two rotten little flattened villages that are perfectly valueless and suffer from all the evils of having our ground overlooked that the Hun has had all this year."*

And a few days later, more good news:

*"G.H.Q. has gone mad again. Absolutely raving this time!*

*It is on the question of the Bosche retirement. The Bosche has very evidently had enough of the Asiago side of the plateau and is very busy making a new line at the foot of his side of the plateau to which he equally undoubtedly intends to retire when it is completed.*

### The Bristol Gunners

*Frank and I know about this reserve line because we have watched the progress on it day by day and have, from aeroplane photos sketched it on our map. I was pointing the whole thing out to the C.O. just before this latest freak of disordered minds came round.*

*At present, the line is only just scratched out i.e. the top layer of turf removed along the line and in places he has dug it a foot or more deep and stakes and wire are being rapidly put out, but he hasn't got cover for a man yet, no dugouts at all.*

*But, of course, G.H.Q. doesn't know this or what the line looks like - they live at Lugo down on the foothills and as the mountains are not transparent and the journey up here to see for themselves is obviously too ridiculously uncomfortable they believe anything that any semi-intelligent deserter likes to tell them. And one came in the other night and said they were likely to retire to this line any night now.*

*So G.H.Q. has ordered all batteries to fill forward positions with ammunition, 600 rounds per gun for us. Our position is where the section used to be, and only five days ago we finished clearing the last of the 7000 odd rounds away and now we are busily taking up 3600 to the racks we have just cleared.*

*Still, c'est la guerre* (that's war) *and if we are doing our best to lengthen it out here, they are undoubtedly shortening it in France and I suppose in the end it will get straightened out."*

Life in the mountains in summer was not all hard work and danger. Gedye:

*"A gorgeous day and hot enough for the plains. I'm on battery duty which means practically nothing after the 8.45 a.m. parade and subsequent walk round the guns, huts, etc.*

*We have been doing well on the wild strawberries lately - each day we have been getting ¾ to a 1lb - all beautifully ripe and some quite large ones.*

*I can hardly believe we have been close on a month up here and then one compares it with last August at Ypres and 1916 on the Somme, it*

### The Bristol Gunners

*comes back to you once again what a wonderful time we are having and have had in Italy.*

*And if a lot of our work here is an utter waste of time, we can't be blamed for that and anyway, we have seen a fair amount of the other sort of war and anytime they like to send us back, we're quite ready for it.*

*Yesterday morning Matt was playing the gramophone on the grass just outside our hut and a crowd of Italian Tommies came round to listen. Two of them spoke Anglo-Yank and were delighted with the Lee White records - "Don't Blame Me "etc. ping-pong is a great hit; we have constructed some racquets of thin wood that are a great success.*

*"Wind" still continues to be vertical with the heads of the various forces here. They believe the Bosche is going back at any moment, but they seem absolutely unable to decide whether to push him a lot further back than he means to go, leave him to go back in his own time and follow him up, or simply to stay where we are."*

The confusion about whether a retirement was to be followed up or not was actually part of a deception plan devised by the overall Italian commander, General Diaz. He was planning an attack on the Austrians, but insisted that only very senior officers were to be informed of his plans. The stockpiling of material for this attack had to be explained without disclosing that an attack was planned. The attack was complicated, and on examination would probably have been foiled by the usual 'fog of war.'

More trench raids were carried out, some on quite a large scale, to find out what the Austrians were up to, and importantly to capture prisoners who could be interrogated for information.

The progress of the counter offensive in France was going well, with the French, British, and American armies advancing steadily and the German Army becoming a spent force.

In early September, the planned attack in Italy was cancelled. Trench raids continued, however. Lieutenant FS Gedye recorded one of several supported by the GVA:

## The Bristol Gunners

*"There was a big raid last night on the same lines as that on the 9th only larger.*

*We had two battalions over, the Bucks and 4th Berks, they captured 210 prisoners including one officer. Our casualties were rather heavy - 12 officers and 100 O.R.s."*

The Austrians were still able to put up a stubborn resistance and both sides suffered casualties, not always from enemy action. Lieutenant Colonel Barnett refers to this in his book:

*"After ten days' rest the Austrians were raided again on the night of 9th September. This time the 4th Oxfords went for Sec, while the 5th Royal Warwicks, employing their whole battalion, made an attempt on the railway cutting at Gaiga. The Oxfords were entirely successful, capturing 31 prisoners with very few casualties. The 5th Royal Warwicks were unlucky. Owing either to faulty timing, or the short shooting of a heavy battery, the leading companies got mixed up in our own barrage, and suffered considerable casualties before reaching their objectives. The Austrians were very much on the qui vive, and severe hand-to-hand fighting took place. Only 10 prisoners and 3 machine guns were brought back, and the battalion had about 90 casualties, but a number of the enemy were killed, and on the balance fared worse than our men."*

Another rumour went round, that the British troops in Italy were to be returned to France, though in the event this did not happen. Gedye records this:

*"The "Back to France" rumour is stronger than ever but as far as we are concerned, has no foundation in fact.*

*I don't think any of us really care a cuss one way or the other though. We either get decently and comfortably frozen to death in Italy [A very painful end for me] or frightened to death very uncomfortably in France, and as we've all died that way so often, there doesn't seem much to it."*

Weather on the plateau was, and still is, variable. In late September heavy rains began, and the weather became much cooler. In mid October, 7th and 23rd Divisions were withdrawn from the Asiago Plateau and redeployed to the Piave River line, leaving 48th Division as the only British troops on the position, and coming under command of the XII

### The Bristol Gunners

Italian Corps, and responsible for all the frontage previously held by two divisions.

October is the month for picking grapes and making wine, and 1918 was no exception. Lieutenant FS Gedye, down on the plain at this time at the wagon line describes why he felt that he should give up drinking wine:

*""Vino" is in full swing here now and the grapes in my billet garden are being picked and vinoed with huge vigour.*

*I've drunk my last glass of it too! What you read in books and see in picture brochures [picshures] is all gospel truth. All the grapes, stems, insects and all, are put in huge vats, and then the dirtiest local inhabitant rolls up his breeks [trousers], slings off his heels slippers, hops in, and squashes the mess. After he has stamped it all into a fine mess, the tap is removed and the juice is poured through a strainer into other tubs and left to ferment."*

As the 48th was now a part of the Italian Army, or at least their command structure, it was decided that the King of Italy (Victor Emmanuel III) would review his forces. Lieutenant FS Gedye was one of the lucky officers chosen to be part of the review, also attended by the Prince of Wales (later Edward VIII):

*"On the 25th, we had a screed in to say that the King of Italy's review would be held on the 29th, and that the 48th would provide one 18 pounder battery, each 18 pr battery in the two brigades providing one subsection.*

*I was detailed as one of the section commanders; of course, from that time on, life was one ghastly rush.*

*We had two rehearsals in a field about 4 miles away - we had to pick our teams, select the harness and men all in about 5 minutes.*

*We trekked to Nove, a village near Marostica, at 8.30 on Saturday. There is a very fine aerodrome there, which was used for the review; otherwise it is a one-eyed hole.*

*I went in advance to meet the G.H.Q. staff captain for billets. The battery arrived about one and the whole brigade went straight into the*

## The Bristol Gunners

*aerodrome for a rehearsal which was rather boring and lasted till 4. The rain came down in floods again just as we got to our field and hastened up the bivouacking no end.*

*Our harness came for the review came by lorry and was so saved from ruin.*

*The Major in command of the battery for the two days was a pukkah swine who entirely spoilt any fun we might have got out of the show. He is one of those loathsome types who went sick before the Somme show in 1916, piled up seniority, and now comes out, never having smelt war, to tell us that his cadets of 18 and 19 could lick us into a cocked hat for efficiency. I realised after about three minutes of his company that we should have a row and was careful to leave him no chance to pick holes in my work going so far as to take a chaff-cutter and a clipping machine to Nove with me for final touches.*

*I dealt with him to my entire satisfaction over the billeting too, I knew he was expecting a room in the village and so I told the Staff Capt when I arrived, and told him in such a tactful way that I knew whoever else got a billet in that most overcrowded village, my B.C. would not be among the number. And so it turned out; after cursing me roundly, he rode off to find a billet for himself and returned very crestfallen an hour later, muttering that the Staff Capt was inefficient and a bounder. I, who had informed the rest of the mess of my action, held a reception in my tent afterwards to receive the thanks of my fellow subalterns.*

*On the day of the show, I clicked for orderly dog. The review was timed for 3.30 but we had to be on parade at 1.30.*

*The turnout was really beautiful. All the harness was perfectly polished and every link burnished, also all the steel-work on the wagons. Even Saunders, the B.C., had to say on parade that the turn-out reflected the greatest credit on every officer, N.C.O, and man.*

*When we got to our place on the review ground, we cleaned the wagons again, rubbed over all the harness, polished the men's boots, oiled the horses hoofs and then sat down to wait for His Maj.*

*The parade was in three huge lines; first, infantry French, English and Italian and an Italian mountain Mule battery, then Field Artillery,*

## The Bristol Gunners

*English, French, and Italian and the last line, Italian heavies, motor transport etc.*

*We [The British] were apparently the only people who thought it necessary to be in spotless review order, the French and Italians were in their familiar state of dirt - the harness the same old mixture of rust, worn-out leather and string.*

*The French battery next to us thought the whole a huge joke and were frightfully tickled to see our final clean-up taking place. After watching us for a time, even that ceased to amuse and they retire to the rear and opening an ammunition wagon, took out a huge flask of vino, and proceeded to have a good swig.*

*When the King arrived, he walked down each line of troops, as he came from the front line towards the British Artillery Brigade our band struck up God Save the King, and all officers stood at the salute.*

*When he got to the French, their band struck up the Marseillaise, and the Iti's came out with the Marcia Reale. Cavan and the Prince of Wales were in the vast crowd that followed him around.*

*Then he went back the Grand Stand and presented medals and finally everyone marched past first the infantry followed by the British Artillery, then the French, then the Italians. We went past at the trot, bumping saddle in the good old style.*

*One of the best shows of the day was a battery of Italian horse-gunners who went past at the gallop in magnificent dressing and style. The Italians are always have a lot of thoroughbred horses and this particular unit had a great lot of nags and the speed at which they passed the stand in a swirl of dust was very fine. We finally got away at 5.30 and returned to our wagon lines next day."*

Trench raids by the 48th Division continued throughout September and into October. A pattern emerged where the raids became easier and more successful. On 24th October a Gloucester battalion raid captured 6 officers and 223 other ranks. The fight seemed to have gone out of the Austrians. Interrogation of prisoners identified that the Austrians were finally going to withdraw to their 'Winter Stellung' (winter defensive position) soon.

## The Bristol Gunners

Despite careful observation, the withdrawal was not seen by the British, but a trench raid on 29th October found the Austrian trenches empty, apart from one soldier with a flare gun whose duty was to send up flares occasionally to simulate that the trench was still occupied.

On 30th October, strong patrols were sent out and advanced beyond the town of Asiago. They approached the winter stellung, expecting the Austrians to defend themselves.

At this time, the Allies had launched an assault further east on the Piave River sector and were advancing steadily, the Austrians staying in contact and fighting. Prisoner interrogations, though, identified a rapid decline in Austrian morale and willingness to continue fighting.

On 30th and 31st October, the Austrian artillery sprang to life and fired extensively at British positions on the plateau.

On the night of 31st October, the French on the right of 48th Division attacked their section of the winter stellung and found that it had no defenders, they had abandoned it. 48th Division immediately prepared to advance in their sector. The attack was totally successful, many Austrians were killed or captured, and much material was captured including 60 artillery pieces.

On the following day attacks were made and ground was captured. The Austrians were withdrawing and the operation developed into a pursuit. The 48th Division followed the Austrians up the Val d'Assa (Valley of the River Assa), and crossed the Italian/Austrian border further up this valley on 3rd November, the first British troops to enter enemy territory during the war. The Austrian Corps Commander, General von Ritter Romer surrendered to 48th Division Commander, Major General Walker at the border post of Osteria del Termine, preferring to do this with the British rather than the Italians.

Elsewhere, the Turks had signed an armistice on 30th October and surrendered in Mesopotamia. The German navy had mutinied and refused to fight anymore. On November 3rd the Austro–Hungarians signed an armistice. Kaiser Wilhelm of Germany was preparing to abdicate and would flee to The Netherlands on November 9th. Austrian Emperor Charles I resigned. Revolution and rioting became widespread in Berlin and other parts of Germany.

## The Bristol Gunners

The war was over, Germany finally signing an armistice that became effective on November 11th.

Lieutenant F S Gedye made this entry in his diary on 30th October when he was down on the plain at the wagon lines:

*"The Austriaco is simply bunking on the Piave, and it is only a question of days before he chucks in.*

*We have heard to-night that Turkey has chucked in and that the Emperor Karl has fled to Hungary.*

*The Czechs and several other mixed breeds have all bagged a town and declared it to be the capital of their country on the "where I eats I sleep" principle as far as one can gather.*

*If an armistice comes off here in the near future and Germany holds on still, I hope we shall either go to France or push up through Austria and start on the Bosche from a new front.*

*Anyway, his last hours are getting nearer and unless we get a move on, I'm afraid we may have seen our last battle!"*

Two days later his diary states:

*"I got back to the wagon-line to-day. The only really amusing feature of the journey was my capture of the hat of Carabinieri from the back of our lorry. One of the gallant band was cycling and without our permission, caught hold of our rear platform for a lift. I have always had a passionate desire to acquire one of these lovely bits of headgear, so I leant forward and removed it. We all tried it on and gave our own impression of how Napoleon looked when in banishment [they are just the right shape for this stirring episode] amidst the terrified bleats of the unhappy victim and then returned it to him after he had passed his destination by some miles.*

*I found them in a state of great excitement here. The Austriaco, usually so well behaved on our front, vanished three nights ago and has not been seen since, at least that is one of the rumours. Anyway, our people had a raid on Asiago and never found a Hun - they walked clean through the town.*

### The Bristol Gunners

*The guns advanced next day, teams being sent up to the mountains at 2 hours notice and the last news from the Major is that the battery is in three section positions.*

*Matthews and one section were at Capitello Mulche, some 500 yards North of Asiago; I don't know where the others are and whether they know where the Hun is seems uncertain.*

*I should have loved to have gone up to-day, but the Major sent down instructions that Rook was to report there to-day and as Todd is acting Staff Capt and we are held in readiness to move at any moment to the Plateau, I couldn't very well do otherwise than stay down here."*

On the day of the Austrian armistice, Gedye was given the task of moving the wagon lines up onto the plateau. He records his feelings:

*"This is, so far, the most wonderful day of the war, although I'm rather too tired to realise it.*

*To start with, we left at 8 a.m. and had, as we expected, a beastly trek, finally arriving at Granezza at 5 p.m.*

*It's a grisly pull up, and sundry overloaded wagons kept dropping to the rear. However, everything finally arrived safely.*

*The arrangements made by a paralytic ass, one Robinson of "B" battery, were the worst I've ever seen, but after numerous troubles, we finally got settled in, in some fashion. Orders at present are that we move on to Asiago to-morrow. I have to report to the battery.*

*After dinner, [Maconochie and toast and jolly fine too] I wandered off to the late Divisional and Div Arty H.Q. and learnt officially that the Armistice commences at 3 p.m. to-morrow afternoon.*

*During my walk, I heard distant cheering and flares, and verey lights were going up, and in spite of my weariness, it gradually dawned on me that something really had happened. By a stroke of unexpected luck, I was very comfortably fixed up with a billet in the hut of the manager of the Y.M.C.A. who had rushed off to spend the night in Austria."*

So, the war was over, no more fighting. What would come next?

249

The Bristol Gunners

## Chapter 7  The Interwar Years

The armistice with Austro-Hungary on 3rd November was the start of another set of problems. The Austrian Army had ceased to operate as a disciplined force; it had taken on some of the characteristics of a rabble. Units disintegrated, stores were looted, and their supply system broke down. All food in their forward areas was quickly consumed, and groups of hungry and undisciplined Austrians were wandering around creating a threat to civilians and Allied soldiers alike.

The GOC of 48th Division, Major General Walker, accepted the surrender of the entire Austrian 3rd Army, at Trento, in Austria itself, and took under his responsibility all the troops and officers in that formation who were now prisoners of war.

The supply route for the 48th Division was precarious. The rapid advance, some seventy miles (one hundred and ten kilometres) in four days, had stretched the ability of the supply organisation to cope, dependent as it was largely on horses. There was just one good road between the supply dumps on the old defensive positions up to Trento, and this was congested with abandoned equipment and groups of soldiers from both sides moving back and forth.

Lieutenant F S Gedye was still with the wagon lines at this time, and describes the scene that he saw when he moved his group up into Asiago on 5th November:

*"When we got back to Granezza about 1 a.m. we found that orders had come in for us to move to Asiago which we did at 2.30.*

*I shared an old Austrian dug-out with Warham, Leslie and Rook and we were a very cheery party.*

*There was an awful squash in the wagon-line there so next morning, I went out and found one for our horses at an isolated farm called Cinque which has a good streamlet of beautiful clear water running through it.*

*In the afternoon I went for a ride with Leslie over the Plateau to Camporovere and had a look at the Val d'Assa.*

## The Bristol Gunners

*Quite interesting but we are still chafing at being an L. of C. unit and missing all the fun. We have seen swarms and swarms of prisoners coming back. Our division alone took 20,000 and 300 guns and lord knows how much transport.*

*It's the first time I've ever felt really sorry for them. A more pathetic-looking mob, I've never seen. Dirty, tired and some of them, half starved, they are a sad and sorry sight streaming up the mountain roads towards Granezza.*

*The advance was so quick that there was no chance to get adequate guards for them and it was no uncommon sight to see 50 or 100 straggling down the road entirely on their own. On the 6th I moved into my new wagon-line and we settled in fairly comfortably*

*This morning, I took an exercise ride out to Gallio Wood and almost to Gallio village and we came back through Pear-shaped Wood.*

*It was interesting to see their wrecks of battery positions where they must have had absolute Hell.*

*The whole road is littered with bits of ammunition boxes, shells, cartridges etc and the wood is quite Ypres-like in its melancholy appearance."*

Luckily for the GVA, it was decided by the Italian Army Supreme Headquarters (Commando Supremo) that they wanted the foreign troops (British, French, and American) to be relieved from operations and returned to the plains. On 8th November, the 48th Division started its withdrawal from the mountains and was back on the Venetian plain by 11th November. It would then trek to join up with the other two British divisions that were being withdrawn from their successful operations further east on the Piave River line.

The three divisions concentrated in the area around the town of Trissino, to the west of Vicenza.

Lieutenant F S Gedye describes the journey:

## The Bristol Gunners

"We moved off in pretty good order at 7 a.m. as a brigade and I had the luck to be leading battery, which makes a lot of difference on a long trek.

We had a stiff climb up to Granezza from Pria del'Acqua and from there on it was an easy job winding down the mountainside. It was a gorgeous day and we rather enjoyed it all. We got into the wagon line about 4 p.m.

David Morgan, who had gone down the line with 'flu had just returned and came in and spent the evening with Todd and myself.

The next day we spent in busily squaring up our part of the show before the battery arrived and I rushed round billets squeezing everyone up. In the afternoon I went in to Thiene to draw pay for the men and arrived back just in time to see the arrival of the Major and Little with one section; Matthews remained behind to bury a horse and arrived an hour later. I was taking the whole stable parade and I've never had a more impossible show. I had arranged that my people should take over the battery as it came in and water and feed their horses, and let their men go off parade at once.

But between the arrival of the Major and Little with the right section and Matthews with the left, a succession of the most extraordinary animals and vehicles entered the lines, which raised yells of delight from the most disorderly parade I've ever had to carry on.

First, a pair of chestnut ponies were led in, then an Austrian G.S. Wagon drawn by two more ponies - a most amazing and shabby vehicle - then a dun outrider and finally an Austrian cooker. All together our bag consisted of one rider, six ponies, a G.S. wagon and a field cooker, not to mention numerous sacks of vegetables, flour, etc. We heard just after they had got down that Germany had signed the Armistice and that fighting had ceased that morning so of course it developed into a rather hectic night. After dinner we went up and visited "C" Bty and then "C" Bty came down to us and somehow "B" and "D" and Headquarters all came up in drafts and it was after midnight before we sorted ourselves out and retired to bed.

Although I can only speak from hearsay of the advance, one or two incidents are worth recording. Apparently, the Italians were very jealous

*of our advance into Austria and in order to preserve the Entente, we had to halt our troops outside Trento in order to wait for the Italians who hysterically insisted on being the first to enter the captured capital.*

*The O/C. Austrian troops, however, outwitted them by sending out a document to our people before the arrival of the Italians officially surrendering the city of Trento to the Officer Commanding 48th British Division.*

*Another rather wonderful story concerns the Colonel of one of the Worcester battalions who rode forward to reconnoitre the country ahead and turning from a side street into the central square of a town and found it absolutely full of Austrian troops, who were assembling to move off on a further retirement.*

*He was apprehended and realising that to be taken a prisoner of war at this late stage of proceedings was too futile to be considered, he called in desperate measures, simulated intense indignation and demanded to be brought before the O/C Troops to whom he let fly on the unspeakable indignity to which he had been subjected winding up an impassioned oration by saying "This is the more inexcusable seeing that I have not come here to fight but to billet my men." The story worked and with many apologies for any misunderstanding he was released.*

*We spent the next three days squaring up the lines, getting rid of surplus stores etc. "G" sub, which we had formed last winter as a home for the staff horses and the transport was split up and returned to the sections and some remounts dished out with the customary amount of grousing and biting sarcasm from the section commanders usual on these occasions. However, Little, Matt and I managed to maintain a most cheery entente and on two spare afternoons, rode into Thiene and played the fool as thoroughly as ever.*

*We had to return all captured vehicles and animals to a divisional rendezvous on the 10th, for return to the Italians, I believe, except the cooker and one pair to draw it.*

*But by a little bit of smart work we did quite well out of the deal and we also kept a priceless little pair of chestnut ponies - one was a perfect heavy draught in miniature.*

## The Bristol Gunners

*On the 26th we received orders to move to Montecchio Precalcino to take over billets from 241 Brigade."*

Now the war was over, thoughts turned to home, and the future.

The demobilisation scheme was, to many, unfair. Priority was given to married men, and those who had a job to return to waiting for them in Blighty. Length of service was given a lower priority, and thus a married conscript with a trade who had maybe been in uniform for less than a year may have left the army earlier than a young unmarried man serving since 1914.

Men were obviously keen to get home as quickly as possible. F S Gedye comments on this in his diaries:

*"This is really quite a good little place and we have good billets. On the 28th the Major had a photographer over and had groups of the battery taken. We had several assortments and it took over 4 hours. Every time the old man wanted to change a plate he had to go down to Rooks billet, where, to Rooks great disgust, he burrowed under his bedclothes in order to do it in the dark - a performance Rook looked on as his own peculiar prerogative!*

*Matthews and I have been busy entering up the new industrial groups and codes in every man's paybook. We are only in the preliminary stages of the demobilisation scheme, but it is already a complicated affair.*

*Hayley, who is only two in front of me on the leave list, tells me he is going on Sunday week, so I should get away soon.*

*The G.O.C. [General Walker] came round the lines yesterday and told Lane there is a rumour that we may be going to Austria as an army of occupation. Innsbruck is the place suggested.*

*If his other rumour, that officers under 30 have to remain in the army for 2 years, is true, I hope we go - it would break the monotony no end."*

The rumour about going as an army of occupation to Austria turned out to be untrue. The demobilisation process worked gradually and slowly. Many men would remain in uniform well in to 1919. Britain had a number of issues to deal with and needed the army to execute on its

## The Bristol Gunners

behalf. There was still much clearing up to be done on the battlefields, and the army would be involved with salvaging equipment abandoned by all sides on every front. They would also be involved in salvaging and dealing with mountains of ammunition and stores left over from the war. And, of course, the battlefields would need to be scoured to recover the bodies of the fallen and a proper respectful burial arranged for each of them. These activities would continue for many years, and, in fact, even today occasional human remains are recovered as well as a steady stream of shells and other munitions are found and require safe disposal.

As is usual with the British soldier, the slow progress of demobilisation gave 'Tommy' a good reason for complaint, an activity that he engaged in at every opportunity. Other activities were brought in to pass the time and keep him active. FS Gedye:

*"The only items of note were a very minute inspection of the battery on Nov 30, which was carried out at 12 hours notice and a very cheery evening at Schio on the 2nd, in which Matt, Fisher, Selby-Lowndes, Brook-Taylor and I took part.*

*The most amusing feature of the C.R.A.'s inspection [which we managed to scrape through without being entirely chewed up] was the capsizing of Blackman, the Sergeant-Major, by his horse in full view of the General.*

*The brightest feature of the time at St Vito was the forming of the "Beatles", a Brigade concert Party that really became excellent - young John Seeley made a most ravishing girl and was reputed to have spent hundreds of lire on underwear - his high kicks were certainly one of the features of the show.*

*A last feat of my decaying memory was to write out for them what I remembered of A.A. Milne's "The Boy Comes Home" that I had seen twice on leave and it was performed several times with great success and no royalties.*

*A dark deed stained our Christmas. We bartered Ikey, our entirely illegal mascot moke who was never shown on the strength of the battery but who, nevertheless lived for some three years on the fat of ration land, together with a sum of money to purchase a complete porker for the mens' Christmas dinners.*

The Bristol Gunners

The original Beatles, the GVA concert troupe who entertained the Brigade post war. John Seeley is probably the figure in the centre.

## The Bristol Gunners

*He went to old Lovato, our billetee who was a nice old kind as Italians go, to his animals and we could not have kept him, even unofficially for many weeks longer.*

*I went back for a few weeks while Lane went on leave. Everything was in the process of disintegration and each week the demob. train took a party away.*

*A battery was formed for the occupation, Bayne-Jardine in command, Lucas-Lucas and Selby-Lowndes being among the officers and Blackman the B.S.M.*

*Weekly there were hectic farewell parties to the people leaving next day.*

*Indignant men used to pop out from the every corner as I made my way to the line with "Please sir, when am I going home?" until I had to make a rule that I would see anyone who wanted information at 6 p.m. and at no other time. And a very unpleasant hour it was too.*

*The most tragic times were the horse sales, when our dear old hairies [also known to the drivers in moments of annoyance as those "long faced – er – blighters"] had to go off in batches to Malo to be sold to the Italians.*

*The less said about the treatment of animals by the southern races the better – sufficient to say that it was simply beastly work to hand over our faithful old nags to their keeping.*

*Canada and Kathleen, my two chargers, who had come out with the battery from England as Major Todd's and Capt Stone's chargers, I got in to the occupation battery; a number of those who had gone blind with the eye disease that so many horses had, were shot, but many were sold.*

*Very big prices were obtained, as the Italians had nothing to compare with the fine build of our heavy and light draught.*

*Mares fetched very high prices and funny old jigs, who looked as though the gift of a lira would cause ecstasy, paid out their thousands of lire for a pair of A.S.C. heavy draught, then went back to buy more.*

*There was a great shortage of meat in Italy at this time.*

## The Bristol Gunners

*We had an old nag, Lomas, a veritable giant among horses, who used to be in the wheel of the G.S. wagon who died slowly of pneumonia and after the post mortem, the village wanted to have the carcase. but Weber, the Vet got the interpreter to explain it was unfit for food [and so it was - very] and we buried it.*

*Next morning when, as orderly officer, I had to detail a party to complete the filling in of the grave which was only partly finished the night before, Lomas had vanished - there was a sinister sequel two days later when the village meat store was literally wreathed with sausages.*

*The other instance was a great feast given by our billetess to some of the local worthies when the piece de resistance was, for each guest, a large slab of polenta over which a single sparrow was roasted on a spit and the bird served complete, feathers and all on the Polenta.*

*Finally, the remnant of the Brigade moved to Tezze and we bade farewell to our nice old billetess, Lovato and Nichola and Rosa.*

*I only stayed a few days in Tezze with them and came home in the early days of March. I believe the final journey to England of what was then called the cadre took place about the beginning of April 1919."*

It is interesting to note the use of the title 'Beatles' for an entertainment group almost fifty years before the name was used again by the famous Liverpudlian pop group.

To the officers and men of the GVA, and all of the army, this gradual deconstruction of an efficient and experienced military unit must have been very difficult, especially to those left behind for the last drafts to return to Britain. It must have seemed like a death of a thousand cuts, added to worries about securing future employment when finally demobilised.

While the GVA was being gradually reduced to a cadre events were proceeding elsewhere. It was a time of great change.

The German Army returned to its Fatherland. To some minds, the Germans (and their allies) had been soundly beaten, and deserved to taste the bitterness of defeat. Some German forces, however, were undefeated at war's end. General Paul von Lettow Vorbeck had led the German and

native forces in East Africa throughout the war. He had achieved his strategic aim of diverting the maximum number of British troops away from the Western Front. His 14,000 soldiers had fought against 300,000 British troops for over four years, and had never been defeated in the field. He would return to Berlin a hero.

**A gun crew from C Battery on the move in Italy post war.**

To many Germans, especially those who had served in uniform, their army had not surrendered but reached an armistice. This failure to accept the real defeat they had suffered would in due time lead to another world war. The belief that the German Army had been betrayed by sections of German society would lead to political and social tensions that would result in the rise of the Nazi party, and all the consequences that this would bring.

The Russians continued with their civil war, the Reds against the Whites, with all the internecine violence and manoeuvring that would result in the Soviet Union. The British Army would be involved in this war, as would many other nations. It would take the Russians many decades to accept that communism was not the panacea for the ills of the old feudal system.

## The Bristol Gunners

The Ottoman Empire of the Turks had failed, and the Turkish nation and its institutions would be rebuilt by Kemel Attaturk, to create a modern state in many ways better than some others of the time.

The Middle East had thrown off the yoke of the Ottomans, and had taken on the hope of freedom and self rule, a hope that was to have mixed results.

The victors, Britain, France, and their allies also had challenges and changes to face.

In Britain, the promise of 'A Land Fit for Heroes to Live in' made by David Lloyd George would not be fulfilled. Many ex servicemen, especially those who had volunteered early on in the war, were unable to find work. Those who suffered wounds, disfigurements, or mental illness as a result of their service fared worse.

Lieutenant Francis Stanley Gedye MC on his charger, Canada, in Italy post war. We rely on his diaries for much of our understanding of the activities of the GVA in The First World War.

The First World War stimulated many social changes. Women had proved themselves totally capable of working alongside men, and had earned the right to participate in the political process, gaining the vote for some in 1918, and eventually on equal terms to men in 1928.

The immediate problem for the victors, though, in 1919, was to formally resolve matters with the defeated nations.

The Paris Peace Conference first met in January 1919, and set the scene for the break up of old regimes and the creation of new states from the remains of the old Austro-Hungarian and Ottoman empires in a series of treaties. Most significantly, it established the concept of war guilt on the Germans, and imposed onerous financial penalties by means of war reparations on them.

### The Bristol Gunners

New countries emerged from this process, and many existing countries changed boundaries. This in turn would lead to stresses and conflicts between peoples, some of which continue to this day. Part of the Italian Irridenta, the Austrian province of Trento, along with smaller territories around Trieste, and Rijeka in Istria (now Croatia) were passed over to Italy. Felice Orsini's aims were realised, if only in part.

The men of the GVA came back to a Bristol that had changed, as had most of European communities. Political, social, economic and cultural changes were in train. It was not the Bristol that they had left.

The 48th Division officially ceased to exist on 26th March 1919. 240th Brigade, RFA, of which the GVA comprised the major part, continued to run down. One battery, made up of volunteers and later recruits, joined 102nd Brigade RFA, a composite force created out of the remaining artillery units in Italy in early March. This was as part of a brigade of occupation. In due course even this military remnant dissolved and the men returned to their homes.

The GVA was disbanded. However, the GVA name lived on, and in March 1920 it was reformed as 1st South Midland Brigade, RFA (TF) with the newly reformed 48th South Midland Division (TF). The Brigade had three batteries in Bristol (261, 262 and 263 Batteries) and one in Reading in Berkshire (264 Battery).

The British Regular Army reverted to its pre-war role of colonial police force. There were around 15,000 Regular troops in Germany as an occupation force in the Rhineland, as well as small detachments in other European countries, but, on the whole, its attention returned to the Empire and Home Defence became the role for the TF again. In October 1920, the Territorial Force was renamed Territorial Army, and the GVA brigade title changed to 66th South Midlands Brigade (TA). Four years later it changed again to 66th (South Midland) Field Brigade, Royal Artillery (TA). Due to this change of title and formal incorporation into the Royal Regiment of Artillery, changes were made to uniforms, buttons and badges. Bandoliers were no longer worn, being replaced by waist belts, and official uniform became the same as the Royal Artillery.

The change to Territorial Army from Territorial Force recognised that the volunteer forces constituted an army in its own right, separate to the

## The Bristol Gunners

Regular Army, and which had its own reserves. The TA had its own role, Home Defence of Britain, and was organised into Territorial Divisions.

In 1924 all artillery units became part of the Royal Artillery, which therefore combined the Horse, Field, and Garrison branches into one Corps. The Royal School of Artillery (RSA) was established in 1920 at Larkhill in Wiltshire as the central training school for all artillery disciplines, though there remained specialist training establishments around the UK under the overall control of RSA. This new organisation ensured that methods and technology could be more easily improved and standardised across the Regular and Territorial Armies and the Empire forces.

When reformed the GVA was commanded by Colonel Balfour, the previous Commanding Officer, and former officers and soldiers were invited to rejoin. A number did and the brigade was initially 80 strong, and reached 140 all ranks by the summer of 1920. Training started straight away, and annual camps were held over the succeeding years at a number of localities.

Initially, while they were building their strength the brigade was attached to a Regular Army brigade at Bulford (24th Battery, 7th Brigade) whose guns and equipment were used for training. In early 1921 six 18 pounder guns were issued to the GVA to enable more extensive training to take place. Batteries were reduced to four guns in 1922. These were replaced by an improved version, the Mark 4 18 Pounder in 1924. The Mark 4 version had seen some limited service in the war, towards the end, but did not enter full service until after the war had finished.

The Mark 4 incorporated several improvements over the earlier marks. It had a box trail rather than the original pole trail, which permitted the maximum elevation to increase from 16 degrees to 37.5 degrees, and a consequent increase in range from 6000 metres to 8500 metres. A better breech mechanism and recuperator was fitted, the latter moving to a new position below the barrel rather than above it. The 18 pounder gun remained in service into the Second World War, and was the basis for the highly successful and reliable 25 Pounder Gun Howitzer. This served the Empire throughout the Second World War and up until the 1990's in a training role.

## The Bristol Gunners

The issue of these guns meant that the GVA had the same weapons as were issued to the Regular Army.

The Army continued to be reliant mainly on horses through into the 1930s. Throughout the Empire, Regular Army fighting and campaigning was carried out mostly in rural and mountainous areas where modern road systems were absent. Animal drawn transport was highly suitable to these areas and the impetus towards mechanisation was reduced, as Britain no longer envisaged a role for its army on the European Continent.

However, the lessons of tank warfare, and the pursuit operations of late 1918, though forgotten by many, had not been entirely ignored by a few more far-sighted officers. Keen intelligence was being applied to foreseeing what mechanisation and other technologies might mean for future conflicts. Military force is most useful in attack. A successful attack relies on force and manoeuvre. Mechanisation offered the potential to improve speed and manoeuvrability for offensive use. It also offered the potential for making mobile some equipments and technology that had previously been immobile. Bringing heavier artillery pieces into the field of battle, for instance.

In 1927 the Regular Army carried out field trials with 'The Experimental Mechanised Force' (EMF, later also called the Experimental Armoured Force). A brigade sized formation was created to examine the issues and opportunities presented by mechanising warfare, especially using armoured vehicles.

This force had an improvised set of motorised equipment. There were light and heavy tanks for reconnaissance and mobile firepower. Infantry were carried in lorries. Artillery guns were drawn by lorries and tracked vehicles. This included gun tractors with caterpillar tracks, and even artillery guns mounted on tank chassis as self propelled artillery (the Birch Gun), an innovation that would not see light of day again until late in the Second World War. This Birch gun was dual purpose, able to be used in the field artillery role as well as an anti aircraft gun.

The EMF was used to see what was needed to make a motorised force effective, how 3C (Command, Control, Communication) needed to change, how logistics would affect operations. It was also used to explore what additional advantages would result from having a faster, more manoeuvrable military formation with a better 'punch.'

## The Bristol Gunners

Though this force identified many important features of motorised warfare, the lessons were not, apparently, valued by the British. The force was disbanded in 1929, and much of the equipment abandoned. The Germans, however, had seen the results, and they took the lessons to heart and built on them. The EMF helped to develop the German Blitzkrieg methods that would be so effective twelve years later in Poland, The Netherlands, Belgium, and France.

Despite the failure to grasp all the lessons of the EMF, the armed forces did recognise that motor horsepower would replace organic horsepower. The use of motorised transport was growing in the civilian world; the use of horses was diminishing. Consequently, in 1932 it was announced that artillery units were to exchange their horses and wagons for lorries as part of a wider motorisation of our forces. The first of these arrived with the GVA in Bristol in April the same year.

**GVA gunners with their newly issued Morris gun tractors, but still with the Mk4 18 Pounder and limber with cart wheels. 1932, Artillery Grounds, Bristol.**

The lorries were, in reality, standard Morris civilian vehicles, though with six wheels. In addition, a number of other vehicles, light cars and motorcycles, were sourced and brought into service over the succeeding months. These vehicles were a direct replacement for the horses, the lorries were used to draw (pull) the same limber and gun arrangement as used previously with horses. One problem was a lack of trained and experience drivers and mechanics. Army drivers were required to be trained and pass a test on light cars before being allowed to progress on

to driving lorries. This was two years before a competency test was required for civilians to drive on UK roads.

There must have been a degree of excitement with the GVA at this time as all these changes came into being, maybe tinged with a little sadness over the passing of the old ways, and the loss of the horses. Some of the excitement was caused by exposure to thrilling new experiences as they witnessed the arrival of mechanisation during training on Salisbury Plain in the summer of 1932. A section from the GVA History:

*"Guns and limbers were borrowed from the pool at Tidworth and extra lorries were hired from the R.A.S.C. All ranks of the 9th Brigade were most helpful, hospitable and instructive. Dragons and Burfords were turned out with regular drivers for two batteries daily - the other two batteries turning out with our own and borrowed lorries. Everybody thoroughly enjoyed these turn-outs and the drivers of the 9th Brigade drove across country with the guns at what seemed a terrific speed with a total disregard of the regulation speed limit. These turn-outs were most instructive and the batteries benefited greatly by the instruction given. The presence of numbers of tanks and low flying aeroplanes added to the general interest of these drill orders."*

66th Brigade (the GVA) were helped and supported by the men of 9th Brigade, a Regular Army unit, during this camp and drivers from 9th Brigade demonstrated their cross country driving skills to impress the men of the Territorial Army. The Dragons referred to were tracked gun tractors, similar to the later Bren Gun Carriers. Burfords were a make of lorry, some of which were fitted with tracks in place of their rear wheels for better cross country mobility.

In succeeding years, further exciting training took place at annual camps. It seems that the need for what is now termed 'all arms training', that is, working with other arms and specialisations during training was recognised, and familiarisation with tanks and other arms was carried out. The GVA History tells us about the annual camp on Salisbury Plain in 1935:

*"The camp was an interesting and instructive one for all ranks, as without moving from the tent lines it was possible to see guns firing and sometimes the shell falling, tanks of various sizes moving rapidly over the*

## The Bristol Gunners

*Plain, infantry marching, aeroplanes and observation balloons in the air all at the same time.*

*A battalion of the Royal Tank Corps was encamped close to the Brigade and parties from the Brigade were allowed to inspect the tanks at close quarters guided by officers and N.C.O.s of the unit. Rides in and on the tanks followed, one of the larger tanks had at least 25 men in and on it whilst it went over the undulating plain."*

And, in 1936:

*"Combined Operations by the Royal Navy, Army, and Royal Air force were held in 1936 after annual training.*

*Vehicles and drivers of the Brigade were attached to units of the Regular Army during these operations.*

*Part of the operations consisted of a landing from ships of the Royal Navy in Studland Bay near Weymouth.*

*In addition to troops, attempts were made to land vehicles.*

*Owing to a very heavy swell running at the time of the landing unloading of vehicles proved very difficult and eventually only one 6 Wheeled Lorry was landed."*

Landing an army from the sea and onto the land across open beaches is a very difficult operation to undertake. Within ten years, the British Army, and the GVA as part of it, would become extremely proficient in this craft. Without these practice sessions, the invasions of North Africa, Sicily, Italy, and France could not have happened.

Through the 1920s and the 1930s the GVA took part in a number of public and civil events as well as carrying out its military training duties.

In 1920 shortly after the Brigade was reformed the first reunion dinner was held. In 1923 a memorial plaque was installed in the drill hall and a book of remembrance was presented to the Sergeants' and the Officers' Messes, containing the names of every GVA soldier who had died in the Great War. This war is sometimes called the Kaiser's War, more commonly the First World War. It is not to be confused with World War

The Bristol Gunners

1 which, for the Americans who use this name, did not start until April 1917.

In 1921 a series of strikes in the docks and mines had caused the TA to be put on standby to assist the civil powers. A composite unit was formed of volunteers from the GVA and the Birmingham Brigade. This unit occupied the Bristol drill hall, but was not called to take any action.

**After reforming the GVA, its officers pose at a training camp in 1923. F S Gedye, by then a captain, is on the extreme left. Note that some officers are still wearing uniforms with rank badges on their forearms, a form of dress that changed during the First World War to rank badges being worn on the shoulder.**

In 1926 a General Strike was held throughout Britain, and many civilians volunteered to assist the civil powers in maintaining transport and supplies to the civil population. Though the Regular Army did assist, there is no record that the GVA were asked to assist, or in fact did so.

Following the General Strike and the Wall Street Crash in 1929 public finances came under strain, and the Army needed to make economies. Pay rates for TA soldiers were cut (as they were for all armed services) and training curtailed. Despite these restrictions, much training was completed including attachments to Regular Army units and courses at

the Royal School of Artillery. On one occasion, in 1932, there was insufficient money to pay for all the attendance at annual camp, and therefore for half the time of the camp all ranks were serving in a completely voluntary and unpaid manner.

In June 1930, a party of 35 former GVA men travelled from Bristol to the battlefields of The First World War in northern France and Belgium. They visited The Somme, Vimy, and The Ypres Salient. They included visits to the cemeteries holding the graves of comrades from 240 Brigade RFA. At this time many memorials and monuments had been completed, or were about to be completed across the former Western Front.

The massive Thiepval memorial on the Somme was being built and would be formally opened in July 1932. The Canadians had started their National memorial atop Vimy Ridge in 1925, it was not completed until 1936. Around Ypres, the Menin Gate memorial had been completed and opened in 1927, while the largest Commonwealth War Graves Commission cemetery at Passchendaele Village, named Tyne Cot by the Northumberland Fusiliers, was still receiving men being found on the battlefields. It had been visited by King George V in 1922 when it already held many thousands of graves.

In their written record of their visit, F S Gedye, now a Captain in the GVA, made the following remarks about these memorials to the fallen:

*"The cemeteries and memorials throughout the area we visited were deeply impressive. Each one appeared to have had individual thought to harmonise its object to its locality, and each with a magnificent simple dignity that is bound to appeal deeply not only to those of us who remember so vividly, but to every generation that sees them in years to come. The years since the war have at least created these moving and unforgettable tributes in a decade has been too full of forgetfulness and disillusion."*

Gedye's comments are insightful, and reflect the feeling of the time by 'old sweats,' that their efforts and sacrifices had not been fully rewarded with a more peaceful and equitable country.

The early 1930's saw an upswing in interest in visiting the battlefields of the Great War. The reasons for this were various, but almost certainly

## The Bristol Gunners

included concerns over increasing unrest and tensions in European countries.

Various church parades and celebration events were held in Bristol at which the GVA were present, during the 1920s and 1930s.

Three officers and 27 other ranks were present on parade at the coronation of King George VI in London. The GVA History states of this:

*"Lt-Col (Bt-Col) C.A.H. Fairbank, B.S.M. Coggins, S/Sgt Collins, and Sgt. Arlett marched in the procession, the remainder lined the route.*

*Coronation Blue uniform was issued to each other rank, consisting of a blue patrol jacket, overalls, Wellington boots, and spurs.*

*Practice drills were commenced 14-4-37 and continued up to Sunday 9-5-37, when the Bristol contingent entrained for London, the Reading portion entraining on Monday 10-5-37.*

*The detachment was encamped in Kensington Gardens, near the Speke Memorial.*

*The weather conditions were bad, rain fell practically continuous up to the day of the Coronation.*

*The Brigade contingent lined the route on both sides of Oxford Street, directly outside Selfridges main entrance and took up position about 10.15 a.m.; the weather was fine.*

*During the waiting period men were allowed to fall out alternatively by odd or even numbers, walk up and down etc; and the period of waiting passed comparatively quickly.*

*After 1.30 p.m. no falling out was allowed, a bag of lunch was served to all troops lining the route; and the procession commenced to pass about 2.30 p.m.*

*The State Coach containing their Majesties passed about 3-15 p.m. The experience was one that will not be forgotten by any of those taking part.*

The Bristol Gunners

*The detachments left for their home stations on Thursday 13-5-37.*

*5 x Coronation Medals were awarded to the Brigade."*

It may seem strange to some that troops were expected to wear Wellington boots on a Royal Parade. In the army, Wellingtons are, in fact, leather calf length boots worn with parade uniform, rather than the more familiar rubber boots.

Discontent existed throughout Europe following the Great War. Revolutions sprung up in Russia and Germany, rioting occurred in many cities. Civil unrest was seen in just about every country. Great Britain was no exception to this. Both the British Communist Party and The British Union of Fascists were prominent during the 1930s. As the Nazis in Germany came to power and demonstrated their determination to reinstate the influence of Germany a cold chill went through every European country. In order to avoid the prospect of another disastrous and costly war many governments adopted a policy of practical appeasement, giving in to the unreasonable demands of Adolf Hitler. Winston Churchill is seen as a lone voice that from the political wilderness sought to warn of the dangers, and in due course he was to be proved correct. However, he was not the only person to be alert to these risks. These others were also astute and, better still, were able to do something practical to prepare the British for the worst eventuality.

Despite the financial stringencies of the 1930s resulting from the Great Depression the British Army, Royal Navy, and Royal Air Force managed to start re-arming and preparing for war. Money was made available, both publicly by government and privately by patriotic individuals and companies to design, build, and introduce new vehicles, ships, and aeroplanes.

Some evidence for this has already been seen, the Army's experiments with mechanised formations in 1927, and the issue of motorised transport to the GVA in 1932. In the early 1930s, mechanisation of the army was completed, the horse becoming obsolete except in very specific situations, such as ceremonial troops and in more remote parts of the Empire.

## The Bristol Gunners

The armed forces were still weak and in transition as the new threats from the fascist governments of Italy and Germany became apparent. The various treaties reached after 1919 had failed to resolve the tensions between nations. New tensions had arisen. The biggest of these factors were the penalties imposed on Germany by the Treaty of Versailles, mainly at the insistence of the French.

As the German threat grew, Britain was forced to respond, reluctantly, and by fits and starts. Nevertheless, respond it did, and great minds turned from thoughts of peace, towards thoughts of how best to meet the threat of war.

The development of aeroplanes in the First World War had shown that the air war would be of increasing importance in any future conflict.

From early 1915 the Germans had sent their Zeppelin airships over to Britain to bomb London and other places. In 1917 Germany had abandoned Zeppelin raids, and had used their Gotha heavy bombers instead, flying from bases in Belgium. The British had used their heavy bombers, the Handley Page Type 0 flown by the Royal Naval Air Service in a number of raids, and were planning a version that could have reached Berlin itself. The bomb load of these planes was relatively modest, but the psychological and morale effects were significant.

Immediately post war, Captains Allcock and Brown flew across the Atlantic for the first time in a modified Vickers Vimy bomber. Lindbergh flew solo across the Atlantic six years later. Other pioneers proved the potential of aeroplanes for international communications and warfare. Aeroplanes became more capable and reliable as time progressed, and scheduled flights were introduced in the 1930s, especially by the British to service the Empire. The aeroplane of 1938 was a very different and more dangerous beast to that of 1918.

Throughout the 1920s and up to 1938 the GVA had trained and prepared for a role as field artillery. In 1938, the nature of the aerial threat that Britain would have to face had become much clearer, aerial warfare was to be the main concern. Home defence, the responsibility of the TA, needed to address this aerial threat. The GVA were needed in a different capability. They were re-roled to become a heavy anti-aircraft (HAA) regiment, 76th (Gloucestershire) HAA Regiment RA (TA). They swapped

### The Bristol Gunners

their old 18 Pounder Field guns for 3.7 Inch Heavy Anti Aircraft guns. They joined Anti Aircraft Command, as part of 8th Anti Aircraft Division.

In the pre-war years other changes were afoot in the Territorial Army in Bristol. In 1934, the Army decided to raise TA Survey Regiments. Survey regiments had the role of locating targets, enemy artillery batteries, using sound ranging, flash spotting, and other technologies. Up to this date, only one Regular Army Survey Company – a battery sized unit – had been in existence. The rationale behind this is supplied in a section from the Defence Surveyors Association:

**"Organisation of flash spotting and sound ranging and other hostile-battery locating units down to the outbreak of World War II**

*In 1915 W.L. Bragg, already, although only in his early twenties, a Nobel Prizewinner (with his father) in Physics, but then a subaltern in a Royal Horse Artillery Yeomanry Regiment, was despatched to France to investigate the French Army's experiments in locating enemy battery positions with what became known as sound ranging. After doing so he was instructed to create similar sound ranging subunits in the British Army.*

*For this purpose he combed the Army for physicists. His Sound Ranging Sections were put into the Field Survey Companies (later Field Survey Battalions) RE although the bulk of the officers were Royal Field Artillery, and the other ranks were from all arms. By the end of World War I there were about 34 Sound Ranging Sections in service. In the early part of World War I Flash Spotting had been invented by H.H. Hemming, a Canadian engineering student serving in the Royal Field Artillery on the Western Front. During the War Observation Groups, similarly recruited and placed in the Field Survey Companies, carried it out.*

*The surveying of our own battery positions and the provision of bearing pickets and aiming points to enable them to undertake predicted fire as developed in World War I was also undertaken by the Field Survey Companies.*

*In 1920 it was decided to transfer all sound ranging and flash spotting and battery survey to the Royal Artillery. A single regular Survey Company RA was formed composed of a Survey Battery, a Flash Spotting*

## The Bristol Gunners

*Battery, (deploying one flash spotting base), and a Sound Ranging Battery, (deploying one sound ranging base). Two similar Territorial Army Survey Companies RA were formed. Shortly before World War II these units were renamed Survey Regiments. To provide one for each projected Corps, a second regular Survey Regiment was to be formed on any mobilisation and early in 1939 each TA Survey Regiment also formed a second Regiment."*

An existing Royal Signals unit in Bristol, 223 (Field Artillery) Section, Royal Signals, was converted to a Royal Artillery Survey section, and eventually became 3rd Survey Regiment Royal Artillery (TA). A second regiment, 5th Survey Regiment RA (TA) was formed in Bristol immediately before the outbreak of war in 1939. While these regiments were not titled Gloucestershire Volunteer Artillery, they do, later, form part of the story of the GVA.

And so, we come to the Second World War.

The Bristol Gunners

## Chapter 8  The Second World War

The GVA had become a part of the immense organisation that was building its strength to defend Britain from air attack. As Neville Chamberlain went to Munich to avert a crisis, as Prague was occupied by the Germans, the GVA learned their new skills and worked hard to become proficient in their new art. In a little over a year they completed their transformation to 'cloud punchers', the army nickname for anti aircraft artillery.

If war came, the GVA were ready and waiting.

As a result of the German air attacks of the First World War a paradigm had developed in air defence thinking in Britain. At first Zeppelin airships, then heavier than air craft, had repeatedly invaded British skies and dropped bombs on London and other locations. The paradigm that 'the bomber will always get through', that is, there was no effective defence against bomber formations, was held to be an inevitable truth. Bombers would have free rein to bomb wherever and whenever they chose to do so.

In the event of war, Britain would bomb her way to victory, by attacking enemy means of trade and manufacture. Of course, this acceptance of the inevitability of bombing attacks meant that Britain would also be open to bombing attack by any enemy. This lead to a fatalistic acceptance that Britain would be bombed and that casualties and destruction would be severe.

Luckily, not every senior RAF officer held to the point of view of bomber invincibility. Some believed that it would be possible to diminish the bombers' power and thereby reduce damage incurred by the defender. In the early 1930s a plan known as 'Scheme F' was introduced, whereby the RAF was to be expanded from under 30 squadrons to 187 squadrons, under the then Chief of the Air Staff, Air Marshall Sir Edward Leonard Ellington. This scheme was still based with an emphasis on bomber squadrons in a ratio of 5 to 2 against fighter squadrons. Nevertheless, the expansion of the RAF had begun. Air Marshall Ellington also re-organised the former Air Defence Great Britain (ADGB) organisation into the more familiar RAF organisation based on commands; Bomber

Command, Fighter Command, Coastal Command and Training Command. Bomber Command would attack our enemies, Fighter Command would protect us from enemy attack, Coastal Command would protect our shipping lanes, and Training Command would ensure that we had a suitable supply of well trained crews to operate our aeroplanes.

In 1937 a new Chief of the Air Staff was appointed, Air Marshall Sir Cyril Newall. Under him aircraft production was increased dramatically, and new, better, aircraft came into service so that by the start of the Second World War Britain at last had an air force that was up to the job, but only just. Air Marshall Newall challenged the then current orthodoxy of bomber supremacy, insisting that a fighter force was equally necessary. He was central in re-equipping Fighter Command with newer and better fighter aircraft – including Hurricanes and Spifires – and more of them than had previously been thought necessary. He also oversaw the provision of comprehensive repair and resupply systems for these aircraft.

Another central character in preparing Britain for effective air defence was Air Marshall Hugh Dowding, Commander in Chief of Fighter Command in the late 1930s. He was perhaps the only person who really challenged the bomber paradigm. Under his insistence and management a comprehensive air defence system was developed. He sponsored the development of radar; he brought together the components of air defence, fighters, artillery, observers, control rooms, barrage balloons into a fully integrated air defence structure. This was the most advanced and effective in the world at that time, and by doing this he saved Britain and the free world. His reward was, of course, typically British. He was sacked from his post, and made to retire.

As the GVA role was now air defence they became part of 8th AA Division (Anti Aircraft Division), which together with other AA Divisions, was part of Anti Aircraft Command (AAC), this being part of RAF Fighter Command. It was decided that the TA would be a good source of manpower to man these new AA forces. A number of TA artillery regiments, and other non artillery regiments, had been converted to anti aircraft regiments throughout the 1930s. The GVA converted towards the end of the process, in 1938.

AAC comprised guns, searchlights, barrage balloons and observer stations. Royal Artillery soldiers manned the guns, Royal Engineers

manned the searchlights, RAF airmen and women operated the balloons, The Royal Observer Corps provided the observers, and RAF personnel operated the radar stations and control systems. All of this was commanded as part of RAF Fighter Command, which enabled a good level of co-ordination with aircraft movements and zones of responsibility. A comprehensive system of control rooms was set up by Fighter Command in order that information from radar and observers could be received and analysed, and decisions made as to what response was appropriate. This would result in the launching of barrage balloons or fighter aircraft, and warnings being sent to searchlights and gun positions in the areas where attack was expected.

Anti aircraft guns had been developed through the First World War. Most weapons were adaptations of existing field artillery pieces. Barrels were put on more suitable mountings for rapid traversing and firing at high angles. Some ammunition types had been developed to improve both range and speed in engagement, but in the early 1930s only a limited range of guns were available, and they were very few in number. With the acknowledgement that Britain was likely to suffer aerial bombardment in a future war, there was a need identified for more modern and effective guns, and for co-ordination with the aeroplanes of the RAF. In consequence, in 1937, new guns were designed, including the 3.7 Heavy Anti Aircraft guns issued to the GVA in 1938, and the Bofors 40mm gun designed in Sweden and manufactured under licence in Britain. The Bofors filled the light anti aircraft (LAA) role, being tasked with engaging aeroplanes flying at lower altitudes.

A section in the HMSO publication in 1943, Roof Over Britain, explains this development of air defences in Britain in the pre-war period:

*"By 1925 the political situation started to look less favourable, and very slowly a start was made to rebuild the air defences. There were now two regular antiaircraft brigades – about 5,000 men – who spent half their year running camps for Territorials. The regulars were not designed for the defence of this country but to go abroad with an expeditionary force. Things gradually began to build up; by 1936 there was one AA Division, and a second division was formed. By 1938 there were five, and they were brought together under one A.A.Corps. In 1939 there were seven Divisions and the Corps became a Command."*

A number of other technologies were being developed that would be used and integrated into the air defences. Radar was developed from the search for a 'death ray' and grasped most energetically by the British. The Germans and Americans were also working on radar, but had not progressed as far or as quickly and were quite some way behind the British in developing practical and effective radar systems. Experiments had been carried out with sound and infra red detection systems, but radar held better and more practical prospects. As war was declared in September 1939 the RAF had constructed a series of fixed radar sites (called Chain Home) on the coast from the Isle of Wight round to Lincolnshire. These first systems were imperfect, but good enough. In time, these early radar systems would be refined to be able to detect aeroplanes at longer ranges and a wider range of altitudes. They also became more able to provide detail on numbers of aircraft. Ultimately, completely mobile systems were developed that could move with the field army, or be fitted to ships and aeroplanes.

Improved balloons and searchlights had been introduced based on First World War experience and more modern materials and technology.

Barrage balloons were placed so as to form a screen around areas needing protection. The threat of collision with the balloons and cables would force enemy aircraft to climb to higher altitudes where their ability to bomb accurately would be diminished. At higher altitudes the heavy guns would have more time to engage aircraft and therefore improve the guns' ability to damage and destroy enemy planes.

Searchlights were employed in close contact with guns. During daylight, searchlight and gun crews could locate and track aircraft by eyesight, optically using binoculars and telescopes of various types, and by sound detectors. At night, the technique was for searchlight units to search for and locate aircraft, shine their lights at the position where they believed the aircraft to be and then follow them so that the guns could aim at the aircraft in the hope of shooting them down.

Shooting at aircraft, though, presents a number of problems, all of which had to be overcome.

The basic problem revolves around the fact that aeroplanes travel through space, relatively quickly, and between the time that a decision is made to

target an aeroplane and the shell arriving and exploding will be many seconds, possibly over a minute. In that elapsed time, the aeroplane will have travelled many kilometres, changed altitude, speed, or its direction. In 1940, a typical bomber could travel at 300 Km per hour, or 5 Km a minute. When the shell exploded the target aeroplane could well be in a completely different piece of sky altogether.

The challenge for the gunners was, therefore, not to aim at an aeroplane, but to aim at a point in the sky where they expected the aeroplane to be some time later. They had to *predict* where the aeroplane would be at the time the shell would explode.

Considerable thought and effort went into working out how this apparently impossible feat of mental and physical agility could be performed by the gunners. At the beginning of the Second World War, a German aeroplane had a less than 1% chance of being shot down by anti aircraft fire. By the end of the war, when London and the south east of England was under intense assault by flying bombs (V1 'Doodlebugs'), 67% of the flying bombs were shot down without reaching their targets. Antwerp was also attacked with flying bombs a few months later, and 97% of them were shot down.

Clearly these brief statistics show how far the art and science of predicting and controlling anti aircraft fire had developed in five years.

How was this achieved?

A combination of factors led to this better performance. Radar improved so that approaching aircraft were identified earlier, with greater accuracy on their speed, height, and direction of travel. Unlike manned aircraft, flying bombs generally followed a steady course, speed, and altitude, making prediction easier. Defensive fighters and guns were given clear zones of freedom to intercept, so that the guns were free to engage anything that flew within range without the delay of having to confirm the identity of the aircraft. By 1945, radar sets were fully integrated with the fire control systems of the guns and men were required only to load the guns, laying and firing became automatic and hydraulically or electrically driven. Better fuses and shells were developed, and the range and rate of fire of guns increased.

## The Bristol Gunners

If the Luftwaffe of 1939 had met the British guns of 1945, they would have run out of aeroplanes and crews within days.

As it was, though, the defences in 1939 were under resourced and still only crudely controlled and co-ordinated. Equipment and manpower of all types were insufficient to meet the expected onslaught, but plans were in place to put this right.

The main emphasis of air defence in Britain in 1939 was the defence of London. Thirty per cent of all heavy anti aircraft guns were placed to defend London – around 350 guns in all. Other cities were lucky if they had one or two regiments (24 guns per regiment) to defend them. Even major naval base towns such as Portsmouth and Plymouth had only one or two regiments to defend them.

A regiment of heavy anti aircraft artillery comprised three batteries; each battery had eight guns in two troops of four guns. Each troop was placed in a prepared gun site around the periphery of the defended city. The four guns of the troop were arranged in a horseshoe pattern with a fire control centre placed at the centre of the horseshoe. The fire control centre identified the targets, calculated the firing data and transmitted this to the guns. The gun layers were tasked with laying the guns on to the data given to them. The other members of the crew were responsible for handling ammunition and loading the gun.

With manual loading and laying rate of fire was only 10 rounds per minute, in 1942 this rose to 20 when automatic fuse setting was introduced. As an aircraft might only be in a position to be fired at for under a minute, rate of fire was important to increase the likelihood of a hit.

Each troop fired all their guns at the same time, so that each 'shot' at an enemy plane would in fact be four shells. When a shell exploded it broke into a number of sizeable metal splinters which flew in all directions at high speed, and it was these splinters that caused damage to a plane. However, if a shell actually hit a plane and exploded inside or alongside it was regarded as a lucky shot, direct hits were not expected.

Anti aircraft fire was also expected to force bombers to change height and direction, take avoiding action, and to distract and upset the crew, so

that when they did release their bombs accuracy was adversely affected. If the bombers flew in formation, accurate AA fire may also disrupt the formation, affecting bombing accuracy, and potentially causing aeroplanes to collide with each other. Lone bombers separated from a formation would also be an easier target for our fighter aeroplanes.

As war clouds gathered over Europe in the summer of 1939 final preparations were made across Britain to prepare for the expected aerial onslaught. Air raid shelters were dug, sand bags were filled and stacked around important buildings, and the TA HAA regiments checked and maintained their guns and equipment.

The GVA in Bristol had their war procedures and gun sites fully prepared and ready for action. The call to mobilise came on 20th August some days before the declaration of war on 3rd September. The GVA were first sent to Southsea in Portsmouth for four days before returning to the Bristol area. They manned their guns at Portbury, but also had some men manning Lewis machine guns at the Filton factory of the Bristol Aeroplane Company.

Bristol had a number of areas which could be regarded as legitimate targets for enemy attack. As well as The Bristol Aeroplane Company, there were a number of other companies making war related products, such as Parnall which made aircraft gun turrets and other aeroplane components. The docks were also an important and likely target. Around the Bristol area there were approximately 24 locations designated and prepared to serve as sites for HAA gun batteries. Some of these were fully built while others were still in need of work in 1939.

Gun batteries were moved between sites in anticipation of raids and to prevent enemy spies identifying where guns were and telling the Luftwaffe where they were so they could be attacked. Having more sites than guns also meant that more guns could be inserted to defend the city at short notice should that become necessary.

The 3.7 inch HAA gun came in two versions, fixed and mobile. The fixed version could travel by road on its own wheeled trailer, but could not deploy or fire while on this trailer. It needed a concrete base fixed with associated buildings and structures to hold ammunition and communications. It also required an electrical supply, telephone

connection, and access for vehicles so that equipment and stores could be easily moved on and off site. A water supply was also needed for the crew, as well as some form of accommodation, as they would be in position for 24 hours per day for extended periods.

The mobile version of the 3.7 inch HAA gun was designed for deployment with the field army and was carried on a trailer on which it could be prepared for firing. It was a mobile system, that is, it was designed and equipped to move with field formations rather than be part of a 'fixed defence.' Most of these types of gun were manned by the Regular Army and sent to France with the BEF when it mobilised.

The GVA were in uniform and fully prepared and deployed in readiness. Therefore, when Neville Chamberlain's ultimatum to the Germans failed to elicit a favourable response. War was declared on 3rd September 1939, and air raid sirens sounded immediately. The people of Bristol, and their GVA guardians, expected raids to take place immediately.

In fact, as we now know, there was to be a period of 'Phoney War' from September 1939 until May 1940. Though there were a few individual German aeroplanes intruding into British skies, they were not intent on bombing and destruction, at least in the short term. These early intruders were mostly tasked with gaining information, through observation and use of aerial photography.

It is not always understood that the German armed forces of 1939 were not large or powerful enough to engage on two fronts at the same time. Their invasion of Poland was using most of their available equipment and manpower, there was little else to use on attacking Britain, or, indeed, any other country.

The late summer and autumn became, therefore, an anticlimax for the people of Britain and Bristol. No massed formations of German bombers came, few bombs dropped, normal life resumed. Children who had been evacuated from the major cities in August gradually returned home, so that by early 1940 most of them were back home with their parents.

The GVA entered into a routine of setting up gun positions, moving to another location, setting up again, with occasional firing practices at safe locations. This continued until mid March 1940, when they were sent to

man their guns on the south coast. Firstly they went to Portsmouth, then Southampton, and then on to the Isle of Wight until the end of April 1940, ending up at RAF Tangmere in May.

On 9th April, the Phoney War ended. The Germans invaded Denmark and Norway. Denmark was quickly occupied and surrendered after only 6 hours, but the campaign in Norway continued until 10th June. The British and French sent troops to assist the Norwegian Army, but were unable to prevent Norway falling to the Germans. There were a few successes, though, including the Royal Navy sinking the bulk of the German naval destroyer forces at Narvik in Norway.

The invasion of Norway was followed on May 10th by the German invasion of The Netherlands and Belgium. The Dutch managed to resist only temporarily, for four days. The British and French crossed into Belgium in order to meet the Germans and fell into a carefully prepared trap. As they advanced northwards, the Germans attacked eastern France through the Ardennes, slicing westwards through the French Army reaching the Atlantic coast near Le Havre and isolating the bulk of the BEF and French in Belgium and Northern France from the rest of the French Army further south. The British and French evacuated as many troops as possible from Calais and Dunkirk in the now famous seaborne evacuation. Most of their equipment was left behind, 338,000 soldiers were saved including 123,000 French soldiers. The bulk of them arrived in Britain with only the clothes that they wore. The best French and British military equipment was left abandoned in France.

Some French and British troops continued fighting in France until 22nd June, when an armistice was reached. Despite Prime Minister Winston Churchill's best efforts and cajolery, the French government was unable to continue the struggle.

Britain was alone.

Yet not completely alone. Many heads of state and governments had escaped and allied themselves with the British, and, in due course, they would mostly help the British and their later cobelligerents by active support in resisting the Germans in their own countries. The British Empire, was, of course, fully committed, and turned its efforts and manpower to the task of defeating the Germans. The Irish Republic,

though technically neutral, allowed many Irish nationals to travel to Britain and join in the fight.

The Americans had already been very helpful in taking contracts for manufacture and supply of aeroplanes, vehicles, guns and munitions, though political differences in the USA made this a sensitive subject.

Many foreign nationals, Poles, Czechs, French, Norwegians, Danes, Dutch, and others, escaped to Britain and volunteered for armed service. Many foreign merchant ships had been sailed to British and empire ports and sided with the British cause by making themselves available to British trade.

Some Polish naval ships had arrived in Britain, manned by Polish sailors.

For many Europeans in German occupied countries, though, difficult choices had to be made. Did they accept the German conquest as a fact and collaborate, or resist? Some chose resistance, but not all were able to do so.

Of the 123,000 French soldiers who escaped via Dunkirk, most went back to France, ending up as prisoners of war. Only around 3,000 chose to stay in Britain and fight on further with Charles de Gaulle's Free French Army (FFL).

While these events took place, the GVA continued to move around the outskirts of Bristol and look at skies largely empty of German aeroplanes. In early June, while Dunkirk was still being evacuated, they had been sent back to Bristol and set up their guns to defend the city.

The German Luftwaffe was designed and operated mostly as an adjunct of the Army. Their aeroplanes and tactics were designed to support their Blitzkrieg tactics, providing close support to troops on the ground. Their bombers had relatively short range and from their bases in Germany, they were unable to reach the Bristol area when carrying a bomb load. Now that they had conquered France, the Luftwaffe was able to use French airfields, and did so with remarkable speed. Luftflotte 3 (German Air Fleet 3) took over airfields in Normandy, across the western approaches. Bristol was now within range of fully loaded bombers.

### The Bristol Gunners

German fighter planes, mostly the Messerschmitt BF109 (Me109), had a very limited range, and at this stage of the war were unable to cross into the West Country, so German bombers arrived unescorted, that is, with no fighters as protection, and mostly at night using darkness for protection. Of course, at this time darkness was a double edged weapon – an aeroplane was hidden from the defences, but also precision targeting was made much more difficult for the bomber.

Over the coming months, raids would increase in size, frequency, and effectiveness. Some of the raids were carried out by small numbers of bombers. These smaller raids, though not effective in terms of physical damage were effective in keeping the defences alert and the civilian population out of their beds. The effect on morale was equally important as everyone, both in and out of uniform, suffered increasingly from tiredness and discomfort. These early raids were intended as precision attacks on very specific military or war production targets. In time, it became clear to the Germans that limiting damage to 'legitimate' targets was impossible, and just as the British and Americans found out later, precision bombing at night was an impossibility with the technology and methods of the time.

The first small raid on Bristol came on the night of 19th / 20th June. A small number of bombers arrived with the intention of attacking the Bristol Aeroplane Company works at Filton. The bombers missed their targets and dropped their bombs in the river Severn.

On 25th June, five people were killed and fourteen injured in another attack on Filton. These first casualties were not, though, at Filton, but in St. Pauls and other parts of the city.

From then the attacks became heavier and more frequent. Bristol was to become the fifth most heavily bombed city in Britain.

GVA Battery Sergeant Major A E Murley of A Battery 76th HAA Regiment kept a diary in which he recorded events. Here are some extracts from this diary, which cover these early attacks:

> *"1940 June 25th Air Raid 5 killed, 14 injured.*
> 
> *June 29th Air Raid fired 13 rounds.*

## The Bristol Gunners

*July 3rd Bombs within 50 yds of camp.*

*July 12th Shot down J U 88, which flew over site at 4,000 ft.*

*July 14th Bombs across gun park. No damage or casualties.*

*July 23rd Raids all night. Fired 100 rounds.*

*August 13th Moved to Cribbs.*

*August 14th Fired 60 rounds.*

*August 24th Fired 29 rounds.*

*September 25th Daylight raid on Filton 20 planes shot down.*

*September 27th Daylight raid on Filton, 6 planes down in flames.*

*October 12th Moved to Rockingham.*

*November 5th Moved to Cribbs.*

*November 6th Lewis gun in action at low flying Heinkel.*

*November 24th Big raid on Bristol, Castle Street.*

*November 25th Avonmouth heavily bombed.*

*November 26th Shirehampton bombed.*

*December 3rd Bomb on Purdown gunsite 2 killed 5 wounded.*

*December 7th Bomb hit gun at Brickfields. 2 men seriously wounded.*

*1941 January 3rd Incendiary raid on Bristol.*

*February 6th Moved to Rockingham.*

*March 11th Shot down Heinkel during raid on Avonmouth.*

*March 16th Raid on Bristol Fired 67 rounds.*

## The Bristol Gunners

*March 17th Shot down Dornier and two Flares Incendiaries in ammo bins.*

*March 29th Raid on Avonmouth. Oil tanks on fire.*

*April. 3rd Raid on Avonmouth. Fired 324 rounds, Gordano Gunsite hit, 1 killed 5 wounded.*

*April 4th Raid on Bristol. Fired 450 Rounds, bomb fell in A hut - no injuries.*

*April 5th Moved to Cribbs.*

*April 11th Blitz on Bristol. Fired 925 rounds.*

*May 8th Raid on Bristol.*

*May 16th Moved to reservoir.*

*June 17th Shot down J.U. 88 over Bristol.*

*September 18th Moved to Rockingham.*

*October 7th Moved to St Georges Wharf."*

The Battle of Britain is generally thought of as lasting from 10th July 1940 to the end of October the same year. If the Germans were to mount an invasion of Britain, the RAF would have to be destroyed. Early German bombing attacks on southeast Britain, the likely location for a German landing, were against RAF fighter airfields. When these attacks failed to prevent Hurricanes and Spitfires flying up to meet and attack the Luftwaffe, German attacks switched to the Chain Home radar stations.

The Germans had a number of fundamental constraints that prevented them from achieving a high kill ratio against British fighters.

Firstly, their fighters had a limited range allowing only a few minutes duration over Britain, so their ability to protect their bombers on deeper targets was limited. A damaged German plane, or an injured pilot, was likely to come down either in Britain or into the sea. Surviving aircrew would therefore have a high probability of being a total loss, that is, being captured by the British or drowning. British fighter pilots, though, if shot

down but uninjured, were more likely to be able to fly again, often returning to their squadrons the same day.

In a similar way, German planes damaged and lost over Britain or the sea were a total loss. Damaged British aeroplanes were more likely to be repairable. British fighter production was always capable of keeping the RAF supplied with enough aircraft. The critical resource for the RAF was pilots, and sufficient of these came from flight training, and from experienced pilots from occupied countries that had escaped to Britain and volunteered to fight with the RAF. There were, of course, pilots who came from the Empire and the USA also to fly with the RAF.

At a critical point, German tactics changed from eroding RAF capability to revenge attacks on London. This allowed the RAF the opportunity to repair airfields and radar stations and replenish aircraft and manpower.

The Battle of Britain was essentially a battle of attrition which the Germans were unlikely to win, though the outcome was a close call.

In any case, the Battle of Britain was fought for a false objective. The German Army was a continental army; it had only limited maritime capability. The Army had used river crossing and bridging techniques with great effect during their attacks on Poland and Western Europe, but they had no capability to cross the Channel. The German Navy was too small to be able to protect an invasion force, especially as the Royal Navy was a strong and effective force that could have intervened and destroyed any German invasion fleet. Half of Germany's naval destroyer force and two cruisers had been destroyed during the Norway campaign. The Germans just could not have mounted an invasion with any chance of success.

German muddled thinking, lack of strategic clarity, and faulty tactics prevented them winning. This is not to diminish anything from the tremendous efforts of RAF fighters and Anti Aircraft Command, and the British people.

A major element of the RAF is often ignored or forgotten when writing the story of The Battle of Britain. Bomber Command (and Coastal Command) continued with their duties throughout this period, attacking German naval ships and invasion barges, with bombs and sea mines.

Bomber Command suffered more casualties during the Battle of Britain than did Fighter Command, a sobering thought. Advances in German anti aircraft defences throughout the war made flying with Bomber Command the most dangerous of activities in the entire British Armed Forces.

In late October 1940, the Germans accepted reality and abandoned their 'Unternehmen Seelöwe' (Operation Sealion), the invasion of Britain.

This did not, of course, mean that German attacks stopped, or even diminished, except when bad weather prevented flying. The attacks continued, especially on London and other cities and towns. This series of attacks became known as the Blitz, and marked German abandonment of the illusion of precision bombing and instead resort to area bombing of mostly civilian areas.

As can be seen from BSM Murley's diary notes, raids continued in Bristol into 1941. He catalogues many of these raids and their effects.

Being an anti aircraft gunner was not, and can never be, a risk free enterprise. GVA gun batteries suffered a number of casualties during the raids. When a raid is expected, most people, especially civilians, are required to seek shelter, in their homes, factories, and public areas. Some people, though, were required to expose themselves to the risks in order to fulfil their duties, and the AA gunners were some of those.

BSM Murley does not mention any deliberate attacks on gun sites, but from his notes, some men were killed or injured by bombs that exploded on gun sites. As well as enemy bombs and bullets that might fall onto a gun site there were other hazards. When an aeroplane is damaged or destroyed in the air, pieces of it will fall to the ground and may land on a gun site. When an anti aircraft shell explodes in the air the pieces will all eventually fall to the ground. Some pieces, splinters and fuses, will have some weight and create a major hazard to anyone in their path. During German raids shell splinter damage to the roofs of houses was a major effect. A shell splinter that can smash a roof tile and penetrate through into the room below would not regard a British steel helmet as much of an obstacle, and AA gunners by the nature of their work were fully exposed to this risk.

## The Bristol Gunners

Bristol was to remain a target for the Luftwaffe for the entire war due to its importance for aircraft and other war production, and for its docks. As the fifth most heavily bombed city in Britain, it suffered over 2,000 fatalities and around 6,000 serious injuries. Three thousand houses were destroyed, and ninety thousand damaged. Production of aeroplanes, engines, and other war materials continued throughout, putting the lie to the old paradigm of the bomber always getting through. They got through but were unable to achieve a decisive result.

A Government publication summarises the Bristol Blitz in its section describing attacks on 'arms towns,'- those towns and cities producing military materials:

> "HMSO 1942, Frontline 1940 – 1941 The Official Story of the Civil Defence of Britain
> 
> Bristol as an 'Arms City'
> 
> Attacks 24th November 1940 50 bombers
> 2nd December 100 bombers
> 6th December 50 bombers
> 3rd & 4th January 1941 150 bombers
> 16th March 150 bombers
> 11th April 150 bombers
> 
> Total 1159 civilians killed to end 1940
> 
> Then there came Bristol, included in the arms towns because air attack on the port was negligible. Its raid of 24th November was the third great provincial attack: it was the city's first and in many ways its worst heavy raid. Though the attacking force was not great and the attack not very long, the damage was heavy, and fires in the city's centre got out of control for a time through the failure of water. The Art Gallery was destroyed, the University's fine hall heavily damaged. The A.R.P. Control Centre had to be abandoned.
> 
> This was a grievous tale of injury to fall suddenly upon a city that only four months earlier, before the fall of France, had been reckoned a westerly haven of refuge, had become crowded with evacuees, and had been reckoned safe enough for use as the BBC's main studio centre. But

## The Bristol Gunners

*Bristol had left nothing to optimism: its civil defence machine was well drilled. It was what Bristol would expect of itself, that the shocks and losses of the first big raid should lead at once to progress based on the lessons learned, and that the shocks should be milder and the losses less with each succeeding attack. Three more heavy ones followed within a few weeks of the first, and soon after the New Year the death toll was about 600.*

*The raid in January took place on a bitterly cold night and produced some strange scenes. Two houses might be seen side by side, one in flames, with the firemen at work on it, the other hung with long icicles where the streams of water had splashed and frozen. The brave and spirited women of the Women's Voluntary Services, taking their canteens out under the bombs with refreshments for civil defenders and anyone else needing it, had their own troubles that night. "The fireman put the cups with dregs down and they froze. We had a choice of being frozen, burned, or blown up, or drowned in tea." These hazards of deep winter were additional to the normal ones that afflicted all who had to move about in the blitz – hidden craters, dark lumps of debris, tangles of firemen's hose, and trailing telephone wires, and the W.V.S. had to learn a new technique of locomotion. One W.V.S. driver used to take her student sons out with her in turn. They lay along the bonnet of her canteen van taking soundings and calling back to her as she nosed forwards.*

*When the real risks involved in fire attack became clear, the Civil Defenders and the people were among the quickest in the country to tackle it at its root – the fire bomb. The sequel was dramatically encouraging. One big attack was thoroughly defeated by this means. On a certain night incendiaries were dropped widely, in an effort to find and light an objective. They were promptly put out everywhere except in one district. A message from the enemy force was overheard, "We have found the target," and it was the offending district, innocent of military objectives, that got the bombs.*

*Later, in one of the heavy raids, the police and other observers were very much struck by the work of civilians in their home neighbourhoods. The police report remarked that "there did not seem to be enough bombs to go round." In the last of the big raids, on Good Friday night, the enemy began as usual with showers of incendiaries. More than one*

*watcher, posted high, saw the white glowing patches all over the target area grow and brighten. Within a few minutes "it was as though someone was drawing a blanket over them. The light died down and disappeared." Three hours later, the bombers were still dropping flares to try and light their target. The bombs fell heavily but blindly. It was a big attack, but damage was limited, and not a single major fire developed.*

*Unhappily, earlier raids had been more harmful. A great part of the centre of the city was completely burnt out, and stands dumb witness to the meaning of total air war as the Nazis taught it to the world."*

The GVA ended their AA defence of Bristol, though, in October 1941 and moved to pastures new. At this period of the war, a number of factors had entered military plans that were to result in new experiences for the GVA.

After the Battle of Britain, the Germans turned their attention once more to their eastern borders. Their long antipathy with the Soviet Russians led to their invasion of eastern Poland beyond the River Bug, occupied by the Russians in 1939, and onwards into Russia, in Operation Barbarossa.

The war was being fought in a number of other places.

As France was falling in June 1940, Italy declared war on France and Britain. It was an opportunist move and the Italian Army had not contributed to defeating either France or Britain, but wanted to share in the spoils of a German victory. In some ways Mussolini, the Italian leader, had mentored Adolf Hitler and been his inspiration in securing the German Chancellorship.

In September of 1940, the Italians crossed the border of Libya into Egypt. Egypt was nominally an independent country, though in reality it was controlled by the British, who had a force of two very weak divisions on the border to defend British interests in the Suez Canal. The British had expected the invasion, and were prepared. Fortunately for the under strength British forces the Italians were even less capable.

Five Italian divisions entered Egypt and then stopped. For three months, the Italians remained static Then a British counter attack drove them back across the border into Libya. Thirty six thousand British, Indian and

## The Bristol Gunners

Australian troops rapidly pushed the Italians back all the way past Benghazi. One hundred and fifty five thousand Italians were taken prisoner. It was a disaster for the Italians, but prompted Hitler to send General Erwin Rommel and his Afrika Korps to North Africa. The Afrika Korps was attended by a sizeable portion of Luftwaffe aircraft. The Germans started to arrive in Libya in February 1941.

In October 1940, Italy had also invaded Greece from Albania, which they had occupied earlier. The Italians had made little progress and were in danger of being defeated by the weaker, but more motivated, Greek Army. The Greeks had pushed the Italians back into Albania and the Italians were poorly prepared for the harsh winter. The Germans decided to invade Greece and they attacked in April 1941 sending their forces via Romania and Bulgaria, countries that were aligned with the Nazis.

Britain was obliged to assist the Greeks and sent forces from Egypt, weakening their position in Libya. Ultimately, the Germans won in Greece and threw the British out. This new commitment, though, also drew off significant numbers of Luftwaffe aircraft.

The German attack on the Russians was launched on June 22$^{nd}$ 1941. It was to be the main focus of the German war effort for the next four years and it was this decision to attack that was the turning point of the war that would lead to Germany's defeat.

The war was far from won in the middle of 1941, but it had not been lost. Britain had survived and its attention started to move from resistance and survival, towards attack and victory. It had gained an ally in Russia, and now the Germans had to fight on multiple fronts at once, a situation long feared by German military strategists.

German air attacks continued against Britain, but at a reduced rate and intensity.

In November 1941, the GVA left Bristol and were sent to man their guns in Dover. For the next eleven months, they were in the Dover area or elsewhere on the south coast. BSM Murley's diary lists events:

"*1941 November 10$^{th}$ Moved to Dover.*

## The Bristol Gunners

*December 10th* Camp hit by German long range shells. One lorry burnt out, no casualties.

*December 16th* Dive bomber attack - 10 Stukas shot down. Shelling from 5pm to 7pm.

*1942 January 3rd* Shelled from 7pm to 8.30pm.

*January 11th* Put up harbour barrage against J.U. 88s, shell landed in camp.

*January 14th* Moved to Yeovil.

*January 28th* Moved to Okehampton for anti - tank shooting.

*February 1st* Moved to Yeovil.

*March 22nd* Moved to Blandford for mobile training.

*April 1st* Moved to Havant with T.T.C.

*May 15th* Battery finished mobile training. Moved to Strood and Oak Street.

*June 10th* Moved to Green Street Green.

*June 29th* Moved to All Hallows.

*July 3rd* Moved to Citadel, Dover.

*July 24th* Surprise raid by 2 x FW 190s. Bombs dropped in Citadel, Dover.

*July 25th* Shelled for two hours - no damage.

*July 30th* Shelled for three hours.

*August 8th* Machine gunned by FW 190s. Balloon on Gunpark shot down in flames.

*August 10th* Battery commenced mobilising.

*August 12th* Shelled in afternoon. Raid 2am to 3.15am.

## The Bristol Gunners

*August 14th Shelled – no injuries.*

*August 16th Shelled E boat fight in channel.*

*August 17th Shelled - no casualties.*

*September 5th 3 x bombs in Citadel - no damage.*

*October 5th Moved to Shorncliffe.*

*October 6 - 8th Battery did 3 day mobile scheme.*

*October 20 - 26th Battery did 8 day mobile scheme."*

Dover is the closest part of Britain to France, and the Germans had guns on the French coast that had the range to fire into the town. The channel between Dover and France was the scene of many air and sea battles as

**A 3.7 Inch HAA Gun of the type used by the GVA prior to going overseas. This is of the fixed type, not the mobile version used in the field army.** (Photo Wikimedia Commons)

British convoys passed through. Dover had a number of gun sites, the Citadel being just one. From BSM Murley's diary, it seems that the GVA were involved in a number of different forms of attack during their periods in residence at Dover. The diaries also bear witness to the change

## The Bristol Gunners

in thinking in the army. There is mention of training in anti tank shooting at Okehampton in January 1942, references to mobile training schemes in March and May 1942.

**A 3.7 Inch HAA gun in its mobile form, as used by the GVA in North Africa, Sicily, and Italy.** (Photo Wikimedia Commons)

The 3.7 inch Heavy Anti Aircraft gun was designed as a specialist gun for shooting at aircraft. It was deemed not to be suitable for use against tanks. However, the German equivalent gun, the 88mm Flak gun had been used in the anti tank role by the Afrika Korps in North Africa to very good effect. There are technical reasons why the German gun was more suited than the British gun, but the British clearly had learned from experience in fighting the Afrika Korps and were trying to apply those lessons. In fact, from 1942 HAA guns in the field army were supplied

with one or two rounds of anti tank ammunition per gun when in service in the field, but were very rarely called upon to fire against tanks in the direct fire role.

The reference to mobile schemes, that is, training in the mobile role is interesting. HAA on fixed installations was the main way of using HAA guns in defence in Britain, but the field army needed their HAA guns to move on the battlefield to defend our own forces as they manoeuvred. The GVA were being trained in the mobile role, which indicates that as early as March 1942 they were probably being prepared for deployment with the field army.

On December 7th 1941, the USA had formally entered the war as a belligerent. They had been attacked by the Japanese at Pearl Harbour in the Hawaiian Islands. Four days later Adolf Hitler made another mistake when he declared war on the USA, encouraging the USA to reciprocate and join forces with the British Empire against Germany.

America was already practically involved in warlike actions before this declaration. American naval ships had been assisting British and Canadian convoys as far as Iceland, and German U-boats had sunk American registered vessels. However, provoking the USA to formally declare war on Germany was a disastrous move by Hitler, though the Americans may have declared war on Germany in any case at a later date.

The only place that the British were in contact with the German Army in early 1942 was North Africa. The battles there moved back and forth between Libya and Egypt with neither side able to land a decisive defeat on the other, mainly due to the basic fact of supply. The further either side advanced, the more difficult became their supply situation. Conversely, the more they withdrew the easier became their supplies as they came closer to their ports and bases.

By July 1942, the Germans had pushed the British back to a position at El Alamein, the last practical defensive position before Alexandria and Cairo. Churchill decided that a new general was needed to take over, and General Bernard Montgomery arrived in Egypt and immediately set about preparing his army for attack. On 23rd October, the British attack started and gradually broke through the German and Italian positions until the enemy were forced to break and run for safety. For Churchill

this was the turning point of the entire war. As he stated in a speech at the Mansion House in November of 1942:

*"Now this is not the end. It is not even the beginning of the end, but it is, perhaps, the end of the beginning."*

As well as attacking the Germans and Italians from the east with the British 8th Army, plans were afoot to land a second army in North Africa, in the west, and the GVA would be part of this force.

Following the fall of France in 1940, the southern part of France (less the Atlantic coast) and French overseas possessions had been governed by a puppet French government, based in the city of Vichy, and led by a First World War hero, Marshall Petain.

The Vichy regime had carefully refrained from taking any belligerent action against Britain, but had assisted the Germans in controlling their part of France for German benefit.

In 1940, after the fall of France, the Royal Navy had been keen to ensure that French warships did not fall into the hands of the Germans, but rather that they sail to join forces with the British. Some French warships were already at anchor in Alexandria and were prevented from action by the British. However, many French warships were based at Oran in Algeria, then under the Vichy French. After the French fleet failed to respond to a request to join the fight against the Germans or to scuttle itself, the Royal Navy opened fire on the port, causing much damage and killing almost 1300 French sailors.

In June 1941, the British with Free French forces had invaded Lebanon and Syria, countries controlled by the Vichy French, in order to prevent the Germans accessing facilities there that may have been of use to them in fighting against the British.

The British were not sure which French senior officers would help them and which would hinder them, partly as a result of the Royal Navy action against the French fleet at Oran in 1940. It was felt prudent for the Americans, who still had diplomatic relations with the Vichy government in Algeria, to carry out discussions and negotiations concerning an

invasion of French North African possessions – Morocco, Algeria and Tunisia.

American General Mark Clark landed clandestinely in Algeria in October 1942 and met with senior Vichy French officers. Another senior Vichy officer, General Giraud, was secretly taken from the French mainland to Gibraltar to meet with General Eisenhower to discuss arrangements. Both these operations were carried out using a British submarine, HMS Seraph, but the pretence was that it was an American submarine in order not to upset the Vichy French.

Support for an allied invasion was secured. As well as the substantial Vichy French forces in North Africa, it was arranged for French Resistance fighters to help out by capturing some coastal defences when the invasion started.

Operation Torch, the invasion of French North Africa, started on November 8th 1942. Invasion fleets sailed both from Britain and direct from the USA. Landings were made in Morocco (Casablanca), Oran and Tangiers. Some Vichy French forces did, in fact resist for a short period. Fighting stopped within two days in most places.

A surprise awaited the Americans in Algiers. As they reached the residence of the senior French commander, General Juin, they found that the Vichy deputy leader, Admiral Darlan, was also there. He had arrived the previous day, ignorant of the impending invasion, to visit his son in Algeria. After some manoeuvring, the two Frenchmen were persuaded to order their forces to cease resistance.

The Vichy forces were divided in their loyalties. Some came over to join the Allies, some became passive and militarily inactive, while some escaped to Tunisia and joined the German forces there and fought with them.

Some Vichy forces in Tunisia, however, were undecided, and left Tunis and sheltered in the mountains west of the city. In due course, these forces were attacked and destroyed by German forces.

## The Bristol Gunners

Some of the French fleet were sunk or damaged during the invasions; some were scuttled by their crews, while a some others came to join the Allies.

Admiral Darlan was appointed by General Eisenhower to lead the French in North Africa, a move that was unpopular with General De Gaulle and the Free French. Darlan was a Nazi collaborator and political opportunist. He was assassinated by a French patriot on December 1942, and replaced by General Giraud.

The GVA were to play their part in North Africa and the defeat of Rommel's Afrika Korps.

The Afrika Korps was already, in November 1942, withdrawing under pressure from General Montgomery's British 8th Army following on from the latter's successful attack at El Alamein. By the time of the Torch landings, the 8th Army was in Libya again and nearing the capture of Tobruk. Now the Afrika Korps was in a pincer movement, under continuing pressure from the 8th Army in the east, and the newly arrived British and American 1st Army in the west.

Over the next six months the Germans and their remaining Italian allies would be pushed back all the way to Tunisia and finally surrender in May 1943. These forces were seriously hampered by shortage of supply, especially of fuel, all of which had to come across the Mediterranean Sea from Italy. At times, most supplies were destroyed before they could reach North Africa, mainly due to air and submarine attack from the British in Malta, as well as attacks from our new bases in Algeria.

The GVA were not part of the first landings of Operation Torch. At the time these actions were taking place the GVA were still in Britain, training in the mobile role at Shorncliffe, near Folkestone, in Kent. BSM Murley's diary notes tell the story of their travel to the shores of Algeria:

> *"1942 November 14th Vehicles moved to port for loading.*
>
> *November 23rd Battery entrained for Glasgow.*
>
> *November 24th Boarded Durban Castle.*
>
> *November 27th Ship sailed at 11pm.*

### The Bristol Gunners

*December 5th Passed through Straits of Gibraltar.*

*December 6th Battery disembarked at Algiers and marched to Barchi.*

*December 9th Transport began to arriving.*

*December 14th C Troop moved to Birmandries.*

*December 15th D Troop moved to Hussein - Dey.*

*December 17th B.H.Q. moved to Birmandries."*

The towns mentioned after December 6th are all close to the city of Algiers. When the Allies occupied Algeria, the Germans characteristically responded quickly and effectively. The Luftwaffe mounted attacks on airfields, ports, and other militarily important sites. Battles were fought between the RAF and the Luftwaffe, every bit as intense and violent as the Battle of Britain. The Allies quickly built up their forces in the country, and having an effective anti aircraft defensive capability was a priority.

The GVA arrived and immediately set up their guns and prepared to meet the German air force under the African sky. They did not have to wait long for action. BSM Murley:

*"1942 December 23rd D Troop shot down J.U. 88 in flames.*

*December 24th Darlan murdered - mounted double guards. [French Admiral Jean-Francois Darlan]*

*1943 January 3rd Rear party landed.*

*January 8th Rear party vehicles unloaded.*

*January 15th. D Troop shot down Heinkel.*

*January 27th C Troop shot down J.U. 88.*

*February 2nd D Troop moved to Maison Blanche."*

## The Bristol Gunners

Maison Blanche was the main airfield just to the south of the City of Algiers, and was the main base for RAF and US Air Force squadrons in Algeria. It was subject to frequent attacks by the Luftwaffe.

The GVA were based at Maison Blanche for just over two months and must have been involved in many actions to protect the aeroplanes based there, though nothing to this effect was noted by BSM Murley – perhaps he was too busy.

While the GVA protected Maison Blanche the Allied forces continued to build up in Algeria.

In January 1943, Churchill, President Roosevelt, General Giraud, and General de Gaulle held a strategic conference on the Atlantic coast of Morocco at Casablanca.

This conference was notable for several reasons. Firstly, there were two French generals present, neither of whom wanted to deal with the other. Giraud had been a collaborator with the Germans in the Vichy government, while de Gaulle had been consistent in his opposition to the Germans and any accommodation with them. The two men were forced to shake hands publicly by President Roosevelt, but they continued to be hostile to each other, even though they were appointed to lead the Free French Forces (FFL) jointly.

Another notable event was the surprise announcement by President Roosevelt that unconditional surrender was demanded of the Germans. This had not been discussed or agreed by Churchill, who thought it unwise, but committed himself to supporting it.

The conference also discussed the next steps for progressing the war. The British and Americans disagreed repeatedly over this issue, but the Americans were persuaded to invade southern Europe as no invasion of northern France was possible at that time. In return, Churchill agreed to increase British forces in the Pacific theatre of operations.

While this conference was in progress, the Battle of Stalingrad was coming to a brutal closure. Stalin had decided not to attend the Morocco conference as he wished to stay in touch with events at Stalingrad from Moscow. German surrender of their 6th Army under General Paulus was a

major blow, 91,000 men were captured by the Russians, and total German casualties for this battle in men killed, wounded and captured by the Russians amounted to over 800,000.

After the Casablanca conference had ended, the American Army in North Africa received its first blooding at the hands of the Germans. The Americans had advanced a little way into Tunisia and were holding positions at an important mountain pass at Kasserine. The British 8th Army had reached Tripoli in Libya on January 23rd, removing the main supply port for the Afrika Corps. Since Operation Torch, the Germans had massively reinforced their forces in Tunisia, and rather than waiting for the 8th Army to arrive decided to secure their western and southern flanks in the Atlas Mountains

In February, the Germans attacked westwards, pushing back French and American forces in a major reverse for the Americans. The Germans used their tactics to good effect, tactics which the British were familiar with and would have had a better idea how to respond. Within two weeks, the German attack was held, though, and some positions recaptured. The Americans subsequently proved that they had learned important lessons from this temporary setback.

The 8th Army had reached the eastern Tunisian border in mid February. The end was in sight for the Germans in North Africa.

In early March the Germans lost heavily when their attack southwards against 8th Army was defeated. General Rommel realised that there was no prospect of winning in north Africa and he decided to request permission to evacuate his forces back to Europe. He left to report to Hitler and did not return. He was replaced as commander of German forces North Africa by General von Arnim.

At the end of March 1943, the Allies started a general advance from both the east and the west against the Germans and Italians who were by then withdrawing into Tunisia. As the 1st Army moved eastwards along the Mediterranean coast the GVA were called forward from Maison Blanche to provide anti aircraft cover for the American II Corps. This Corps was now commanded by General George Patton, its former commander having been sacked due to his poor performance at the Battle of Kasserine. Patton would become famous for his dash and thrusting

## The Bristol Gunners

manner, and his personality clashes with the more systematic and cautious Bernard Montgomery.

BSM Murley recorded the movements of the GVA as it moved eastwards along the northern coast of Algeria and into northern Tunisia:

*"1943 April 9th  Battery moved off and arrived at Palestro.*

*April 10th Battery moved on to Side Emberak.*

*April 11th Battery moved on to Ain M'lila .*

*April 12th Battery moved on to Souk -Ahras.*

*April 13th Battery deployed at Le kef. Total journey 485 miles.*

*April 20th Battery deployed at Djebel Abiod.*

*April 26th Battery constructed sites under fire at Sedjenane.*

*May 7th Battery moved off, bivvied 10 miles E of Mateur.*

*May 8th D Troop deployed in Bizerta, while enemy still in town.*

*May 9th C Troop and B.H.Q. moved into Bizerta."*

The towns listed by BSM Murley chart the progress of the GVA. The final days of the Afrika Korps were somewhat chaotic, but they did manage to remain an effective fighting force almost to the end, and the Allies had to fight hard to subdue them, until the final three days when order collapsed and the German forces disintegrated as an effective army. 230,000 German and Italian soldiers went into captivity. Massive quantities of supplies, equipment, tanks, and aeroplanes also fell in to Allied hands.

In six months, the Germans had lost over one million of its troops in Russia and North Africa. The Allies, mostly British and American, had learned how to fight alongside each other, and how to win. This was the first joint campaign, and it was to set the pattern for many more successful collaborations over the coming two years.

## The Bristol Gunners

At this stage, the Allied forces were truly multinational, and would continue to be so. The Empire was represented by British, Canadian, New Zealand, Indian, South African, and troops from many other countries. As well as Americans from outside the Empire, there were many French, Polish, and Greek soldiers.

The sea and air links between the German forces in Tunisia and their main supply base in Sicily were effectively broken in the last weeks of the campaign. Allied control of the skies and seas prevented the vast majority of supplies reaching the Germans, and prevented the evacuation of Germans from Tunisia.

While the campaign in Tunisia was drawing to its close, the Allies had been deciding where exactly to attack next. Now that the entire shore of North Africa was in Allied hands, many options were open to them. They could mount an invasion anywhere from the south of France, to Italy, the Balkans, or Greece. The Germans knew that they were coming, but where would they land next?

Churchill and Roosevelt had agreed that it was to be Sicily followed by Italy. In order to trick the Germans into spreading their by now diminished forces as thinly as possible British Intelligence carried out an operation to deceive them as to where the next invasion would occur.

This operation was called Operation Mincemeat. A body, supposedly of a Royal Marine officer carrying 'secret' documents, was released by submarine off the Spanish coast. The body was washed ashore, and the content of the documents was passed by the Spanish authorities to the Germans. Spain was technically a neutral country, but as the government was fascist, it retained strong links with the Germans.

The documents were drawn up to indicate that the next invasion would be in Greece and Sardinia. The Germans took the documents as genuine, and therefore the actual site, Sicily, was only lightly defended when the Allies arrived offshore on 9th July 1943.

The Allies had accumulated considerable forces in North Africa, but they were spread over long distances along the Mediterranean shore. Supplies, equipment, warships, transport ships, and landing ships had to be accumulated ready for action. Invasion convoys were to be loaded and set

### The Bristol Gunners

sail from a number of North African ports, and so, the GVA started their preparations.

In late June, they were issued with the supplies they would need for landing in Sicily and on 29th June they spent time waterproofing and organising their vehicles and equipment for transport to the beaches. BSM Murley:

> "1943 June 29th Waterproofing of guns and vehicles commenced.
>
> July 12th Moved to concentration area in Sousse, up V track.
>
> July 16th Moved to Brentford Assembly Area.
>
> July 17th Moved to Charlton area.
>
> July 18th Battery embarked on L.S.T.s at Sousse. Sailed at 11pm.
>
> July 20th Battery disembarked at Syracuse at 8 am. Troops deployed at Augusta by 2pm."

Operation Husky, the invasion of Sicily, started on 9th July with paratroop and glider landings inland to secure important bridges and other sites. Sea landings were made at two locations, by the Americans under Patton on the south coast, and by the British and Canadians on the east coast near Syracuse. Seven divisions were landed on the first day, almost as many as would land in Normandy on D-Day eleven months later..

The sea landings were largely unopposed as the Italian forces were positioned inland, though the airborne element of the invasion suffered losses through anti aircraft fire from Allied naval ships as they flew overhead.

The Americans advanced westwards along the coast round to the northern side of the island while the British took the eastern side of the island.

The Allies benefitted from effective air cover from planes operating from Malta and Pantelleria (an Italian Island captured in a preparatory action) and the Italian and German air forces were unable to cause significant problems, though there was work for the GVA to do.

## The Bristol Gunners

Sicily was fully occupied within two months and many Italians went into captivity, though the bulk of the Germans – around 60,000 – managed to escape across the Straits of Messina to the Italian mainland.

The GVA arrived as part of 8th Army, in the port of Syracuse on the east coast, ten days after the invasion had started, on 20th July. They deployed the same day to Augusta, coming into action immediately. Augusta is another port town north across the bay from Syracuse. BSM Murley recorded the actions that the GVA dealt with in his diary:

*"1943 July 21st Big raid on Augusta, fired 320 rounds and shot down 1 plane.*

*July 22nd Big night raid fired 654 rounds.*

*July 23rd Raid on Augusta. Fired 100 rounds. Troops deployed at Syracuse.*

*July 25th Raid on Syracuse.*

*July 26th Night raid.*

*July 27th Raid – fired 500 rds.*

*July 28th Raid – fired 600 rounds.*

*August 10th Raid fired 800 rounds D Troop shot down 1 plane."*

On 17th August the Allies had completed their occupation of the island, and preparations started for the move to the mainland of Italy.

Three weeks later, on 3rd September, the Allies returned to the mainland of Europe. Landings were made at three places. The first landing was across the straits of Messina in Calabria directly opposite Sicily by 8th Army. The next main landing was at Salerno, south of Naples, on 9th September by 5th Army. This site was chosen as it was the furthest north while remaining within fighter aeroplane range from Sicily, so that the landing could be properly protected by air cover. Another landing by 8th Army, at Taranto, the main Italian Navy base in the instep of Italy's boot was made also on 9th September.

The Bristol Gunners

Opinion within the Allies was divided over the wisdom of committing substantial forces to Italy rather than using them to invade France across the English Channel. Strains were showing with Stalin, the Russian leader, who wanted an invasion into France as soon as possible to weaken the German forces ranged against his armies in Eastern Europe. The British and American armies were not yet ready to invade France – it was seen as a much harder target to invade than Italy. Churchill called the Mediterranean theatre the 'soft underbelly' of German occupied Europe and a better place to invade in 1943 and at least a way of demonstrating to Stalin that the Allies were doing their part to defeat the Germans.

In time, the soft underbelly would turn out to be 'a tough old gut' according to American General Mark Clark, the commander of the 5th Army.

The landings at Calabria and Taranto were successful and met very little opposition, the Germans had held most of their forces further north nearer Rome. The 8th Army rapidly advanced and occupied all their objectives, including the port of Bari on the east coast.

Salerno, though, was a more difficult position. The landings there were a mix of American forces from Sicily and Algeria and British troops sailing from Tunisia and Libya. The Germans had anticipated a landing in Salerno but were not initially holding defensive positions in great strength there. Once the landings started, though, the Germans responded rapidly and resisted with their normal efficiency. The situation became critical, and General Mark Clark at one point prepared orders to re-embark the troops and abandon the landing. This crisis passed, though, and the balance swayed in favour of the Allies. The Germans started to withdraw.

The Italian King Victor Emmanuel III had realised that the Italians could no longer stay in the war on the side of the Germans, and started secret negotiations with the Allies for an armistice. He dismissed Mussolini and had him arrested. He sent emissaries to Sicily to negotiate with the Allies. An armistice was signed on 3rd September and announced on 8th September, the day before the Salerno landings.

### The Bristol Gunners

Italian forces had not been forewarned of the armistice and no orders had been issued to them. Many Italian troops allowed themselves to be overrun by the Allies, while some others sided with the Germans and continued to fight alongside them. The Germans immediately started to transfer troops from northern Europe and the Balkans to Italy in order to oppose Allied advances.

The Italian King and his new government abandoned Rome and travelled to Brindisi in southern Italy.

The GVA crossed the Straits of Messina, the shortest distance between Sicily and the mainland, on September 23rd, and travelled across the south of Italy to the port of Bari, on the east coast, five days later. BSM Murley:

> *"1943 September 21$^{st}$ Battery moved off and bivvied at Santa Teresa.*
>
> *September 22$^{nd}$ Battery bivvied at Messina.*
>
> *September 23$^{rd}$ Battery crossed the straits of Messina., in L.C.M.s and L.S.T.s and bivvied at Gallies nr Reggio.*
>
> *September 24$^{th}$ Battery moved to Pizzo.*
>
> *September 25$^{th}$ Battery moved to Catanzaro Marina.*
>
> *September 26$^{th}$ Battery moved on to Strongoli.*
>
> *September 27$^{th}$ Battery moved on to Torrente Saracen.*
>
> *September 28$^{th}$ Battery moved on to Bari.*
>
> *September 29$^{th}$ Battery deployed in defence of Bari."*

Bari was to become a major port and supply centre for Montgomery's 8$^{th}$ Army. It needed to be protected from air attack in order that equipment and supplies could be landed there and thus shorten the supply route to the divisions at the front. By the time that the GVA took up their positions around the city the front had moved further north. They were to remain defending Bari for the next 8 months.

### The Bristol Gunners

Once the 8th Army (responsible for the right flank on the east side of Italy) had moved up to join the 5th Army at Salerno (5th Army had responsibility for operations on the west side of Italy) a general advance was started. The German strategy was to establish a series of defensive positions across the width of Italy in succession from south to north. Italy is a mountainous country, and only 160 Km wide for most of its length. Mountains form a central spine with narrow plains on the coasts. Italy has been described as having a geography designed for defence, and the Germans were to exploit this potential to the full.

Some of these German defensive positions were intended only to delay the Allies' advance, giving time for the Germans to prepare particularly strong positions at the best locations.

Progress in Italy was never going to be easy, but the Allies made what progress they could. By the end of 1943, the Allies had come up against a main German defence line, named the Gustav line. This had been partly breached by the 8th Army to the east of the central Apennine Mountains, but further progress was halted by winter weather and the strong German positions in front of 5th Army around the town of Cassino. Both armies would continue to batter away at this position for five months until they finally managed to break past it and capture Rome on June 4th 1944.

While the front line troops were pushing up to the Gustav line, the GVA continued in position some 280 Km (175 miles) behind the front at Bari, defending the port and other installations from air attack.

At this stage of the war the German Luftwaffe was starting to suffer from a shortage of aeroplanes, manpower, and fuel. It was, though, still an effective and dangerous force. Bari seems to have been mostly free from attack by the Luftwaffe while the GVA were at the port, with one exception, noted by BSM Murley, in his usual terse style:

*"1943 December 2nd Big raid on harbour - 1000 killed, 15 ships sunk in harbour."*

The full details of this raid on Bari were not generally known until many years after the war had finished.

As Bari was so far behind the front, and the Luftwaffe had not been present in the battles to a significant degree it appears that the attention

## The Bristol Gunners

given to air defence at Bari was inadequate. There were no fighters dedicated to its protection, and anti aircraft artillery was thin on the ground. There had been some Luftwaffe attacks on other ports closer to the front, such as Naples and Salerno, on the west coast.

Bari harbour is quite small, and the quantity of stores, vehicles and equipment needed to pass through it to keep the armies fighting was large. At any one time, more ships than was prudent were unloading or moored in and around the harbour. At night, lights were used freely to facilitate continued unloading.

On 2nd December, a single Luftwaffe aeroplane was sent on reconnaissance to the port and reported back that the harbour offered an excellent opportunity as a target. Later that same evening over one hundred German bombers arrived over the port and proceeded to sink or seriously damage around 40 ships. The port was out of action for several weeks. Ammunition ships exploded, and fuel stores were ignited causing serious damage and casualties.

One embarrassing feature was that earlier the same day, the British RAF commander, Air Marshal Sir Arthur Coningham had stated in a press conference that in his opinion the Luftwaffe would not be able to attack the port.

As if the loss of ships, supplies, and equipment were not bad enough, there was one cargo that was secret and highly dangerous, and which was on a ship destroyed in the attack.

The Allies were concerned that the Germans may resort to the use of chemical weapons. They had secretly decided send stocks of mustard gas bombs to Italy for use in retaliation should the Germans use chemical weapons.

This mustard gas was released because of the destruction of the ship carrying it. Many casualties were in the water of the harbour having jumped off their own ships. Many of these men were contaminated with mustard gas mixed with oil from damaged ships, and were rescued by naval ships and treated on board and in shore hospitals, without anyone realising the contamination. Oil released into the water from damaged

ships acted as a solvent for the mustard gas and helped it to stick to skin. Mustard gas also escaped as a gas cloud and this blew into the town itself.

Within a day, many hundreds of military casualties, medical staff, and civilians from the town, developed symptoms of mustard gas exposure, including blistering, blindness, and other skin and lung complaints.

It took some time for the military authorities to understand what had caused the injuries as the crew of the ship had all been killed and the cargo had not been listed correctly on the manifesto.

All records of the event were suppressed and not released until 1967. Even today, apparently, many citizens of Bari are unaware of the full nature of the events of that time. Bari has the dubious distinction of being the only European town during the whole of the war to suffer from chemical warfare.

BSM Murley understated the losses, around two thousand died according to some sources, though the actual numbers are still unknown.

Once the port had been brought back in to operation things returned to normal for the GVA, with very little in the way of targets to shoot at.

As spring came in Italy, despite the disaster at Bari, military thoughts turned to ways of overcoming the problems that they were facing, and would face in the future.

The first attacks on the Gustav line at Cassino were made in January, and despite tremendous efforts by American, French, and British troops the Germans were still in position. A way round the western side of the position was made by making a further seaborne landing up the coast at Anzio. This move failed to unlock the door, and the fighting at Anzio would continue for five months. Further attacks were made at Cassino, but still the Germans obstinately refused to withdraw. The famous and historical monastery was bombed to rubble, making the situation worse for the Allies The rubble provided the German defenders with better protection and a more effective defensive position.

The Luftwaffe, despite being able to mount effective raids from time to time, such as that on Bari in December, was being seen less and less over

### The Bristol Gunners

Allied territory. Anti aircraft gunners were spending most of their time staring at a sky that was empty of enemy aeroplanes.

**GVA Sergeants pose in Italy 1944, out of the line perhaps, but not out of the mud.**

In addition, plans were being developed for the invasion of France, and that would need the Allies to make sure that every resource available made a full and positive contribution to success. Experienced formations, notably 7th Armoured Division, the Desert Rats, had been sent from Italy the previous November to Britain to spearhead the invasion of northern France on D-Day. As well as the landing planned for Normandy in June, troops were needed for a landing in the south of France in August. In the spring of 1944, the Allies in Italy withdrew a number of American and French divisions to form an invasion force for the south of France,

leaving the 5th and 8th Armies with fewer and less experienced troops for the tasks in hand.

As a result, the GVA went for further training and a change in role. They were sent a little north from Bari in the middle of February 1944 to train as field artillery, using their anti aircraft guns in the indirect fire support role.

It made a lot of sense if guns and artillerymen that were underemployed as anti aircraft were able to take on the dual role of both anti aircraft and field artillery. There were a couple of issues, though, that would need to be resolved before this could be done.

The first problem was that HAA batteries were not equipped with fire control equipment suitable for indirect fire. This would need to be supplied. The officers and men needed to be re-organised, re-equipped, and trained for indirect fire. Equipment needed included vehicles and radio communications – observers needed to be forward in the front line and had to get there and be able to communicate with the guns as well as the infantry that they were supporting.

A second problem, which surfaced as the GVA went into action as field artillery was that anti aircraft fire has a very different pattern than field artillery. Anti aircraft fire entails short periods of firing with long periods, maybe days, with no firing. Field artillery is in action more often – several fire missions per day, and always on call. A field gun may fire dozens of rounds on a single mission, or continuously over several hours. The barrels of the anti aircraft guns were found to get extremely hot when used in extended fire missions, so hot that the started to visibly droop and had to be taken out of action and cooled down.

A third problem also related to the barrels of the guns. To reach high altitude an anti aircraft shell has to be fired at a much higher speed than is normal for a field gun. Higher speed requires more propellant and the friction creates more barrel wear. Whereas a field gun would need a new barrel at around 10,000 rounds fired, a barrel firing high velocity shells could be worn out after 1,000 rounds.

Despite these issues, the guns were needed at the front, and so the GVA undertook the training and drew up the extra equipment they would need.

### The Bristol Gunners

In May 1944, a final attack was launched at Cassino and this time it was successful. The Gustav line had cracked and the Allies could advance once more, to the next German defensive line. The troops in the Anzio beachhead broke out and the Germans quickly withdrew to the north of Rome.

As the Cassino battle was coming to an end the GVA travelled up from Bari, crossed the Apennine Mountains, and went into position near Cassino. By the time they arrived, though, the battle was moving northwards, and over the next few days they moved on up the west coast and were deployed in the anti aircraft role outside Rome.

Rome had been occupied on 4th June, just two days before D-Day in Normandy, so the news of its capture was overwhelmed by what many saw as the bigger story.

Once again, the Allies were involved in a slow advance up the length of Italy, with the Germans taking full advantage of the landscape and natural obstacles to slow them down.

The next major German defensive position, called the Gothic Line was 20 kilometres north of the River Arno, which runs through Florence to the sea at Pisa, some 360 Km (225 miles) north of Rome. The Gothic Line was placed on the southern side of the Apennine Mountains where they run down to the coast north of Viareggio, across the mountains blocking the pass between Florence and Bologna, and on across the centre of Italy to the Adriatic coast just north of Pesaro.

Firstly, though, the Allies came up to a delaying position, the Arno Line, on the north bank of the River Arno in late July 1944. They started to attack the Gothic Line defences in August after they had pushed the Germans off the Arno Line.

The GVA were deployed in the field role on 27th July just south of the River Arno and supported the attacks to cross the river and push up to the Gothic line further north.

Their first position was south of Pisa, and on 23rd August they moved 20 Kilometres further east up into the mountains towards Florence. BSM

Murley's diary notes give some flavour of the conditions they encountered after many months of having little contact with the Germans, something perhaps of a rude awakening:

*"1944 July 27th Troops deployed in field roll against enemy on N. side of Arno.*

*August 3rd Shell landed 10 yards from No 3 gun D Troop – no damage.*

*August 4th D Troop had 150 shells on site – no damage.*

*August 6th C Troop mortared – no casualties*

*August 7th C and D Troops Shelled – no damage.*

*August 11th D Troop had 20 shells, 1 lorry hit.*

*August 12th D Troop shelled again 1 Matador and a motorcycle damaged.*

*August 23rd C and D Troops in action near La Serra, south of San Miniato.*

*August 25th B.H.Q. and Troop rear echelons moved to vicinity of Paloia, B.H.Q. had 9 shells in camp. Tents ruined, dinner blown up, kit holed but no casualties. B.H.Q. moved to alternative position.*

*August 27th B.H.Q. Shelled – No damage.*

*September 4th Troops in action just N. W. of Lamporecchio against Gothic line."*

The last mentioned position, Lamporecchio, was north of the Arno and about 20 Kilometres west of Florence, and at this time the GVA were involved with the assault on the main Gothic Line.

The Gothic Line was to prove almost as hard a position to break through as the Gustav Line at Cassino. The aim for the Allies now was to break through a last defensive line. It was the last natural obstacle before the Lombardy Plain. If they could just break the Gothic Line, and reach the Plain, the rest of northern Italy would be open to them, and they could

## The Bristol Gunners

cross the Plain and the Po River and push up through the Dolomites into Austria, liberating that country before the Russians arrived.

Unfortunately, it was not to be. The Germans also realised the importance of retaining their positions, and the consequences of losing them. They had concerns, though, that the Allies could and would break it, possibly by outflanking it by another seaborne landing further up the coast.

The Gothic Line was 15 Kilometres deep, consisting of layers of belts of barbed wire, machine gun bunkers, tank turrets mounted in concrete, anti tank ditches, mortars, self propelled guns, anti tank guns, all arranged with the normal German thoroughness. In addition, the Germans generally held the higher ground overlooking the Allies lower down on the mountain slopes and could therefore interfere with artillery fire if a target appeared.

The Germans did have some disadvantages though. Italian partisans were very active behind the front, and made life quite difficult, especially for small groups of Germans moving around and less able to defend themselves. Senior officers had less freedom to move, and some were ambushed and killed by the partisans. It is also said that the quality of concrete used in the fortifications was poor using local materials. Whether this was a result of deliberate action by local suppliers, or just a fact of life in Italy is not clear.

There was a pause in the Allied advance while stores and preparations were completed. The attack was to be in two phases. The first, a diversion, was to be along the Adriatic coast by 8th Army to draw off German reserves from the centre, the road to Bologna through the mountains. The second phase would then be to attack towards Bologna against a more weakly held defence along the mountain road.

The 8th Army started their drive on Rimini on 25th August, and initially made some progress along the coast. Progress inland, in the foothills of the mountains was harder and slower.

At the same time the 5th Army started to probe forward in the mountains on the road to Bologna. The 5th Army, though nominally American, was a true multinational force, as was the nominally British 8th Army.

The Bristol Gunners

For the next nine months the GVA would remain part of the American led 5th Army under General Mark Clark.

Clark was an ambitious soldier, and probably more than a little selfish. He had commanded the troops in the Anzio beachhead when the 8th Army were battering their way through the Cassino position. When the Gustav line fell, he had been tasked with bursting out of the beachhead and advancing eastwards across the Italian peninsula in order to cut off and capture the German forces retreating from Cassino. In the event he decided instead he would race to Rome for the honour of being the liberator of the 'Eternal City.' He therefore failed to achieve a strategic success for the Allies by taking out a good proportion of the best German troops. He had mismanaged one of the few good opportunities presented to the Allies in the Italian campaign, and it is possible that the war in Italy could have been completed in 1944 rather than drag on into 1945 as it did.

5th Army had three corps, two American and one British, plus some assorted units as corps troops. The American II Corps was all American. US IV Corps had American, Brazilian, and South African divisions within it, as well as Italian units. The third corps, British XIII Corps, consisted of British, Indian and Canadian units. No doubt, scattered around in staff positions, and on attachment within units were men from other nations. Included within the American forces were African Americans in combat roles, unusual for the American forces which were highly segregated and African Americans were mostly used in logistical and non combat roles. There were also Japanese Americans, referred to as 'Nisei.' Many African American and Japanese Americans distinguished themselves in the fighting in Italy.

8th Army had within it British, New Zealand, Indian, Jewish, Italian, Canadian, Greek, and Polish formations and units.

Though most troops had British or American weapons, and therefore ammunition needs, the supply of rations caused many issues, as not all troops could consume all types of food. There was no common diet allowed by cultural or religious requirements.

## The Bristol Gunners

The Germans had a common set of weapons and dietary preferences, which gave them an advantage especially when moving troops to different parts of the battlefield.

The GVA were involved with 5th Army's attack on the Gothic Line, initially supporting 6th South African Armoured Division in its attacks on the Monte Albano massif. Despite its South African name, the division also contained a brigade of British infantry from the Guards Regiments, 24th Guards Brigade, and it seems that it was this brigade that the GVA supported for most of the action.

Once again we rely on BSM Murley for some of the detail of actions at this time:

*"1944 September 4th Troops in action just N.W. of Lamporecchio against Gothic line. Sites in front of Guards Brigade and 25 pounders.*

*September 6th B.H.Q. and rear echelons move to Ponto Elsa.*

*September 8th All bridges over Arno washed away by rainstorm. Much difficulty getting ammo and rations across.*

*September 10th C and D Troops in action at Montecatini.*

*September 12th D Troop moved to new position 1 mile W. of Montecatini.*

*September 4th Shells in town, 8 shells landed within 100 yards of B.H.Q. – no damage.*

*September 13th D Troop mortared by Coldstream Guards registering D.F. task. No damage. [Defensive Fire] 10 shells landed just beyond B.H.Q., 1 in C Troops Wagon lines.*

*September 14th Troops fired murders in support of Guards brigade attack on Gothic Line. More shells in town.*

*September 15th Fired more murders for Coldstreams.*

*September 16th Fired counter battery bombards for 6th South African Armoured Division.*

### The Bristol Gunners

*September 18th More shells in town, 5 South Africans killed.*

*September 19th More shells - no damage.*

*September 26th C and D Troops moved to new positions in mountains N. of Bagnols."*

A 'murder' is an army slang term of the time for a fire mission where all available guns in range concentrate on a single target in the hope of overwhelming it. It was at this period of the war that the anti aircraft guns of the GVA came under their most intense and protracted usage. The heating up of barrels became a real problem, as the infantry attacks required the guns to keep firing over many hours.

As well as using heavy anti aircraft guns as field artillery, light anti aircraft guns were found a role in attack. Their shells were really too small to have a useful effect in ground bombardment, but they had the useful characteristic of being tracer rounds. Tracer ammunition, also used in machine guns and other smaller calibre weapons, was useful in helping a gunner, a spotter, or an observer, to see where shells were going in relation to an intended target. Therefore, corrections could be made to the aim and hits more easily made and verified. The British had developed the technique in deliberate attacks for light anti aircraft guns to be fire over the heads of our attacking forces to indicate either the direction to take, or the boundaries of each unit. This had first been used, very successfully, at the Battle of El Alamein in October 1942, and by this period was standard practice.

In addition, the Allies had an advantage in the number of tanks that they had, though the quality of these was poor compared to German tanks and German anti tank guns. Tanks are most suitable in open country where their advantage in gun range over enemy infantry can best be used. In the mountains they were vulnerable to concealed anti tank guns. Narrow roads on mountains meant that a single tank knocked out could prevent all further vehicle movement until it had been cleared. Often tanks were used as artillery instead. They would be lined up and would fire continuously on indirect targets. As with anti aircraft guns, tank guns were not designed to fire continuously, and barrel heating and excessive wear was a problem. Nevertheless, the extra firepower, especially at critical times, was most welcome and effective.

### The Bristol Gunners

Co-ordinating all the guns and supporting fire for an attack had become highly organised by this stage of the war, and the extra anti aircraft guns would be controlled and organised with heavy artillery into AGRAs – Army Groups Royal Artillery. The weight of fire from the AGRA could be applied to whichever part of the front needed it, and this ability, particularly by the British, was highly feared and respected by the Germans. They were of the opinion that British artillery was the most dangerous hazard on the battlefield.

BSM Murley's note of September 13th is instructive. Infantry battalions had some integral artillery of their own, 3 inch mortars. Mortars have a shorter range than artillery guns, but can fire at very high rates and put down very effective high explosive, smoke, or illumination rounds with very fast response times. It seems that either their calculations or observational powers were somewhat in error when they seem to have fired at the GVA positions while registering a defensive fire task. For this to happen, the GVA must have been very close to the front line at the time.

The Allies were unable to make the important breakthrough to the Lombardy Plain, though some small advances were made. As winter came on the weather intervened and military activity ground to a halt. On the right flank, on the Adriatic side of the mountains, the 8th Army had broken the Gothic Line but a succession of rivers swollen by heavy rains made further progress unlikely. In the mountains, the 5th Army had moved past the Gothic Line, but again the weather had defeated further progress, and supply across the mountains became extremely difficult.

The Germans and the Allies looked at each other in the mountains south of Bologna and pondered what the spring would bring.

For the GVA, the closure of the advance in 1944 meant a move to the seaside, or at least nearer the coast. In early October they left the mountains, and travelled westwards down the Arno valley. They then moved northwards up the Tyrrhenian Sea coast, through the stylish seaside resort of Viareggio (meaning 'King's Road') to take up positions in the hills overlooking the town. Though the Allied attacks were further to the east, on the other side of the Apennines, it was not a quiet sector. The Germans were active, as were the GVA. BSM Murley:

## The Bristol Gunners

*"1944 October 5th  C and D Troops moved to new positions in mountains 7 miles N. of Viareggio.*

*October 6th  C Troop shelled with airburst, 1 rifle and 4 tents damaged.*

*October 8th  B.H.Q. established 5 miles N. of Viareggio on coast road.*

*October 12th  C Troop moved to new position 1½ miles S. of Forti del Marni.*

*October 13th  C Troop shelled with airbursts, water trailer holed in 4 places.*

*October 15th  C troop shelled again, No.2 gun cables cut.*

*October 20th  C Troop had 55 shells on site. No.2 gun put out of action with damaged elevating gear. 155mm shells dropped near B.H.Q.*

*October 21st  C Troop again shelled. No damage.*

*October 22nd  C Troop again shelled No 3 gun out of action with damaged recuperator.*

*October 23rd  C Troop shelled again No 1 gun had holes in buffer tank, elevating gearbox and recuperating casing. C Troop moved to alternative position.*

*October 25th  Shells fell on C Troops old site when flash simulators fired.*

*October 26th  Flash simulators on C Troop old site drew more fire.*

*November 11th  Sites recced in Poretta Terme area, steep and mountainous.*

*November 21st  Torrential rain - guns flooded out of pits.*

*November 24th. Shells fell near B.H.Q. No casualties.*

*December 16th  C Troop shelled by 88mm. Control room got direct hits Taylor P.C. wounded in back, Bdr. Cook hit in head. Predictor and Height Finder put out of action.*

### The Bristol Gunners

*December 20th Picked up 6 Germans off the shore in a small boat.*

*December 21st C Troop shelled by 155mm. 2 gun cables cut and 20 rounds exploded no casualties.*

*December 23rd Picked up 5 Italians civilians landing in small from Spezia.*

*December 28th C Troop moved to site 2 miles W. of Canviore. German attack on Serchio Valley, expected to extend here."*

BSM Murley's comment for November 11th is interesting. The village that he mentions is back up in the mountains overlooking Bologna. In the event the GVA were not to move into that area again, but clearly someone considered that a move there was possible, perhaps to relieve another unit in need of rest and recuperation.

The German attack that he mentions in the Serchio Valley did not develop into anything serious, but it did demonstrate that the Germans were still active and in an aggressive mood.

The use of flash simulators in late October was maybe a ruse to help our own guns to locate and eliminate the German battery that had been firing at C Troop. A flash simulator was a small explosive device, similar to a thunderflash firework, used to look like a gun being fired. If the German observers could see this, they would call down their own artillery to fire at that spot. It seems that C Troop, having been fired at for a few days had moved to a more healthy location out of site of the Germans. When the German artillery fired on their old position, where the flash simulators were used, it gave our artillery Survey Regiments an opportunity to locate their guns using flash spotting techniques or sound ranging techniques. These methods had been developed to a high degree by this stage of the war and were regularly used to identify enemy guns and then give the location to our own medium and heavy artillery for a counter bombardment. Royal Artillery Survey Regiments are known to have been very active in the area and at this time, including 3rd and 5th Survey Regiments that had been raised in Bristol pre-war, and of whom we heard briefly at the end of the last chapter in this book.

C Troop seems to have been either very unlucky, or careless, as it seems to have had more than a fair share of German counter battery fire.

## The Bristol Gunners

The notes referencing picking up Germans and Italians in boats offshore is intriguing. It is not clear whether they were spies or deserters, but at this late stage in the war, they are more likely to have been the latter.

The situation for Italians, especially civilians, was difficult. There were two governments in existence, one supporting the Germans and one in the south aligned with the Allies. Some aspects of the war in northern Italy in the last two years of the war could be likened to a civil war.

Benito Mussolini had been dismissed as Prime Minister by King Victor Emmanuel III in September 1943 when the Allies had invaded the Italian mainland. Mussolini had been in declining personal popularity well before this time. His army had suffered humiliation on the battlefield by the British in North and East Africa in 1940, and by the Greeks and Albanians in 1941. When the Germans had invaded Russia in June 1941, Mussolini sent many of his troops to the Eastern Front to help the Germans, but more to help his own reputation and that of the Italian nation. He hoped to secure easy spoils of victory and re-establish his reputation. What happened, of course, was that the poorly equipped Italians suffered severely in the conditions of the Russian winter and the intense and brutal battles.

Supplies of fuel and food had become very short in Italy and a large black market economy had developed. There was serious discontent among the ordinary Italian people. By the time of the Allied invasion of Italy, Mussolini's status was under threat, and the Italian people wanted the war to end. Many Sicilians and Italians welcomed the arrival of the Allies, especially the Americans, as liberators. The King had no real alternative than to arrest and imprison Mussolini and try to get the best possible deal from negotiations with the Allies.

Mussolini was held in a mountain resort in Abruzzo, to the east of Rome. Two months later, he was rescued by German paratroopers who landed in the mountains by glider and took Mussolini north to meet with Hitler, who forced him to remain nominally in charge of what Italian forces and territory remained under German control. Mussolini took up residence on Lake Garda, and became in reality a puppet of Hitler, with no real control or influence.

## The Bristol Gunners

Much of northern Italy was under direct German control, and much of the Irridenta that had been gained by Garribaldi and aspired to by Felice Orsini were lost. After the war some would be regained but some parts in Istria (now Slovenia) were to be lost forever.

The front between the Germans and Allies remained static throughout the winter. The Allies further reduced their forces due to problems elsewhere. Some had gone to Greece (British, Indian, and Greek divisions), where the Germans had withdrawn, and civil war between royalists and communists had broken out. The Canadians and a British division had been withdrawn and sent to France where it was felt the need was greater. There had been some new formations arriving, a Brazilian division, and the American 10$^{th}$ Mountain Division, but more had departed than had arrived. Supplies of reinforcements – battle casualty replacements – were well below actual requirements. Every unit had been in continuous action for two years, and war weariness was a concern. At this stage of the war, all combatant nations were suffering from the attrition of their armed forces, especially in the infantry. In some cases artillery and tank units were converted to infantry to try to make up the deficit.

This fate was not to befall the GVA. In January, they came out of the line and were sent to Lucca just behind the front near Pisa and back in to the HAA role. Why this should be is not clear as the Luftwaffe was mostly absent from the war, and the risk from bombing raids must have been very low.

Manpower needs were being met from a variety of sources. Significant numbers of soldiers from the Empire who had not previously been required in a combat role were pressed into service. The GVA received a draft of men from South Africa, from what is now Botswana, and this is recorded by BSM Murley who refers to them as 'Bechuanas:'

*"1945 January 23$^{rd}$ Battery moved to Lucca in A.A. role. Very quiet.*

*February 19$^{th}$ Bechuanas joined the battery.*

*March 13$^{th}$ Battery moved up to Viareggio again D troop at Mintonte, C Troop at Fiumetto.*

*March 26$^{th}$ White troops in exchange for Bechuanas, left the battery."*

## The Bristol Gunners

In late March the GVA were again going into the field artillery role, and the black South African soldiers probably had not been trained in that role, so were withdrawn again, no doubt being sent to another unit elsewhere. This type of augmentation of manpower was common at this time in the British Army.

In early April 1945, the Allies started what would be their last attacks. The GVA were on the left flank, on the coast north of Viareggio, with 5th Army. The attack that they were involved in supporting was a diversion. The intention was to draw German reserves over to the west and east coasts, and then to attack the Germans in the centre where they would then be weaker. The attacks were successful, and by 20th April the mountain position had been passed and the Allies were moving onto the Lombardy Plain below. BSM Murley records this period of the battle, including the unfortunate injury to the commanding officer, Major Chapman:

*"April 5th Attack started with barrage at 5am. Both troops busy. Coast O.P. shelled by 170mm.*

*April 7th Coast O.P. hit by 170mm mortar shells and bullets in vicinity - no casualties.*

*April 8th C.O. had leg blown off in minefield. [Major Chapman]*

*April 10th D Troop moved to new site over the Cinquale. C Troop in new site near coast O.P.*

*April 12th B.H.Q. moved to Fiumetto.*

*April 13th Troops moved to new site N. of Marina De Massa.*

*April 14th First into Avenza with one 3 tonner and two motorcycles.*

*April 23rd Battery moved to Marina Di Carrara."*

After emerging from the mountains onto the Plain, the next major obstacle was to be the Po River. On 24th April, the GVA withdrew from the line on the coast, and travelled across the mountains, first to Bologna, then north of Modena to deploy to protect an important bridge on the River Po at San Benedetto, just south of Mantova. The Germans and their

## The Bristol Gunners

remaining Italian troops were in headlong retreat, and advances by the Allies were fast.

Organisation within the German occupied remnant of Italy descended into chaos. Germans surrendered in large numbers, but others were intent on escaping into Austria, Germany, or elsewhere including Benito Mussolini. He, with his mistress Clara Petacci, had gone west from Lake Garda and was trying to reach Switzerland via the mountains north of Lake Como. Their intention was to fly from Switzerland and seek refuge in Spain, which was also a fascist country. They were intercepted by Italian partisans on 27$^{th}$ April, and executed the next day without any form of legal process. Their bodies, along with a dozen or so other fascists, were taken to Milan and strung up on meat hooks in a square that had been used as the place of execution of anti fascists.

The war, for Mussolini at least, was over. For the GVA war's end would come a few days later.

BSM Murley:

*"April 24$^{th}$ 11am battery moved through Viareggio, Pistoia, Bologna, Modena, to San Benedetto Po, in defence of bridge.*

*May 2$^{nd}$ Battery moved to Piacenza in defence of bridge there. Germans in Italy surrendered.*

*May 4$^{th}$ Germans in Holland, Denmark and Northern Germany surrendered.*

*May 5$^{th}$ Germans in South Austria surrendered.*

*May 8$^{th}$ Churchill spoke at 3pm giving official news of Germany's surrender.*

*Troops had "Cease Fire.""*

Another war was over. The GVA had played their part in full, once again.

As at the end of the First World War, the GVA found themselves in northern Italy, and demobilisation would take some time to complete. The aftermath of this war also needed trained and organised manpower to establish law and order, the collection and processing of multitudes of

prisoners of war, and the repatriation of our own POWs and other displaced persons. The task allotted to the GVA was to become prison warders:

*"May 14th Moved to Pesaro to join 7th A.G.R.A."*

*May 17th Battery began guarding surrendered enemy personnel in cages at Cesenaties and Cessna.*

*November 24th Regiment officially ordered to go into a state of "Suspended Animation"*

*Personnel of the battery posted to 51st H.A.A. Regt."*

Therefore, at the end of 1945 76th HAA Regiment ceased to exist. For the men, it was time, yet again, to return to Bristol and start their lives over again. For Britain, the end of the war brought new challenges and uncertainties.

**1955, former GVA BSM Murley, by then a captain, points to something of interest to five visiting British and foreign generals during range practice. Most of the information relating to the actions of the GVA in the Second World War are based on BSM Murley's records.**

The Bristol Gunners

## Chapter 9  From Then Until Now

Britain ended the war on the winning side. It had declared war on the Germans to defend its own interests. Allies had come, and allies had gone, such as Poland and France, though the Free French stayed with Britain throughout the difficult times, and many Poles fought with the British throughout the war. Enemies had come and gone, both the Italians and the Russians had started as enemies, and ended as Allies. Other Allies arrived at our sides to help, and were still with us at the conclusion of hostilities.

However, Britain, having won the war, had also lost. Many of the fruits of British invention had been given over to the Americans in return for their continued support. Britain also had entered into a period where the inevitability of the end of Empire became accepted.

Britain and the British people were tired, bloodied, but definitely unbowed. There was much for them to be proud of, some regrets of course, with mixed optimism and pessimism. Britain had experienced many of the worst aspects of war, save that of occupation (except, of course, in the Channel Islands). The countries that had been occupied, along with the losers, had to reflect on what had caused the descent into war, its consequences, and what to do next. Some countries had been rent in two. Some were riven socially and politically, others, like Germany, rent in two by the physical barriers of the Iron Curtain.

The technologies of the pre war days had progressed dramatically under the impetus of survival. Radar had become a working technology, useful both in warfare, and in more peaceful pursuits. Traditional explosives had become more effective and deadly, but none more deadly than the atomic weapons used against the Japanese in the last weeks of the war. Just as the paradigm of the invincible bomber dominated defence thinking in the 1930s, the apparent inevitability of nuclear war was to come to dominate the second half of the twentieth century.

In 1945 and 1946, the service men and women started to return from duty, swapping khaki or blue uniforms for a civilian suit or overalls. For most of them their thoughts were not on the far future, but on the very near. How to get back into family life, how to take up, yet again, the routine of

## The Bristol Gunners

everyday life without the danger and disruption. Rationing, of food especially, would continue for many years. British civil and community life had changed.

A baby boom started, and for the next ten years the British population, at least the younger element of it, would procreate and fill the gaps. Many displaced persons born in foreign lands would stay and settle. Even former enemies, having been in prison camps and now allowed freedom to interact with local people, decided to stay and settle in Britain.

Over the coming decades, the Empire and its ending meant that more people, from further afield, would make Britain their home.

The military mind also turned to thoughts of peace, or, at least, what to do now that peace of a sort had returned. The Territorial Army, as the main agent for home defence, was resurrected. Divisions of 'Terriers' were to be reformed, as well as Anti Aircraft Command. Though the immediate threat had been removed, more threats could emerge and we needed to be ready for them. The TA was reformed around a reduced number of divisions. The pre war TA had seventeen divisions, the post war TA had only ten divisions. This would soon be further reduced to eight. The old 48th South Midland Division, in which the GVA had fought during the First World War and served up to 1938 was not reformed. It had gone to France with the BEF in 1940, evacuated via Dunkirk, and had not served abroad again. It was disbanded in 1944.

Though the Empire, and the need to police it, was a diminishing prospect in the late 1940s, the Regular Army would find itself involved in many conflicts between then and now. They have fought wars far away, in Korea, in Borneo, in Malaya, in Africa, in Arabia, in the Middle East, and in the cold waters of the South Atlantic Ocean. They have also fought wars closer to home, in Northern Ireland, and in the Balkans.

The longest and ultimately most successful war was against their former enemy-ally, the Soviet Union. The Cold War was fought at many levels. Casualties were relatively light, especially between the main adversaries, but proxies, such as Koreans and Vietnamese, sometimes suffered massively. However, win the Cold War we did. The world has been offered a better prospect because of that.

### The Bristol Gunners

Newer conflicts arose after the demise of Communism. Terrorism, radicalism, religious intolerance, greed, poverty, and hunger were motivations. Wars are no longer mainly fought between nations, but within nations, or between ideologies.

All this we now know, but in 1946 the sense was 'what do we do now?'

During the Second World War, the military had learned how to shoot down bombers and other aeroplanes with increasing degrees of success. Britain would need to keep its anti aircraft defences intact and at the ready. In 1947, when the TA was restructured, the Heavy Anti Aircraft regiments reformed and took up the tools of their trade. One among them was the GVA. As after the First World War, the men of Bristol were asked to volunteer their services to serve in the GVA, and they did so enthusiastically.

The GVA changed its title, from the former 76th HAA Regiment (TA) to 266 (Mobile) HAA Regt RA (TA). This was the first time that the '266' title number was used in relation to the GVA. The '(Mobile)' part of the title distinguished the regiment as a mobile one, that is, its weapons were designed to move and deploy into positions wherever required, with the field army.

The guns that the GVA used were essentially the same 3.7 Inch Heavy Anti Aircraft guns that they had used previously, though improved by alterations to equipment and ammunition brought in during the war.

Advances in technology during the war demonstrated that unmanned missiles, such as the V2 rockets used by the Germans, would form a new kind of threat. In 1947 there was no immediate way to counter this threat, a solution would have to be found.

Aeroplanes had also become faster, more agile, and flew higher, and out of practical range of a conventional ground fired artillery shells. The British and the Americans had been experimenting with developing supersonic aircraft since 1942. The Americans broke the sound barrier in 1947. The message was clear, present equipment was not going to be good enough to counter these faster, higher-flying aircraft.

## The Bristol Gunners

Some work was done post war to improve the existing heavy anti aircraft guns, but all efforts were stopped in the late 1950s in favour of guided missiles. These were becoming viable systems, and the only realistic prospect for defence against fast high flying aircraft. Heavy anti aircraft guns were replaced by two missile systems in Britain's forces. Both were the results of private company projects. The Bristol Bloodhound project was begun in 1949, and it was ready for introduction into service in 1958. The Bloodhound, then the main weapon for UK Air Defence, was operated by the RAF, and initially they were deployed into fixed positions in Britain. A later version was mobile and could be deployed with an expeditionary force.

In 1960, the Army took into service another type of high level anti aircraft missile, the Thunderbird, supplied by the English Electric Company. Thunderbird was a mobile system, designed to be able to accompany the Army wherever it was needed.

Guns were to be retained for low level anti aircraft duties, and the reliable Bofors was worked on a little by the Bristol Aircraft Company at Filton. However, their designs were eventually dropped in favour of an improved version developed by the Swedish Bofors company. This improved weapon, fully powered and radar controlled was taken into British army service as the L40/70, which remained in service until the mid 1970s, being replaced in its turn by missile systems.

The GVA persisted with their guns until 1960, training as hard and as diligently as always. They changed their unit title in 1956 to 311 (Bristol) HAA Regt RA (TA), retaining their 3.7 Inch guns. However, the writing was on the wall for these weapons, and when the end came for them the GVA needed to change their role, and their name, once again.

The GVA were never issued with any Thunderbirds. On the introduction into service of this missile in 1960 the GVA's role in Heavy Anti Aircraft ceased. Thunderbirds were to be an exclusively Regular Army weapon. The TA lost its role in national air defence, the RAF had the Bloodhound, and no longer needed help from the Army.

As a result, the GVA changed role and name again, in 1961, this time to become 883 (GVA) Locating Battery RA (TA). The men of the GVA could stop looking to the skies for targets, and in future would fulfil another important role for the Royal Artillery.

The role of 883 (GVA) Locating Battery was to use a range of equipment and methods to locate enemy mortars and artillery positions, pass this information to medium or heavy gun batteries to enable them to counter bombard the enemy positions and thereby remove them from the battlefield.

GVA Green Archer radar system drawn by a Humber 1 Ton armoured truck, deploying on exercise in the 1960s, probably on Salisbury Plain Training Area.

The need to do this had first been recognised in the First World War, as we have previously seen. Methods and equipment had developed to improve the speed and accuracy of the work. A locating battery was organised into three troops. The first of these was a Locating Troop (Loc. Tp.), equipped with Green Archer radars. These radar sets were able to plot a mortar bomb in flight and calculate its trajectory, extrapolating this back to the origin, that is, the point on the ground from where the mortar bomb had been fired.

The second troop was a Sound Ranging Troop (SR. Tp.) This used sensitive ground microphones set out in a line on the ground several kilometres long. When an enemy gun is fired, the sound of its firing will reach each microphone at a slightly different time based on the distance

## The Bristol Gunners

from the gun muzzle to each microphone. Knowing the speed of sound at the time (it varies with air density and air temperature) enables the operator to triangulate back to the location of the gun, and once again, this information is used to counter battery the enemy gun's position. Forward OPs are required to initiate recording, and these forward observers 'flash spot' if the enemy are foolish enough to fire their guns in sight of these observers. By comparing the direction from two or more observers to each flash, a triangulation can be made to the gun position. Counter bombardment results, as before.

The GVA, and the Royal Artillery, used a variety of vehicles. Here two GVA NCOs rescue their Matchless G3WD motorcycle from a stream, and they seem to be enjoying themselves doing so.

The third troop was a Survey Troop. In Britain, national survey was a military activity; hence our best maps are produced by the Ordnance Survey organisation, originally part of the Corps of Royal Engineers. Maps in other countries are generally not as good or accurate as our excellent OS maps. For positioning radars, sound bases, OPs, guns and many other pieces of military hardware to be effective in their work it is important to have them accurately surveyed and located on the map in use. Often, in war, British military survey troops need to produce an accurate survey and amend the maps in use.

## The Bristol Gunners

A Locating Battery would normally form part of a division's Artillery Group HQ.

The GVA title was now being applied to a battery, rather than as previously, a regiment. As 266 (HAA) Regiment, and later as 311 (HAA) Regiment, it had been much bigger, having four batteries. The reduction in size was further complicated by the amalgamation of the GVA with 883 Battery, successor unit to the two Survey Regiments (3rd and 5th) that had been raised in Bristol just before the Second World War.

We heard earlier that before the Second World War, in 1937, two Royal Artillery Survey Regiments had been formed in Bristol as TA units. Both of these served throughout the War. The two regiments then amalgamated in 1947 as 376 Observation Regiment RA (TA). In 1959, this regiment was reduced to battery size, renamed 883 Locating Battery, and was organised to become part of the 43rd Wessex Division Royal Artillery Headquarters. 43rd Wessex Division was one of the Territorial divisions that were reformed after the Second World War, and each division required a Locating Battery as part of its Royal Artillery Headquarters.

The Royal Artillery used the terms 'Survey', Observation' and 'Locating' to title and describe these units. This can be very confusing to the casual observer. In fact, all these terms refer to the same type of unit with the same role, the changing nomenclature purely reflecting changing thinking within the military. Survey, Observation, and Locating batteries and regiments essentially do the same thing. They are responsible for finding (locating) the enemy's artillery and mortars so that they can be destroyed by our own artillery.

3rd Survey Regiment RA (TA) had been formed in Bristol before the Second World War, and served in the Italian campaign as did the GVA. They never served in the same locations as each other, but 3rd Survey Regiment did great work for the divisions that it served in 8th Army. Major J R Jenner, who served with the regiment during the war wrote a record of its war time adventures. He summarises its work thus:

> "To sum up the work of the Regiment, the campaign in Italy proved that survey, which had had a sticky beginning in the early stages of the war, really worked and that Flash Spotting and Sound Ranging were

The Bristol Gunners

*quite indispensable adjuncts to any Counter Battery Organisation. Sound Ranging in particular had exceeded the wildest hopes of its most optimistic supporters and had produced excellent results in the most adverse conditions. Reports from other theatres proved that the lessons which we had learned in Italy were exactly the same as those learned in NW Europe.*

*We were lucky during the war in Italy to have as CCRA 13 Corps, Brigadier Greene who had once commanded the Survey Company and so knew what we were trying to do. He said that 3rd Survey was the most Territorial Regiment in the British Army and how much he liked visiting any of our detachments. He also said that wherever he went in Italy he always met at least one truck with the distinctive 33 sign but that these trucks were always driven well and at a reasonable speed and so never did anything about it. Actually they were generally on the hunt for vino and other welfare supplies."*

Thus, in 1961, the GVA of 311 HAA Regiment RA (TA) amalgamated with the existing 883 Locating Battery RA (TA) to form the re-titled 883 (GVA) Locating Battery RA (TA). This unit also incorporated the Counter Battery Troop from 43rd (Wessex) Division HQRA staff.

While a seasoned military person would have little difficulty dealing with these somewhat arcane variations of name and format, a casual observer would at this point be sighing heavily and wondering how on earth we managed to win a war. There is a military saying, 'if in doubt, reorganise', and it seems that in the 1950s there was more than a modicum of doubt.

In any case, the GVA had a new role, new equipment, and once again entered into the spirit of things with an energetic response. Much training and socialising completed the conversion and amalgamation.

At this time there were many other regimental amalgamations and reductions taking place, in both the TA and in the Regular Army. Famous regimental names disappeared from active service as the Army adjusted to the realities of the time.

National Service, that is, universal conscription of 18 to 21 year old males, in the UK had ended in the late 1950s. By 1963, the last National Servicemen had left and the Army, both professional and amateur was

much smaller, and all volunteer. A reduced manpower pool, and reducing (and possibly, clarifying) responsibilities drove many of these amalgamations.

The Empire was in the process of shrinking as colonies and other overseas possessions took their independence and set out on the path of self determination. Some would make good use of this opportunity and their citizens would thrive. Others, of course, would make the worst of it and would descend into decades of poverty, corruption, and famine. While the bulk of this reduction took place by the early 1960s, some would have to wait until the end of the century to be released from the Empire's embrace.

Britain needed fewer soldiers to police, and defend, a reduced empire. The nature of threats to Britain and its worldwide interests was changing. Europe was a much more peaceful place, with the prospect of a future free of internecine conflict. There was a dark shape on the eastern horizon, though. Despite the fact that Russia had fought (eventually) on the side of the anti fascists and had liberated many peoples from totalitarian government in one form, it had chosen to continue on the path of its own totalitarian domination of these countries and peoples. Tensions between the former allies, Russia, and the West, grew. Proxy wars had broken out in the Far East (Korea); nationalist wars were being corrupted in the name of Communism (Vietnam) and would lead to America's worst humiliation on the battlefield.

Britain had kept troops in Germany from 1945, initially as an ersatz civil administration, latterly as a defence force. This force, reduced in size, was to counter the threat of invasion from the east by the Russians. The Western Europeans and North Americans had formed the North Atlantic Treaty Organisation (NATO) in 1949 to commit themselves to mutual defence – all for one and one for all. In their turn, the Soviets had formed the Warsaw Pact in 1955 to assure themselves from invasion from the west. West Germany, the part occupied and in the care of the Allies (Britain, France and the USA) had been politically rehabilitated and admitted to NATO in 1955 as a sovereign power, and able to establish its own armed forces once again. Gradually the Cold War clarified, and would form a basis of defence policy in Britain for the following forty years.

Land invasion was one concern, however low its actual probability was. The major emerging threat of the time was nuclear weapon armed ballistic missiles, capable of being fired from one continent to attack another. These were called Inter Continental Ballistic Missiles (ICBMs). In 1959, the first operational ICBMs came into service, somewhat crude in performance, but a threat nonetheless. Over time, they would become more capable, more accurate, more of a threat. Britain and America developed manned aeroplanes capable of delivering nuclear bombs in attack or retaliation, these were to prove a temporary measure, and missiles would eventually rule the nuclear roost.

A paradigm was to dominate relations between the two Superpowers, summarised and suitably abbreviated to 'MAD.' Mutual Assured Destruction would be the watchword for decades, until we all emerged from that particular aberration into the last years of the Twentieth Century.

The British Army on the Rhine (BAOR), as our German based troops were known, was reduced to a corps sized commitment (around 60,000 troops) in 1949. Even with the assistance of other Western European and North American troops permanently positioned on the Continent, BAOR would be insufficient to stop and repulse a land invasion from the Warsaw Pact nations. British military reserves would be needed to reinforce BAOR if war threatened.

The TA divisions were tasked with reinforcing BAOR in the event of war with complete and self contained divisions, such as the 43$^{rd}$ (Wessex) Division, in which the GVA served. To be able to fulfil their role alongside the Regular Army divisions they needed to have the same capability and equipment. Therefore, in 1961, the GVA, as 883 (GVA) Loc. Bty. RA (TA) became part of 43$^{rd}$ Wessex Infantry Division (TA). In the event of the threat of war in Europe, they would deploy along with the other units of the division to Germany. Their role would be to use their locating radars, sound ranging equipments, and survey skills to identify the locations of Warsaw Pact artillery positions and pass that data to the medium and heavy artillery regiments for them to counter battery (CB) the enemy.

Further changes fell on the British Army in the late 1960s. The 1966 Defence White Paper announced the end of the Territorial Army, it being

replaced by the Territorial and Army Volunteer Reserve (TAVR). The TAVR would have four parts. TAVR I would be units with a commitment to be used for all military purposes, TAVR II units would be NATO units for support to BAOR, TAVR III units were for home defence only, and TAVR IV was a collection of bands and training units, such as the OTCs.

As a result of this (yet another) reorganisation, the GVA were placed in TAVR III, for home defence, as a sub unit of a Yeomanry Regiment, The Royal Gloucestershire Hussars, as their A (GVA) Squadron.

**HRH Queen Elizabeth II inspects the men of the GVA during a visit to Bristol, believed to be 1956.**

Two years later, in 1969, TAVR III was disbanded, the units being reduced to cadres of about eight men. At this point there was a real danger that the GVA, and its association with the Royal Regiment of Artillery would be lost forever. Fortunately, in the way of old soldiers everywhere, the old sweats kept their heads down, got on with things, in the hope of better times ahead. An unofficial GVA cadre set up the Bristol Royal Artillery Club and continued to meet in the bar at the

## The Bristol Gunners

Artillery Grounds on Friday evenings, thereby keeping the GVA name and spirit alive through the darkest period of its history.

During the post war period up to 1989 Britain and the West felt themselves under threat from the Soviet Russians. While some in our society were resolved to resist and counter this threat, the response of others to was challenge the use of military strength. They saw nuclear disarmament as the best way for us to establish a moral ascendancy. Along with this there was a general revision of the rightness of our resistance to the challenges that brought about the First and Second World Wars. The performance of our generals and soldiers was also brought into question. The false paradigm of 'Lions led by Donkeys' of the First World War developed, and the perception that the bombing of cities like Dresden, Hiroshima and Nagasaki were somehow voluntary and wanton acts. A country or regime that starts a war, and which uses any and every means in its power to win can expect its adversaries to use any means at their disposal to shorten and win that conflict.

Soldiers, sailors, airmen, are sent to fight our enemies. They are citizens and soldiers, fighting on behalf of every other citizen. They are not free to chose the means by which they will win, but win they must. And, in many conflicts, they have carried this responsibility well, and we must all be proud of them, and what they have done on our behalf.

In 1968, former Trumpeter Harold Essex Lewis (nicknamed 'Bungy' by his GVA comrades), by then a retired Lieutenant Colonel, was moved to write an article for the Bristol Evening Post newspaper, which is reproduced here. Bungy could speak with some authority on matters as seen by the soldier who served his country. He mobilised with the GVA in August 1914, served throughout the First and Second World Wars, was wounded, and rose to a senior rank. In the article he stated:

*"15th November, 1968. Article by Lt Col H. Essex. Lewis.*

*As The Golden Jubilee week of the First World War Armistice draws to a close, there remains one last question: Was it Worth it?*

*Many of us who served in the Kaiser War still find it difficult to believe that half a century has passed since the Order – "Hostilities will cease at 11.00 hours on November 11, 1918" brought an end to the fighting on*

## The Bristol Gunners

the Western Front and a sense of incredulous bewilderment to those in actual combat.

And now 50 years later we ask was it worth it?

Was it worth the expenditure of life, of treasure, of the many unknown sacrifices, the misery and sorrow which our generation suffered during those years and in some respects is suffering still?

As a Gunner who served through that war in batteries which were involved in most of the major events on the Western Front I think that I can speak for my generation of our Army when I say that it never occurred to us to think in that way at all.

Do the doctors and nurses caught up in a cholera or some other fearful epidemic where their very ministrations have exposed them to infection and death ask "Was it worth it?" The onset of fire, flood pestilence or foe affords no time for argument.

As each occurs it must be met, dealt with and if humanly possible, overcome. And as the men of the fighting services went to deal with their task they knew that the alternatives were submission or defeat.

They saw then as we have seen again more recently, just what either would mean to their country, their homes and their people.

### Slaughter

Their conditions of life, mud-locked, verminous and with constant exposure to death in more than one unpleasant form, have been the subject of books by clever young men then unborn. They have written them off as fools driven like sheep to the slaughter by a High Command whose foolishness they are pleased to prefix by one of the words now in common use but once considered to be confined to the soldiery.

So almost every year these young men seem to return to their "Was it worth it?" and we smile among ourselves and agree that we never gave it a thought. What we know and remember with pride is that with us an order was an order and not a basis for argument, and that we carried out our orders wherever they took us and groused as soldiers must have done since man first bore arms. Those years taught us to know our

## The Bristol Gunners

*fellow man for what he was and from the fire of that experience has emerged the gold of friendship.*

Lt Col H. Essex-Lewis Nov 15, 1968.

Lest we Forget"

The threat from the East was to continue for another twenty one years from the date of Bungy's article. Other threats were developing, and would become clearer as time passed and the end of the century drew closer.

In 1971 a further change in military perceptions occurred. The TAVR was expanded, and a new GVA unit formed, centred on the Bristol Royal Artillery Club cadre. This new incarnation was 266th (Gloucestershire Volunteer Artillery) Observation Post Battery, Royal Artillery (Volunteer). The 'Volunteer' part of this somewhat elongated and convoluted name referred to the unit status as part of TAVR II. TAVR III units had been 'Territorials', whereas TAVR I & II units were 'Volunteers.' For everyday convenience, the new unit title was written as 266 (GVA) OP Bty RA (V).

The GVA had returned to be a full member of the British defence community, prepared once again to fulfil its duty.

Their new role reflected some appreciation of practical and budgetary realities within the Army.

Keeping soldiers in Germany was expensive. TAVR soldiers were much cheaper as they only had to be paid for the time they chose to serve each year, with no added costs for family, travel, education, accommodation and so on in foreign currency. The role was for the GVA to train twelve OP parties, each of one officer and six non commissioned soldiers in the OP role. These OP parties, fully trained and equipped to the same level as their Regular Army counterparts would be used to supplement each Regular Army artillery regiment in times of exercise and war. Each Regular Army artillery gun battery required three OP parties on operations. Two of these would be Regular Army troops, and the third would come from the TAVR. The TAVR parties would train for most of the year with their own guns, but on annual exercises would join their regular regiment and become a part of their organisation.

The Bristol Gunners

There were to be two of these OP batteries in Britain, providing in total twenty four TAVR OP parties to Regular Army artillery regiments in BAOR.

The TAVR OP batteries needed guns with which to train. On weekend camps, live fire would be provided by real guns making real bangs so that training would be as realistic as possible. In the normal way of things in the British Army, instead of issuing the OP batteries with the weapons currently in use in the Regular Army, the 75mm Pack Howitzer, the OP batteries were each given three Second World War era QF 25 Pounder Gun-Howitzers to play with. As it happens, the 25 Pounder was probably the better gun, and was very popular with the gun crews. As well as training the twelve OP parties (totalling 84 all ranks), the GVA needed a half battery of guns with their gun crews and command post operatives. These forty or so trained soldiers would, in war, go as individual reinforcements to BAOR artillery regiments. In reality, there was little strict delineation between 'Gun End' and 'OP End', and many individuals were trained to perform equally well whether serving the guns or observing in a trench at the 'front.'

One bonus that the GVA enjoyed was a generous supply of ammunition. The QF 25 Pounder gun had been used by the thousand during the Second World War. At the end of that war there had been massive stocks of ammunition in store. Some of this had been dumped in the Irish Sea, along with many other types of surplus military stores. Some more had been fired on operations in Korea, Suez, and a dozen other minor wars, but the British Army still retained large stocks of 25 pounder shells. The two OP batteries were the last units in the British Army to be equipped with these guns and to use them regularly for live fire. Consequently, supplies of ammunition for live firing practice was more than generous, and the average TA OP party fired many more live rounds in training than even their Regular Army colleagues.

Another unusual feature of these OP batteries was the very high proportion of officers. A normal battery sized military unit would have around five or six officers. An OP battery was staffed by around twenty officers, which meant that it had an officers' mess almost as large as that of a regiment, without the restraining influence of the presence of a

Commanding Officer (Lieutenant Colonel) to moderate the spirits during times of celebration.

In this guise, the GVA returned to its old ways of hard and enthusiastic training, preparing for the unwelcome possibility again being called to resist the forces of the Queen's enemies.

Annual training camps for the guns were generally held in the UK, though occasional overseas camps were also included from time to time, such as the 1975 annual camp in Cyprus. In the early days, most supported Regular Army regiments were based in Germany, so OP parties spent their annual camps on the Continent, either travelling by road from Bristol to northern Germany, or flying there. Over time, BAOR was reduced in size, and some BAOR Divisions became UK based, but still with a BAOR war role. In consequence, some OP parties came to support UK based artillery regiments. One of these, 4$^{th}$ Regiment, went to the South Atlantic as part of the Falklands task Force in 1982. Unfortunately for the GVA, 4$^{th}$ Regiment's war increments were drawn from other regular regiments rather than the GVA.

In 1979 there were further changes in the role and nomenclature of the TAVR. The Territorial Army title was reintroduced, though a major change was that it was no longer an army. The new version of the TA would not provide combat divisions to the Regular Army or for home defence. Instead it would provide individual and small group war increments (such as OP parties), minor (company, squadron or battery sized) and major unit (battalion or regiment sized) war increments to Regular Army divisions, as well as specialist units not required in times of peace, such as engineer, logistic and medical units. For the GVA, though, it would continue more or less on the same path and role.

As an OP battery, the GVA were issued with much equipment and technology to play with, identical to that supplied to their Regular Army colleagues. Occasionally they would be issued with a new generation of equipment before the Regular Army. In the 1980s a revolution had started in mobile electronics, and a range of new equipments began to arrive to help OP parties to do their work. Laser range finders, better radios, gun data computers, image intensified observation devices, lightweight radar equipments, and a little later, GPS equipment.

## The Bristol Gunners

For twenty years the GVA, as an OP battery, helped win the Cold War. Through the 1980s Soviet communism gave up the competition with NATO (largely through the efforts, it has to be said, of the Americans very ably led by President Ronald Reagan). In 1989, the Berlin Wall was broken, and the peoples of Eastern Europe were released from the Bear's iron grip. The Warsaw Pact was abandoned, and it was clear that the Soviet threat had passed.

**GVA Officers' Mess silver and trophy display.**

Very quickly, it became obvious to the government of the time that there was to be a 'peace dividend', the military contingencies of the previous forty years were no longer required. Unfortunately, for the military planners, the threat situation was to change and become more complex and diffused. No longer the old East/West tensions, but a newer and more complex situation has developed. Old assumptions have needed to be abandoned, and so far, every new assumption has proved to be wrong.

The rise of fanaticism, terrorism, gangsterism, greed, inequality, intolerance, desire for freedom, and many other factors previously suppressed or hidden have surfaced in many parts of the world. The new

threats are less easy to define accurately, predict, and prepare for. It is clear that the Cold War conflict between ideologies had kept some of these forces for change subdued. Removing Superpower interest and involvement from the less developed areas of the world has resulted in an increase of conflict and uncertainty.

**A GVA OP party on exercise in their FV432 APC, probably at the Royal School of Artillery, Larkhill, Salisbury Plain, in the mid 1980s.** (Photo Clive Gamlin)

Such it was in 1990, just as the Western World was starting to feel more secure, the Middle East started into conflict with the Iraqi invasion of Kuwait. Unrest of various origins in that region continues to this day, with no final resolution predicted or expected in the near future.

For the GVA the fall of communism in the early 1990s led to another change of role. The reduction in scale and likelihood of war deployment for BAOR reduced the need for additional OP parties to be supplied to the Regular Army. The two OP Batteries were converted to gun batteries, losing their obsolete (but still popular) QF 25 Pounder guns and replacing them with the modern L118 Light Gun. As a gun battery the GVA became the fourth battery for a regular regiment, 7th Regiment Royal Horse Artillery (shortened to 7RHA). Despite being a 'horse artillery'

regiment, 7 RHA did not support a cavalry formation, but was instead the artillery support for the Airborne Forces. As 'Airborne', they trained as parachutists, wore the red beret of the Airborne Forces, and identified themselves as 'Airborne Gunners' in every way. In fact, the Bristol base housed only a half battery of guns and the battery headquarters. The other half battery of guns was in Romford in Essex. For peacetime organisation 266 (GVA) Parachute Battery RA (TA) was part of 100 (Yeomanry) Regiment RA (TA).

**An OP Party from the GVA taking part in a military demonstration at the RSA, Larkhill, in the mid 1980s. They are sitting around a camouflaged OP trench.**
(Photo Rick Barthelmie)

The GVA entered their period of support to 7th Regiment RHA with great enthusiasm, and many of them gained the cherished red beret. This relationship continued until the early years of the twenty first century when another change of military thinking placed the GVA more logically to support 29th (Commando) Regiment Royal Artillery, which is based in Taunton in Somerset. Same guns, but some differences in training and deployment. They swapped the risk of air sickness for that of sea sickness.

## The Bristol Gunners

Once again the GVA changed name, but not its spirit. The current title is 266 (GVA) Commando Battery RA. They are once again fully accommodated in Bristol.

The fact is that for the last few years the GVA has not been tasked to field a full gun battery in the event of war. The various financial and other realities have meant that units such as the GVA are pressed into service as sources of trained artillerymen to serve as war increments to artillery regiments that are preparing for operations, in the Balkans, in Iraq and in Afghanistan. In this, GVA men have served in The Second Gulf War, in Iraq, in the Balkans, and in Afghanistan. No doubt, as future requirements occur, they will continue to keep the GVA name in the front line.

In 2009, as a reward for 150 years of association with, and service to, the City of Bristol, the GVA was given the Freedom of the City of Bristol. They continue to be headquartered in the same location on Whiteladies Road in Bristol as when Major HBO Savile first called the men of Bristol to serve. It is hoped that they will long continue to do so.

At the time of writing this book the GVA are preparing for yet another change in role. Under the Defence Reform changes introduced by the British Government in 2013 the GVA are to change from a gun battery to a battery operating MUAS (Miniature Unmanned Aerial Systems) aerial drones. These are used in locating potential threats to our forces in direct support of infantry and other troops in the field. In this role they are changing their place in the overall Army structure to become part of 104 Regiment Royal Artillery, based in Newport in Gwent. This regiment is also part of what is now to be known as Reserve Forces, volunteer soldiers with an important and integrated role within the overall defence structure. It is hoped and totally expected that the men (and women) of the GVA will continue to make the people of Bristol proud of them.

The great lesson from history, especially in military matters, is 'Prepare for the Unexpected.'

One thing that can be confidently assured, is that when the next call comes, the GVA will stand ready to serve. They will continue to be

*Fidus et Audax.*

The Bristol Gunners

## Glossary

| Term | Meaning |
|---|---|
| 3C | Command, Control, and Communication. |
| 15 Inch How | A very large calibre gun mounted on a railway mounting. |
| 4.2, 4,2 Inch | Four point two inch gun, a German medium artillery gun. |
| 4.5, 4,5 Inch | British 4.5 Inch medium artillery howitzer. |
| 5.9, 5.9 Inch | Five point nine inch gun, a German heavy artillery gun. |
| 6 Inch | A British artillery gun with a barrel bore of 6 inch (150mm) diameter, a heavy gun. |
| 60 Pounder | A British medium artillery gun, firing a shell of 60 pounds (about 25 Kg) in weight. |
| 7.2 Inch | A large German gun of 7.2 inches barrel diameter. |
| 75, 75mm | A French field gun of 75mm bore, also referred to in French as 'soixante quinze,' equivalent to the British 18 Pounder. |
| 88, 88mm | 88 millimetre, a German anti aircraft gun of the Second World War. |
| 9 Inch | A British artillery gun with a barrel bore of 9 inches (225mm) diameter, a heavy gun. |
| 9.2, 9.2 Inch | A British heavy artillery gun with a barrel bore of 9.2 inches. |
| AA | Anti Aircraft, sometimes Ack Ack from the phonetic alphabet in use in the British military at that time. |
| AAC | Anti Aircraft Command, the organisation in Britain responsible for ground based anti aircraft forces between 1939 and 1953. |
| Ack Ack | AA, Anti Aircraft fire. |
| Ack, Beer, | British military phonetic alphabet for the letters 'A' and 'B.' |
| Ad hoc | Improvised for a specific purpose. |
| Adjutant, Adjt. | Officer, normally a captain, responsible for the administration of an infantry battalion, cavalry regiment or artillery brigade (or regiment). |
| Advance party | Part of a military unit which deploys first, making reconnaissance and preparing facilities for the main part of the unit. |

### The Bristol Gunners

| | |
|---|---|
| AGRA | **A**rmy **G**roup **R**oyal **A**rtillery, artillery guns grouped together and commanded at corps or army level as opposed to divisional artillery. |
| Alfresco | From Italian language, in the open air. |
| Allies, Allied Powers | Collective term for the countries that fought on the same side as the British. |
| ANZAC | **A**ustralian & **N**ew **Z**ealand **A**rmy **C**orps, a British military formation mostly comprised of Australian and New Zealand troops in the First World War. |
| AOC, Ordnance | **A**rmy **O**rdnance **C**orps, the organisation in the British Army responsible for storing and maintaining bulk stores of ammunition, food, and other materials. |
| APM | **A**ssistant **P**rovost **M**arshall, a senior military policeman. |
| Archie | British military nickname for anti aircraft guns. |
| Army | A military formation, generally comprising two or more corps, and commanded by an officer with the rank of General, and totalling up to 200,000 men. |
| Artificer | Military Mechanical Engineer. |
| Arty. | Abbreviation for artillery. |
| ASC | **A**rmy **S**ervice **C**orps, the arm of the British Army responsible for loading, unloading and transport of supplies, later titled with 'Royal' to become RASC. |
| Austriaco | Military slang term for the Austrians used in the First World War. |
| BAC | **B**rigade **A**mmunition **C**olumn, the wagons, horses and men responsible for storing and transporting ammunition in an artillery brigade. |
| Back stud | Metal stud used to attach a separate collar to a shirt. |
| Bandolier | An item of military uniform, a belt worn diagonally across the chest carrying small pouches for holding rifle ammunition. |
| BAOR | **B**ritish **A**rmy **O**f the **R**hine, British forces permanently stationed in Germany after both world wars. |
| Barrage | Shellfire used to form a barrier to movement on the battlefield. |
| Battalion, Battn., Bn. | An infantry unit, approximately 1,000 men commanded by a Lieutenant Colonel. |
| Battery | An artillery unit comprising between four and eight guns and the men, horses, vehicles, and equipment to |

The Bristol Gunners

operate them, approximately 100 men in total.

| | |
|---|---|
| Battery Captain, BK | The second in command of an artillery battery, a captain. |
| Battery Commander, BC | The officer commanding an artillery battery, usually a major. |
| Bde. | Abbreviation for 'brigade.' |
| Bdr., Bombardier | Royal Artillery rank equivalent to corporal. |
| Beaten zone | The area within which projectiles from a weapon will strike the ground. |
| Bersaglieri | Italian Army soldiers in the light infantry, with distinctive uniforms, including a feathered hat. |
| BGRA | **B**rigadier **G**eneral **R**oyal **A**rtillery, a Staff Officer at Corps level, responsible for field artillery matters. |
| BHA | **B**rigadier **H**eavy **A**rtillery, a staff officer at corps level responsible for the use of heavy artillery. |
| BHQ, B.H.Q. | Battery, or battalion, headquarters, the position from where a senior officer commanded his unit. |
| Billet | Military term for accommodation, normally a building. |
| Bivvy, bivouac, bivouacking | Military term for a temporary shelter, normally a waterproof sheet or groundsheet, or small tent. |
| Blighty | Military term for Britain. |
| Blighty one, a Blighty | Military slang term for a wound sufficiently serious to need hospital treatment in Britain. |
| Blind | Noun, can refer to a 'dud' shell, one that has been fired, but has not (yet) exploded. |
| Blind | Verb, to prevent an observer from being able to see a piece of ground, usually by the use of smoke shells or smoke projectors. |
| Blitzkrieg | Literally 'lightning war' in German, a method of combining aircraft, tanks, artillery and infantry in attack so as to advance very rapidly. |
| Bosche, Boche | French term for German soldiers also used by the British, contracted from the term for 'German cabbage.' |
| Bounty | A payment to Territorial soldiers, paid annually for reaching the required standard, or on mobilisation for war service. |
| BQMS | **B**attery **Q**uarter**M**aster **S**ergeant, a senior NCO responsible for drawing supplies and issuing stores and equipment within a battery, also responsible for feeding arrangements. |

### The Bristol Gunners

| | |
|---|---|
| BRA | **B**rigadier **R**oyal **A**rtillery, a staff officer at division level responsible for advising the GOC on artillery matters. |
| Brass hats | Army slang for senior officers, from the braid worn on the peaks of their uniform hats. |
| Breech | In artillery, the rear opening of the barrel into which the ammunition is placed before being fired. |
| Breech block | In artillery, the metal component that closes the gun breech after the gun has been loaded and seals the barrel so that the force of the propellant drives the shell forward. |
| Brevet, Bt | A military term used when an officer is appointed temporarily to a higher rank, e.g. Bt Col, Brevet Colonel. |
| Brigade (Infantry or Cavalry) | A formation made up of infantry, artillery and cavalry, between 3 & 6 thousand men in strength and commanded by a brigadier. |
| Brigade (Artillery) | In artillery and prior to the Second World War, a number of batteries commanded by a lieutenant colonel, equivalent to an artillery regiment from 1920s onwards, about one thousand men strong. |
| (To) Brigade | Verb, military term, to organise a number of units into a larger formation. |
| British Warm | A knee length wool topcoat worn by British officers as a trench coat. |
| BSM | **B**attery **S**ergeant **M**ajor, a senior NCO, responsible for administration and discipline in an artillery battery. |
| Bty. | Abbreviation for Battery, an artillery unit comprising between four and eight guns and the men, horses, and equipment to operate them. |
| Bully | British Army term for tinned beef, canned or 'corned' beef. |
| Bully | As in 'bully for him', military term for 'well done.' |
| Bunker | Military term for an underground shelter for troops. |
| Buvette | French bar, for example, at a railway station. |
| Cadre | A small core group, in military terms, the smallest number of people who could represent a unit during formation or dissolution. |
| Café au Cognac | Coffee with cognac brandy. |
| Capt. | Abbreviation for the rank of captain. |

The Bristol Gunners

| | |
|---|---|
| Carabinieri | Italian armed police responsible for both military and civil policing. |
| CB | Counter Battery, firing artillery at the enemy's artillery in order to destroy it or prevent it from firing at our troops. |
| CBSO | Counter Battery Staff Officer, a staff officer at corps level responsible for co-ordinating CB. |
| CCS | Casualty Clearing Station, a British Army medical facility for treating casualties out of the front line and evacuating them to base hospital. |
| Central Powers | Collective term for the countries which fought on the same side as the Germans, including Austro-Hungary, Turkey, Bulgaria. |
| Charger | A military officer's horse. |
| Chit | British Army term for a piece of paper, often to record information or a transaction. |
| CO | Commanding Officer, usually of a major unit such as a regiment or battalion, of the rank of Lieutenant Colonel. |
| Coastal artillery | Artillery guns and men used to defend ports and coastal installations. |
| Col. | Colonel, a senior military rank. |
| Concentrate, concentrating | Military term for bringing together a formation and preparing to deploy tactically. |
| Contact | Military term for opposing forces firing at each other. |
| Corps | A military formation generally comprising three divisions and other corps troops, totalling around 50,000 men, and commanded by a Lieutenant General. |
| CRA | Commander Royal Artillery, a staff officer at corps (or divisional) level responsible for advising the corps commander on artillery matters. |
| Crump Hole | Shell hole. |
| Cwt. | Abbreviation for an Imperial measure of weight, the hundredweight, 112 pounds, or about 50Kg. |
| DA | Divisional Artillery, the brigades of artillery that are a permanent part of a division, normally made up of field and howitzer batteries. |
| DAC | Divisional Ammunition Column, the men, horses and vehicles responsible for transporting and supplying ammunition within a division. |

### The Bristol Gunners

| | |
|---|---|
| Dago | Derogatory term for men of Spanish, Portuguese or Italian ethnicity. |
| DCM | **D**istinguished **C**onduct **M**edal, a gallantry medal for non commissioned soldiers. |
| Dead ground | Ground which is not visible due to being hidden by hills or dips in the ground obscuring the observer. |
| Defilade | Protection from fire or observation provided by natural or artificial obstructions. |
| Dejeuner, petit dejeuner | French for lunch, breakfast. |
| Demob, demobilisation | The process for releasing men from military service at the conclusion of war. |
| Der Tag | German 'The Day', usually means the first day of an assault when infantry go 'over the top' and start their attack. |
| Destruction | In artillery, to damage an enemy's equipment to the point where it will no longer function. |
| Detrain | Military term for unloading vehicles, animals, equipment, men and stores from railway transport. |
| Direct fire | Firing at an enemy who is seen by the firer. |
| Division, div. | A military formation commanded by a major general, comprising many infantry, cavalry, and artillery units and a manpower strength of between ten and twenty thousand. |
| Divisional artillery | All the artillery (and mortars) forming an integral part of an army division. |
| Dossing | Sleeping in the open or in make-shift accommodation. |
| Draft | A group of soldiers moving between units as reinforcements or for demobilisation. |
| Drop short | A shell that strikes the ground too close to own troops, causing them danger, also derogatory term for the artillery used by infantry soldiers. |
| DSO | **D**istinguished **S**ervice **O**rder, a British medal for senior officers for distinguished or meritorious service in wartime. |
| E Boat | A type of German naval craft, a fast and well armed small patrol vessel. |
| Elastic Defence | A concept for a defensive position where an attack can be absorbed and then repulsed without resort to a hard crust of defences. |

The Bristol Gunners

| | |
|---|---|
| Elephant Hutting | A method of constructing underground bunkers using semicircular preformed cast metal sections. |
| Enfilade fire | Small arms or artillery fire applied to a target on its longer dimension, such as lengthways along a trench. |
| Entente | French word for 'agreement', sometimes refers to 'Entente Cordiale', an informal agreement between the French, British and Russians to co-operate militarily, before and during the First World War. |
| Entrain | Military term for loading vehicles, animals, men and stores onto railway transport. |
| Estaminet | French tavern or inn, serving drink and food. |
| FAH | Fresh Air Habit, the dangerous tendency for soldiers to sleep out in the open and at risk from shrapnel or sniper fire. |
| Felice Orsini | 19th Century Italian political activist, his aim was achieving expansion of the Italian State into the Irridenta. |
| FFL | Forces Francaise Libre, Free French Forces, the French who escaped the fall of France in 1940 and committed to fighting on against the Germans. |
| Field Ambulance | British military medical unit responsible for treating casualties between Regimental Aid Posts and Casualty Clearing Stations. |
| Field Artillery | Artillery that is mobile, generally with smaller calibre artillery weapons, and supporting infantry formations. |
| Field Hospital | A military hospital established some miles behind the battle front, where casualties can be treated over many days or weeks. |
| Field trial | Trying out new equipment or techniques in realistic situations on exercise 'in the field.' |
| First light | Dawn. |
| Flanders, Flandres, Vlaams | The region of low lying ground on the border areas of both France and Belgium on the North Sea Coast. |
| Fleabag | Military slang for a sleeping bag or blankets. |
| Fog of war | Generally used to describe the confusion and chaos that develops once battle is started. |
| Foot(soldier) | Infantry. |
| Forward slope | The face of a hill or valley that faces, and is in sight of, the enemy. |
| Funkhole | Underground troop shelter. |

## The Bristol Gunners

| | |
|---|---|
| Fw190, Focke Wolfe 190 | A type of German fighter aeroplane used in the Second World War. |
| Gas suit | Outer uniform clothing for protection from poison gases such as mustard gas. |
| Gazette(d) | To publish a military promotion or award in the London Gazette which is the publication of record for British military announcements. |
| GOC | General Officer Commanding, the officer commanding a division (or military district), in the rank of Major General. |
| Gorblimey | Normally refers to a form of British Army peaked cloth headwear that was not very smart. |
| Graze fuse | A fuse for an artillery shell that explodes the shell very quickly on light contact with the ground, so that it explodes on the surface rather than in the ground. |
| GS, GS wagon | General Service, a horse drawn wagon that was used for carrying supplies, the standard horse drawn wagon used by the British in the First World War. |
| Gun tractor | Vehicle for pulling guns into and out of action. |
| Gunner | Base rank in the Royal Artillery, equivalent to private in an infantry regiment, also used to refer to anyone in the artillery. |
| Gunpark | Place where guns are parked when out of the line. |
| HAA | Heavy Anti-Aircraft Artillery, a branch of artillery with guns capable of firing at aeroplanes at high altitude. |
| HAG | Heavy Artillery Group, the heavy artillery batteries controlled at corps level and having larger calibre guns. |
| Hairies, hairy ones | British military slang for heavy draught horses. |
| Hate | A short but intense period of shelling, sometimes using every weapon in range. |
| HE | High Explosive, either a type of shell that explodes, or the material used in making an explosion. |
| Heinkell 111, He111 | A type of German bomber aeroplane used in the Second World War. |
| Horse Artillery | Artillery that is mobile and supports cavalry. |
| Howitzer | Artillery gun that fires at the high angle so that shells land vertically, used more for destruction missions and on targets that lie behind hills. |
| Hun | A derogatory term used by the British to describe Germans. |

The Bristol Gunners

| | |
|---|---|
| HV | **H**igh **V**elocity, a projectile that travels at or above the speed of sound (over 340 metres per second). |
| Indent | Requisition. |
| Indirect fire, Indirect target | Firing at an enemy that cannot be seen by the firer, usually needs a forward observer who can see the enemy and report on the accuracy and effectiveness of the fire. |
| Irridenta | The part of 'natural Italy' that was not part of the Italian state, and which the Italians wished to own. |
| IS, Imperial Service | A scheme in the British Army whereby Territorial and Volunteer soldiers could opt for service overseas in return for a higher rate of pay. |
| Iti's | Slang for Italians. |
| Jack Johnson | A German shell which burst with black smoke named after a famous black American Boxer. |
| Ju87 | Junkers 87, a type of German dive bombing aeroplane, also known a Stuka, used in the Second World War. |
| Ju88 | Junkers 88, a type of German aeroplane used for bombing and other roles, in the Second World War. |
| Khaki Drill | Lighter weight military uniform intended for use in hot climates. |
| LAA | **L**ight **A**nti-**A**ircraft Artillery, a branch of artillery with guns intended to engage aircraft at lower altitude. |
| Lachrymatory | Tear gas, literally 'making tears.' |
| Last light | Dusk. |
| LCM | **L**anding **C**raft **M**echanised, a naval craft designed to land vehicles and tanks onto a beach. |
| Leaders | The horses at the front of a team drawing a gun or wagon. |
| Liaison | A duty whereby an officer from a sub-unit is based at the next senior HQ so as to ensure commands and information pass quickly and accurately. |
| Line | Telephone cable, or, line of trenches, or, story, or, a unit recruited after war has been declared, such as second line unit. |
| Little Willie | Shell from a German 77mm field gun, named after Kaiser Wilhelm II's son, Crown Prince Wilhelm. |
| LoC, L of C | **L**ine **of C**ommunications, the zone behind the battle area where supply and command units operate. |
| Lorry hop | Hitch hike, getting lifts from military lorries. |

The Bristol Gunners

| | |
|---|---|
| LST | Landing Ship Tank, a flat bottomed ship used to carry heavy vehicles with a ramp so that they can land and drive off over a beach. |
| Lt. | Lieutenant, a junior officer rank. |
| Lt. Col. | Lieutenant Colonel, a senior military officer's rank, normally commanding a battalion or regiment. |
| Luftwaffe | The name for the German Air Force, literally 'Air Arm.' |
| Machonochie | A variety of tinned stew issued to the British Army in the First World War, named after the manufacturers in Aberdeen. |
| Matador | A British army lorry used to draw artillery guns. |
| MC | Military Cross, a medal awarded to junior officers for acts of exemplary bravery during action. |
| Mess, messing | Military term for feeding and accommodation, officers' mess is where officers would eat and sleep. |
| Messerschmitt 109, Me109 | A type of German fighter aeroplane used in the Second World War. |
| Meteor | Military meteorological officer, responsible for collecting and disseminating meteorological data to other parts of the army. |
| Minnie | Minnenwerfer, a German trench mortar, literally 'mine thrower.' |
| Mixed dress | The military term for apparel that is not to uniform requirements, often means mixed civilian and military clothing. |
| Mobilisation | The term used for the process of putting an army onto a formal war footing, bringing all regular and reserve forces into action. |
| Mobus | Slang for **mo**tor **bus.** |
| Moke | Slang for donkey. |
| Monte | Italian for mountain or 'mount.' |
| Mountain how(itzer) | An artillery gun that fires in high angle and can be dismantled for easier transportation by mule or manpower in mountainous areas. |
| MT, M.T. | **M**otor **T**ransport, a military term for all forms of motorised transport vehicles. |
| Murder | Second World War term for an artillery fire mission using all available guns in range to create maximum weight of fire on a single target. |

The Bristol Gunners

| | |
|---|---|
| Nab | Capture or take possession of. |
| NCO | Non Commissioned Officer. |
| Neutralisation | Military term, to prevent a target from acting, firing, or responding. |
| No Man's Land | The territory between two opposing forces which neither occupy. |
| OC | Officer Commanding, normally in the rank of Major, commanding a minor unit such as an artillery battery, infantry company, or cavalry squadron. |
| Officers' servant | Batman or mess orderly, a soldier employed to administer for officers' needs. |
| Oloffbereitschaft | The meaning of this is not clear, but it may refer to a bunker used as a place for sentries to use. |
| OP | Observation Post, a place where military officers can observe the enemy and either control artillery fire or report enemy activity. |
| Open sights | Using the sighting equipment of an artillery gun to fire directly at a target that can be seen. |
| OR | Other Rank, usually any rank below sergeant. |
| Orderly dog | On duty officer or senior NCO. |
| OTC | Officers Training Corps, Territorial Army units based in universities used for training students up to commissioned officer rank. |
| Outrider | A type of horse, not used for draught or in a team. |
| Over the top | Military term for getting out of a trench and moving around on the surface, in attack, or between trenches in defence. |
| Overalls | Military uniform trousers worn on formal parades, with a coloured stripe down the outside of each leg. |
| Parados | The rear wall of a trench or fortification. |
| Parapet | The front wall of a trench or fortification. |
| Patrol jacket | A blue military jacket worn on ceremonial parades, sometimes referred to as 'blues.' |
| Picardy | A region of northern France which includes the areas on either side of the Somme River. |
| Pillbox | A hollow concrete construction, normally partly above ground, to shelter troops and weapons. |
| Pioneer | Soldiers whose role is the construction of defences, roads and other military installations. |
| Plugstreet | British nickname for the town of Ploegsteert in |

The Bristol Gunners

| | |
|---|---|
| | Belgium. |
| Poilus | Nickname for French Army infantry soldiers, literally means 'the hairy ones.' |
| Pool | A military term for a central store from where vehicles or equipment can be drawn for temporary use, that is, a source of shared resources. |
| POW | **Prisoner Of W**ar. |
| Premature | A shell that explodes earlier than intended, sometimes with disastrous results if it is close to the firing gun or own troops. |
| Pukka, pukkah | British military term (from India) to mean real, or genuine. |
| Pursuit | A rapid advance against an enemy who is withdrawing quickly. |
| Q | Quartermastering, the role of storage and supply of all materials to army units. |
| QM | **Q**uarter**M**aster, an officer in a battalion or regiment responsible for stores and supply, normally a captain or major. |
| QMS | **Q**uarter **M**aster **S**ergeant, a non commissioned officer responsible for food and supplies in a unit. |
| Qui vive | Alert, aware, from the French Army sentry's challenge 'Qui Vive?' who lives? or, who goes there? |
| RAF | **R**oyal **A**ir **F**orce, the British arm responsible for air warfare, formed in 1918 from the former army Royal Flying Corps and the Royal Naval Air Service. |
| Railhead | A railway station where men and supplies are unloaded, normally also a main supply storage site. |
| RAP | **R**egimental **A**id **P**ost, a medical post serving an infantry battalion providing first aid to casualties. |
| RASC | **R**oyal **A**rmy **S**ervice **C**orps, the army organisation responsible for transporting stores and equipment. |
| RE | **R**oyal **E**ngineers, a British military Corps responsible for field engineering. |
| Rear party | The residual part of a military unit which stays behind during action or deployment. |
| Reconnaissance | Military term, a noun, for the results of exploring and gaining information, especially of enemy territory. |
| Reconnoitre, recce. | Military verb for exploring and gaining information, especially of enemy occupied territory. |

The Bristol Gunners

| | |
|---|---|
| Redoubt | A strong point in a defensive system. |
| Regiment | A major unit of Infantry, Artillery or Cavalry, approximately 1,000 men strong commanded by a lieutenant colonel, or a part of the army that recruits soldiers wearing the same cap badge. |
| Regt. | Abbreviation for Regiment. |
| Relieve, relief | Military term for the operation where one unit takes over a position from another unit. |
| Remount | Horse, a replacement horse in a military unit. |
| Remount Officer | A military officer whose role was to procure and supply additional horses. |
| Retirement | Military term for a deliberate rearward movement of troops. |
| Retreat | Withdrawing as a result of enemy action, but doing so in good order and with discipline. |
| Reverse slope | The face of a hill or valley that faces away from the enemy and is therefore out of sight to him. |
| Revett(ing) | Wood, corrugated iron or other material used to reinforce the sides of trenches to prevent them collapsing. |
| RFA | **R**oyal **F**ield **A**rtillery, the part of the Royal Artillery that is mobile and supports infantry troops (until 1922). |
| RFC | **R**oyal **F**lying **C**orps, a British Army corps responsible for aerial warfare up to 1918. |
| RGA | **R**oyal **G**arrison **A**rtillery, that part of the Royal Artillery responsible for heavy and fixed artillery, such as in coastal defence, or siege artillery (until 1920). |
| RHA | **R**oyal **H**orse **A**rtillery, that part of the Royal Artillery that is mobile and supports cavalry. |
| Roll (call) | A military procedure whereby everyone in a unit is checked off by name to find out who is present (and correct). |
| Rosso | Italian word for red, often vino rosso = red wine. |
| Rotate | Military term for the process whereby units take turns in occupying a particular position. |
| Rout | The withdrawal of a military force as a result of enemy action, and where military discipline breaks down and the force ceases to be effective militarily. |
| Royal Observer Corps | A British civil defence volunteer organisation tasked with observing aircraft movements and reporting these |

The Bristol Gunners

to a central control centre (1925 to 1995).

| | |
|---|---|
| RSA | The **R**oyal **S**chool of **A**rtillery at Larkhill in Wiltshire. |
| RTO | **R**ailway **T**ransport **O**fficer, a military officer responsible for rail transport arrangements. |
| S.O. | **S**taff **O**fficer, military officer part of the higher level organisation and not part of a regiment or corps. |
| S.Q. | It is not clear what this refers to, it could be 'Staff Qualified', an officer earmarked for future promotion. |
| S/Sergt., S/Sgt. | Staff sergeant, a senior military non commissioned rank. |
| SAA | **S**mall **A**rms **A**mmunition, rifle, machine gun, and other ammunition used in small weapons, including grenades. |
| Sabot | A form of wooden footwear, such as clogs, enclosing the whole foot, historically associated with poor or working people in Europe. |
| Screed | Military slang for a set of orders or instructions. |
| Screen | Hessian or other material used alongside a road or other position to hide movement from observation. |
| Section | Part of a unit, a sub-unit, in an artillery battery it would be half a battery. |
| Sergt., Sgt. | Sergeant, military rank, a senior non commissioned officer. |
| Servant, Officer's Servant | A batman, an orderly whose role is to administer one or more officers. |
| Shrapnel | Lead balls that are expelled from a shrapnel shell at high speed, named after the inventor of the shell, Major General Henry Shrapnel. |
| Siege artillery | Heavy Artillery that is immobile, and fires a heavy shell for destruction of major defence constructions, or roads, rail, etc. |
| Smoke candle | A device for releasing smoke so as to obscure or blind observation of our own troops by the enemy. |
| Smoke helmet | Gas mask. |
| SNCO | **S**enior **N**on **C**ommissioned **O**fficer, sergeant or staff sergeant. |
| Soixante-Quinze | French artillery gun, 75 mm bore, equivalent to the British QF 18 Pounder. |
| SOP | **S**tandard **O**perating **P**rocedures, the rules and routines that determine how things are done within a military unit or formation. |

The Bristol Gunners

| | |
|---|---|
| SOS | A call from the infantry to fire at their most vulnerable point, guns are aimed at this point when not engaged on any other target so as to ensure a very fast response when needed. |
| SOS rocket | A coloured flare fired by the infantry to instruct the artillery to fire at the SOS target. |
| SOS target, SOS line | An artillery target agreed with the infantry which will be fired at on request to protect the infantry at their most vulnerable point. |
| Sous officer | French non commissioned officer, literally 'under officer.' |
| Sqn., Sq. | Abbreviation for the military term squadron, a unit of cavalry or engineers approximately 100 strong. |
| Stand to, standing to | A military action whereby all troops man their defences and are fully prepared in case of attack, routinely at dawn and dusk, but also when ordered. |
| Strafe, strafing | From German for 'punishment', British military term for firing at a target. |
| Stuka | A German dive bomber of the Second World War, also called Junkers 87 or Ju87. |
| Stunt | A military attack, or manoeuvre, or, in flying, a complicated, tricky or skilful display. |
| Sturmtruppen | German for storm troopers or assault troops, elite German infantry using special tactics. |
| Subaltern | Junior officer below the rank of captain, a second lieutenant or lieutenant. |
| Sub(unit), Subsection | A military unit that is part of a minor unit, in an artillery battery (minor unit) it would be an individual gun and crew. |
| Switch | A position behind and connected to the front line trenches, which can be used to create a new defensive position if the enemy penetrate the front trench. |
| TD | Territorial Decoration, an award for long service in the Territorial Army. |
| TF | Territorial Force, part of the British Army recruited in peacetime from civilian volunteers, and committed to home service defence, between 1908 and 1920. |
| Thunderflash | An explosive firework making a loud bang, used in military training to represent grenade, mortar, or shell fire. |

## The Bristol Gunners

| | |
|---|---|
| Time, time fuse | Refers to fuses in artillery shells than are set to explode after a defined time in flight, the intention is that they explode in flight before hitting the ground. |
| Tin hat | Slang for steel helmet, official name was 'shrapnel helmet', that is, for protection from shrapnel bullets. |
| Tommy | Generic nickname for the British soldier. |
| Topping, top hole | Military slang for 'very good.' |
| Tp. | Abbreviation for the military term troop, a part of a squadron or battery. |
| Trail | The part of a gun extending rearwards, in contact with the ground, and supporting the weight of the gun. |
| Trap | Small one horse carriage. |
| Trek, Trekking, Trekked | From Afrikaans for 'pull', travel by horse drawn wagon over distance, generally on roads or tracks. |
| Trench bridge | A bridge built over a trench to enable vehicles and horses to pass over, used especially in the attack and advance to enable guns and supplies to be brought forward. |
| Triple Alliance | The countries that agreed to co-operate in war, Germany, Austro-Hungary, Italy (Italy soon left this alliance and joined the Entente). |
| U/S, US | Un Serviceable, not working. |
| Uscita | Italian for 'exit.' |
| Vento Verticale | British Army slang for 'wind up' from Italian language, meaning panic or excitement. |
| Verey, Verey light, Very | A flare fired from a specialised pistol, flares normally being of a particular colour (red, green, white). |
| Vermouth | A form of wine fortified and flavoured with herb extracts popular in Italy and France. |
| Vin Ordinaire | Everyday quality wine. |
| Vin, vino | French and Italian words for wine. |
| Vinoed | Slang for making wine, or being drunk having consumed wine. |
| Visual station | Heliograph signalling apparatus, using reflected sunlight or lamp light on a mirror to send messages in Morse code. |
| W, X, Y, Z Day | British system for indicating the days relative to a specific day, Z (Zero) Day normally being the day of the main attack. |

### The Bristol Gunners

| | |
|---|---|
| Wagon line, WL | Position to the rear of a defensive or gun position where the horses and wagons are sent during action, also from where supplies are despatched forwards. |
| War reparations | The act of making a defeated nation pay money to the victorious nations as a penalty or compensation. |
| Wash out, washed out | Cancelled, degraded. |
| Wellington boots | Military leather calf length boots worn on ceremonial parades. |
| Wheeler | A horse in a team drawing a cart or trailer that is closest to the cart, that is, at the rear of the team, and provides braking and steering for the team. |
| Wind up | Nervous (see also *vento verticale*). |
| Winter stellung | German for winter line or position, defensive position where the German or Austrians chose to spend the winter season. |
| Wipers | British military nickname for the city of Ypres, in Belgian Flanders. |
| Wire | Telephone cable, or, barbed wire used in defence. |
| Woolly Bear | A German (4.2 inch) artillery shell that part explodes in the air releasing shrapnel, and part also explodes on the ground, with a characteristic pink smoke. |
| Wurst | German sausage. |
| XPM | e**X**panded **P**ierced **M**etal, a form of sheet metal mesh used to construct or reinforce defensive structures such as trenches. |
| Zero line | In a gun battery, the compass direction which is the centre of the arcs within which the guns will fire. |
| Zone | The area allocated to an observer for which he is responsible for keeping under observation, also the area allocated to guns at which they are expected to fire. |

The Bristol Gunners

# Bibliography

| | |
|---|---|
| 240 Brigade War History | An Outline of the War History of the 240th (1st South Midland) Brigade R.F.A.(T), FS Gedye, CE Boyce, H Essex-Lewis, 1933 |
| FS Gedye diaries | Private diaries of Lieutenant F.S Gedye based on letters to his family 1914 to 1919 |
| EL Gedye diaries | Private diaries of Lieutenant E L Gedye based on letters to his family 1914 to 1916 |
| 48th Division Italy | With the 48th Division in Italy, George Henry Barnett, William Blackwood & Sons, Edinburgh, 1923 |
| The White War | The White War, Mark Thompson, Faber & Faber, 2008 ISBN 9780571223343 |
| Military Operations Italy | Military Operations Italy 1915 - 1919 Brigadier General Sir James E Edmonds and Major General H R Davies, IWM, 1991, ISBN 0901627747 |
| Command and Control | Command and Control on the Western Front, Gary Sheffield and Dan Todman, Spellmount, 2007, ISBN 9781862274204 |
| Artillery in the Great War | Artillery in the Great War, Paul Strong & Sanders Marble, Pen & Sword, 2011 ISBN 184415949-3 |
| History of the First World War | Liddell Hart's History of the First World War, BH Liddell Hart, Pan, 1972 ISBN 0330233548 |
| Boyce Diary | Private document written by Captain Boyce, adjutant 1912 to 1915 |
| Roof Over Britain | The Official Story of Britain's Anti-Aircraft Defences 1939-1942. HMSO 1943 |
| Anti-Aircraft | Anti-Aircraft A History of Air Defence, Ian V Hogg, Macdonald and Jane's London 1978 ISBN 0354011634 |
| Frontline 1940 - 1941 | HMSO 1942 The Official Story of the Civil Defence of Britain |
| The War North of Rome | The War North of Rome June 1944 - May 1945, Thomas R Brooks, Sarpedon 1996, ISBN 1885119267 |
| The Bristol Gunners website | http://www.thebristolgunners.webspace.virginmedia.com |

Lightning Source UK Ltd.
Milton Keynes UK
UKOW01f2132150715

255265UK00005B/105/P